Christianity and Criminal Law

This collection, by leading legal scholars, judges and practitioners, together with theologians and church historians, presents historical, theological, philosophical and legal perspectives on Christianity and criminal law.

Following a Preface by Lord Judge, formerly Lord Chief Justice of England and Wales, and an introductory chapter, the book is divided into four thematic sections. Part I addresses the historical contributions of Christianity to criminal law drawing on biblical sources, early church fathers and canonists, as far as the Enlightenment. Part II, titled Christianity and the principles of criminal law, compares crime and sin, examines concepts of *mens rea* and intention, and considers the virtue of due process within criminal justice. Part III looks at Christianity and criminal offences, considering their Christian origins and continuing relevance for several basic crimes that every legal system prohibits. Finally, in Part IV, the authors consider Christianity and the enforcement of criminal law, looking at defences, punishment and forgiveness.

The book will be an invaluable resource for students and academics working in the areas of Law and Religion, Legal Philosophy and Theology.

Mark Hill QC practises from Chambers in the Inner Temple, London, and is Associate Professor at Cardiff University, UK; the University of Pretoria, South Africa; King's College London, UK; and Notre Dame University Law School, Sydney, Australia.

Norman Doe is Professor of Law at Cardiff University, UK, and Director of its Centre for Law and Religion.

RH Helmholz is Ruth Wyatt Rosenson Distinguished Service Professor of Law at the University of Chicago, USA.

John Witte, Jr is Woodruff University Professor of Law, McDonald Distinguished Professor of Religion and Director of the Center for the Study of Law and Religion at Emory University, USA.

Law and Religion

The practice of religion by individuals and groups, the rise of religious diversity and the fear of religious extremism, raise profound questions for the interaction between law and religion in society. The regulatory systems involved, the religion laws of secular government (national and international) and the religious laws of faith communities are valuable tools for our understanding of the dynamics of mutual accommodation and the analysis and resolution of issues in such areas as: religious freedom; discrimination; the autonomy of religious organisations; doctrine, worship and religious symbols; the property and finances of religion; religion, education and public institutions; and religion, marriage and children. In this series, scholars at the forefront of law and religion contribute to the debates in this area. The books in the series are analytical with a key target audience of scholars and practitioners, including lawyers, religious leaders and others with an interest in this rapidly developing discipline.

Titles in this series include:

Ecclesiastical Law, Clergy and Laity
A History of Legal Discipline and the Anglican Church
Revd Neil Patterson

Christianity and Global Law
Edited by Rafael Domingo and John Witte, Jr.

Christianity and Criminal Law
Edited by Mark Hill QC, Norman Doe, RH Helmholz and John Witte, Jr

Law and the Christian Tradition in Italy
The Legacy of the Great Jurists
Edited by Rafael Domingo and Orazio Condorelli

For more information about this series, please visit:
www.routledge.com/Law-and-Religion/book-series/LAWRELIG

Christianity and Criminal Law

Edited by Mark Hill QC,
Norman Doe, RH Helmholz
and John Witte, Jr

Routledge
Taylor & Francis Group
LONDON AND NEW YORK

Produced by the Center for the Study of Law and Religion, Emory University

First published 2020
by Routledge
2 Park Square, Milton Park, Abingdon, Oxon OX14 4RN

and by Routledge
52 Vanderbilt Avenue, New York, NY 10017

Routledge is an imprint of the Taylor & Francis Group, an informa business

British Library Cataloguing-in-Publication Data
A catalogue record for this book is available from the British Library

Library of Congress Cataloging-in-Publication Data
Names: Hill, Mark, 1965- editor. | Doe, Norman, editor. | Helmholz, R.H., editor. | Witte, John, Jr., 1959- editor. | Emory University. Center for the Study of Law and Religion, sponsoring body
Title: Christianity and criminal law / edited by Mark Hill, Norman Doe, R.H. Helmholz and John Witte, Jr.
Description: Abingdon, Oxon; New York, NY: Routledge, 2020. | Series: Law and religion | "Produced by the Center for the Study of Law and Religion, Emory University" | Includes bibliographical references and index.
Identifiers: LCCN 2020002866 (print) | LCCN 2020002867 (ebook) | ISBN 9780367858254 (hardback) | ISBN 9781003015260 (ebook)
Subjects: LCSH: Criminal law–Philosophy. | Law–Christian influences. | Criminal liability–Religious aspects–Christianity. | Justice–Religious aspects–Christianity. | Christianity and law.
Classification: LCC K5018 . C47 2020 (print) | LCC K5018 (ebook) | DDC 261.8–dc23
LC record available at https://lccn.loc.gov/2020002866
LC ebook record available at https://lccn.loc.gov/2020002867

ISBN: 978-0-367-85825-4 (hbk)
ISBN: 978-1-003-01526-0 (ebk)

Typeset in Galliard
by Deanta Global Publishing Services, Chennai, India

In Memoriam

The Right Honourable Sir John Laws
Sometime Lord Justice of Appeal
1945–2020

Jurist, scholar and friend
Husband, father and grandfather

Requiescat in pace

Contents

Contributors

Albert W. Alschuler is the Julius Kreeger Professor Emeritus of Criminal Law and Criminology at the University of Chicago Law School, USA. He has also taught at Northwestern, Texas, Colorado, Penn, Berkeley, Michigan, NYU, Columbia, Brooklyn and San Diego. Alschuler has written on plea bargaining, sentencing guidelines, the exclusionary rule, jury selection, police hunches, confessions, bribery, campaign funding, Oliver Wendell Holmes, William Blackstone, the privilege against self-incrimination and other topics, most of them in the field of criminal justice. A convert from agnosticism to Christianity at age 48, he is currently Moderator of the Congregational Church in Cumberland, Maine (UCC).

Markus Bockmuehl is the Dean Ireland's Professor in the Exegesis of Holy Scripture at the University of Oxford, UK, and a Fellow of Keble College; he has also served as Associate Head of the university's Humanities Division (with responsibility for graduate studies). Until 2007, he was a professor at the Universities of Cambridge and St Andrews, and previously taught at Regent College and the University of British Columbia, Canada. Among his books is *Jewish Law in Gentile Churches* (2003); more recent titles include *Simon Peter in Scripture and Memory* (2012), *Ancient Apocryphal Gospels* (2017) and *Creation ex Nihilo: Origins, Development, Contemporary Challenges* (2018, ed. with G.A. Anderson). His teaching covers the New Testament as well as Jewish and early Christian studies, while his current research focuses on aspects of early Christian eschatology.

Nathan S. Chapman is Associate Professor of Law at the University of Georgia, USA. He was formerly Executive Director of the Stanford Constitutional Law Center. His scholarship focuses on due process of law, religious liberty, and Christianity and the law. He holds degrees in law and theology from Duke University, and is a McDonald Distinguished Fellow at the Center for the Study of Law and Religion at Emory University, Atlanta.

His Honour Peter Collier QC is a recently retired Senior Circuit Judge, having for over 10 years been the Resident Judge at Leeds Crown Court and the Honorary Recorder of Leeds. He sat as an additional judge in the Court of Appeal Criminal Division 2011–2018. He had spent the previous 35 years as a barrister practising principally in the area of criminal law, and was appointed Queen's Counsel in 1992. He is also a diocesan chancellor (Wakefield 1992–2006; Lincoln 1998–2006; and currently York since 2006) and Vicar General for the Province of York since 2008. He is a member of the Legal Advisory Commission of the General Synod of the Church of England.

Norman Doe is Professor of Law at Cardiff University, UK, and Director of its Centre for Law and Religion. His books include *Fundamental Authority in Late Medieval English Law* (1990), *The Legal Framework of the Church of England* (1996), *Canon Law in the Anglican Communion* (1998), *The Law of the Church in Wales* (2002), *An Anglican Covenant* (2008), *Law and Religion in Europe* (2011), *Christian Law* (2013), *The Legal Architecture of English Cathedrals* (2017) and *Comparative Religious Law: Judaism, Christianity, Islam* (2018). A Visiting Professor at Paris University, he was a Visiting Fellow or Scholar at Trinity College Oxford (2011), Corpus Christi College Oxford (2015) and Jesus College Oxford (2018), and founding member of the Colloquium of Anglican and Roman Catholic Canon Lawyers (1990). He is Chancellor of the Diocese of Bangor and Director of the LLM in Canon Law at Cardiff Law School which he established in 1991.

David Etherington QC read Jurisprudence at Keble College, Oxford, UK, followed by a Special Diploma in Public and Social Administration in which he was awarded a distinction. He joined the Chambers of Michael Havers, then Attorney General and later Lord Chancellor, in 1982 and took Silk in 1998. He specialises in fraud and serious organised crime, and was appointed a Recorder of the Crown Court in 2000. He served on the Professional Conduct Committee and Professional Practice Committees of the Bar Council and was chairman of both for several years. He is Chancellor of the dioceses of Norwich and St Edmundsbury & Ipswich and Deputy Chancellor of Ely. David has advised a number of television dramas and other legal programmes including *Kavanagh QC*, *Judge John Deed*, *Hypotheticals* and Channel 4's *The Trial – A Murder in the Family*, and lectures on both advocacy and professional ethics.

Richard W. Garnett is the Paul J. Schierl/Fort Howard Corporation Professor of Law, Concurrent Professor of Political Science and the Director of the Program on Church, State & Society at the University of Notre Dame, USA. He was raised in Anchorage, Alaska, and received his BA in philosophy *summa cum laude* from Duke University in 1990 and his JD from Yale Law School in 1995. He served as a law clerk to the Chief Justice of the United States, William H. Rehnquist, and to Chief Judge Richard S. Arnold of the United States Court of Appeals for the Eighth Circuit. In 1999, he joined the faculty at Notre Dame Law School where he teaches and writes about criminal law, constitutional law and the freedoms of speech and religion. His current book project, *Two There Are: Understanding the Separation of Church and State*, will be published by Cambridge University Press.

RH Helmholz is Ruth Wyatt Rosenson Distinguished Service Professor of Law at the University of Chicago, USA. A graduate of Princeton University, Harvard Law School and the University of California, Berkeley, he teaches the modern American law of real and personal property, including the law of natural resources. However, most of his research interests have been devoted to the history of the European *ius commune*, with particular attention to its place in the development of the English legal system. Working from their manuscript records, he has taken a hand in tracing the history of the jurisdiction of the ecclesiastical courts in England from their beginning in the thirteenth century to their temporary abolition in the 1640s. His most recent book is *Natural Law in Court* (Harvard University Press, 2015), in which he traces the role played by the law of nature in the legal practice of the courts of Europe, England and the United States from 1500 to the mid nineteenth century.

Mark Hill QC is Associate Professor at Cardiff University, UK; the University of Pretoria, South Africa; King's College London, UK; and Notre Dame University, Sydney, Australia; and a Fellow of the Center for the Study of Law and Religion at Emory University, USA. He is Chairman of the Ecclesiastical Law Society and Vice-President of the International Consortium for Law and Religion Studies. He holds various judicial appointments including a Recorder assigned to the Midland Circuit hearing criminal, civil and family cases, and sits as a judge in the Consistory Courts of the dioceses of Chichester and Leeds. His recent publications include the fourth edition of the practitioner text *Ecclesiastical Law* (2018), *Religion, Law and Security* (2018), *Great Christian Jurists in English History* (2017), *The Confluence of Law and Religion* (2016) and *Magna Carta, Religion and the Rule of Law* (2015).

Lord Judge was Lord Chief Justice of England and Wales from 2008 until his retirement in 2013. He was called to the Bar by Middle Temple, elected a Bencher in 1987 and served as the Treasurer in 2014. He was appointed a Justice of the High Court in 1988, assigned to the Queen's Bench Division. In 1996, he was appointed a Lord Justice of Appeal, becoming a Privy Councillor. He was the Senior Presiding Judge from 1998 to 2003, and appointed the first President of the Queen's Bench Division in 2005. Lord Judge is the convenor of the crossbenchers in the House of Lords. He is an Honorary Fellow of Magdalene College, Cambridge, and an Honorary Doctor of Laws at Cambridge University, where he is the Commissary of the university. He is a Distinguished Fellow and Visiting Professor at King's College London. He was President of the Selden Society between 2007 and 2013. He is co-author of *Magna Carta Uncovered* (2014) and the author of *The Safest Shield* (2016).

Chloë Kennedy is Senior Lecturer in Criminal Law at the University of Edinburgh, UK. She holds a PhD and LLM from the University of Edinburgh and an LLB (hons) from the University of Glasgow. Chloë's research is mainly focused on criminal law, legal theory, legal history and the relationship between these areas. She is also interested in the interrelations between law and religion and law and gender. As well as authoring various articles, Chloë is co-editor of *Scottish Feminist Judgments: (Re)Creating Law from the Outside In*. Chloë currently holds an Arts and Humanities Research Council early career research leader fellowship, during which she is researching and writing a critical history of identity deception.

David McIlroy is a barrister specialising in banking law, including civil claims for fraud, at the English Bar. He is Visiting Professor at Queen Mary University of London, UK, having previously taught banking law for 19 years at SOAS University of London. He holds Master's degrees in law from the Universities of Cambridge and Toulouse and a PhD in theology from the University of Wales. In addition to his work on banking law, David's other major research area is the theology and philosophy of law. As well as numerous articles, he is the author of *A Biblical View of Law and Justice* (2003), *A Trinitarian Theology of Law: In Conversation with Jürgen Moltmann, Oliver O'Donovan and Thomas Aquinas* (2008) and *The End of Law* (2019). He is an Associate Tutor at Spurgeon's College where he teaches a course on the Mission of Justice and the Theology of Law.

Jeffrie G Murphy is the Regents' Professor of Law, Philosophy and Religious Studies at Arizona State University, USA. He has written extensively on Kant's moral and legal philosophy, the philosophy of crime and punishment, the moral emotions, forgiveness and mercy and (most recently) humility as a moral virtue. He is a past president of the American Philosophical Association and was invited by the Divinity Faculty at the University of Cambridge to present the 2010 Stanton Lectures. His most recent book is *Punishment and the Moral Emotions—Essays in Law, Morality, and Religion*.

Daniel Philpott is Professor of Political Science at the University of Notre Dame, USA. He conducts scholarship on religion and global politics, with emphasis on reconciliation, religious freedom, theories of the political behaviour of religious actors and religious political ethics. Among his books are *God's Century: Resurgent Religion in Global Politics* (2011), *Just and Unjust Peace: An Ethic of Political Reconciliation* (2012) and *Religious Freedom in Islam? The Fate of a Universal Human Right in the Muslim World Today*. Since 2014, he has co-directed the *Under Caesar's Sword* initiative, a global research project on Christian responses to persecution. He has also facilitated faith-based reconciliation in Kashmir and the Great Lakes Region of Africa, and is conducting research on Christian political theology.

Heikki Pihlajamäki is Professor of Comparative Legal History at the Faculty of Law, University of Helsinki, Finland. He has written on themes such as the history of evidence law and lay judges, police law and different aspects related to the history of criminal law. Recently, his interests have increasingly shifted towards the history of commercial law and the theory of comparative legal history. Comparative aspects have been important throughout his production, and geographically his work comprises not only Scandinavia and Europe, but also the United States and Latin America. He was co-founder of the journal *Comparative Legal History*, and is a member of the Finnish Academy of Science and Letters and of the Teachers' Academy of the University of Helsinki.

Sir John Saunders is a member of the Parole Board for England and Wales. He is a retired High Court Judge and has presided over a number of high-profile trials in recent years, including those concerning abuse of parliamentary expenses and telephone tapping by the media. He began practice at the criminal bar on the Midland Circuit in 1972 and was appointed Queen's Counsel in 1991. He became a Senior Circuit Judge and the Honorary Recorder of Birmingham in 2004 and was elevated to the High Court Bench in 2007. He is President of the Court of Appeal of St Helena, and chairs the public inquiry into the deaths of the victims of the Manchester Arena Attack in 2017.

Mathias Schmoeckel is Professor for Civil Law and Legal History in Bonn University, Germany, corresponding member of the Istituto Lombardo, board of directors of the Stephan-Kuttner-Institute and teaches also in Paris and Catania. He focuses on the relationship of Christianity and law since the Church Fathers, mostly in matters of evidence, procedure, private and international relation. He is co-editor of the commentary on the history of the German Civil Code, and of the *Zeitschrift für Rechtsgeschichte – Kanonistische Abteilung* as well as of the *Revue d'histoire de droit français et étranger*. He has authored, among other books, *Jugend der Justitia* (Tübingen: Mohr Siebeck, 2013) and *Recht der Reformation* (Tübingen: Mohr Siebeck, 2013), and has edited over 30 volumes on the history of German and canon law.

John F. Stinneford teaches and writes about legal ethics, criminal law, criminal procedure and constitutional law. His work has been published in numerous scholarly journals, including the *Georgetown Law Journal*, the *Northwestern University Law Review*, the *Virginia Law Review* and the *William & Mary Law Review*. Stinneford's work has been cited by the United States Supreme Court, state supreme courts, federal courts of appeal and numerous scholars. In the fall of 2015, he was a Visiting Scholar at the Georgetown Law Center, Center for the Constitution. Stinneford clerked for the Hon. James Moran of the United States District Court for the Northern District of Illinois. He teaches first-year courses in criminal law and constitutional law, and upper-level courses in professional responsibility, criminal procedure, federal criminal law, law & literature and white collar crime.

Brent A. Strawn is Professor of Old Testament at Duke Divinity School and a Professor of Law at Duke University School of Law in Durham, North Carolina, USA, where he also has a secondary appointment at the Law School. He has authored *What Is Stronger Than a Lion? Leonine Image and Metaphor in the Hebrew Bible and the Ancient Near East* (2005), *The Old Testament is Dying: A Diagnosis and Recommended Treatment* (2017) and *The Old*

Testament: A Concise Introduction (Routledge, 2020). He has edited more than 20 other volumes, including *The Bible and the Pursuit of Happiness: What the Old and New Testaments Teach Us about the Good Life* (2012) and *The Oxford Encyclopedia of the Bible and Law* (2015), which won the American Library Association's Dartmouth Medal for Excellence in Reference (2016). He was one of the editors and translators for the *Common English Bible* (2011) and serves on the editorial boards of various monograph series, including *Old Testament Theology* (Cambridge University Press). He is an ordained elder in the United Methodist Church.

Jeroen Temperman is Professor of International Law and Religion and Head of the Department of International and European Union Law at the Erasmus School of Law, Erasmus University Rotterdam, the Netherlands. He is also the Editor-in-Chief of *Religion & Human Rights* and a member of the Organization for Security and Cooperation in Europe's Panel of Experts on Freedom of Religion or Belief. He has authored, among other books, *Religious Hatred and International Law* (Cambridge: Cambridge University Press, 2016) and *State–Religion Relationships and Human Rights Law* (Leiden: Martinus Nijhoff, 2010); and edited *Blasphemy and Freedom of Expression* (Cambridge: Cambridge University Press, 2017) and *The Lautsi Papers* (Leiden: Martinus Nijhoff, 2012).

John Witte, Jr is Woodruff University Professor of Law, McDonald Distinguished Professor of Religion and Director of the Center for the Study of Law and Religion at Emory University, USA. A leading specialist in legal history, family law, religious liberty, human rights, and law and Christianity, he has published 260 articles, 18 journal symposia and 32 books. Recent titles include *The Western Case for Monogamy over Polygamy* (Cambridge University Press, 2015); *Religion and the American Constitutional Experiment* (Oxford University Press, 4th ed., 2016); and *Church, State, and Family: Reconciling Traditional Teachings and Modern Liberties* (Cambridge University Press, 2019).

Preface

Lord Judge

The Temple, where the London symposium met to debate drafts of the chapters which follow,[1] is quite literally the very same ground trodden by King John, the Barons, loyal and rebel, Archbishop Langton and the Princes of the Church as they tried to negotiate a settlement, thrashing out a solution for the dispute between the King and the Barons and embodying it in a charter, which in the following June became the first clause of Magna Carta itself.[2] Our brilliant, emblematic Temple Church had only just been consecrated. The Temple was a place of sanctuary. To shed blood here would have been a sin imperilling the immortal soul. It was also somewhere the immortal soul – and the day of judgment was inevitable – would probably feel safe to negotiate.

And it is in this church that one of the great unsung heroes of history, William Marshal, was laid to rest, unsung although without him Magna Carta would have been a mere footnote in history, just one of many charters to much the same effect as those that were dished out by mediaeval European rulers.[3] We all know its provisions that justice was not to be denied or delayed or sold: but the charter also provided that people would not be at risk of any penalty unless they had contravened the law of the land – not some generalised law of God, but the law of the land. The judges were required to know that law and uphold it; and law enforcement officials, such as sheriffs and bailiffs, were not to act in a judicial capacity. Those principles stand today: quite what the law in 2018 orders and prohibits has become more convoluted. One simple phrase in Chapter 2 in this volume says it all: "Criminal law is a vast subject".[4]

1 This Preface comprises the lightly edited text of the introductory remarks made by Lord Judge at the opening of the Christianity and Criminal Law symposium convened in Inner Temple, London on 13–15 October 2018.

2 See generally Anthony Arlidge and Igor Judge, *Magna Carta Uncovered* (London: Bloomsbury Press, 2014).

3 See various of the essays in Robin Griffith-Jones and Mark Hill, eds., *Magna Carta, Religion and the Rule of Law* (Cambridge: Cambridge University Press, 2015).

4 Chapter 2, Brent Strawn, "Criminal Law in the Old Testament: Homicide, the Problem of *Mens Rea* and God", p. 13.

Here in England, and no doubt elsewhere in what I shall describe as the Christian world, we are now inundated with prohibitions or directions which, disregarded, may produce a penalty. Where there were once Ten Commandments, we now have tens of hundreds, thousands of criminal offences, well in excess of five figures. They range from laws against driving at a prohibited speed, to a relatively recent law prohibiting anyone from causing a nuclear explosion.[5] Quite who will survive to investigate the crime, bring the perpetrator to whichever court has survived the explosion, and where the judge, the jury, the prison and prison officers to keep the defendant secure will be found are not explained. But one could argue that both speeding and causing a nuclear explosion are derived from continuing attention to the exhortation to us all to love our neighbour. With the distinction that in many situations, exhortation is no longer believed to be adequate and enforcement by criminal penalties is deemed necessary.

The following chapters represent a fascinating group of studies: stimulating, learned, provocative and profound. I have had the privilege of reading them. They make a scholarly read. My attention has been drawn to Aeschylus, war veteran of the Battle of Marathon, whose plays I tried reading at 17 years of age, and which I never did complete, to Kubrick's *Clockwork Orange*, which I never saw. I have noted *Bushell's Case*,[6] which I know well, and *Barnette's Case*,[7] of which I was ignorant. Today's world has been represented by commentary among many others on restorative justice and plea bargains and presidential pardons. We have been enlightened from Plato to the modern day via all the Fathers of the Church. Christianity is some 2000 years old, but its roots are found in mysticism from the Middle East, Greek philosophy, Roman law and, of course, Judaism. This history and these foundations and the inexorable revolution of time have commanded concentrated attention, and they have received it.[8]

Where to begin? As more than one of the chapters does, perhaps we should start at the very beginning, the Book of Genesis itself. The Garden of Eden, where the first crime was committed, the first trial took place and the first sentence was imposed. The defendants were not represented. If you were defending Adam and Eve, your mitigation plea would have proceeded along the lines that this was mere theft of an apple, no doubt one of many on the same tree, and unless eaten, an apple which would have become a wizened windfall by the end of the summer. This message was undoubtedly given to the defendants by the serpent, which it is not to be forgotten was itself part of God's creation. With forensic courage, the advocate might have asked why such an evil creature was created at all. In any event, the serpent was largely to blame for introducing the idea, offering the temptation and distorting their judgement. The Prosecution

5 Nuclear Explosions (Prohibition and Inspections) Act 1998.
6 (1670) 124 ER 1006.
7 *West Virginia State Board of Education v Barnette* (1943) 319 U.S. 624.
8 See e.g. Diarmaid MacCulloch, *A History of Christianity: The First Three Thousand Years* (London: Penguin, 2010).

argument would have been quite different. This was not eating any old apple. This was not a minor offence against property. This was eating an apple from a particular tree. It represented direct defiance of the only law in the Garden, a law of utmost simplicity, and constituted an irremediable breach of trust. The motive was shameful, seeking knowledge which would have made them almost Godlike. The offence constituted a terrible threat to the whole of His magnificent creation. Every judge trying criminal cases has listened to beguiling but mutually contradictory submissions of this kind. And must resolve how, justly, to balance them.

The sentence was expulsion from the Garden, with the additional physical punishment on Eve, extended to all her daughters for eternity. Beyond that, all children, every boy baby and every girl baby, were marked with original sin. All humanity's tribulations followed. The very next crime was fratricide, when one of their sons, Cain, killed another son, Abel. Was that not a direct consequence of the expulsion, just for eating an apple? Or was it an inevitable consequence of man's fall? Or both? So that raises the question whether the sentence for stealing an apple, even this particular apple from this particular tree, was excessive? Did it do any good? Should there have been a short period outside the Garden – to show the defendants what the world outside would be like? But would not any period outside have contaminated their innocence irretrievably? So, maybe a warning would have sufficed? In the High Court of Eden, mercy did not temper justice. So what was the point of the expulsion sentence? Was it simply the vindication of the law, a better society, with future generations understanding or having a clear understanding of the need to earn eternal life? Maybe a truly merciful sentence was not realistically available. Or again, maybe mercy was indeed shown. They were not executed. They were given the opportunity to earn ultimate redemption, assuming that is that they were not predestined to fail. Again, any sentencing judge will identify with these problems. And it can perhaps be argued that the fact that problems like these are identified daily in the criminal justice process, and are expected to be so identified, may itself be derived from the long history addressed in the following chapters.

In passing, I underline that there was no mitigation plea. The defendants were unrepresented. The judge who had laid down the law himself concluded that they were guilty and he himself passed sentence. In the Garden of Eden the trial process was unfair. It is perhaps too late for a prerogative pardon.

The story of the first crime provides a vivid illustration of the societal impact of crime. Every society, even the most primitive, has laws. And breaches of society's laws, even when based exclusively on religious belief, it was very quickly discovered, could not just be left to the hereafter. Even a theocracy enforces its laws on Earth. It does not leave what are asserted to be divine laws to divine justice, but rather purports to imbue the enforcing authorities on Earth with the investment of divine agency.

This volume directly addresses Christianity and criminal law. Today, Christianity includes numerous, not always consistent beliefs and traditions, which include, let us not forget, among others, the Coptic Church and the Greek Orthodox Church, and in the Western world not least Protestantism and Catholicism with their different manifestations and beliefs. Men and women died horrible deaths because of their belief in or rejection of predestination, or the alternative belief, free will. In this history, the Reformation is really pretty recent, and over 20 centuries the authority of the Christian Church, or more accurately Churches, has varied within different societies, sometimes waxing, sometimes waning.[9]

The secular arm of the State and religious authority have at times been virtually indivisible, at others, at loggerheads. Usually that is a consequence of the struggle for power, political power, often dressed up as a religious issue, but sometimes the struggle for political power is directed to a moral issue. Was Henry VIII in breach of the law of God when he married his dead brother's wife, and so cursed? The short answer is that he cannot have been, because he became, and apparently always had been, the Supreme Head of the Church in England. So, it was just the marriage that was cursed. In passing, everyone ignores that his second marriage was equally cursed, because before he met Anne Boleyn, he had slept with her older sister; instead of dismissal suffered by Catherine of Aragon, Anne Boleyn faced trumped-up charges of infidelity. But Henry's struggle with the Pope, however dressed up in biblical texts, was about power. If the Pope would not provide him with the outcome he wanted , then that power should be placed where the desired outcome could be guaranteed.[10]

Every society has had to address the immediate problem, the daily problem, of the appropriate way to deal with the individual who has committed an offence. That responsibility is ultimately carried by judges, themselves fallible fellow human beings. With the possible exception of cases involving children, and the very rare cases involving life and death decisions, if you asked most judges to identify their most burdensome responsibility, it would rarely be the law, however complicated and difficult that may often be, but how to deal with the post-conviction decision. So many factors are in play. There is the crime itself and how contemporary society views the crime; there is the victim and the consequences for and impact of the crime on that individual, and sometimes on wider society; there is the defendant, with all their history, and their level of culpability and their intention at the time when the crime was committed; there is the future as well as the past. What is most appropriate, punishment or rehabilitation? This obligation to carefully balance many factors, some of which at least are in conflict (and I could give an entire lecture on the subject), is a responsibility shared by every judicial authority, the pagan and Christian, Mohammedan or atheist, whether society has or does not have a religious foundation, or indeed is a theocracy.

One of the constant themes in this volume is achieving the appropriate balance between justice and mercy. Assessing the proper balance between them is an awesome responsibility, and perhaps throughout these discussions we should bear in mind that in every Christian country, every day, every week, men and women will be exercising it. For them all, the Christian heritage does not diminish the

9 See e.g. Euan Cameron, *The European Reformation* (Oxford: Clarendon Press, 1991).
10 See e.g. Arthur Geoffrey Dickens, *The English Reformation* (London: Batsford, 1964).

burdens. I began practice at just about the time when the death penalty was abolished and went to the Court at Nottingham the day after one of the very last such sentences had been imposed. The atmosphere was bleak. The court where that sentence had been passed was shut. I was told that the judge, a member of the Anglican faith, was spending the whole of that day praying in the nearby church.

The story of sin and crime, and their possible overlap and the confusion between them has been a vivid aspect of history. To me, one of the most interesting aspects of studying the chapters that follow has been the distinction between the crimes which constitute offences against what might fairly be described as religious crimes (alleged to be against God in Heaven) and those which are crimes against the Church on Earth (for example, sacrilege), and the impact of the distinction on developing thinking. On a personal level, I remember with fondest love my Catholic grandmother, the most devout of women, with a burning faith and belief in the afterlife who would have been much more concerned about sin, which she would have seen as an offence offered to God, an insult to Our Saviour, who died on the cross to expiate our guilt, than about the place occupied by such a sin in the list of crimes. To her, I suspect, suicide was a sin, a mortal sin, and by comparison with mortal sin the question whether it was a crime or not, would have been trivial.

Largely, today, we live in a secular society in which that authority of the Christian Church has significantly diminished. Our beautiful churches, every single village offering testament to the worship and devotion of previous generations, are now largely empty. How many really believe, as my grandmother did, that this present life is a mere testing ground for eternity, with the immortal soul facing judgment by the Almighty, just as Adam and Eve did? The continuing role to be played by Christianity, or indeed any other faith, in the development of the criminal law will inevitably become less intense than it once was. Even if it were to diminish to extinction, even if we no longer believe in sin, as the following distinguished chapters demonstrate, Christianity's continuing influence on criminal justice in Western society will abide.

Acknowledgments

This volume on *Christianity and Criminal Law* is one of several new introductions to Christianity and Law commissioned by the Center for the Study of Law and Religion at Emory University. Each volume is an anthology of some two dozen chapters written by leading scholars. The volumes contain historical, doctrinal and comparative materials designed to uncover Christian sources and dimensions of familiar legal topics. Each is authoritative but accessible, calibrated to reach students, scholars and instructors in law, divinity, graduate and advanced college courses as well as educated readers from various fields interested in what Christianity has, can and perhaps should offer to the world of law. Earlier titles in this series include *Christianity and Law* (2008); *Christianity and Human Rights* (2010); *Christianity and Family Law* (2017); and *Christianity and Natural Law* (2017). Other titles are forthcoming on Christianity and: Conscience, Constitutionalism, Economic Law, Global Law, International Law, Migration Law and Private Law. We aim, over time, to commission other such volumes on Christianity and bankruptcy law, education law, elder law, environmental law, health law, labour law, procedural law, remedies and other familiar legal topics.

This volume on *Christianity and Criminal Law* – together with the parallel volumes in press on Global Law and Private Law – was made possible by a generous grant from Fieldstead and Company, a private California foundation. We give thanks to the Fieldstead board and directors for their generous support, and to the programme officers, Dr Stephen Erikson and Dr Joe Gorra, for their wise counsel as we planned these volumes. We are deeply grateful to Dr Hester Higton for so generously sharing her superb editorial talents in copyediting this manuscript. We also express our warm thanks to Ms Anita Mann and Ms Amy Wheeler for their skilful administration of this and other scholarly projects.

It was a joy for us to work with such a range of leading scholars from North America and Europe who contributed fresh and perceptive chapters to this volume. Our collective efforts were greatly enhanced by the two round-table conferences held at Emory University in 2017 and in Mark Hill QC's Chambers at the Inner Temple, London, in 2018. Those intense discussions helped us identify the major themes for this study of Christianity and Criminal Law, a topic which has not been well explored in recent scholarship. We give thanks to our Emory colleagues, Professor Rafael Domingo and Dr Justin Latterell, for their help in the first Emory conference, and Dr Robin Griffith-Jones, the Reverend and Valiant Master of the Temple, for his generous hospitality during the second symposium in the heart of legal London, not least for designing a splendid service of choral matins at which Professor Witte preached a rousing sermon.

The purpose of the round-table sessions was to stress-test the views expressed in a multi-disciplinary hot-house environment. Hence, the discussions were robust and demanding, not unlike doctoral defences. The idea was not to produce a comprehensive narrative of every conceivable interaction between Christianity and the criminal law. Such would be an impossible task. Each discrete subject is vast, subjectively understood and amenable to a range of interpretations. The hope was that by selecting leading experts in the field of Christian theology and criminal law and practice, each contributor would bring an insightful perspective on a particular matter, in territory which was often contested. Thus, this volume represents a gallery of individual canvasses, and not a complete holistic mural. In some instances, the chapters talk to one another both within and across the two principal disciplines. But each contributor brings his or her own voice such that the chapters can be read independently, unlocking one or more aspects of the rich and enriching world of Christianity and criminal law, and pointing the reader to further reading on the subject.

We are delighted to publish this volume and several others in Routledge's distinguished Law and Religion series edited by one of the world's preeminent scholars of law and religion, Norman Doe. Professor Doe and his many colleagues in the Centre for Law and Religion at Cardiff University have been vital trans-Atlantic allies with the Emory Center for the Study of Law and Religion. We are grateful for their leadership in this expanding global field of inter-disciplinary legal study, and for their partnership with the Emory Center in publishing this and parallel volumes on law and Christianity. We are also deeply grateful for the generous collaboration of Dick Helmholz, the world's leading historian of English ecclesiastical law, and a scholarly giant in the study of legal history, and of law and religion on both sides of the Atlantic. His wise counsel and contributions throughout the preparation of this volume have greatly improved the pages that follow. The mundane but essential task of organising the round tables, managing the contributors and ensuring consistency of style throughout the manuscript fell on the lead editor, Mark Hill QC, a long-standing friend and collaborator. While this book was in production, he was made honorary chief of the Erinmo people in Nigeria by their king, The Elerinmo of Erinmo, and given the title *Bameto*, which translates as "an adept organizer with understanding of religion". Although with characteristic modesty he rarely uses his chieftain's title, it neatly encapsulates Mark's contribution to this and many other projects.

Finally, we express our warm thanks to Alison Kirk, Emily Summers and their colleagues at Routledge in taking on these volumes and applying their usual standards of excellence in their editing, production and marketing of this one in particular.

Mark Hill QC and John Witte, Jr
Center for the Study of Law and Religion
Emory University

Feast of the Epiphany, 2020

1 Introduction

Mark Hill QC[1]

In the view of the famous student of comparative law Henry Sumner Maine (1822–88), the earliest days of European criminal law were marked by a decidedly religious character.[2] It was God who first instructed men that they were not to commit murder. It was God who alerted men to the dangers of perjury. If a king issued a similar law, he did so as God's chosen ruler, giving specific form and force to what was at bottom a religious command. Maine was far from alone in this characterisation of religion's early link to law. Indeed, variations of the theme of religion's relevance to the growth of Western legal systems continue to appear in the works of modern historians.[3] Maine's view also long held the field among European and American lawyers, theologians and historians. Brent Strawn's chapter, which opens this volume, supports our recognition of Maine's characterisation of the historical tie between law and religion. The law of crimes, Strawn demonstrates, is "profoundly godlike when seen through ancient eyes".

Today's law, however, appears to have lost this ancient character. Making a causal connection between our criminal law and religious commands is a habit we are widely regarded as having outgrown. Time and opinion move on. Religion now belongs within the private side of modern lives, not the public world of courts and crime. The Age of Enlightenment's signal achievement was to break the existing link between law and religion. Heikki Pihlajamäki's magisterial contribution to this volume explores the complexity of this subject. He shows that

1 This introduction is the work of several hands – those of Norman Doe, Dick Helmholz and John Witte, as well as my own. Not only have they brought into the light the points of continuity and similarity we had identified in planning this project, but they have also uncovered several additional connections which emerged from the revised drafts of the chapters. I am grateful for their help and for their company in completing this project.

2 Henry Sumner Maine, *Ancient Law: Its Connection with the Early History of Society and Its Relation to Modern Ideas*, 1st ed. 1861, republished in Beacon Series in Classics of the Law (Boston: Beacon Press, 1963), 1–19.

3 See, by way of example, James Q. Whitman, *The Origins of Reasonable Doubt: Theological Roots of the Criminal Trial* (New Haven and London: Yale University Press, 2008); Reinhard Zimmermann, ed., *Der Einfluss religiöser Vorstellungen auf die Entwicklung des Erbrechts* (Tübingen: Mohr Siebeck, 2012); Thomas Oakley, *English Penitential Discipline and Anglo-Saxon Law in Their Joint Influence* (New York: Columbia University Press, 1923).

religion did remain a force to be reckoned with even among most Enlightenment thinkers. Subject to this amendment, a significant one, Pihlajamäki's chapter does not deny the gradual impact of secularism on this subject. He would agree. To many recent commentators the Christian religion appears to stand as an obstacle in the way of reaching desirable goals within their own systems of criminal law. Religious history – replete with witch hunts and incineration of heretical dissenters – is thought to be ample evidence of the wisdom of religion's relegation to the sidelines of public life and penal law.

Why, then, does it make any sense to produce a volume devoted to investigating the relationship between Christianity and the criminal law? And once produced, why should anyone read it? Answers to this objection are found in the chapters which follow, but it is worthwhile identifying some of the threads that tie them together. Several good reasons exist for undertaking an investigation into the connections between crime and religion. Different sorts of readers will take an interest in the subjects found in this book's chapters. Some of these interests will seem immediately obvious to most of us. Others require more thoughtful consideration of religion's legitimate role in modern criminal law. While more challenging, they are also the more deserving of scholarly attention and thought.

1.1 The immediate interests of the subject

Several groups of potential readers will profit in an immediate way from the essays in this volume. The first is made up of the men and women whose professional careers intersect with its subjects – religion and criminal law. The clergy are the most obvious members of this group. Virtually all Churches – Catholic, Protestant and Orthodox – have canons. They contain rules and legal principles touching offences and offenders.[4] They establish court systems, enact procedural rules and provide definitions of both wrongful conduct and available remedies and penalties. Norman Doe's chapter draws upon his own pioneering spade work in exploring this subject,[5] and several other chapters in the volume add to what he has done. The chapter by R.H. Helmholz on the mediaeval canon law's treatment of criminal law provides an historical example. A good number of basic Western criminal law concepts of *mens rea*, *actus reus* and causation, as well as basic crimes against persons, property, religion and morality have roots in the mediaeval Christian sources and their antecedents in the first millennium.[6]

A real need exists today for greater knowledge of this subject among the parochial clergy. Few would dispute that this knowledge is too often slight or even non-existent, and Doe's chapter provides an attractive starting point. Not only

4 See, e.g. Mark Hill, *Ecclesiastical Law*, 4th ed. (Oxford: Oxford University Press, 2018).

5 See most recently Norman Doe, *Christian Law: Contemporary Principles* (Cambridge: Cambridge University Press, 2013).

6 See, e.g. R.H. Helmholz, *The Spirit of Classical Canon Law* (Athens, GA: University of Georgia Press, 2010).

that. The book's utility may prove immediately useful to the clergy in several ways. For instance, it provides an abundance of material that is of potential use to the clergy in their capacity as preachers. Some of it will enliven their sermons. John Stinneford's chapter, to take just one example, includes the fascinating showing that today Adam might have been convicted of the English offence of "scrumping" (taking fruit from a common orchard or garden). This is, at most, a misdemeanour, a minor infraction of the law, but the story in the Book of Genesis reminds us that God's commands go beyond simple obedience to existing law. A comparison with Adam's action and the modern law of scrumping will bring that point into dramatic focus. His fate will confirm the preacher's point. This book is full of such treasures.

Another group of professional men and women who will profit in an immediate way from the essays that follow are lawyers – lawyers whose practice includes disputes in matters connected to religious life. This has been a perennial field of contention, and it remains an area of litigation to this day. It sometimes seems to be growing in frequency and importance. The laws of most Western countries guarantee religious freedom to its citizens. What, then, happens when that freedom comes into conflict with secular laws? This is not a new question. It has a long history. Consider, for instance, the example and the effects of the fourteenth-century English statutes of Praemunire.[7] They sought to curtail the Church's freedom of action by restricting rights of appeal to the papal court. Nathan Chapman's chapter on crimes against the State addresses similar large questions which laws like this one now raise. It is a continuing problem, one that involves conflicting but legitimate loyalties. His analysis begins, as does that of several other of the present authors, with the writings of St Augustine. The treatment of this subject by the ingenious Bishop of Hippo is not identical with what today's analysis will yield, but the chapter demonstrates both how old the question is and how varied Christian responses to it have been. Augustine also still has something of value to say about the legal treatment of the conflicts that arise, and this volume provides a ready entry into his thought on the subject.

A further group of readers who will find subjects of immediate utility in this volume's chapters consists of the students and teachers in universities and law schools that offer courses and seminars in law and religion. This has become a growing field of study. The current *Directory of Law Teachers* in the United States lists 104 teachers of courses and seminars on the subject, and the Association of American Law Schools' section on law and religion claims more than 450 members.[8] Academic centres devoted to the study of law and religion have also sprung

7 25 Edw. III, st. 3, c. 22 (1351); 27 Edw. III, st. 1, c. 1 (1353); 16 Ric. II, c. 5 (1392). See also W.T. Waugh, "The Great Statute of Praemunire of 1353", (1922) 37 *English Historical Review* 173–205; E.B. Graves, "The Legal Significance of the Statute of Praemunire of 1353", in Charles Taylor, ed., *Anniversary Essays in Mediaeval History by Students of Charles Homer Haskins* (Boston and New York: Houghton Mifflin, 1929), 57–80.

8 See *The AALS Directory of Law Teachers 2017–2018* (Washington, DC: West Publishing and Foundation Press, 2018), 1567–8.

up to become established institutions at several American universities – Emory, Brigham Young, Pepperdine, St John's in New York, Notre Dame and Villanova, for example. Since 1998, Cardiff University in the United Kingdom has had a successful Centre for Law and Religion, and other centres have popped up on the Continent, in South Africa, Southeast Asia and Australia. There is now an International Consortium for Law and Religion Studies, together with various regional consortia. Several of the chapters in this volume will help students in these institutions go beyond a concentration on the constitutional disputes that test the limits of religious freedom. The breadth of its essays, including both history and future possibilities for change, will help lawyers and theologians gain an inside look at the character of religious law itself. Such a look will also take them well beyond the current case law. It will put current controversies into a larger perspective.

A still further group of readers who will find material of interest in this book's chapters is that made up of men and women who take a serious interest in their own religion. Although there has been an apparent decline in the size of this population over the last 50 years, the professedly Christian share of the population in the United States is still over two-thirds.[9] How many among that number take a serious enough interest in the faith they profess, to prompt them to take up and read a volume about law and religion is anyone's guess. No surveyor's list attempts to distinguish between the nominal and the serious. The latter cannot be an empty category, however, and the chapters that follow will interest its members in several ways. Lord Judge's Preface to this volume is testimony to the interest the contents of this volume have had for him, and his is only one example among many. There are readers who have found and will find interest in the intersection of past and present thought about crime and religion. What is laid out in the books of the Bible and is explored in the works of interpreters of Scripture is capable of deepening the faith of religious men and women. Likewise, the second of Nathan Chapman's chapters, which concludes the volume, raises questions over the participation of Christiansin matters of governmental judgment, firm in the faith that God uses human judgment. What better note on which to finish but to return to the profoundly theological questions which are ever-present in the intersection of Christianity and the criminal law, which will continue to be asked in the current and future generations.

1.2 The wider interests of the subject

The worth of this volume's chapters is more than a matter of immediate utility. They provide a good deal of food for thought, thought that both can and should have real consequences. Law and the Christian ministry are learned professions.

9 In 2014, it stood at 70.6%; see the statistics compiled by the Pew Research Center, "America's Changing Religious Landscape", 12 May 2015, https://www.pewforum.org/2015/05/12/americas-changing-religious-landscape.

To be complete, even to be respectable, each field of inquiry requires some familiarity with history. Several aspects of current criminal law are hard to understand without it. Theology is also shallow and unconvincing if its history is ignored. The nature of both professions thus invites attention to basic questions of legal theory. It is natural for us to ask why certain acts deserve to be condemned and punished while other apparently similar acts do not, and religion always requires thinking seriously about the basic problems of right and wrong. This volume helps in the process of giving serious consideration to the future possibilities of present actions. Richard Garnett's thoughtful and fascinating study of today's law dealing with attempts to commit criminal acts provides one example. In fact, several of the book's chapters also illustrate the possibilities for profiting from the subject's past, as well as shedding light on some questions of current moment and dispute. Three particular themes, found in several of the following chapters, demonstrate the volume's value.

The first of the three is the ubiquity of concern in the chapters for questions of criminal law in the works of the great theologians of earlier centuries. A concern for law and crime appears in the works of virtually all the greatest Christian thinkers. The treatment of crime in the works of St Augustine, Thomas Aquinas, Martin Luther, John Calvin and many other theologians from the past figures prominently in several of the chapters. As a matter of course, these theologians dealt with crimes against God and the Church, religious matters such as simony, blasphemy and heresy. That coverage was almost as a matter of necessity. The need is made explicit in Jeroen Temperman's chapter on the subject. He shows how inevitable and valuable criminal law's inclusion in the thought of Christian theologians and canon lawyers has always been. The questions they touched on ranged widely, well beyond subjects intimately tied to the immediate interests of the Churches. For instance, most crimes were also sins. Their inclusion in manuals used to direct human beings' conduct in the world was only to be expected. It is also worthy of particular note in the Protestant tradition. The great reformers discussed in the volume's pages were not antinomians. Even Martin Luther, whose scathing remarks about lawyers and Christianity are sometimes quoted to demonstrate his antipathy towards law, actually had useful and positive things to say about law's value, not excluding its criminal side.[10] As the volume's chapter by Mathias Schmoeckel convincingly demonstrates, Luther differed from his Catholic opponents about the proper forum for administering a public regime suited for the detection and punishment of criminals. He did not differ with them about its necessity.

Perhaps the most thought-provoking examples of the volume's utility for serious thought are those chapters that discuss aspects of the modern criminal law that have their origins in Christian law and thought, but which in their modern form have largely lost touch with those origins. We have forgotten

10 See also John Witte, Jr., *Law and Protestantism: The Legal Teachings of the Lutheran Reformation* (Cambridge: Cambridge University Press, 2002).

where they came from. A person's right to remain silent in the face of a charge of criminal conduct, a privilege enshrined in the Constitution of the United States, found initial support in the mediaeval Church's laws. *Nemo tenetur prodere se ipsum* (no-one is bound to betray himself):[11] confession of one's private sins was owed to God, but not to one's temporal governors – just one of the several similar examples brought forward and discussed in Peter Collier's helpful chapter in this volume, in which the practical experience of recently serving judges and practitioners augments the high-vaulted scholarship of the academy. Nor has this connection entirely disappeared from modern law. David McIlroy's chapter on the historical influence of Christianity on the development of *mens rea* as a requirement for punishing criminals provides a clear example, even though modern criminal lawyers rarely recognise the connection.[12] Chloë Kennedy's essay also demonstrates that many parts of modern criminal law have their roots in traditional Christian beliefs. What she calls the "tenacity of Christian norms" is illustrated by the modern resistance to permitting assisted suicide. Suicide (self-murder according to mediaeval ways of thought) is no favourite of our own legal systems. Few of us living today would wish to see a stake driven through the heart of the man or woman who has committed suicide, but we still punish anyone who drives the stake at the request of a volunteer. Similarly, David Etherington's chapter, which deals with several aspects of our law's treatment of offences against the person, opens up a subject of continuing importance by exploring its roots in its Christian past.

A second long-term appeal of this volume, one touched upon by several of its contributors' essays, is the help Christianity provides in the evaluation, criticism and reform of modern systems of criminal law. Not all imperfections of the past have disappeared, and the Bible itself invites the justified criticism of some of today's practices, as Markus Bockmuehl's chapter demonstrates in scholarly detail. The trial of Jesus provides the most prominent of the several examples upon which his essay touches. Condemnation at the behest of a mob is a stain upon the administration of justice in any age, and Pilate's capitulation to one stands as a warning against it. The possibility has not gone away. The "War on Crime" that was declared by American President Lyndon Johnson in 1965, and re-voiced by Prime Minister Tony Blair in the 1990s, as a way of combatting urban unrest may have had some positive results, but it also went too far by a large margin. Too often, people have been imprisoned for trifling offences. Today, the United States imprisons the same number of people with criminal records as it has four-year college graduates. Nearly half of black American

11 See *Decretales Gregorii* IX (the *Liber Extra* of 1234), at X 5.1.14 (*Veniens ad sedem*), in Aemilius Friedburg, ed., *Corpus iuris canonici*, 2 vols. (Graz: Akademische Druck- und Verlagsanstalt, 1959), 2:col. 737.

12 See Elizabeth Papp Kamali, *Felony and the Guilty Mind in Medieval England* (Cambridge: Cambridge University Press, 2019).

men have been arrested for criminal activity by the age of 23.[13] At bottom, the dramatic overcrowding and inhuman conditions in American prisons that have followed this Declaration of War have been the unfortunate aftermath of a surrender to the crowd. The chapter by Sir John Saunders gives a detailed account of the current intent of the English system of parole, whereby offenders are rehabilitated into life outside the overcrowded and under-funded prison regime.

A particularly telling criticism of the misuse of a religiously inspired institution is also found in Albert Alschuler's exploration of the current exercise of the pardoning power vested in the American president and also in the governors of most U.S. states. Mercy in the exercise of jurisdiction over crime is a part of the inheritance of Christianity. There is little doubt about that. Jeffrie Murphy's authoritative chapter explores the benefits which the Christian duty of showing mercy brings to all those who administer the criminal law. The law itself can sometimes go very wrong when this duty is forgotten or ignored. The example of Jesus' treatment of the woman taken in adultery is one example among many. God himself is merciful (Deut. 4:31). "Blessed are the merciful, for they shall receive mercy" (Matt. 5:7). The Christian roots of the modern pardoning power, the power to temper justice with mercy, are evident in its history.

However, as the chapters also demonstrate, these are powers that can be misused. Alschuler shows that in the United States today they are being misused. The power to pardon was meant to be a force for good. It was designed to remedy individual injustices. Instead, recent American presidents have employed it to reward those who have made large monetary contributions to their own political and personal funds. Pardons, like mediaeval indulgences, seem to be for sale. As his chapter demonstrates, the biblical records make it clear that Jesus "would have disapproved of partisanship towards the rich and powerful in granting clemency". An analogy with the sin of simony – the payment of money for obtaining a spiritual office – also provides a telling argument against the modern misuse of a religiously based institution. The connection between law and Christianity provides a way, perhaps the best way, of demonstrating that the right to pardon was not meant to be converted into a fund-raising technique.

A third source of interest in the contents of this volume inheres in Christianity's power to generate new ideas and institutions in the administration of criminal law. Daniel Philpott's chapter is particularly eloquent on this score. It shows the utility that initiatives based on the Christian duty to forgive have served in the commissions established in the wake of transitions from dictatorships to democratic regimes. South Africa's Truth and Reconciliation Commission led by Archbishop Tutu is the most celebrated of these transitional bodies. There

13 See Matthew Friedman, "Just Facts: As Many Americans Have Criminal Records as College Diplomas", 17 November 2015, https://www.brennancenter.org/our-work/analysis-opinion/just-facts-many-americans-have-criminal-records-college-diplomas.

have been a surprising number of them, as Philpott's chapter demonstrates, and a connection with the Christian religion has been a feature of many of them. He treads on solid ground in finding the inspiration for their establishment in "God's willingness continually to restore his covenant with the people of Israel". Both institutions have within them a similar mixture of mercy and practical sense. The commissions not only promote forgiveness and reconciliation, but they also call for the public recognition of past wrongs on the part of the perpetrators of those wrongs. This requires an open admission of guilt, wherever it is feasible, by the men who have done wrong. It is not "cheap grace". Open repentance is required. These commissions provide an example of Christian principles being put to a novel and profitable use.

John Witte's chapter on what he calls "sex crimes" provides an equally fascinating example of religious law's capacity for new uses. Adultery, sodomy and the like were long public crimes in Western law, acts condemned and punished in the courts of both Churches and kings. The justification given for their criminalisation is spelled out in his chapter's exploration of the thought of Thomas Aquinas, who stated it clearly and connected its purposes with the law of nature. Somewhat surprisingly, Aquinas also provided a partial justification for permitting the practice of prostitution. Attempts to abolish it, he held, and the consequences would be worse. "[T]he carnal appetite is always alive" and "prudential and practical concerns" must be considered in shaping the law designed to govern human conduct. In recent centuries, as Witte recognises, the "modern secular State" has undone most of the traditional criminalisation of sexual offences, including most aspects of prostitution. But his chapter also shows that this development has not rendered Christianity irrelevant. The Churches have a responsibility to promote a higher standard of behaviour than does much of our criminal law. Their members should not be silent simply because a question of criminal law has arisen which conflicts with religion. There are also contentious modern questions of public law where the voice of Christianity still needs to be heard. The question of polygamy's possible legalisation in Western law, a question once thought to have been settled in the negative by its conjunction with the growth of the Church of Latter Day Saints in the nineteenth century, is bound to arise again. Witte's contribution calls for Christian voices to be heard when it does.[14]

1.3 Conclusion

Each chapter in this collection of essays is followed by a list of books and articles which provide fuller treatments of the themes covered in the chapter itself. In a few cases, they lead to fuller treatments written by the authors of the chapters themselves. In all cases, they amplify and refine what is found in each of the texts that precedes them. These references are well worth following up. Taken

14 For fuller treatment, see John Witte, Jr., *The Western Case for Monogamy over Polygamy* (New York: Cambridge University Press, 2015).

all together, they demonstrate that this volume is more than the sum of its parts. Virtually all of its subjects demonstrate that the connection between law and religion, one akin to the connection that Henry Sumner Maine perceived so many years ago, is worth study today. Christianity's place in the criminal law has been diminished. But it has not been wholly lost.

Part I

Historical contributions of Christianity to criminal law

2 Criminal law in the Old Testament

Homicide, the problem of *mens rea* and God

Brent A. Strawn[1]

Since much contemporary jurisprudence goes back in one way or another to its forebears, both recent and ancient, it is no surprise that criminal law, specifically, also owes much to antique legal traditions and corpora.[2] This point is even truer when the framework in question is an explicitly Christian approach to (criminal) law, since Christianity has, from its inception, looked to Holy Scripture for inspiration and guidance, correction and instruction. As is well known, the words "Scripture" and "Scriptures" in the Greek New Testament almost invariably refer to what Christians now call the Old Testament,[3] and it is readily apparent that the Old Testament contains far more legal material, generically speaking, than the New. So, if one is looking for biblical materials pertaining to crime and delict, such matters will be found most easily and extensively in the Hebrew Bible.[4]

Criminal law is a vast subject – in the biblical world no less than today – and so what follows is but a brief introduction to the subject that focuses on several aspects of Old Testament criminal law within its cultural environment.[5] I will

1 My thanks go to the editors for their assistance and to my fellow contributors for helpful remarks at the conference in London. I am especially grateful to Chloë Kennedy and Albert Alschuler for their thoughtful feedback

2 See, inter alia, Brent A. Strawn, ed. *The Oxford Encyclopedia of the Bible and Law*, 2 vols. (Oxford: Oxford University Press, 2015) (henceforth *OEBL*), esp. 1.xiii–xviii; also Harold J. Berman, *The Interaction of Law and Religion* (Nashville: Abingdon, 1974); and John Witte Jr., *God's Joust, God's Justice: Law and Religion in the Western Tradition* (Grand Rapids: Eerdmans, 2006).

3 A possible exception is 2 Peter 3:16, which may include Paul's writings as part of that designation ("as also the other scriptures"), though perhaps here the term is more generic: "writings". See Richard Bauckham, *Jude–2 Peter*, rev. ed. (Nashville: Thomas Nelson, 2014), 333; and Lewis R. Donelson, *I & II Peter and Jude: A Commentary* (Louisville: Westminster John Knox, 2010), 281, for discussion.

4 In the present essay, I use "Hebrew Bible" and "Old Testament" interchangeably, but favour the latter, given the Christian orientation of this volume.

5 For the United States, see, inter alia, Guyora Binder, *Criminal Law* (Oxford: Oxford University Press, 2016). For a convenient presentation of the range and specifics of biblical law, see Tikva Frymer-Kensky, "Israel", in Raymond Westbrook, ed., *A History of Ancient Near Eastern Law*, 2 vols. (Leiden: Brill, 2003), 2:975–1046, esp. 1027–42; see also Richard H. Hiers, *Justice and Compassion in Biblical Law* (New York: Continuum, 2009), 61–164. For

first provide an orientation to the legal sources preserved in the Old Testament, including some discussion of a few of the problems besetting the proper interpretation and use of these texts. I will then consider the main texts on homicide in the Pentateuch with an eye on those self-same interpretive problems before turning to a particularly tricky issue: the problem of the mental element in the determination of culpability and punishment. In the final section, I consider one of the main differences between contemporary law and biblical law – God's role in law – to draw some possible, though perhaps unrecognised and under-theorised, connections between modern jurisprudence and Scripture, and what such connections might mean for a Christian approach to criminal law.

2.1 The biblical sources for criminal law and a few of their interpretive problems

The late biblical and ancient Near Eastern scholar Tikva Frymer-Kensky helpfully collected the biblical data pertaining to crime and delict, including penalties for the same. According to her categories, the Bible addresses the following crimes (a few representative biblical citations are included):

Homicide: Exodus 21:12; Leviticus 24:18; Numbers 35:16–19.
Injury, especially by striking: Exodus 21:18, 22–25; Leviticus 24:19–20; Deuteronomy 27:24.
Sexual offences, including adultery, rape, seduction and forbidden sexual partners: Exodus 22:16; Leviticus 18 and 20; Deuteronomy 22:22, 25–27.
Theft, including kidnapping, burglary and fraud: Exodus 21:16; 22:1–2, 3, 8; 23:4; Leviticus 19:11, 35; Deuteronomy 24:7; 25:13–16.
Damage to property, including injury to slaves and animals: Exodus 21:20–21, 26–27, 33–34; 22:4–5, 13–14; Leviticus 24:18.
Falsehood and *slander*: Leviticus 5:20–26; 19:16; Numbers 5:31; Deuteronomy 19:18–19; 22:19; 27:25.
Witchcraft, *blasphemy and other misuses of God's name*, *apostasy* and *idolatry*: Exodus 22:17; Leviticus 19:26, 31; 24:10–23; 26:1; Deuteronomy 13:2–12, 13–19; 16:21; 17:1–5; 27:15.
Rebellion against authority: Exodus 21:15, 17; 22:27; Leviticus 19:32; Deuteronomy 17:9–13; 21:18–21.[6]

introductions to ancient Near Eastern criminal law, see, inter alia, Russ VerSteeg, *Early Mesopotamian Law* (Durham, NC: Carolina Academic Press, 2000), 107–28; and Russ VerSteeg, *Law in Ancient Egypt* (Durham, NC: Carolina Academic Press, 2002), 151–86.

6 Frymer-Kensky, "Israel", 2:1029–42. See also Ze'ev W. Falk, *Hebrew Law in Biblical Times*, 2d ed. (Provo, UT: Brigham Young University Press/Winona Lake, IN: Eisenbrauns, 2001), 67–82.

Other schematisations are possible, but Frymer-Kensky's are useful and helpful. However these offences are categorised, the punishments due them could be through divine or human sanctions. The former "were left to the hand of God", with the latter differentiated as to capital, corporal, talionic or pecuniary measures.[7]

Frymer-Kensky's presentation already highlights two important aspects of biblical criminal law: first, that it contains a good bit of material that would not count as criminal law today (simply because much here is decidedly and thoroughly *religious*); and second, that at least some of what the Bible treats as criminal law would, by today's categories, be considered private law. This latter point is true not only with regard to certain topics (e.g. torts) but also for how such matters were handled legislatively: in many cases, resolution was left largely, if not entirely, to private parties.[8]

The last-mentioned point is not universally true. The Old Testament knows of legal authorities who are sometimes identified, though not all of these figures should be considered "official" by our standards.[9] Some, for example, are simply referred to generically as village "elders" (Hebrew *zĕqēnîm*). Be that as it may, in a decent number of instances the clearest data we have about legal authority generally, or about specific legal authorities is found in *non*-legal material: narratives, to cite one example, not legal texts proper. Legal "storyettes", as Frymer-Kensky calls them (e.g. Lev. 24:10–23; Num. 15:32–36; 1 Sam. 30:22–25),[10] are therefore an important resource for law in the Old Testament, as is the legal information that can be gleaned from the prophetic or wisdom books, though these materials are oftentimes less clear and certainly less direct than the texts that are more obviously, if not also by definition, legal in nature.[11] Unfortunately, even a more limited focus on just the legal texts of the Pentateuch is beset by a number of interpretive difficulties. Five deserve brief discussion.

First and foremost, biblical law belongs to a wider cultural environment that also preserved a great deal of legal material.[12] Most scholars deem it likely that at

7 Frymer-Kensky, "Israel", 2:1027 9. Note her inclusion of pollution and bloodguilt under the rubric of "penalties". See further below.

8 This likely reflects the fact that much of ancient Israelite life was rural, without regular interaction with State-sanctioned authorities who would enforce law. See, inter alia, Douglas A. Knight, *Law, Power, and Justice in Ancient Israel* (Louisville: Westminster John Knox, 2011).

9 See Reinhard Achenbach, "Legal Experts: Ancient Near East and Hebrew Bible", in *OEBL*, 1:518–27; also Frymer-Kensky, "Israel", 2:981–93.

10 Frymer-Kensky, "Israel", 2:979–80.

11 See, e.g. Tova Ganzel, "Law in the Prophets", in *OEBL*, 1:479–84; F. Rachel Magdalene and Bruce Wells, "Law in the Writings", in *OEBL*, 1:485–95; and James K. Bruckner, *Implied Law in the Abraham Narrative: A Literary and Theological Analysis* (Sheffield: Sheffield Academic Press, 2001). Note also the legal ostraca that have been recovered from ancient Israel/Palestine – see Frymer-Kensky, "Israel", 2:981; and Christopher A. Rollston, "Epigraphic Texts", in *OEBL*, 1:266–71.

12 For introductions to this material, see, inter alia, Kenton L. Sparks, *Ancient Texts for the Study of the Hebrew Bible: A Guide to the Background Literature* (Peabody,

least some of what is found in ancient Near Eastern law directly influenced what is now found in the Bible.[13] Much can be gained, therefore, by a close comparison between biblical law and its ancient Near Eastern antecedents, though such comparison is often difficult with the results controverted.[14]

A second issue is that in the present form of the Pentateuch, all law is placed in the time of the wilderness wanderings between Israel's departure from Egypt and its arrival in Canaan, with a special focus on the stay at Mount Sinai. This is odd if only because it generates an unexpected disjuncture between the literary setting of the law and a good bit of its specific content, much of which clearly relates to and dates from a very different historical setting(s): a time of settled life in towns and houses with officials and rulers, agriculture and business, and so on and so forth. One effect of the literary setting of Pentateuchal law – apparently the result of intentional editorial activity (see below) – is that *almost the entirety of biblical law is ascribed directly to God*, even if Moses often serves as God's intermediary. In truth, it is the *divine origination of biblical law*, far more than its *editorially located geography*, that differentiates what one finds in the Torah from so much ancient and contemporary jurisprudence. While various gods are sometimes found in ancient Near Eastern legal collections, it is primarily the monarch, not the deity, who is responsible for authoring and promulgating law in the ancient Near East, in sharp contrast to what one finds in the Old Testament.[15]

MA: Hendrickson, 2005), esp. 417–34; John H. Walton, *Ancient Near Eastern Thought and the Old Testament: Introducing the Conceptual World of the Hebrew Bible*, 2d ed. (Grand Rapids: Baker Academic, 2018), esp. 269–91; and Westbrook, *A History of Ancient Near Eastern Law*, *passim*, esp. the introduction by Raymond Westbrook, "The Character of Ancient Near Eastern Law" (1:1–90). For a convenient collection of the pertinent cuneiform texts, see Martha T. Roth, *Law Collections from Mesopotamia and Asia Minor*, 2d ed. (Atlanta: Scholars Press, 1997). See also, more generally, Meir Malul, *The Comparative Method in Ancient Near Eastern and Biblical Legal Studies* (Kevelaer: Butzon & Bercker/ Neukirchen-Vluyn: Neukirchener, 1990).

13 See, e.g. David P. Wright, *Inventing God's Law: How the Covenant Code of the Bible Used and Revised the Laws of Hammurabi* (Oxford: Oxford University Press, 2009). In various writings, Raymond Westbrook has argued for a "common law" tradition that existed across the ancient world (e.g. "Character of Ancient Near Eastern Law"). For critical engagements, see Bernard M. Levinson, ed., *Theory and Method in Biblical and Cuneiform Law: Revision, Interpolation, and Development* (Sheffield: Sheffield Academic Press, 1994); and Samuel Jackson, *A Comparison of Ancient Near Eastern Law Collections Prior to the First Millennium* BC (Piscataway, NJ: Gorgias, 2008)

14 Bernard S. Jackson, "Reflections on Biblical Criminal Law", in *Essays in Jewish and Comparative Legal History* (Leiden: Brill, 1975), 63: "The differences may be easily ascertained. Their interpretation is more difficult". Jackson's essay was a response to Moshe Greenberg, "Some Postulates of Biblical Criminal Law", in *Studies in the Bible and Jewish Thought* (Philadelphia and Jerusalem: Jewish Publication Society, 5755/1995), 25–41 (first published in 1960), who subsequently replied to Jackson in Moshe Greenberg, "More Reflections on Biblical Criminal Law", in Sara Japhet, ed., *Studies in Bible 1986* (Jerusalem: Magnes Press, Hebrew University, 1986), 1–17.

15 See Greenberg, "Some Postulates of Biblical Criminal Law", 27–9; also Yochanan Muffs, *The Personhood of God: Biblical Theology, Human Faith and the Divine Image* (Woodstock,

It goes without saying that in secular constitutional democracies the divine world plays virtually no role whatsoever; perhaps, in light of biblical law, it might be said of the contemporary situation that the State has arrogated to itself powers that at one time in history were seen as transcending it (see further in Section 2.4).

The third interpretive difficulty is that there are ***several distinct legal corpora in the Bible***, even if these now appear within the one Sinai + Wilderness setting within the Pentateuch. Scholars have identified no fewer than four major blocks of legal material:

1 the *Book of the Covenant* or *Covenant Code* (Exodus 20:22–23:19);
2 the *Deuteronomic Law* (Deuteronomy 12–26);
3 the *Priestly Law* (Leviticus 1–16 + Numbers 1–9); and
4 the *Holiness Code* (Leviticus 17–27).[16]

The presence of overlapping material and obvious discrepancies between these blocks reveal that the texts come from diverse circles, if not also from vastly different time periods.[17] Biblical scholars disagree on the (relative and absolute) dating of these four blocks of texts and their precise delineation. Where overlapping topics or texts differ, scholars also debate whether the later law (if the chronology can be determined) was meant to supplement the earlier legislation or to completely eradicate and replace it.[18] Beyond the niceties of these reified academic debates, the major takeaway is that readers must frequently reckon with ***multiple understandings*** of any one specific criminal law in the Bible.

A fourth issue concerns actual legal practice. For some time now, scholars have posited that the ancient Near Eastern legal collections are just that – "collections" of laws, not legal "codes" properly so-called, with the correlate being that it is uncertain if these collections were ever meant to be consulted, let alone

VT: Jewish Lights, 2005), 35–44. For examples of the gods in prologues to Mesopotamian legal collections, see Roth, *Law Collections*, 15, 25, 80–1.

16 For overviews, see Eckart Otto, "Book of the Covenant", in *OEBL*, 1:69–77; Daniel I. Block, "Deuteronomic Law", in *OEBL*, 1:182–95; William K. Gilders, "Priestly Law", in *OEBL*, 1:166–75; and Jeffrey Stackert, "Holiness Code and Writings", in *OEBL*, 1:389–96; as well as the book-length treatments in Dale Patrick, *Old Testament Law* (Atlanta: John Knox, 1985); and William S. Morrow, *An Introduction to Biblical Law* (Grand Rapids: Eerdmans, 2017).

17 Two famous examples, among others, are: the laws on profane slaughter (Lev. 17:1–8 vs. Deut. 12:13–16, 20–22) and the laws on slave manumission (Exod. 21:2–6 vs. Deut. 15:12–18 vs. Lev. 25:39–43).

18 For replacement theories, see, e.g. Bernard M. Levinson, *Deuteronomy and the Hermeneutics of Legal Innovation* (Oxford: Oxford University Press, 1997); and Jeffrey Stackert, *Rewriting the Torah: Literary Revision in Deuteronomy and the Holiness Legislation* (Tübingen: Mohr Siebeck, 2007). For supplementation, see Joshua A. Berman, *Inconsistency in the Torah: Ancient Literary Convention and the Limits of Source Criticism* (Oxford: Oxford University Press, 2017); and Brent A. Strawn, "Moses at Moab, Lincoln at Gettysburg? On the Genre of Deuteronomy, Again", (2018) 24 *Zeitschrift für Altorientalische und Biblische Rechtsgeschichte* 153–210.

implemented.[19] Given this situation in the case of the great cuneiform traditions, scholars have posited that the same may have obtained for ancient Israel and for biblical law. But what would the purpose of ancient law – biblical or otherwise – be if it wasn't for actual practice? Assnat Bartor has recently summarised three main options: (1) "the laws were part of royal propagandistic literature", meaning they had little practical value and were meant for public recital at festivals or ceremonies; (2) the laws were a type of "professional literature", a kind of legal textbook of precedents; or (3) the laws were "a literary genre that emerged out of scribal schools", meant to inculcate morality and also develop legal thinking – only later did these "general principles of moral advice" become "a binding set of laws".[20] It is difficult to determine which of these options is most likely correct; perhaps some of them may be fruitfully combined. Writing specifically of "everyday law" in biblical Israel, Raymond Westbrook and Bruce Wells note the difficulties but nevertheless assert that "the laws in the Bible represent... what people at the time considered the law to be, and even if not always put into practice, they reveal the underlying processes of juridical thought that were prevalent in the society".[21] Of course, in light of the third interpretive difficulty above, concepts such as "people *at that time*" and "thought... prevalent *in the society*" are moving targets until matters of chronology are decided.

The final interpretive issue concerns the nature of biblical law, especially in light of the preceding considerations. On the one hand, much of what takes place in terms of punishment in biblical law seems to depend on private parties. In the modern perspective, this effectively makes much biblical criminal law into what we would call private law.[22] On the other hand, the geographical setting of divine law coupled, especially, with its divine point of origin problematises any notion of private law in the Bible because *God is always somehow involved*, and one could

19 Thousands of judicial decisions are preserved in Akkadian but none directly cites the most famous of ancient Near Eastern legal collections: the Laws of Hammurabi (henceforth LH). For texts and discussion, see Remko Jas, *Neo-Assyrian Judicial Procedures* (Helsinki: Neo-Assyrian Text Corpus Project, 1996); Victor Avigdor Hurowitz, "Hammurabi in Mesopotamian Tradition", in Yitschak Sefati *et al.*, *"An Experienced Scribe Who Neglects Nothing": Ancient Near Eastern Studies in Honor of Jacob Klein* (Bethesda, MD: CDL Press, 2005), 497–532; and Klaas R. Veenhof, "'In Accordance with the Words of the Stele': Evidence for Old Assyrian Legislation", (1995) 70 *Chicago-Kent Law Review* 1717–44.

20 Assnat Bartor, "Legal Texts", in John Barton, ed., *The Hebrew Bible: A Critical Companion* (Princeton: Princeton University Press, 2016), 176. See also Anne Fitzpatrick-McKinley, *The Transformation of Torah from Scribal Advice to Law* (Sheffield: Sheffield Academic Press, 1999).

21 Raymond Westbrook and Bruce Wells, *Everyday Law in Biblical Israel: An Introduction* (Louisville: Westminster John Knox, 2009), 3.

22 See Bruce Wells, "Law and Practice", in Daniel C. Snell, ed., *A Companion to the Ancient Near East* (Oxford: Blackwell, 2005), 193: "As opposed to most modern systems, the legal systems of the Ancient Near East do not appear to have had a distinction between civil law and criminal law".

hardly imagine a more official authority than the Deity.[23] This divine presence seems to redefine or at least de-emphasise notions of privacy or private law in the case of biblical law, but God's involvement in Israelite jurisprudence also impacts the notion of criminal law. Among other things that might be said, the literary presentation found in the Pentateuch, which makes all law God's law, makes crime look more and more like sin.[24]

Definitions are important at this point. Today, a basic definition of *criminal law* would be in terms of "offences against the community at large",[25] though more would need to be said to round this out, including, perhaps, "the feeling of danger to the community; the public character of the prosecution; the nature of the penalty; and the inability of the victim to pardon or compromise".[26] In ancient Israel, it is even harder to offer a precise definition of criminal law.[27] Similar difficulties obtain for any attempt to define *sin*, though that term refers most basically to violating religious law or otherwise offending a divine entity.[28] By that definition, (criminal) law in the Pentateuch, given its setting and divine point of origin, would indeed seem to qualify as sin, though one should exercise caution, since it is clear that, at least in some texts surrounding purity legislation, not all religious impurity counted as sin.[29] For present purposes, it must suffice to note these terminological and definitional problems, while still acknowledging that the divine origin of Pentateuchal law casts a distinctively religious light on *all* biblical legislation. One practical effect of this is that human sanctions for

23 See Brent A. Strawn, "Biblical Understandings of Private Law", in Robert F. Cochran Jr. and Michael Moreland, eds., *Christianity and Private Law: An Introduction* (Abingdon and New York: Routledge, forthcoming 2020).

24 The reverse may also hold: sin looks more and more like crime with God as divine judge.

25 Bryan A. Garner and Henry Campbell Black, eds., *Black's Law Dictionary*, 10th ed. (St. Paul: Thomson Reuters, 2014), 456; see there for Fletcher's useful distinction between criminal law and penal law, with the former the more capacious category. See further Binder, *Criminal Law*.

26 Jackson, "Reflections on Biblical Criminal Law", 55, with reference to Anthony Phillips, *Ancient Israel's Criminal Law: A New Approach to the Decalogue* (Oxford: Basil Blackwell, 1970), 10–11.

27 See Jackson, "Reflections on Biblical Criminal Law", 55–62, who states that, for "historical [legal] systems, it is more useful to isolate a single criterion. The victim's inability to pardon or compromise is sometimes seen as the real test" (55). See also Falk, *Hebrew Law in Biblical Times*, 71: "crime is … those acts the suppression of which is the concern of the community", a definition that is immediately problematised by the fact "that most crimes were originally dealt with by private vengeance" (see above).

28 See, e.g. Mark Biddle, *Missing the Mark: Sin and Its Consequences in Biblical Theology* (Nashville: Abingdon, 2005); Mark Boda, *A Severe Mercy: Sin and Its Remedy in the Old Testament* (Winona Lake, IN: Eisenbrauns, 2009); and Karel van der Toorn, *Sin and Sanction in Israel and Mesopotamia: A Comparative Study* (Assen/Maastricht: Van Gorcum, 1985). See also Julian Morgenstern, *The Doctrine of Sin in the Babylonian Religion* (San Diego: Book Tree, 2002; first published 1905), 1: "whatever incites the anger of the gods, is sin".

29 See Jonathan Klawans, *Impurity and Sin in Ancient Judaism* (New York: Oxford University Press, 2000).

law-breaking, insofar as they too are ultimately mandated by the Deity, are also divine sanctions.

A closer look at a specific topic in biblical law is in order, in part as a way to exemplify, but also negotiate, the five difficulties outlined above. Homicide is an excellent test case for several reasons: its universal recognition as a crime, for example, and the fact that, even in the Bible, at least some of what takes place after homicide appears to be adjudicated by authorities of one sort or another. Most importantly, biblical homicide is attested in several different texts – indeed, in each of the four major legal corpora found in the Pentateuch, as well as in an important sequel in the Book of Joshua. One would be hard-pressed to find another crime so well described and cross-attested. Still further, the biblical laws on homicide afford unique insight into the mental element of crime, something that other biblical criminal laws leave mostly undiscussed. An investigation of homicide can be both illustrative and informative, therefore, for other laws in the Bible that are less theorised.

2.2 Homicide in the biblical degree

While various non-legal texts might also be adduced, the most extensive laws concerning homicide occur in the Book of the Covenant, the Deuteronomic Code, the Priestly Law and Joshua 20.[30] I exposit each below before focusing, in Section 2.3, on the problem of criminal intention.[31]

2.2.1 The Book of the Covenant: Exodus 21:12–14

This passage, presumably the earliest biblical law pertaining to homicide, is terse compared to the more extensive treatments in Deuteronomy and Numbers. The murder is defined as an act of striking (*makkēh*, from *n-k-h*) that results in death (*wāmēt*, "and he dies"; v. 12a). The talionic penalty is also death: "he shall surely be put to death", an emphatic construction in Hebrew (*môt yûmāt*, v. 12b). There is an immediate qualification, however, or perhaps two: (a) if the killing was not premeditated – the killer had not been lying in wait for, or perhaps better "hunting", the victim (*lōʾ ṣādāh*); and/or (b) it was "an accident allowed by God" – a difficult and ambiguous phrase in Hebrew – then the unintentional killer can escape to "a place" (v. 13) presumably for sanctuary, maybe even to *a* or *the* sanctuary given the mention of God's altar in verse 14. There is no refuge, however, for someone who *plots* (*z-y-d*, a verb often used for arrogant

30 Within the legal texts of the Pentateuch, the Sixth Commandment of the Decalogue is obviously an important law pertaining to homicide; I touch on it briefly below. Note also, but far more briefly, Lev. 24:17, 21 (which belong to the Holiness Code): "If anyone kills (*n-k-h*) another person, they must be executed … Someone who kills (*n-k-h*) an animal must make amends for it, but whoever kills (*n-k-h*) a human being must be executed" (Common English Bible).

31 See further (and for some of what follows), Brent A. Strawn, "Intention", in *OEBL*, 1:433–45.

or presumptuous actions) against another person to *slay* (*h-r-g*) them *on purpose* (or "cunningly" or "treacherously"; *bĕʿormāh*, v. 14). This kind of intentional homicide can find no sanctuary, not even at God's own altar (see also 1 Kgs 1:50–51; 2:28–34), perhaps because the victim is described in very intimate terms: "another person" may also be translated as "his friend/companion/neighbour" (*rēʿēhû*, Exod. 21:14). The people responsible for the execution of the killer are apparently the community since the "you" in verse 14 is plural.

Already in the Book of the Covenant, then, we have a distinction between first- and second-degree murder, along with some criteria for how these two types of homicide are distinguished and punished. But, as one might expect with early law, much is left unclear that will require further elaboration. Can more be said about the mental state of the killer, for instance? "Not hunting/lying in wait" is obviously to be contrasted with "plotting to slay on purpose", but what does "an accident allowed by God" mean? And what about the unspecified "place" God will designate to which an unintentional killer can escape? Subsequent legislation – not surprisingly – fills in many of these gaps.

2.2.2 The Deuteronomic Code: Deuteronomy 19:1–13

Much is familiar in this text if one has already read Exodus 21. The victim is again called *rēʿēhû*, "his friend/companion/neighbour" (vv. 4, 5, 11) and the killing is defined once more as a matter of striking (*n-k-h*, vv. 4, 11), though this is clarified in a second instance as striking "mortally" (*n-k-h* with *nepeš*, v. 11; see also v. 6).

There is also a good bit of new information in Deuteronomy 19: what was a non-descript "place" (*māqôm*) in the Book of the Covenant is here a system of three asylum cities, appropriately distributed throughout the land of Israel so as to give an unintentional killer a reasonable chance to make it to safety (see Deut. 4:41–43 and further below).[32] New language appears for the murderer in the Deuteronomic Code: he is called a "killer" (*rōṣēaḥ*, a participial form from *r-ṣ-ḥ*) and the verb from the same root is used in both Deuteronomy 4 and 19 to describe the actions of such a *rōṣēaḥ*. This same verb is also found in the Sixth Commandment of the Decalogue earlier in Deuteronomy 5: *lōʾ tirṣaḥ*, "Don't kill!" (v. 17; also in Exod. 20:13). But the absolute stringency of the Sixth Commandment aside, the Deuteronomic Code is aware that killing does sometimes take place; if so, what matters is *how* it takes place. Deuteronomy 19 contributes to that discussion by rounding out the brevity of the Book of the Covenant by means of a more common verb for ambushing (*ʾ-r-b*, v. 11) and, most importantly, by adding that a key determinant is whether the killer

32 Scholarly discussion of the asylum cities is large and complicated. For a beginning, see John F. Quant, "Asylum", in *OEBL*, 1:33–7; Pamela Barmash, *Homicide in the Biblical World* (Cambridge: Cambridge University Press, 2005), 71–93; and Francesco Cocco, *The Torah as a Place of Refuge: Biblical Criminal Law and the Book of Numbers* (Tübingen: Mohr Siebeck, 2016).

meant to commit the act. Two factors are crucial in making this determination about intent: whether the killer hated the victim previously (vv. 4, 6, 11) and whether the person performed the act "without knowledge" (***biblî-da'at***, v. 4; see also 4:42), which, in this context, is the equivalent of "without meaning to".[33] Inadvertency is further illustrated by what is presumably a representative (if somewhat fantastic) example in the vignette about the axe-head (19:5).[34]

In these sorts of scenarios the killing is deemed accidental, or, at least, the killer must not be punished by the "blood avenger" (***gō'ēl haddām***), a murky figure – most likely a relative of the victimn, not a formal agent of the State – who is, understandably, enraged over the death.[35] If the homicide is unintentional, however, avenging the blood of the victim is forbidden in both *legal* and *religious* terms – if these are, in fact, differentiable in the ancient world.[36] There is, first, "no death sentence" (***'ên mišpaṭ-māwet***, 19:6) decreed in the case of unintentional murder and, second, to kill an unintentional homicide would be to spill "innocent blood" (19:10, 13). The blood*shed* of the innocent subsequently becomes blood*guilt* that will be required of the Israelites (19:10); hence, it must be "removed" or "burned away" (*b-'-r*, 19:13).[37]

2.2.3 The Priestly Law: Numbers 35:9–34

This is the latest of the three homicide laws according to most scholars. If nothing else, the length of the unit is noteworthy; that is apparently the result of the lapse of time and the process of further legal reflection. The most important pieces of new information can be summarised as follows:

1 The escape cities are now explicitly identified as places of "refuge" or "asylum" (***miqlāṭ***, vv. 11–15, 25–28, 32; see also v. 6).
2 The length of asylum is limited to the balance of years left in the life of the high priest (vv. 25, 28, 32).[38] Once the priest dies, the unintentional killer

33 See Strawn, "Intention", 1:436.
34 See also Westbrook, "Character of Ancient Near Eastern Law", 1:71, on how "the intellectual method of the codes was to set out principles by the use of often extreme examples".
35 This rage is *not* assuaged in the least by determination of intent. The blood avenger is perceived as one who will desire the death of the *rōṣēaḥ* regardless of their mental state. Note also that the avenger's retributive act is described *in the same way* as the initial act: as a case of mortal striking (v. 6). For more on these matters, see Assnat Bartor, "Bloodguilt and Blood Feud", in *OEBL*, 1:64–68, esp. 66–7; also Barmash, *Homicide in the Biblical World*, 20–71.
36 See Brent Nongbri, *Before Religion: A History of a Modern Concept* (New Haven: Yale University Press, 2013).
37 See also Deut. 21:1–9 which concerns an unsolvable murder case: a body is found but the killer is unknown. The passage is highly ritualised, involving the sacrifice of a heifer, a statement of innocence on the part of the elders of the nearest town and a request that God forgive and not hold them guilty for innocent blood.
38 There is debate over whether the passage has one (Jerusalemite) high priest in mind or the chief priest in the local town; note that verse 32 omits any mention of "high".

may return to his own land (v. 28). This information thus specifies a limit to the period of sanctioned blood revenge killing.

3 Lack of intent is specified by means of three new phrases: "by accident" (*bišgāgāh*; vv. 11, 15), "without meaning to" (*bělōʾ rěʾôt*)[39] and "he did not want to harm" the victim (*lōʾměbaqqēš rāʿātô*, v. 23).

4 Accidental killing is, first, *contrasted with* non-accidental scenarios:
   a striking with an iron object of any sort or with a stone or wooden object that could "cause death": these three cases warrant the death penalty (vv. 16–18);
   b even if no object is involved – the striking is by hand only – if it is "out of hostility" (*běʾêbāh*), then it, too, warrants the death penalty (v. 21);
   c pushing "out of hatred" (*běśinʾāh*) and throwing "with malice" (*běṣdîyāh*) also warrants the death penalty (v. 20).

5 Accidental killing is, second, *defined* as:
   a pushing without prior planning ("suddenly") and "without hostility" (v. 22a);
   b throwing any object "without malice" (v. 22b);
   c dropping a stone on someone without meaning to, without being at odds and without desiring to do them harm (v. 23).

6 These delineations are referred to as "the case laws" (*hammišpāṭîm*, v. 24) and "regulations and case laws" (*ḥuqqat mišpāṭ*)[40] that are said to be valid "for all time" and throughout the land (v. 29).

7 "The community" (*hāʿēdāh*, vv. 12, 24, 25) is the body that is to employ these rules when judging (*š-p-ṭ*) between the killer and the blood avenger in v. 24, and, presumably, also in the earlier "judgment" (*mišpāṭ*) in v. 12 that must take place before any killer is executed.

8 The blood avenger (*gōʾēl haddām*, vv. 19, 21, 24, 25, 27; *gōʾēl* alone in v. 12) is the only explicit instrument of execution in the case of a guilty verdict. Blood vengeance is carefully circumscribed, however: it is sanctioned for intentional homicides and allowed for unintentional homicides if the latter killer ventures outside the region of the asylum city before the death of the high priest (vv. 26–28a). Blood revenge outside these circumstances apparently incurs "bloodguilt" (*dām*, v. 33, see v. 27).

9 Blood or bloodguilt (both *dām*) is said to "defile" the land (*ḥ-n-p*, v. 33). The prohibition of making the land "unclean" (*ṭ-m-ʾ*, v. 34) is apparently a synonymous formulation.

10 Capital cases cannot be decided on the basis of one witness alone; instead, there must be more than one: "witnesses" (*ʿēdîm*, v. 30) is plural but unspecific.

39 More woodenly, "without seeing" – that is, without seeing where the stone was being dropped.

40 Baruch Levine, *Numbers 21–36: A New Translation with Introduction and Commentary* (New York: Doubleday, 2000), 558, takes this construction as hendiadic: "a judicial statute".

11 "Ransom" (*kōper*, from *k-p-r*) – presumably payment of some sort – cannot be accepted in the case of a death penalty verdict (v. 31); neither can one pay to be released from the requirement to stay in an asylum city (v. 32).[41] There is also no ransom (*yĕkuppar*, from *k-p-r*) for the blood (bloodguilt) shed in the land except by shedding the blood of the original killer (v. 33).[42]

And yet, despite these new items – and the details familiar from Exodus 21 and Deuteronomy 19 – perduring questions and unresolved ambiguities remain. Consider, with reference to ambiguity, the fact that the term *rōṣēaḥ* describes *both* the killer who kills accidentally *and* the killer who kills intentionally. In the case of the latter, there is something equivalent to a legal pronouncement: *rōṣēaḥ hûʾ*, "he is a killer" (vv. 16–18) – though one is tempted to translate that phrase here, given the context, as "he is a murderer". The verbal root *r-ṣ-ḥ* is also used to describe the implementation of the death penalty itself (v. 30), whereas most instances of that act employ a form of the root *m-w-t* ("to die"). Now one might argue that the literary context and grammatical adjuncts clarify, at least here in Numbers 35, which kind of *rōṣēaḥ* and which kind of "*r-ṣ-ḥ*-ing" are forbidden and which are permitted, but the point stands that both *rōṣēaḥ* and *r-ṣ-ḥ* are, in themselves, at least bivalent. This fact means that, in briefer, less-developed examples – including, above all, the laconic Sixth Commandment (*lōʾ tirṣaḥ*) – there remains a good bit of uncertainty as to precise meaning: is *all* killing forbidden or only what we would today call first-degree murder?[43]

2.2.4 A Coda on Joshua 20

Although it lies outside the Pentateuch and is more of a legal storyette than a law proper, Joshua 20 brings the biblical laws on homicide to an apt conclusion. The chapter records the setting up of six asylum cities (*ʿārê hammiqlāṭ*, v. 1; see also v. 2 and vv. 7–8), in compliance with the Pentateuchal legislation. In so doing, the chapter also repeats and combines in brief compass most of what is found in the other homicide texts: the killer who qualifies for asylum is a *rōṣēaḥ* (vv. 2, 5) who "struck mortally" (*n-k-h* with *nepeš*, vv. 2, 9; *n-k-h* alone in v. 5) his friend/companion/neighbour (*rēʿēhû*, v. 5) "by accident, without knowledge" (*bišgāgāh biblî daʿat*,[44] v. 3; *biblî daʿat* alone in v. 5; *bišgāgāh* alone in v. 9) – a

41 See also Falk, *Hebrew Law in Biblical Times*, 72: "The stay in these places was, thus, a kind of punishment rather than an enjoyment of divine protection".

42 Cf. Gen. 9:5–6, which Greenberg ("Some Postulates of Biblical Criminal Law", 31) deems a "precise and adequate formulation of the jural postulate underlying the biblical law of homicide".

43 Contrast later rabbinic discussion which is considerably more developed – for example, the Mishnaic tractate *Makkot*.

44 The combined formulation is odd without a conjunction, and the second part, "without knowledge", is missing in some manuscripts. See Richard D. Nelson, *Joshua: A Commentary* (Louisville: Westminster John Knox, 1997), 226–8; see also the next note.

point that is demonstrated by the fact that there had been no hatred between the two theretofore (v. 5). The avenger of blood (*gōʾēl haddām*) is still in hot pursuit (v. 5), but Joshua 20 provides crucial new information on legal procedure. The unintentional killer who flees to an asylum city must go to the city gates (the place of juridical review) and plead his case (*d-b-r... dĕbarayw*, "speak his words/ deeds") before the city elders (*ziqnê hāʿîr*, v. 4a). The assumption is that the killer in this instance is telling the truth; the elders will take the killer in and provide a place (*māqôm*) for him, and he is permitted to remain there (v. 4b). The elders are explicitly forbidden from handing the killer over to the blood avenger *because* (*kî*) the killing was unintentional (v. 5; see also v. 9). The killer must stay in the asylum city until he stands for "judgment" (*mišpāṭ*) before "the congregation" (*haʿēdāh*, v. 6; see also v. 9) and/or[45] until the death of the high priest (v. 6). After that point, the killer can return to his own house and the hometown from whence they had fled originally (v. 6). A final important detail is that the asylum cities are explicitly designated not only for Israelites but also for any immigrants who reside among them (v. 9).

2.3 The mental element: the problem of intention

Ancient Near Eastern law does not express the same level of concern with regard to intentionality in homicide that is evident in the biblical laws,[46] though intention is a factor in the Hittite Laws (HL). In HL ##3, 4, II and III there is mention of different scenarios in which killing was "by accident" (*keššaršiš waštai*),[47] terminology that indicates that the killings described earlier (HL ##1–2), which lack this language, must be considered intentional, even if not premeditated (both concern a quarrel).[48] This same phrasing occurs in HL #V–VI with reference to accidental blinding.

The presence of the mental element in non-homicide cases such as blinding in HL serves as an apt entrée into the problem of *mens rea* more generally in ancient Near Eastern law, where the topic is encountered not infrequently, especially in cases of personal injury. Consider, for example, the Laws of Hammurapi (henceforth LH) ##206–7:

45 The Hebrew lacks a conjunction and the entire second clause about the death of the high priest is missing from some manuscripts. See Nelson, *Joshua*, 226–8, and the previous note.

46 For Egypt, see VerSteeg, *Law in Ancient Egypt*, 169–72; and James Hoch and Sara E. Orel, "Murder in Ancient Egypt", in Sara E. Orel, ed., *Death and Taxes in the Ancient Near East* (Lewiston: Mellen, 1992), 87–128. For Mesopotamia, see VerSteeg, *Early Mesopotamian Law*, 108–11; Jackson, *A Comparison of Ancient Near Eastern Law Collections*, 180–8; Samuel Greengus, *Laws in the Bible and in Early Rabbinic Collections: The Legal Legacy of the Ancient Near East* (Eugene: Cascade, 2011), 160–83; and Barmash, *Homicide in the Biblical World*, esp. 207–19, for 47 different cuneiform sources on homicide.

47 More woodenly, "his hand sins". See Harry Angier Hoffner Jr., *The Laws of the Hittites: A Critical Edition* (Leiden: Brill, 1997), 170, for discussion.

48 See Hoffner, *Laws of the Hittites*, 17–18, and his translation of HL in Roth, *Law Collections*, 213–40 (217).

> If an *awīlu* should strike another *awīlu* during a brawl and inflict upon him a wound, that *awīlu* shall swear "I did not strike intentionally", and he shall satisfy the physician (i.e. pay his fees). If he should die from his beating, he shall also swear ("I did not strike him intentionally"); if he (the victim) is a member of the *awīlu*-class, he shall weigh out and deliver 30 shekels of silver.[49]

The punishment for the crime depends not only on the outcome of the blow, to be sure, but also on the intention of the striker, who must swear that he did not intend harm. The language used here is the Akkadian equivalent to what is found in Deuteronomy 4:42; 19:4 and Joshua 20:3, 5, since it, too, concerns lack of *knowledge*: "I did not strike knowingly" (*ina idû la amḫaṣu*).

Punishments for other types of assault and injury are also often mitigated on the basis of intent: lack of intent leads to lighter punishment. The mechanism by which the intent is determined, however, is rarely clear. In LH, the perpetrator simply swears (*itamma*, from *tamû*) to this effect – probably a reference to a formal oath of some sort.[50] This supposition takes on increased likelihood not only given the use of *tamû* in other legal contexts,[51] but also from how intention plays a role in other kinds of ancient Near Eastern texts, particularly religious ones: hymns, prayers and ritual/cultic texts where the oath in question is taken *before the gods*. One might note, for example, negative confessions of sin, such as that in the Egyptian *Book of the Dead*, chapter 125, which often employ language of "not knowing" about wrongdoing in an apparent attempt to motivate the gods to forgive the human supplicant. If there was an *actus reus*, that is, there is nevertheless no accompanying *mens rea* according to these texts. While many of these texts are admittedly religious and not legal, there is, again, considerable overlap in these arenas in antiquity, generally speaking, even if the specific textual genres remain differentiable. What such texts show, regardless, is that the gods, too, were evidently open to arguments concerning intention when it came to religious crimes (i.e., sins).

On the one hand, then, there is something approaching *strict liability* in these cases: the petitioner has (presumably) done something wrong and is responsible for it in some fashion; on the other hand, there is some awareness, even if it is not yet fully developed, that there are mitigating factors and these should matter in how things move forward.[52] So, while there was nothing like an insanity defence

49 Roth, *Law Collections*, 122.

50 See G.R. Driver and John C. Miles, *The Babylonian Laws*, 2 vols. (Oxford: Clarendon, 1968), 1:412, also 1.61–5. See also F. Rachel Magdalene, *On the Scales of Righteousness: Neo-Babylonian Trial Law and the Book of Job* (Providence: Brown Judaic Studies, 2007), 78–84.

51 See Michael P. Streck and Martha Tobi Roth, eds., *The Assyrian Dictionary of the Oriental Institute of the University of Chicago*, vol. 18: *T* (Chicago: Oriental Institute of the University of Chicago, 2006), 159–65; see also Andrew R. Davis, "Oaths and Vows", in *OEBL*, 2:149–56, as well as the Ninth Commandment against false testimony.

52 See also Roscoe Pound, *An Introduction to the Philosophy of Law*, rev. ed. (New Haven: Yale University Press, 1954), 79, who argued that it was certain intellectual developments in the

proper,[53] there were nevertheless "acts of God",[54] and there were also different mental states. The gods should take these latter into consideration when they dole out punishment for religious infraction since they bear directly on culpability. The situation in the Bible may be put in even stronger terms: given the literary setting of Pentateuchal law, in which all law is divine in origin, the God of Israel is *not* the one who must be convinced of these mental states by human petitioners; rather, the God of Israel is *the one who legislates* such considerations, even for the most heinous of crimes: homicide.[55] That is to say that, in the Bible, God legislates about *mens rea* not just *actus rea*. It comes as no surprise, then, to encounter discussion of intention in other contexts in the Old Testament, from the ritual (see Leviticus 4–5) to the poetic (see Ps. 19:12–13; 90:8; 119:10, 21, 67, 118; Job 6:24; 19:4).[56] What the biblical and ancient Near Eastern materials demonstrate, therefore, is that ancient people reckoned with the problem of the mental element in law and therefore were not nearly as rigid in their understanding of cause and effect when it came to (religious) misfortune as is sometimes claimed.[57] If someone "did not mean to do it" – whatever "it" was, even if quite

nineteenth century that shifted "a positive, creative theory of developing liability on the basis of intention" to "a negative, restraining, one might say pruning, theory of no liability except on the basis of intention. Liability could flow only from culpable conduct or from assumed duties. The abstract individual will was the central point in the theory of liability … The bases of liability were culpable conduct and legal transaction, and these came down to an ultimate basis in will. The fundamental conception in legal liability was the conception of an act – of a manifestation of the will in the external world". It should go without saying but should nevertheless be underscored that ancient understandings of individuality, selfhood and will are not the same as modern ones. See, inter alia, Charles Taylor, *Sources of the Self: The Making of the Modern Identity* (Cambridge, MA: Harvard University Press, 1989); along with Susan Niditch, *The Responsive Self: Personal Religion in Biblical Literature of the Neo-Babylonian and Persian Periods* (New Haven: Yale University Press, 2015); and Michael Carasik, *Theologies of the Mind in Biblical Israel* (New York: Peter Lang, 2005).

53 Falk, *Hebrew Law in Biblical Times*, 69: "No special provision was made for criminal lunatics". See also Brent A. Strawn, "What Is It Like to Be a Psalmist? Unintentional Sin and Moral Agency in the Psalter", (2015) 40 *Journal for the Study of the Old Testament* 61–78.

54 See, e.g. LH ##45, 48, 249, 266; see also the odd phrasing in Exod. 21:13.

55 The story of Cain and Abel in Gen. 4:1–16 is significant at this point (see also Barmash, *Homicide in the Biblical World*, 12–19). It may be that Cain has played the part of God by taking Abel's life, a point he tries to avoid by disclaiming the role of "keeper". But in the Old Testament, *God* is the one who is most often said to keep humans and thus attends to the deceased's cry for justice. See Ps. 121:4; and Paul A. Rieman, "Am I My Brother's Keeper?", (1970) 24 *Interpretation* 482–91; also Gen. 9:5–6 and Gen. 50:15–21.

56 See Strawn, "Intention", 1:440–2; Strawn, "What Is It Like to Be a Psalmist?".

57 See Strawn, "What Is It Like to Be a Psalmist?"; also Fredrik Lindström, *Suffering and Sin: Interpretations of Illness in the Individual Complaint Psalms* (Stockholm: Almqvist & Wiksell, 1994); and Fredrik Lindström, *God and the Origin of Evil: A Contextual Analysis of Alleged Monistic Evidence in the Old Testament* (Lund: CWK Gleerup, 1983). Contrast Morgenstern, *Doctrine of Sin in the Babylonian Religion*, 1: "Misfortune of all kinds was the result of the divine anger … If evil came, the god was angry. What could have caused this? Sin! This is one of the fundamental principles of the Babylonian religion, if not of all primitive religions".

awful – that fact should matter. This realisation, evident in the texts, opens up a fissure, even if only a very slight one, that will lead to larger legal and theological issues with regard to culpability and punishment, sin and responsibility. The fact that the divine world attended to (or *should attend to*) the mental element in crime and sin is an appropriate segue to the final section on God(s) and the law.

2.4 God(s) and/as law, law and/as god(s)

The relationship between the divine world and the legal one is ancient; it is also quite close in the way the Bible, at least, portrays God as divine legislator. This point was not lost on later writers speaking of God and the law – Eike von Repgow, for instance, wrote "God is Law itself, therefore justice is dear to him",[58] and Thomas Aquinas spoke of God in terms of, if not actually as, eternal law.[59] To be sure, it is not only the presentation of law in the Pentateuch that underlies such sentiments, but also texts such as Psalm 11:7:

> Because the LORD is righteous (*ṣaddîq*),
> he loves righteous acts (*ṣedāqôt*),
> the upright (*yāšār*) will see his face.

It is without doubt the close connection between the divine world and the law, both inside and outside the Bible – and thus the bleed-over between crime and sin – that led to religious pleas regarding *lack* of intent. In the Priestly system, after all, intentional sins were precisely the ones that were deemed *un*forgivable.[60]

Contemporary legal systems, of course, have been largely scrubbed of divine agents though they retain a divine or semi-divine agency[61] – particularly vis-à-vis criminals – insofar as the law has the power to declare guilt or innocence, enforce

58 Eike von Repgow, *Sachsenspiegel, Prologus*, translation from Mary Dobozny, *The Saxon Mirror: A Sachsenspiegel of the Fourteenth Century* (Philadelphia: University of Pennsylvania Press, 1999), 67; see also 208–9. The original reads: *Got is selber recht, dar umme is im recht lip.*

59 Thomas Aquinas, *Summa Theologiae: Latin Text and English Translation, Introduction, Notes, Appendices, and Glossaries*, vol. 5: *God's Will and Providence (1a. 19–26)*, ed. Thomas Gilby and Ian Hislop; repr. ed. (Cambridge: Cambridge University Press, 2006), 74–5 (I, 21, 1): "God is a law unto himself" (*Deus autem sibi ipsi est lex*). See also *Summa Theologiae*, II-I, 93–108; R.J. Henle, ed., *Saint Thomas Aquinas: The Treatise on Law* (Notre Dame: University of Notre Dame Press, 1993).

60 See Strawn, "Intention", 1:440–1, on Leviticus 4–5 and Numbers 15:22–29; see further Jacob Milgrom, *Numbers* (Philadelphia: Jewish Publication Society, 5750/1990), 122, also 405–6; Jacob Milgrom, *Leviticus 1–16: A New Translation with Introduction and Commentary* (New York: Doubleday, 1991), 424, 457–60.

61 See also Rémi Brague, *The Law of God: The Philosophical History of an Idea*, trans. Lydia G. Cochrane (Chicago: University of Chicago Press, 2008). Not unrelated discussions include Charles Taylor, *A Secular Age* (Cambridge, MA: Harvard University Press, 2007); and George Steiner, *Real Presences* (Chicago: University of Chicago Press, 1989). See also Rafael Domingo, *God and the Secular Legal System* (Cambridge: Cambridge University Press, 2016).

payment of damages to victims of torts and even inflict physical punishment for crimes, up to and including total control over an offender's life through, say, a lifetime in prison or, still more ultimately, by means of execution. The power of law is, in this sense, profoundly godlike when seen through ancient eyes,[62] but the same is true today and for the very same reasons. It seems important, therefore, to recognise this godlike power of even secular law and, correlatively, the implicit theology at work even in *a*-theological systems. As Umberto Eco has asserted:

> behind every strategy of the symbolic mode, be it religious or aesthetic, there is a legitimating theology, even though it is the atheistic theology of unlimited semiosis or of hermeneutics as deconstruction. A positive way to approach every instance of the symbolic mode would be to ask: which theology legitimates it?[63]

Modern legal systems may not always be "instances of the symbolic mode", but ancient ones surely were.[64] And yet, insofar as even secular legal systems exercise godlike power over their subjects, it seems that these systems, too, traffic in the theological (per Eco) even if that is not always at the level of explicit awareness and so, potentially at least, might do so in a manner that might be deemed dangerous. The theological aspect of that statement relates to the near absolute power wielded by law, again on certain matters and some subjects. Such a situation is dangerous, according to the Bible – even just according to Old Testament law by itself – since nothing and no-one should come before God (Exod. 20:3 // Deut. 5:7; see also Deut. 6:4–5; etc.). When humans or human institutions mistake this situation and favour another, the results are consistently deleterious, according to Scripture. This may be one more reason, to come full circle, why *all* law in the Pentateuch is presented as *God*'s law.

62 In fact, in some systems the gods themselves were subject to law, which makes the law *supra*-divine, somehow above the gods and thus a god as well, if not the highest of gods and most supreme of deities. See Greenberg, "Some Postulates of Biblical Criminal Law", 27–8, on the Mesopotamian material, and note Pindar who spoke of Nomos ("law") as king of all (Frag. 169), and Plato, who called the law *theos* ("god") in *Ep.* 8.354e. The same might be said for certain aspects of Second Temple Judaism (e.g. Ezra 9:37; Gal. 4:4–5, etc.) and later rabbinic thought, where God is subject to the Torah and to legal insights into the Torah generated by the rabbis. See Christine Hayes, *What's Divine about Divine Law? Early Perspectives* (Princeton: Princeton University Press, 2015), for how the roots of such a perspective lie in the Bible. A good example is the story of the daughters of Zelophehad (see Num. 27:1–11; 36:1–12). See also Lisbeth S. Fried, "The Torah of God as God: The Exaltation of the Written Law Code in Ezra-Nehemiah", in Nathan MacDonald and Izaak J. de Hulster, eds., *Divine Presence and Absence in Exilic and Post-Exilic Judaism* (Tübingen: Mohr Siebeck, 2013), 283–300.

63 Umberto Eco, *Semiotics and the Philosophy of Language* (Bloomington: Indiana University Press, 1986), 163.

64 See Thomas Kazen, *Emotions in Biblical Law* (Sheffield: Sheffield Phoenix, 2011); and Åke Viberg, *Symbols of Law: Contextual Analysis of Legal Symbolic Acts in the Old Testament* (Stockholm: Almqvist & Wiksell, 1992). See also Hayes, *What's Divine about Divine Law?*

Another way to put this theology of even secular law is that whether (mono) theistic or not, there's always a god; the question is whether it is a *legal god* or *how legal the god* in question may be. Or, to reverse the terms, the question may be how *divine* the law really is. To return to the matter of intention, it is clear that intent mattered to the gods (in the ancient world) and to God (in the world of Scripture) and so one expects that it should continue to matter whenever the law performs divine or semi-divine functions vis-à-vis its subjects. In the end, then, one way that law might be more aware of its godlike powers, and less dangerous in exercising them, would be to pay increased attention, whenever possible, to the problem of intention.[65] It seems clear, in any event, that Christianity, on the basis of its sacred Scripture, can and must support those places where the law – criminal or otherwise – functions to create, order and maintain the kind of society that was also, and earlier, envisioned, even legislated, by its Lord.

Further reading

Barmash, Pamela. *Homicide in the Biblical World* (Cambridge: Cambridge University Press, 2005).

Burnside, Jonathan. *God, Justice, and Society: Aspects of Law and Legality in the Bible* (Oxford: Oxford University Press, 2011).

Falk, Ze'ev W. *Hebrew Law in Biblical Times*, 2d ed. (Provo, UT: Brigham Young University Press/Winona Lake, IN: Eisenbrauns, 2001).

Frymer-Kenski, Tikva. "Israel", in Raymond Westbrook, ed., *A History of Ancient Near Eastern Law*, 2 vols (Leiden: Brill, 2003), 2:975–1046.

Greengus, Samuel. *Laws in the Bible and in Early Rabbinic Collections: The Legal Legacy of the Ancient Near East* (Eugene: Cascade, 2011).

Hayes, Christine. *What's Divine About Divine Law? Early Perspectives* (Princeton: Princeton University Press, 2015).

Knight, Douglas A. *Law, Power, and Justice in Ancient Israel* (Louisville: Westminster John Knox, 2011).

Morrow, William S. *An Introduction to Biblical Law* (Grand Rapids: Eerdmans, 2017).

Strawn, Brent A., ed. *The Oxford Encyclopedia of the Bible and Law*, 2 vols (Oxford: Oxford University Press, 2015).

Westbrook, Raymond, ed. *A History of Ancient Near Eastern Law*, 2 vols (Leiden: Brill, 2003).

Westbrook, Raymond and Bruce Wells. *Everyday Law in Biblical Israel: An Introduction* (Louisville: Westminster John Knox, 2009).

65 See, inter alia, J.L.J. Edwards, *Mens Rea in Statutory Offences* (London: Macmillan, 1955); Itzhak Kugler, *Direct and Oblique Intention in the Criminal Law: An Inquiry into Degrees of Blameworthiness* (Burlington, VT: Ashgate, 2002); and Mohamed Elewa Badar, *The Concept of Mens Rea in International and Criminal Law: The Case for a Unified Approach* (Oxford: Hart, 2013).

3 Conflicting criminal jurisdictions in early Christianity

Markus Bockmuehl

Jesus was crucified in April 30 or 33 on a Roman cross immediately outside the walls of Jerusalem, under the official charge sheet or *titulus* publishing his crime as one of political insurrection: “King of the Jews”. While this is one of antiquity’s better-documented executions, rather less can be said with certainty about the fate of his apostolic college of 12 closest followers. The first among the 12 to die was James the son of Zebedee, beheaded in Jerusalem by Herod’s grandson Agrippa I in March or April of the year 41 or 42. There are grounds for believing that the disciples’ spokesman Simon Peter suffered crucifixion in or near the Circus of Nero in Rome between 64 and 67, purportedly upside down (as the *Acts of Peter* asserts a century later). Other accounts are of more legendary quality but eventually include the martyrdom of all but 1 of the 12 (John the son of Zebedee).

Several other close followers of Jesus fared no better. The Book of Acts lists Stephen as the first martyr, stoned to death apparently by a mob following a trial in the mid 30s. Around the year 58, Paul of Tarsus was placed under Roman arrest in Jerusalem and imprisoned in Caesarea amid a swirl of Jewish popular and legal opposition before his transfer to Rome two years later to face an imperial court (Acts 21–28). Christian sources of the later second and subsequent centuries consistently claim his eventual Roman execution by decapitation (*decollatio*; *capitis amputatio*), a fate shared with James the son of Zebedee and a number of other early believers (see also Rev. 20:4). James the brother of Jesus is known from the Jewish historian Josephus, as well as early Christian sources including Hegesippus, to have been controversially condemned, thrown from the Temple wall and likewise stoned to death under the high priest Hanan ben Hanan in the year 62 (*Antiquities* 20.200). Over the next century, other Christian leaders followed including Saints Ignatius of Antioch, Polycarp of Smyrna and Justin Martyr, as well as lesser-known individuals and communities in North Africa and Gaul; all fell foul of the supposed agents of Roman justice in one way or another.

Historical difficulties aside, we may readily acknowledge that accounts like these often make it impossible to distinguish with confidence between formal criminal proceedings on the one hand and kangaroo justice or mob violence on the other. And few of these early martyrdom stories, even when taken at face value, help adjudicate contested questions such as the relative prevalence or otherwise of official persecution, to some extent even for the notorious third century.

Nevertheless, an experience of conflict with criminal law of one definition or another – or indeed of more than one definition – is never far from the surface. This is particularly clear if we allow for a relatively broad understanding of that concept: in any legally constituted society, criminal law addresses actions considered sufficiently harmful that they are formally proscribed by statute and subject to prosecution and punishment by lawful authority.

A further glance at the evidence under this heading reveals an additional important insight on the New Testament. Not only was early Christianity entangled with diverse legal challenges from its earliest origins, but also the nature of these entanglements turns out upon momentary reflection to be confusingly complex and multi-layered – certainly in Palestine but arguably in other parts of the Roman Empire too.

There are a number of significant but relatively straightforward tensions between followers of Jesus as victims of crime or as perceived (or, rarely, real) perpetrators. Under each of these headings, the texts attest plenty of experience with a problematic apparatus of criminal justice, from unjust laws to miscarriages of justice and sham trials to arbitrary impositions of violence. The body of potential evidence here is enormous and the task of engaging it far exceeds what can be attempted in this short essay.

Instead, I would like here to explore another, possibly less familiar, but in any case strikingly formative aspect of this complexity: pre-Constantinian Christianity's relationship to criminal law was inevitably articulated against the backdrop of several *overlapping criminal jurisdictions and legal systems* – typically at least two, but sometimes more.

To some extent the conflict between divine law and the law of the land – or the law of the occupiers – had been readily apparent in Jewish and Israelite history for at least half a millennium, both in the Holy Land and in far-flung regions of the Mesopotamian and Egyptian diaspora. And from the perspective of Roman law, which also reflected extensively on customary international law under the heading of *ius Gentium*, the experience of disentangling relations with indigenous legal frameworks was also not particularly unusual. In the New Testament, however, the relationship with not just one but multiple outside legal authorities becomes particularly formative for the shape of the emerging Church.

I begin by examining this phenomenon of diverse criminal jurisdictions in the trial and execution of Jesus, before exploring this in relation to penal sanctions in the experience and teaching of the Apostle Paul. Finally, I hope to venture a couple of suggestions about how Christians of the second and third centuries began to develop notions of public justice in relation to the criminal law and legal administration of the dominant power.

3.1 Overlapping criminal jurisdictions in the Jesus tradition

In relation to the ministry and death of Jesus, different jurisdictions not only overlap but also convict the accused of markedly different offences. Three or four main points of reference merit brief discussion.

3.1.1 Pharisaic disputes

The first of these may seem particularly familiar to readers of the Gospels, but turns out upon closer examination to be something of a red herring for this purpose. Jesus spends a good deal of his Galilean ministry in sometimes acrimonious legal controversy with Pharisaic challengers about his teaching and praxis. More often than not, these debates concern the interpretation of positive biblical laws specifically about sabbath observance, about vows or about purity – all of which were matters of considerable and heated contention between rival first-century Jewish groups – and even between particular constituent factions of those groups (such as the Hillelite and Shammaite branches of Pharisaism).

Christian interpreters of quite diverse commitments have often used these narratives to feed a trope of Jesus' conflict with Judaism and indeed the abolition of the Law in favour of varying agendas of supersession – whether traditional ones of grace and justification by faith or progressive ones of social inclusion. On this account, Jesus runs afoul of Jewish criminal law and jurisprudence because he is a good Christian, or perhaps more recently because he is a good liberal.

Perhaps unfortunately for this still fondly held historical misconception, the views Jesus espouses are typically well within the range of attested Jewish legal debate, whether in the first century or in subsequent rabbinic thought. On some matters (including divorce), later rabbinic legal norms eventually resolve that debate rather differently; but on others (healing on the sabbath; vows depriving parents), the normative consensus ultimately vindicates or at least tolerates positions compatible with those of Jesus.[1]

But the issues at stake in these Galilean controversies only rarely, if ever, directly concern "criminal" cases: biblical law has few if any properly *penal* sanctions for the laws concerning impurity or diet, divorce or exorcisms; and its definitions and remedies regarding sabbath observance were for the most part so broad and unspecific as to require extensive elaboration in Jewish legal debate.

Jesus certainly appears to claim a surprising degree of interpretative authority, quite plausibly breaching what some factions would have regarded as the acceptable boundaries for the laws at issue. But the debates explore boundaries and definitions of proper legal practice among controversialists for whom the validity and even the observance of the statutes in question are not themselves contested. Perhaps the only partial exception to this rule is the episode of Jesus and the adulterous woman in John 7:53–8:11 – a highly influential story whose place in the ministry of Jesus is difficult to establish in view of its late and secondary manuscript attestation in the Gospel of John. (It also raises interesting questions about

1 See e.g. Markus Bockmuehl, *Jewish Law in Gentile Churches: Halakhah and the Beginning of Christian Public Ethics* (Grand Rapids: Baker Academic, 2003); William R.G. Loader, "Jesus and the Law", in T. Holmén and S.E. Porter, eds., *Handbook for the Study of the Historical Jesus*, 4 vols. (Leiden and Boston: Brill, 2011), 3:2745–72; and Angelika Strotmann and Markus Tiwald, "Das Matthäus-Evangelium: eine Paulus-Polemik? Überlegungen zum Toraverständnis des ersten Evangelisten", in M. Ebner *et al.*, eds., *Quaestiones disputatae* (Freiburg im Breisgau: Herder, 2016), 64–106, along with literature cited there.

whether Jesus' response is one of blanket remission, as Christian homilists like to assume, or more a counsel of *nolle prosequi* in the face of compromised witnesses. Conviction in such cases was complicated, as were requirements placed upon witnesses. Conversely, easy assumptions of a blanket remission tend to ignore the social and relational costs to the husband, the other wife, respective children and so forth.)

Most telling, perhaps, for the "red herring" status of Jesus' legal disputes with Galilean Pharisees is that neither those conflicts nor indeed those Pharisees appear at his trial in Jerusalem. One might have imagined that charges about his sabbath praxis, supposed magic and sorcery, or false prophecy would surface at his trial, as some of them repeatedly do in later Jewish anti-Christian polemic (invoked, for example, by the important second-century pagan critic Celsus). Even Matthew, for whom the conflict with the Pharisees takes on iconic importance, never attributes to them the prosecutorial agency emphatically exercised by his "chief priests and elders" (Matt. 26:3, 47, 57, 59; 27:1, 20 etc.; contrast 27:62). Conversely, even some of Jesus' most startling statements in Galilee (such as encouraging a potential follower to abandon burying his father; 8:22) appear to elicit neither criminal nor any other sanction from Matthew's Pharisees.

All this suggests the relative remoteness of Jesus' sometimes unconventional halakhic teaching and praxis from any properly *criminal* injunction. The halakhic interpretation of particular cases is no doubt intensely contested, sometimes because of the different principles brought to bear on the relative prioritisation between conflicting biblical laws. Yet, while accusations of subverting the Torah are launched in both directions, each party acknowledges the Torah to be the determining legal framework. As William Loader puts it, there was

> nothing in Jesus' reported approach to the Law which would warrant the conclusion that Jesus set aside Torah or even set aside parts of Torah. Controversies concern different ways of interpreting Torah, different priorities. If Jesus had abandoned Torah or set parts of it aside or in other ways breached it in a major way, we might expect to have some indication of this in the accounts of his trial and execution. This is not the case.[2]

3.1.2 Roman judgment and execution

This brings us to a necessarily brief discussion of the trial of Jesus. He is tried, convicted and executed as a criminal, even if the legal validity of the trial has, of course, been roundly challenged since antiquity. Notably, it is *Roman* judicial and executive power that takes charge of the death of Jesus: especially in their combination, both the published charge on the *titulus* and the penalty for a non-citizen are recognisably Roman. Scholars widely relate this to the fact that the Jewish Sanhedrin at this time probably had no formal right to carry out

2 Loader, "Jesus and the Law", 3:2767.

executions (see also John 18:31). This matters considerably, however complicit its officials may have been with Roman legal force: it is ironic, and in due course bore tragic consequences, that Christian texts even from the earliest period imply or affirm that it was Jews who killed Christ (note already 1 Thess. 2:15; Matt. 27:25; John 19:15–18).

The proceedings and indeed the charges also make good sense within a provincial Roman setting. Here even more than in the capital, criteria of criminal liability and conviction might well be nebulous, while proceedings were highly adversarial without minimum requirements about subtleties such as pre-trial discovery, witnesses or rules of evidence.[3] As for the identification of that criminal charge against Jesus, among the plausible possibilities most scholars have opted for *maiestas* (a crime of treason against Rome that came into its own in the later Republic and was then increasingly associated with the person of the emperor) rather than *perduellio* (a rarely prosecuted offence concerned with misconduct in public office or related detriment to the political order).[4] This offence of treason appears to have been interpreted more loosely, and capital punishment applied more readily, from the time of Tiberius: its meaning and application became "both uncertain and deadly".[5]

Biblical law and the overwhelming bulk of subsequent Jewish practice do not envisage crucifixion among the available forms of the death penalty. Rather exceptionally, it appears, Alexander Jannaeus (103–76 BCE), authoritarian ruler of the temporarily independent Jewish State of the second and early first centuries

3 See Andrew M. Riggsby, "Criminal Law, Roman", in *Oxford Classical Dictionary* (Oxford: Oxford University Press, 2017), http://oxfordre.com/classics/abstract/10.1093/acrefore/9780199381135.001.0001/acrefore-9780199381135-e-8153?rskey=6DoAM0&result=1 (accessed 15 January 2019).

4 See recently Callie Williamson "Crimes Against the State", in P.J. de Plessis *et al.*, eds., *The Oxford Handbook of Roman Law and Society* (Oxford: Oxford University Press, 2016), 337–40; Andrew M. Riggsby, "Public and Private Criminal Law", in P.J. de Plessis *et al.*, eds., *The Oxford Handbook of Roman Law and Society* (Oxford: Oxford University Press, 2016), 310–21; Riggsby, "Criminal Law, Roman"; and previously O.F. Robinson, *Penal Practice and Penal Policy in Ancient Rome* (London: Routledge, 2007), ch. 5. For legal aspects of the trial and execution of Jesus, see e.g. David W. Chapman and Eckhard J. Schnabel, eds., *The Trial and Crucifixion of Jesus: Texts and Commentary* (Tübingen: Mohr Siebeck, 2015); John Granger Cook, *Crucifixion in the Mediterranean World* (Tübingen: Mohr Siebeck, 2014); Simon J. Joseph, *Jesus and the Temple: The Crucifixion in Its Jewish Context* (Cambridge and New York: Cambridge University Press, 2016).

5 Jill Harries, *Law and Crime in the Roman World* (Cambridge: Cambridge University Press, 2007), 79 (see generally 77–80). Peter Garnsey, "Why Penalties Become Harsher: The Roman Case, Late Republic to Fourth Century Empire", (1968) 13 *Natural Law Forum* 141–62, influentially discussed the late Republic and early Empire's increasingly harsh penal regime; Jean-Jacques Aubert, "A Double Standard in Roman Criminal Law? The Death Penalty and Social Structure in Late Republican and Early Imperial Rome", I J.-J. Aubert and A.J.B. Sirks, eds., *Speculum Iuris: Roman Law as a Reflection of Social and Economic Life in Antiquity* (Ann Arbor: University of Michigan Press, 2002), 94–133, applies this to the early Christian experience.

BCE, had in fact adopted it. At the behest of Sadducean advisers, he famously had 800 Pharisees crucified, slitting their wives and children's throats before their eyes while he himself watched from his elaborate banquet – an episode also remembered with revulsion even by an anti-Pharisaic document in the Dead Sea Scrolls.[6] By contrast, even the notoriously murderous pro-Roman regime of Herod the Great appears not to have resorted to this quintessentially Roman mode of execution. Romans, by contrast, crucified routinely.

3.1.3 Preceded by a conflicting Jewish trial

As for the criminal proceedings themselves, a Jewish trial or informal hearing consistently and plausibly *precedes* the Roman one in all four Gospels. The phenomenon of parallel Jewish and Roman jurisdictions involved in the crucifixion of Jesus has, of course, been the subject of extensive discussion.[7] Since Jewish authorities sought to hand Jesus over to Pilate broadly on the grounds of insurrection, it made sense for them to seek to establish a suitable charge against him. While even casual Roman justice would have little trouble with a capital charge of *maiestas* for a "King of the Jews" (the term *basileus* was also the Greek title of the emperor), this clearly could not be a Jewish capital crime.

Once again, the juridical setting of an apparently hurried night-time hearing looks informal at best and would, by the standards of subsequent rabbinic law, have been illegal on several counts including such matters as the publication of the charge, the timing of the trial (both at night and, if the Synoptic Gospels are to be believed, on the holiest night of the Passover festival) and the nature and quality of witnesses. Few of the circumstantial details look historically discoverable with any degree of confidence. But be that as it may: what decides the fate of Jesus here is not his politics nor even any claim to (messianic) kingship.

Instead, the first, unsuccessful charge relates to Jesus' supposed threat to the Temple. The evangelists are not wholly consistent in describing the charge: for Mark, *false* and contradictory witnesses assert that Jesus actively planned to destroy the Temple and build another "made without hands" in three days (14:56–59). Matthew turns them into true witnesses who follow a host of false ones; but their allegation is merely the less problematic one that Jesus claimed the *ability* to destroy and rebuild the Temple (Matt. 26:60–61). Luke's abbreviated account of the Jewish trial has no witnesses at all, although the false charges resurface in his account of Stephen's trial in Acts 6:13–14.

In John, the theme features only in the form of a challenge to Jewish interlocutors that if *they* destroy the Temple, Jesus would rebuild it (2:18–22). It is not

6 Josephus, *The Jewish War* 1.97–8, 113; *Antiquities* 13.380–3, 410–11. See also 4Q169 (4Q Nahum Pesher) 3+4.i.7–9.

7 See n. 2 and also Peter Egger, *"Crucifixus sub Pontio Pilato". Das "Crimen" Jesu von Nazareth im Spannungsfeld römischer und jüdischer Verwaltungs- und Rechtsstrukturen* (Münster: Aschendorff, 1997).

obvious how in any of its forms such a verbal (and hypothetical) claim, however offensive to vested political and commercial interests, could really constitute a capital offence against normative Jewish law. This point may be tacitly acknowledged when, having unsuccessfully challenged Jesus to defend himself, the investigating high priest moves on to what ostensibly becomes the actionable charge of blasphemy. The more credible political calculus was not that there was any likelihood of Jesus destroying the Temple, but that the riot he might cause could induce the Romans to do so (John 11:48).

Recent years have seen a great deal of research on the question of what lies behind the high priestly charge of blasphemy and on what basis it could be valid.[8] In Mishnaic law (*m. Sanh.* 7.5), a conviction for blasphemy must both be *witnessed* and involve an explicit utterance of the divine name which in biblical texts is represented by the tetragrammaton YHWH. This was in first-century religious parlance most likely expressed by the reverential Hebrew circumlocution *Adonai* ("Lord") or the equivalent Greek *kurios.* While the blasphemy law's stated development in the first century is difficult to ascertain, studies of contemporary texts suggest that the Mishnah's relatively stringent criteria were not yet in place.

The precise meaning and validity of this charge are impossible to confirm either legally or historically. But the narratives seem unambiguous in their suggestion that the Sanhedrin is convened in a hurried, irregular and contrived session as a kangaroo court, content to seize on the first available Jewish legal justification that will smooth Jesus' transfer for execution under Roman law and authority.

The Fourth Evangelist, not implausibly, pictures the high priest Caiaphas as presiding judge to be thoroughly and perhaps coldly pragmatic. His associates voice fears that "If we let him go on like this, the Romans will come and destroy both our holy place and our nation". Caiaphas, cool as a seasoned practitioner of realpolitik, responds by chiding his underlings' uncomprehending hysteria: "You know nothing at all! You do not understand that it is better for you to have one man die for the people than to have the whole nation destroyed" (John 11:48–50). The claim entailed in Jesus' apocalyptic assertions about the Messiah and Son of Man exercising divine judgment and power at God's right hand (Mark 14:62; Matt. 26:64) seemed convenient enough to underwrite that outcome.

3.1.4 *Guilty as charged?*

Roman and Jewish criminal law are thus seen to overlap, as perhaps Jesus also envisages them to do in the coming prosecution of his disciples under both Roman and Jewish law (Matt. 24:9; Mark 13:9; Luke 21:12–15). Decisively for the outcome of the proceedings for him personally, Jesus is convicted of a capital

8 E.g. Darrell L. Bock, *Blasphemy and Exaltation in Judaism and the Final Examination of Jesus* (Tübingen: Mohr Siebeck, 1998); Michael Theobald, "'Ihr habt die Blasphemie gehört!' (Mk 14:64)", (2016) 58 *Novum Testamentum* 233–58, citing extensive earlier literature.

crime under both jurisdictions. For the execution of criminal justice, that proves convenient.

But these two judgments overlap plainly at cross purposes as far as the administration of justice is concerned in the case of Jesus. Indeed, it is difficult to exaggerate the extent to which the two jurisdictions on the one hand collaborate while on the other hand they deliver legal results that directly collide and contradict each other. The crime for which Jesus is executed in one jurisdiction would not be a capital crime in the other and vice versa: blasphemy of the Jewish God could never have constituted a Roman offence.

So was Jesus guilty of either crime? As in many pre-modern contexts, legal definitions and rules of evidence do not permit a confident answer. As we saw above, the legal definition of blasphemy and rules for conviction are very difficult to pin down in first-century Jewish law – as perhaps they have been for codes of law throughout the centuries. In this case, it does not appear to be a precise criminal charge but a more vaguely perceived offence against God.

On the Roman side, Pilate's miscarriage of justice seems more evident. He freely acknowledges his scope for acquittal but appears as a man swayed by undue influence. Enemies of the accused need only hint vaguely and implausibly at denunciation: "If you release this man, you are no friend of Caesar" (John 19:12). Philo of Alexandria and Flavius Josephus characterise him as inflexible, self-centred and cruel, misappropriating Temple funds for Roman infrastructure projects, subject to bribes and evidently very vulnerable to rebuke and eventual deposition by Rome (Philo, *Embassy to Gaius* 301–2; Josephus, *Antiquities* 18.88–9). The question of Jesus' guilt or innocence of the criminal charges against him cannot be resolved on the assumption of a properly functioning administration of justice and the rule of law.

That said, it remains notable for our purposes that Jesus is at least notionally convicted at both trials. The effective history of this singular patent miscarriage of justice has left an enormous footprint on the cultural history of Christendom, indelibly imprinting on it an expectation – if not always the delivery – of the scrupulous machinery of a fair trial for all, especially the guilty, and even perceived enemies of the people.[9]

3.1.5 *Messianic criminal law?*

Several other relevant dimensions of criminal law could fruitfully be discussed. Among these is the strikingly recurrent motif of debt prison and how to avoid it, which surfaces in several of the parables and discourses of Jesus. Disciples are instructed to settle with their adversary on the way to court to avoid imprisonment,

9 J.H.H. Weiler, "The Trial of Jesus", (2010) 204 *First Things*, https://www.firstthings.com/article/2010/06/the-trial-of-jesus (accessed 15 January 2019), acknowledges this point in an essay arguing that paradoxically both the Sanhedrin and Jesus sought to fulfil the will of God by their actions – and both were needed to achieve that aim.

apparently in a case involving unsustainable financial obligations (Matt. 5.25; Luke 12.58); similarly the parable of the unforgiving servant invokes the punishment of long-term debt prison pending repayment of a re-activated debt.[10]

My final brief point under this heading, however, amounts to little more than a thought experiment about the possibility that the Jesus tradition may already attest the emergence of an embryonic third criminal jurisdiction that continues to gain in significance through the second and third centuries in advance of the Constantinian turn. Ernst Käsemann (1969) noted the persistent recurrence in the New Testament of what he called "sentences of holy law", i.e. in his view typically pronouncements made by an early Christian prophet within a eucharistic setting. The concept as such came in for significant criticism for a variety of reasons, partly because of unwarranted assumptions about its fixed form and the mode of its delivery. But it does seem clear that even the Jesus tradition had already developed incipient quasi-legal or even quasi-statutory statements of authoritative rulings which in some cases attracted sanctions or penalties for infractions. Some such principles governed early Christian communities in ways that resemble the conventions and norms of Jewish halakhah.[11] As with Jewish and biblical law, it is far from clear whether the sanctions were ever systematically intended or applied. Sometimes, the penalty falls to eschatological rather than human judgment: those who "cause one of these little ones to stumble" will find their fate worse than being drowned with a millstone around their neck (Mark 9:42; Matt. 18:6; Luke 17:2). But, in any case, the theme of Christ as legislator is strongly implicit in the New Testament (beginning with Matt. 28:19 and John 13:34) and before long seems evident not only to Christians but also to Roman outsiders.[12]

At other times, quasi-juridical proceedings are envisaged within the community of the followers of Jesus. While the Jesus of the Synoptic Gospels speaks forcefully about divorce and adultery, about the sanctity of vows and non-resistance to violence, it is not always clear what he expects to happen when these things do occur. But at least in Matthew, Jesus clearly begins to establish for his messianic community a divinely endorsed juridical function that has its apostolic focus on Peter's endowment with the authority of "binding and loosing",[13] an authority that is also assigned to an "ecclesial" messianic assembly whose sanction includes expulsion from the community (18:17–19). While this perhaps remains a long way from formal criminal proceedings, it does in certain respects resemble

10 Matt. 18:23–34. On debt prison in the teaching of Jesus, see further Nathan Eubank, "Prison, Penance, or Purgatory: The Interpretation of Matthew 5.25–6 and Parallels", (2018) 64 *New Testament Studies* 162–77.

11 I tried to develop this argument in Bockmuehl, *Jewish Law in Gentile Churches*.

12 E.g. Lucian (*c.* 125–*c.* 180), *Passing of Peregrinus* 13.

13 Matt. 16:18–19 – an authority strikingly echoed in pronouncements of divine judgment (Acts 5:1–11) or resistance to hostile power in the Acts of Peter.

principles and mechanisms of excommunication and extirpation in biblical law.[14] As such, it also sheds interesting light on analogous developments in Paul and other early Christian texts, foreshadowing a day when Christians would be called upon to think about the administration of criminal justice.

3.2 Paul's engagement with Jewish and Roman criminal law

The case of St Paul furnishes no particularly close analogies with that of Jesus, but here too it is possible to observe engagement with two or more incompatible systems of criminal law.

3.2.1 Paul prior to Christ?

The Book of Acts is more explicit than Paul's own letters about the extent to which the apostle himself at various times fell foul of both Roman and Jewish law. This may, in fact, already pertain to the pre-Christian Paul, whom Luke describes as an accomplice or accessory to the mob execution of the first Christian martyr Stephen (7:54–59). Although the Torah sanctions stoning as a penalty for blasphemy (Lev. 24:23) and one or two other offences, in the absence of a court verdict Stephen's stoning was clearly extrajudicial and unlawful, like that of Naboth (1 Kings 21:11–13) or the prophet Zechariah son of Jehoiada (2 Chr. 24:21) in the Old Testament. Luke also reports a violent pre-Christian Paul "breathing threats and murder" against the fledgling Greek-speaking church in the diaspora (Acts 9:1; 22:4) – a striking choice of words that finds an interesting resonance with the young Saul's violence against the primitive Church noted in an early Jewish-Christian account,[15] raising the question of whether the actions of Paul the youthful militant would have been above criminal prosecution under Roman law. Paul himself does repeatedly allude to his past role as a "zealot" and violent persecutor of the Church (Gal. 1:13–14; Phil. 3:6; see also 1 Tim. 1:13, 15), though without offering details.

3.2.2 Paul the Apostle

The Roman legal context of the Christian Paul's trial and imprisonment(s) has been the subject of repeated careful study.[16] We begin with the narrative in Acts before turning to the apostle's own writings.

14 See William Horbury, "Extirpation and Excommunication", in W. Horbury, ed., *Jews and Christians in Contact and Controversy* (Edinburgh: T&T Clark, 1998), 43–66.

15 *Pseudo-Clementine Recognitions* 1.70–2.

16 Most extensively by Harry W. Tajra, *The Trial of St. Paul: A Juridical Exegesis of the Second Half of the Acts of the Apostles* (Tübingen: Mohr Siebeck, 1989) and *The Martyrdom of St. Paul: Historical and Judicial Context, Traditions, and Legends* (Tübingen: Mohr Siebeck, 1994), in a significant advance on older works including A.N. Sherwin-White, *Roman Soci-*

3.2.2.1 Paul in Acts

Acts has Paul beaten and briefly imprisoned overnight by Roman authorities after his exorcism in Philippi, on a charge of disturbing the city as Jews introducing unlawful customs. In addition to the account of the miraculous night-time destruction of the prison due to an earthquake, Paul and Silas resist the order to release them quietly by demanding that the magistrates give an account for their unlawful beating and imprisonment without conviction of two Roman citizens (Acts 16:16–40).

There is very limited evidence[17] for other arrests or criminal proceedings prior to Paul's detention in the late 50s during a visit to Jerusalem on the occasion of the Jewish festival of Pentecost or *Shavuot* (20:16; 21:30–33). Once again, the Roman and Jewish legal jurisdictions stand in some tension. Jewish charges against Paul on that occasion appear vague and somewhat variable: he initially incurs the crowd's ire above all on the false rumour that he had offended against the regulation prohibiting the introduction of "foreigners" into the Court of the Israelites on pain of death (21:28–30).[18] Luke implies that the Jewish charges against Paul, which eventually focus on his role as an agitator and supposed desecrator of the Temple (24:5), appear vague, incoherent and incomprehensible to the Roman authorities (21:30; 22:29), here depicted as acting properly throughout. The protection of Paul's safety is in view for both his arrest and subsequent transfer to Caesarea, where he is kept under guard for two years pending the required proper trial (note also 25:16). With repeated hearings involving successive Roman governors and Jerusalem barristers (24:1; 25:1, 7), the proceedings are eventually brought to a point when Paul is given the option of a trial in Jerusalem (25:9). Luke has Paul's reply implicitly play the Roman citizenship card (explicitly noted only at 22:25–29; 23:27; see also 16:37), appealing to Caesar in order to trump the claims of Jewish criminal justice with those of Roman jurisdiction. This is presumably on the calculus that Jerusalem lawyers might be unlikely to travel to Rome and that a court in the capital would find no reasonable grounds to convict him (25:10–12, 25–27). That said, the first-century legal context is complex and Paul's *provocatio* (or *appellatio*) is both historically and legally problematic, as commentators amply document.[19]

---

ety and Roman Law in the New Testament (Oxford: Clarendon Press, 1963). See also Erika Heusler, *Kapitalprozesse im lukanischen Doppelwerk. Die Verfahren gegen Jesus und Paulus in exegetischer und rechtshistorischer Analyse* (Münster: Aschendorff, 2000), on Luke's Roman legal adjustments to his trial narratives of Jesus and Paul.

17 Most commentators rightly view the cryptic reference to "fighting wild animals at Ephesus" (1 Cor. 15:23) as metaphorical, given that Roman citizens could not be thrown to the beasts.

18 A well-known inscription prohibiting the entry of "foreigners" (*allogeneis*) on pain of death was publicly displayed on signs repeatedly described by Josephus (*Jewish War* 5.194; *Antiquities* 15.417), two of which survive (CIIP 2). On the prohibition, see also Philo, *Embassy to Gaius* 212.

19 See Richard I. Pervo, *Acts: A Commentary*, 611–13, rather too sweepingly; contrast more cautiously Harries, *Law and Crime in the Roman World*, 28; Brian Rapske, *The Book of Acts*

At least one earlier episode attests Luke's pattern of competitively juxtaposing Paul's engagement with the Roman and Jewish criminal jurisdictions. In the year 51, Paul's Jewish opponents in Corinth attempt to denounce him before the proconsul Gallio, perhaps on the grounds of "atheism" or the illegal perversion of religion. Gallio's dismissal of the case is striking: it concerns only *Jewish* law and involves no Roman crime or grave misdemeanour (*adikéma ti è radiourgéma ponéron*; Acts 18:14). The account in Acts famously ends without a trial or formal conclusion after a further two years of relatively open detention.

3.2.2.2 *The Pauline letters*

For the most part, Paul himself makes only passing direct reference to questions of *Roman* criminal law in his extant letters. Thus, he may allude in 1 Corinthians 5:1 to the Roman extension of the law of incest to relations by marriage (*adfines*), including stepmothers and concubines.[20]

Most explicitly, perhaps, Paul addresses the question in general terms in his influential and hotly debated remarks to Christians at Rome about loyalty to legitimate secular government (Rom. 13:1–7). He writes in particular to urge the payment of taxes, apparently with reference to the recent tax riots in Rome that in the late 50s instigated Nero's reforms of indirectly levied taxes whose collection had been outsourced to revenue farmers (see Tacitus, *Annals* 13.50–1). Government, even secular government, is instituted by God: and its tax authorities therefore are "ministers of God" (Rom. 13:6). In this role, government exercises criminal judgment and "bears the sword… to execute wrath on the wrongdoer". This seems a clear allusion to the legitimacy in principle of Roman criminal law. Much speculative ink has been spilled on the question of whether the apostle's view of the Roman sword would have remained just as sanguine when the same emperor deployed it against the Roman Church, and his near successor against the city and Temple of Jerusalem. Paul certainly articulates a position of support for the (notably contingent) authority of secular government that is well attested in contemporary Jewish sources.[21] Before long, in any case, that Roman sword would arrest the apostle in Jerusalem and keep him imprisoned in

and Paul in Roman Custody (Grand Rapids: Eerdmans/Paternoster, 1994), 47–56; Tajra, *Trial of St. Paul*, 142–51. See further Heike Omerzu, *Der Prozess des Paulus. Eine exegetische und rechtshistorische Untersuchung der Apostelgeschichte* (Berlin and New York: De Gruyter, 2002), 17–52, 53–110.

20 Philippe Moreau, *Incestus et prohibitae nuptiae. Conception romaine de l'inceste et histoire des prohibitions matrimoniales pour cause de parenté dans la Rome antique* (Paris: Belles lettres, 2002), part II, notes a gradual extension of the incest law to include step-parents; relatives by marriage, concubinage or former marriage; and slaves; as well as illegitimate and adoptive relations.

21 While a similar point of reference might be in view at 1 Tim. 1:8–11, the nature of the crimes there regulated by "the law" seems more likely to envisage Jewish rather than Roman law, and any related jurisprudence appears internal to the Church.

Caesarea, transfer him to Rome and detain him at least temporarily at the hands of the Praetorian Guard (Phil. 1:13), and, in due course, apparently terminate his ministry by severing his head from his body.

At least in passing, however, Paul does hint at brushes with both Roman and Jewish law in the course of his ministry, listing multiple imprisonments,[22] "countless" (extrajudicial?) floggings and three beatings with rods, as well as five Jewish punishments with 39 lashes and one (extrajudicial?) stoning (2 Cor. 11:23–25).

Jewish criminal law surfaces repeatedly in Paul's letters. For reasons of substance as well as space, we may here leave aside his extensive theological and moral polemic around the Jewish law. Paul mostly discusses it in relation to a Gentile audience to whom much of it is not applicable as statutory law upheld by a governing human authority: he either ignores or indeed emphatically discounts laws about calendrical, agricultural, dietary, purity and circumcision-related matters (few of which are perhaps properly "criminal" to begin with).

Flogging appears in biblical law to have represented the default punishment in the absence of other prescribed penalties (Deut. 25:2). To eliminate arbitrariness in its application and to protect its character as an instrument of correction rather than retribution, a standard penalty of 39 (three times 13) rather than the biblical 40 lashes was formulated in rabbinic law.[23] This came to be prescribed for a variety of specific offences including false vows or breach of a Nazirite vow, cursing, incest and certain other sexual acts, as well as working on the sabbath or festival days (*m. Mak.* 3.1–9); it served more generally for crimes meriting divine extirpation or excommunication, for which the Mishnah envisages flogging as a substitute (*m. Mak.* 3.15). It is not possible to reconstruct the first-century development of the law in detail, and in any case the nature of Paul's specific culpability is difficult to establish. That said, the precedent of Jesus and Stephen suggests the possibility of an accusation of blasphemy, which the Mishnah associates with excommunication (*m. Ker.* 1.1). Of course, one cannot rule out the possibility of extrajudicial violence. But one intriguing possibility is that these five otherwise unattested episodes may belong to the early "unknown" years of Paul's ministry between Damascus and Antioch, when his mission to Jews in Syria, Cilicia and Arabia may have incurred punishments resembling those he had previously meted out to Greek-speaking Jewish Christians as their persecutor. Importantly, the limited nature of Jewish criminal jurisdiction in the diaspora means that this punishment is only possible where both parties affirm and desire continued membership of the synagogue.

Other Jewish criminal laws are still very much in play for Paul, notably including stipulations about idolatry, sexual offences, bloodshed or certain property and family laws that the Torah itself finds implicitly or explicitly applicable to Gentiles. To ignore these laws, he shows, results in the positive sanction of exclusion from

22 Acts knows of only one of these prior to his detention in Jerusalem, Caesarea and Rome (16:23–40); 1 Clement 5.6 claims a total of seven.

23 *m. Mak.* 3.10; see already Josephus, *Antiquities* 4.231, 244.

the kingdom of God (e.g. 1 Cor. 5:9–11; 6:9–12; 10:8–12, 21). They bear in this connection the weight of *criminal* law, but the juridical authority is internal to the Church: Paul explicitly envisages ecclesial law courts (1 Cor. 6:1–6). An unreconciled offender persisting in an incestuous relationship is thus on one occasion excommunicated on the apostle's authority in absentia (1 Cor. 5:3–5), in a way reminiscent of Matthew 18. Yet, in these and all other cases, the more definitive judgment turns out to be, for Jews as well as for Gentiles, eschatological and divine.

Unlike in Acts, the legal circumstances of Paul's period of imprisonment are rarely to the fore in his own writing. Philippians reflects briefly on his detention by the Praetorian Guard (1:7, 13, 17), a situation from which Paul hopes to be released (1:25; 2:23–24). Aside from the brief note to Philemon, the additional captivity letters may or may not stem from his own pen. In any case, only one of these provides any insight into Paul's legal situation: the plausibly Pauline or near-Pauline[24] letter known as 2 Timothy recalls his acquittal at a first trial despite being abandoned by his supporters (4:16–17), but Paul now expects to suffer execution within weeks or months (4:6, 9, 21) – and to face the divine judgment in the assurance that what awaits him is a crown of reward.

Finally, the question of penal sanction in that divine judgment famously also elicits Paul's theological thought at its most radical. He applies to this judgment his interpretation of the redemptive death and resurrection of Jesus through a rich cluster of metaphors, several of them drawn from legally significant contexts. Remission or pardon is for Paul far from cost neutral, but involves a high sacrificial price paid by the divine pardoner. Paul connects that death not only to the deliverance of Passover (1 Cor. 5:7; see also 11:23–25) but also to the sin-bearing sacrifice of the Day of Atonement (Rom. 3:24–26), to the purchase of a slave's freedom (1 Cor. 6:20; 7:23; Gal. 1:4; 5.1) or the transfer from one master to another (Rom. 6:16–20; 7:6, 25), or indeed to the work of reconciliation between hostile parties (Rom. 5:10–11; 2 Cor. 5:18–20; Col. 1:22). It is this radical interpretation that grounds Paul's defining conviction about the singular incongruity of God's transforming gift of grace regardless of the recipients' worth or symbolic capital – unconditioned by their worth though not unconditional upon their response.[25]

24 Note the work of Jens Herzer, "Den guten Kampf gekämpft: das Ende des Paulus im Spiegel des Zweiten Timotheusbriefes und der frühchristlichen Überlieferung", in R. Hoppe and M. Reichardt, eds., *Lukas – Paulus – Pastoralbriefe. Festschrift für Alfons Weiser zum 80. Geburtstag* (Stuttgart: Katholisches Bibelwerk, 2014), 339–69; also e.g. Luke Timothy Johnson, *The First and Second Letters to Timothy: A New Translation with Introduction and Commentary* (New York: Doubleday, 2001); J. Murphy-O'Connor, *Paul: A Critical Life* (Oxford and New York: Oxford University Press, 1996), 358–61.

25 See John M.G. Barclay, *Paul and the Gift* (Grand Rapids: Eerdmans, 2015), the most important recent treatment of this subject.

3.3 Concluding outlook

Both Paul and the Jesus tradition engage Jewish *as well as* Roman criminal jurisdictions, at times in quite deliberate contrast, and in addition to any internal Christian disciplinary proceedings. If space and leisure were granted, one could pursue this point in relation to additional New Testament writers, including 1 Peter and the Book of Revelation. Jewish law co-existed, often uneasily but on the whole straightforwardly, with Rome's law of the land. By contrast, the Christian experience of competing criminal jurisdictions tended to differentiate the early Church significantly from most ancient Jewish communities, for whom Rome tends to represent more clearly a *singular* legal Other. The "Venn diagram" for the earliest Church's relationship with external criminal jurisdiction seems markedly more complex.

For Christians, especially in parts of the East, this awareness of legal pluralism and experience of competing jurisdictions may have continued throughout the pre-Constantinian period. By the year 100, the majority of the world's Christians (numbering fewer than 10,000) may still have been ethnic Jewish residents of Palestine and Syria. But even as late as the year 400, substantial numbers of Christians in the Holy Land evidently maintained close if often fractious relations with Jewish synagogues: writers such as Jerome (*Epistle* 112.13) and Chrysostom (*Against the Jews* 1.5) confirm this clearly if grudgingly, while on the rabbinic side one finds direct as well as indirect evidence of persistent if at times problematic contact – including, notably, in legal and halakhic questions.

More interesting for the emergence of Christian reflection about criminal law is the phenomenon of an increasing co-optation and critique of Roman criminal justice in the context of persecution. Second-century Christian public intellectuals and apologists had already begun to claim a mantle of public discourse in philosophy and in ethics. This is a development one might not have anticipated from either Jesus or the Pauline letters (in contrast to the Paul of Acts). Perhaps in view of the persistent impetus in both Paul and the Jesus tradition for an *internal* penal jurisdiction, pre-Constantinian Christians never simply abdicated or "outsourced" criminal justice to Rome. Nor, on the other hand, did they enter public service themselves – a repeated point of recrimination for their second- and third-century critics.

Yet, even in the absence of their own shared system of public law, Christian apologists gained increasing confidence in their engagement of Roman criminal justice on its own terms. While there was also an important quietist strain of resistance that deliberately withdrew from such engagement, the patent legal injustice of persecution emboldened legally trained writers such as Tertullian (*c.* 160–225) and later Lactantius (*c.* 250–325) to publicly assert their own superior citizenship and *Romanitas* while castigating Rome's failure to abide by its own best principles. Tertullian, the apparent inventor of that initially derogatory term (*De Pallio* 4.1), challenges Roman authorities for perverting their own lawful notions of due process and precedent. In the persecutions, their usual custom of torturing criminals to elicit a confession is perversely further corrupted into torturing the innocent in order to procure a denial (*Apol.* 2). It is for him a patent offence against natural justice that freedom of religion is granted to all except Christians (*Apol.* 24). As in some respects is the case for the Book of Revelation, the heat of Tertullian's rhetoric about criminal justice derives in part from the fire in his belly about the impending *eschatological* judgment from heaven, in which Christ is not victim but judge – an image that is already vitally central to his eschatological role in the Gospels (e.g. Matt. 25:31–46). Tertullian is famously willing to grant that Rome's legitimate government now serves public peace as the "restrainer" of the Antichrist mentioned in Paul's letters (2 Thess. 2:7). But thereby hangs a tale for another occasion, which also relates to the troubling question of why, despite Tertullian's strictures against public office, Christians after the Constantinian turn were so quick to co-opt and enact State violence.

Further reading

Aubert, Jean-Jacques. "A Double Standard in Roman Criminal Law? The Death Penalty and Social Structure in Late Republican and Early Imperial Rome", in I.J.-J. Aubert and A.J.B. Sirks, eds., *Speculum Iuris: Roman Law as a Reflection of Social and Economic Life in Antiquity* (Ann Arbor: University of Michigan Press, 2002), 94–133.

Cook, John Granger. *Crucifixion in the Mediterranean World* (Tübingen: Mohr Siebeck, 2014).

Egger, Peter. *"Crucifixus sub Pontio Pilato". Das "Crimen" Jesu von Nazareth im Spannungsfeld römischer und jüdischer Verwaltungs- und Rechtsstrukturen* (Münster: Aschendorff, 1997).

Heusler, Erika. *Kapitalprozesse im lukanischen Doppelwerk. Die Verfahren gegen Jesus und Paulus in exegetischer und rechtshistorischer Analyse* (Münster: Aschendorff, 2000).

Horbury, William. "Extirpation and Excommunication", in W. Horbury, ed., *Jews and Christians in Contact and Controversy* (Edinburgh: T&T Clark, 1998), 43–66.

Joseph, Simon J. *Jesus and the Temple: The Crucifixion in Its Jewish Context* (Cambridge/New York: Cambridge University Press, 2016).

Loader, William R.G. "Jesus and the Law", in T. Holmén and S.E. Porter, eds., *Handbook for the Study of the Historical Jesus*, 4 vols (Leiden/Boston: Brill, 2011), 3:2745–2772.

Omerzu, Heike. *Der Prozess des Paulus. Eine exegetische und rechtshistorische Untersuchung der Apostelgeschichte* (Berlin/New York: De Gruyter, 2002).

Rapske, Brian. *The Book of Acts and Paul in Roman Custody* (Grand Rapids: Eerdmans/Paternoster, 1994).

Tajra, Harry W. *The Martyrdom of St. Paul: Historical and Judicial Context, Traditions, and Legends* (Tübingen: Mohr Siebeck, 1994).

Tajra, Harry W. *The Trial of St. Paul: A Juridical Exegesis of the Second Half of the Acts of the Apostles* (Tübingen: Mohr Siebeck, 1989).

4 Crime and the canon law

RH Helmholz

4.1 Introduction

This chapter describes the place of crime and criminal procedure in classical canon law, the law of the mediaeval Church. It has two primary goals. The first is to demonstrate the existence of a canon law on crime and criminal procedure, describing briefly its character and reach. The second is to assess its place in the long history of jurisprudential thought and legal practice in Continental Europe, England and North America. The chapter's larger aspiration is to suggest to students of criminal law, even including those in their first year of law school, that Christian religious thought has occupied a meaningful place in the development of our law on this subject. Study of the history of the canon law of crimes will enrich, although it may also complicate, any student's thinking about the resources and the goals of today's criminal law.

To some potential readers, this chapter may appear to be a pointless undertaking. Today, the law of the Church appears to have only the most tenuous connection with the criminal law in force. Morality based upon religious sentiment does play a part in its administration, as several chapters of this book demonstrate, but the formal law by which the Church and its clergy are governed does not. Ideas such as the value of forgiveness, ideas inspired by the Christian Scriptures, may influence the administration of modern systems of criminal justice,[1] but the Church's canon law exists in a quite different world. This is the common modern assumption, even though the existence of canon law is sometimes brought into public attention, as in the current controversies over the prosecution of pederast priests. However, good reasons exist for questioning the relevance of current assumptions on this subject. Many of the chapters in this volume provide ample justification for examination of Christianity's place in the formation of our own law of crime. They include specific references to the Church's law. Moreover, the assumptions of the present day do not always mesh with those of the past. Historically, both as an institution and as a source of legal ideas, canon

1 See the readings, some criticising the loss of a Christian perspective of criminal law, in Jeffrey Brauch, *A Higher Law: Readings on the Influence of Christian Thought in Anglo-American Law*, 2d ed. (Buffalo: Hein & Co., 2008), 193–283.

law mattered.[2] It is a subject worth exploring. One should begin, however, with a short description of its contents.

4.2 The sources and character of the Church's criminal law

It is possible to point both to the existence of disciplinary rules and to the statement of large principles of justice dating from the earliest days of Christianity's existence, but the formulation of a working system of canon law occurred only in the years which coincided with the recovery of classical Roman law at Bologna in the eleventh and twelfth centuries. Canons had been enacted and collected together in many circumstances at various times during the early Middle Ages, but their authority was unclear, their invocation infrequent and their coverage incomplete. No system of public courts existed. It was the arrival of the movement for reform within the Church led by the papacy and the revival of learning in the twelfth century that set the Church's disciplinary law on a more ambitious course. A signal event in its evolution was the compilation of the *Concordia discordantium canonum* (*c.* 1140), a law book traditionally attributed to Master Gratian of Bologna. This collection of canons, apparently designed for use in teaching at the nascent university of Bologna, adopted the dialectic method of Abelard's *Sic et Non*. It then set forth existing canons and other decrees of the Church, and where these formal laws seemed contradictory, its compiler added comments and distinctions in an attempt to reconcile them.

Gratian's *Decretum*, as it was and is called, was followed by developments of immediate and lasting importance. One was the rise of the papal decretal as a primary source for the Church's law. It was capped by the promulgation in 1234 of the *Liber extra*, a collection of decretals and conciliar decrees commissioned by Pope Gregory IX and edited for clarity and consistency by Raymond of Peñaforte. He organised the decretals according to their subject matter and placed them within five books, each book divided into titles and chapters. The first dealt with the constitution and organisation of the Church; the second with questions of jurisdiction and procedural rules; the third with regulation of the clergy, the sacraments and ecclesiastical obligations; the fourth with marriage, divorce and domestic relations; and the fifth (which is the principal subject of this chapter) with the penal law of the Church. The *Liber extra* built upon the *Decretum*, not diverging from it on most points, but enlarging it and filling gaps in the coverage of the earlier work. It also reflected changes in the Church's law (as in the law of marriage) that had occurred between 1140 and 1234. The same pattern was followed by later collections of papal decretals, primarily the *Liber sextus* (1298) and the *Clementines* (1317). Together, these collections of decretals and conciliar decrees made up the *Corpus iuris canonici*. It was the subject

2 Its relevance is recognised, for example, in the classic work on the history of the subject: James Fitzjames Stephen, *History of the Criminal Law of England*, 3 vols. (London: Macmillan, 1883; repr. New York: Burt Franklin, 1964), 2:396–445.

of instruction in European universities, and its texts were applied in ecclesiastical courts throughout Europe from the thirteenth century onwards.[3]

Three particular justifications were found in these books for the creation of an ecclesiastical law of crimes and criminal procedure. The first was the existence of biblical precepts. The Ten Commandments were authoritative. They laid out the correct path for men and women to follow. This assumption was shared across Christian Europe, and it had concrete results. God had spoken to Moses, commanding him to communicate to his people rules of human behaviour, and Moses had done so. Churchmen in later ages therefore took it for granted that this biblical precedent meant something. Their own responsibility extended to seeing that God's commandments were kept. To the mediaeval canonists it was evident that all positive law should take serious account of the scriptural dictates, or at least stand in accord with them. It is telling that mediaeval jurists continued to refer back to the Decalogue in dealing with the justification for the Church's jurisdiction over crime. A pithy conclusion taken from a much later source stated the long-accepted connection to these Commandments with clarity. It held "the great general division of crimes by the Canon law was according to the tables of the Decalogue into those against God, and those against man: the former comprising simony, heresy, schism, apostasy, witchcraft, sacrilege; the latter [comprising] homicide, adultery, theft, usury, perjury, fraud and the like".[4] All of these fell under the Church's ban.

Another reason for the existence of the Church's criminal law grew out of the existence of a clerical privilege. The mediaeval canon law asserted that members of the clerical order enjoyed a general privilege not to be summoned before secular courts. Best known in English history from the conflict between King Henry II and his archbishop Thomas Becket in the twelfth century,[5] this privilege rested upon a conviction that the clergy constituted an order of men and women endowed with a special responsibility and special privileges. Those rights and duties were held to require their exemption from many secular burdens. It was a contentious claim, but Becket's martyrdom established that principle's place in English criminal law, where it soon became the source of what is now called "benefit of clergy". Lay courts were required to hand over clergy accused of having committed a crime to their bishop for discipline within the Church itself. Similar but not identical rules

3 The following abbreviations are used in this chapter to refer to its contents:

Dist. 1 c. 1	*Decretum Gratiani*, Distinctio 1, can. 1
C. 1 q. 1 c. 1	———, Causa 1, quaestio 1, can. 1
X 1.1.1	*Decretales Gregorii IX*, Lib. 1, tit. 1, cap. 1
Sext 1.1.1	*Liber sextus*, Lib. 1, tit. 1, cap.1
Extrav. 1.1.1	*Extravagantes* (of Pope John XXII and Communes), Lib. 1, tit. 1. cap. 1
gl. ord.	*glossa ordinaria* (standard commentary on texts of the *Corpus iuris canonici*)

4 Arthur Browne, *Compendious View of the Ecclesiastical Law of Ireland*, 2d ed. (Dublin: R.E. Mercer, 1803), 400.

5 The most important documents relating to the controversy are found in translation in Thomas Jones, ed., *The Becket Controversy* (New York: Wiley, 1970). The canonical principle is found at X 2.1.8.

were applied in other mediaeval European lands. As a practical matter, this system of bifurcated jurisdiction required a law to deal with clerical crimes and also with clerical defendants in such matters. Simply put, if clerics were to be tried by their bishops, the bishops needed a law capable of being applied. Moreover, the clergy were bound by many rules that did not apply to the laity, as for instance rules restricting their participation in tournaments or duels (X 5.13.1–2; X 5.14.1–20), or requiring observation of high standards in clerical dress and behaviour.[6] Both the existence of these special crimes and benefit of clergy itself also required the development of a law of criminal procedure by which clerics could be tried. Some parts of that procedure were borrowed from Roman law; other parts were created by ecclesiastical legislation. What emerged was not identical with that which was applied in the courts of the English common law, but it was in use in English ecclesiastical courts and some other tribunals for centuries. Although its extent came to be limited by a growing list of crimes in which the privilege could not be claimed, benefit of clergy was formally abolished in England only in 1827, when it fell to the force of the great movement for reform.

A further reason for the existence of an ecclesiastical law of crime was a result of the overlap between sinful conduct and criminal behaviour. The mediaeval Church regarded it as a responsibility to define, and indeed to punish, sinful behaviour, particularly where the temporal law was inexact or in need of guidance and support. Heresy is the best known of such ecclesiastical crimes, but there were several others. For instance, incest and infanticide both required definition, and like heresy, both were regarded as requiring detection and punishment in circumstances where the temporal law was deficient.[7] The law of the Church filled a gap. It was within the penitential forum of the mediaeval Church that this duty of correction was most fully implemented, and canon law was relevant there.[8] It clarified what conduct amounted to sinful behaviour. In addition, because some public sins were thought to require public penance, canonical texts were needed to secure that the requirement was met. This led naturally to the creation of canon laws defining and punishing illicit conduct. Within the mediaeval context, therefore, it was natural, even inevitable, that canon law should have contained substantive laws defining criminal behaviour and providing procedures for its enforcement, as it did in fact.

4.3 The contents of the canon law of crimes

The fifth books of both the *Liber extra* and the *Liber sextus* contained lengthy coverage of individual crimes. They were devoted to defining the reach and

6 A helpful exposition of this theme is found in James A. Brundage, *Medieval Canon Law* (London and New York: Longman Press, 1995), 70–97.

7 See, e.g. C. 2 q. 5 c. 20; X 5.10.3; many examples of these prosecutions are found in R.H. Helmholz, "Infanticide in the Province of Canterbury during the Fifteenth Century", (1975) 2 *History of Childhood Quarterly* 379–90.

8 See, e.g. F. Broomfield, ed., *Thomae de Chobham Summa Confessorum* (Louvain and Paris: Nauwelaerts Press, 1968), 664–76.

stating the consequences of violation of those laws. Specific crimes were defined and methods of proceeding against men and women accused of having committed them were laid out. Although it is sometimes supposed that Continental criminal law, including canon law, treated accused men and women as guilty until they could prove their innocence, in fact it did not do so except under quite limited circumstances. Ordinarily, the *onus probandi* in criminal cases lay with the prosecution.[9] The Church's law did permit consideration of circumstantial evidence of guilt, including public clamour. That might have been strong enough to require defendants to undergo canonical purgation as an earnest expression of their innocence (X 5.1.24; X 3.2.8). In time, this concession to the difficulties inherent in proving some crimes did lead to some of the abuses modern writers associate with the Roman and Spanish Inquisitions; however, in its inception, the inquest procedure was regarded as a necessary remedy for the weakness of an inherited system in which private individuals bore the burden of initiating and proving the guilt of those accused of a crime.[10]

The substantive coverage of crimes in the Church's law books was quite widely ranged. Indeed, many of the crimes included had little to do with specifically religious matters. The canonical texts extended from homicide to unlawful hunting (X 5.12.1–25; X 5.24.1). Canons placed within the decretals dealt with adultery and with false boasting (X 5.16.1–7; X 5.31.9). Crimes discussed ranged from forgery to blasphemy (X 5.26.1–2; X 5.20.1–9). These compilations also contained an extensive treatment of the sanction of excommunication – its variations and its effects (X 5.39.1–60). The Gregorian Decretals dealt with the proper ways of proceeding against those who had committed these crimes, seeking to uncover an efficient and fair-minded way to deal with men and women who came under the Church's ban.

Specific examples from the decretals provide the best indication of their coverage and character. One that is illustrative was found in the title of the fifth book of the decretals, which dealt with theft. Surprisingly, it contained only five chapters. The first was an extract from the Bible (Ex. 21:16) which states that if one man "steals another man and sells him ... he shall surely be put to death". This stated the seriousness of the crime, but the *glossa ordinaria* qualified this rule, stating first that it applied only if the stolen man was actually free, citing a text excluding the death penalty under those circumstances from the Digest (Dig. 48.15.7) and also one from *Decretum Gratiani* (C. 33 q. 2 c. 6), stating that under canon law no man had the right to kill his wife because she had

9 See Richard Fraher, "'Ut nullus describatur reus priusquam convincatur': Presumption of Innocence in Medieval Canon Law?", in Stephan Kuttner and Kenneth Pennington, eds., *Proceedings of the Sixth International Congress of Medieval Canon Law* (Vatican City: Biblioteca apostolica Vaticana, 1985), 493–506.

10 See Richard Fraher, "The Theoretical Justification for the Criminal Law of the High Middle Ages: 'Rei publice interest ne crimina remaneant impunita'", (1984) *University of Illinois Law Review* 577–95; Albert Shannon, *The Medieval Inquisition*, 2d ed. (Collegeville, MN: Liturgical Press, 1991), 98–122.

committed adultery. It added that the courts of canon law were not necessarily governed by the temporal law on this subject because they "possessed no sword but a spiritual sword, one which does not kill but gives life". The second was an extract from the decrees of a church council, announcing that if thieves and robbers were caught and killed while committing a crime, they were not to be prayed for by the Church. It went on, however, to state that if they were killed (or only wounded) and confessed to a deacon or a priest before dying, then they should be remembered in the Church's prayers and be given a Christian burial. Forgiveness was thus possible, even required if the circumstances were right. The gloss to this text added two points to the first – not only that the Church should not pray for a person who died in the very act of committing a mortal sin, but also that his confession need not be made to a cleric; even a layman would do if time was short and the reasons urgent. The third dealt with a classic dilemma of the natural law – taking property that belonged to someone else out of necessity, as in the theft of food by a hungry man. It held that this act was still a wrong, although the gloss added that in the opinion of some jurists, the criminal himself should be held blameless where his hunger had been so overwhelming as to be irresistible. The next dealt with receivers of stolen goods, stating that they too were included in the Church's ban, and the fifth and final chapter came from a decretal letter of Pope Alexander III (d. 1181), permitting a thief to be ordained if three conditions were met – the thief must have made restitution of the stolen goods; he must have confessed his own wrong and done penance for it; and he must demonstrate to the satisfaction of his bishop that his crime was not a matter of public scandal among those he would be required to serve. The last of these requirements was thought to be for the protection of the Church itself. Its shepherd must not be the source of harm to his flock, and this might happen if his promotion in the face of damning evidence from his past life encouraged members of the flock to believe they themselves could sin and suffer no lasting consequences.

As this example demonstrates and as even the most casual perusal of the title's contents will confirm, the Church's law on crimes was very far from a comprehensive code. Indeed, it was incomplete and unclear in many respects. It failed to distinguish sufficiently between the "external forum" of public courts and the "internal forum" of confession. Also, its coverage was uneven. Some crimes – simony and heresy for example – were treated at length and in detail (e.g. X 5.3.1–46; X 5.7.1–14), whereas other crimes – witchcraft and infanticide for example – were accorded only two or three canons (X 5.21.1–3; X 5.10.1–3). Much had to be left to resources drawn from the Roman law, further development contained in the *Liber sextus*, discretion exercised by individual judges and customary practices in courts where canon law was in force. The *Corpus iuris canonici* was far from a true code. Often, its coverage was quite incomplete, leaving room for change and experiment, such as occurred in the development of summary procedure and the organisation of the legal profession. Many texts were treated as illustrative of certain principles – important principles – but ones that left room for choice in individual cases.

In assessing the nature of canon law's contributions to the historical development of our criminal law, it is useful to recall that when Raymond of Peñaforte had completed his great work in compiling the Gregorian Decretals, what he had produced was sent to the law faculties at European universities. It was not directed to the bishops or the ecclesiastical judges before whom criminal cases would come. That choice may seem strange to modern readers, but in fact it was not inappropriate at the time. Both the decretals and Gratian's *Decretum* left many aspects of the canon law of crimes open to dispute and development. In the Middle Ages, the law faculties were regarded as the normal venue for this process to take place. The result was a large body of academic works devoted to crime and to criminal procedure.

4.4 Historical importance of the canon law

This section assesses the role played by the canon law of crimes in the development of modern criminal law. If it did so at one time, the question is whether any of that contribution has lasted? The European Enlightenment, the growth of a division between the common law and the European *ius commune* and great changes in public attitudes towards crime and morality all intervened between the time when canon law was formulated and the present era. Are there nevertheless connections to be made in this field? Are there plausible reasons today for paying any attention to mediaeval canon law? The history of the subject suggests that there are.

4.4.1 Specific historical examples

Individual rules and long-established practices give reasons for thinking that there have been such connections. Examples of judicial and scholarly recognition of the place of canon law in the law of criminal procedure and in the substantive law of crimes suggest that the canonical influence outlasted the Middle Ages. When the eminent Italian criminologist Julio Claro (d. 1575) came to the subject of proper criminal procedure involving the use of inquests to determine questions of guilt and innocence, he turned for authority and guidance to the innovations introduced by canon law and also to its interpretation by Pope Innocent IV (d. 1254).[11] In this almost reflexive action, Claro had much company. Hugo Grotius (d. 1645), for example, called upon the *Decretum Gratiani* in discussing the reasons that required proportionate levels of punishment for crimes.[12] Similarly, Jodocus Damhouder (d. 1581), the Flemish author of another much used treatise on the law of crimes, began his treatment of the law

11 *Practica criminalis*, Lib. V, Quaest. 5, no 4 (Venice: Paul Ugolinus, 1595), 68.
12 P.C. Molhuysen, ed., *De iure belli ac pacis* (Leiden: A.W. Sijthoff, 1919; repr. 2016), 373, Lib. II, c. xx § 10.2.

of homicide with a discussion of the biblical example of Cain and Abel.[13] Lord Judge's Introduction to this volume calls our attention to another example: the story of Adam and Eve's expulsion from the Garden of Eden also long served as an authority, indeed it was the focal point among Continental jurists for the start of their analysis of criminal procedure. God had laid down a law forbidding the taking of forbidden fruit. When Adam disobeyed, God formally summoned the offenders. It was interpreted as a lesson to all judges. They were required to do the same. Then, God listened to Adam's attempt to justify his own actions. So must judges listen. As unlikely as it may seem today, this story was used by generations of writers on the law of crime. It was understood to state the basic requirements of due process in criminal procedure.

In assessing the practical side of this subject, it also seems pertinent to make reference to a rule that was to have a lasting effect on the development of the European and English criminal law. Canon law excluded the use of professional lawyers to represent those accused of crimes at trial (X 5.1.15).[14] The rule was also a part of Roman law (Dig. 48.1.13). The result was that, except in special circumstances, lawyers could not be appointed to act in criminal trials.[15] Both the accuser and the accused must be present and speak for themselves. Lawyers, it seemed to the canonists, too often served as obstacles to discovery of the truth. They actually prevented the condign punishment of guilty men and women. Adam had no lawyer to speak for him. Perhaps that was a meaningful precedent. At any rate, this rule barring defence counsel was long accepted. The struggle to overcome it is, of course, known to any student familiar with the history of English common law, but its origin in (or at least its coincidence with) the law of the mediaeval Church has rarely been remarked upon by modern historians. Perhaps it should be.

Even in England, where common law precedents and parliamentary statutes, not the *ius commune*, were normally the chief sources of criminal law, several post-Reformation statutes nevertheless preserved the criminal law jurisdiction that had been developed in the ecclesiastical courts, thus effectively safeguarding the substance of several parts of the canon law rules defining and punishing crimes.[16] The English laws against usury, for instance, were dependent upon the laws on the subject found in the laws of the Church.[17] The great English jurist

13 See his *Praxis rerum criminalium opus absolutissimum* (Antwerp: Belleri, 1601; repr. Aalen, 1978), 163–6, ch. LXVII.

14 For fuller discussion and examples of the several exceptions to this rule, see Nicolaus de Tudeschis (commonly known as Panormitanus), *Commentaria in libros decretalium* (Venice, 1615), ad id.

15 See C. 5 q. 3 q. 2 and Dig. 48.1.13; J.P. Lancellotus, *Institutiones iuris canonici* (Venice, 1704), Lib. III, tit. 2, no 12: "Regulariter in causis criminalibus non potest intervenire procurator".

16 See, e.g. the statements in Ferdinand Pulton, *De pace regis et regni* (London: Stationers' Company, 1609; repr. New York and London: Garland Publishing, 1978), 8, tit. Of Menaces, Assaults, Batteries, etc., nos. 26–7.

17 See Robert Filmer, *A Discourse on Usury* (London, 1678; repr. New York and London: Garland Publishing, 1978), 27–9, making repeated use of Roger Fenton's 1611 *Treatise* on the subject.

of the eighteenth century, William Blackstone (d. 1780), critical as he was of the "sanguinary laws" against doctrinal heresy contained in the mediaeval canon law,[18] nevertheless made effective use of the Church's laws in praising the abolition of ordeals as a means of deciding guilt or innocence in criminal cases.[19] That advance had been, as he recognised, a contribution of the Fourth Lateran Council of 1215. And when Blackstone took up a recurring problem within criminal law, for example the defence of coercion in a prosecution for the commission of a criminal act, he turned to the "constant man" test taken from the mediaeval *ius commune* for a definition of the degree of force necessary for successful invocation as a defence in a prosecution of a criminal act.[20]

4.4.2 General themes

Such fragments of evidence, capable of multiplication though they are, do not fully reach the more important task of seeking out major themes and possible contributions of canon law in the evolution of modern criminal law. All that they truly show is that, historically, canon law was a necessary part of the *ius commune* and was not ignored by generations of civilians. But there is more to say. Respectable evidence suggests that there have been three principal ways in which the mediaeval canon law played an active role in shaping modern law.

The first has been by establishing the desirability and even the necessity of using the criminal law to shape and control human behaviour. This is a controversial question today, and it has been so since the rise of legal positivism and the widespread acceptance of what is called the harm principle, the view that the sole legitimate purpose of the criminal law is to deter behaviour that causes harm to others. Most famous in recent history, this basic conflict came to the surface in the "Hart–Devlin Debate" over the criminalisation of homosexual behaviour and prostitution.[21] Historically, canon law stood firmly on the side of using the law to promote the cause of morality. This stand was not simply a reflexive reaction of a celibate clergy's desire to condemn sexual sins. Canon law did draw a line between sinful and criminal conduct; only public conduct specified in the existing laws that was subject to prosecution in a public court fell within the sphere of courts with criminal jurisdiction. Thoughts and purely private acts did not. However, this left many public offences that were crimes against morality. Most of them have all but disappeared from modern criminal law. Included in earlier centuries were the crimes of blasphemy, fornication, simony, heresy, usury, schism, apostasy, witchcraft and sacrilege. Today, with the partial exception of usury, these are all matters of either private choice or outside the law's domain.

18 *Commentaries on the Laws of England* (Oxford: Oxford University Press, 2016), *46, Lib. IV, c. 4.

19 Ibid., *338, Lib. IV, c. 27, citing C. 2 c. 5 q. 7 and X 3.50.9 and *gl. ord.* ad id.

20 Ibid., *30, Lib. IV, c. 4.

21 The dispute and other examples of the clash of views are well described in Russell Sandberg, "Towards a Jurisprudence of Christian Law", in Norman Doe, ed., *Christianity and Natural Law: An Introduction* (Cambridge: Cambridge University Press, 2017), 227–30.

This, however, is a relatively recent development. One of the professed goals of the mediaeval canon law was to teach men (and women) how to live, how to live well and peaceably in company with others (X 1.31.13). Not only that; they would one day be called upon to account before God for the conduct of their lives, and the law of the Church was meant to help put them on the right path in anticipation of that fateful day. Norman Doe's chapter in this volume contributes to our understanding of this feature of religious law.

It also shows that this way of thinking has largely passed out of sight in modern academic discussions of the goals of the criminal law.[22] However, our criminal law has not banished the objective of encouraging morally responsible behaviour from the legitimate goals of criminal law. Many of the "dignity offences" in modern American law seem designed to change the behaviour of persons as much as they do to prevent actual harm to others. Laws such as those against the use of narcotic drugs, loitering, bestiality or the possession of child pornography have so attenuated the meaning of the "harm principle" that it may be better – it certainly seems more honest – to treat them for what they seem to be – offences against morality. Not all of these modern crimes can claim a specific canonical pedigree. They are not found in the *Corpus iuris canonici*. However, they do fit within the objective goals which canon law endorsed in earlier centuries.

A particularly interesting "hold-over" that does have a link with canon law is the crime of public drunkenness. Its canonical ancestor has an intriguing history. The texts of the mediaeval canon law prohibited and penalised persistent and personal drunkenness of the clergy, suspending offenders from their offices and benefices for repeated and serious infractions.[23] The canonists devoted their efforts to defining and condemning the offence. For them, as for us, definitions of punishable drunkenness were not exact. They could not be. Difficulties inherent in defining the offence did not, however, prevent expansion of the canon law's jurisdiction to encompass the problem. In England, the neglect of prior centuries gave way to a sterner regime in the sixteenth century, and the resources of the Church's law played a part in the process. Public drunkenness of ordinary men and women became a criminal offence, first in the courts of the English Church,[24] and soon thereafter also in secular tribunals.[25] A man could be summoned to appear before either a consistory or a common law court to respond to this charge and then to suffer appropriate sanctions if it were true. It remains

22 On the variegated history of this subject in the law of the United States, see Herbert Hovenkamp, *Law and Morals in Classical Legal Thought* (Chicago: University of Chicago Press, 1997).

23 X 3.1.14; *Decretum Gratiani*, d.a. Dist. 35, c. 1. See also Josephus Mascardus, *De Probationibus* (Frankfurt, 1593), Lib. II, concl. 578 (to the effect that proof of conduct worthy of punishment under the crime of drunkenness was "difficilis et ardua").

24 Marjorie McIntosh, *Controlling Misbehavior in England, 1370–1600* (Cambridge: Cambridge University Press, 1998), 32; Martin Ingram, *Carnal Knowledge: Regulating Sex in England, 1470–1600* (Cambridge: Cambridge University Press, 2017), 354.

25 4 Jac. I, c. 5 (1606–07); 21 Jac. I, c. 7 (1623–24).

a criminal offence in several American jurisdictions to this day, sometimes under the rubric of disorderly conduct, sometimes on its own.[26] Of course, it is true that drunkenness of a man or woman may have negative consequences for others, but the crime itself does not require proof of any. Few modern lawyers would see a connection between the mediaeval canon law and this offence under our law, but in fact there is one. We have simply forgotten what it was.

A second contribution to the development of modern criminal law derives from its role in the transmission of basic notions of procedural fairness in criminal law. This was not, of course, a role exclusive to the law of the Church. Other sources may have played an equal or a greater part – the law of nature for one, the Roman civil law for another. But the multiplicity of possible sources is no reason to ignore canon law entirely.[27] A good example of the evidence, one that should be added to the use of the story of Adam and Eve discussed above, is the principle of proportionality in punishment. Gratian's *Decretum* and its accompanying *glossa ordinaria* stated the basic rule at several points. When the offences of two or more persons are equal, so should their penalties be (C. 36 q. 2 c. 6). Greater delicts are to be subject to greater penalties, lesser delicts to lesser penalties (C. 24 q. 1 c. 21). Punishments should be determined in part by the status of the person being punished (C. 14 q. 6 c. 1). In other words, under canon law the ideal punishment was to be proportionate both to the nature of the offence and the status of the offender.[28] The extent of its actual influence on jurisprudential thinking in Europe is difficult to evaluate, and how fully it was implemented in the administration of justice is also open to doubt. The canonists themselves did not regard the cited texts as absolute in character. At the very least, however, one can say that canon law was mentioned as authoritative in discussions of the application of this principle. Lawyers used it in their arguments.[29]

A particularly likely means by which this sort of transference appears to have occurred is found at the end of Book V of the *Liber sextus*. Under its title *De regulis iuris*, the Sext provided 89 rules of law for use in the courts of the Church. Many of them were drawn from the equivalent section of the Roman law's Digest (Dig. 50.17.1–211) – one example of the important role that substantive and procedural rules taken from Roman law played in the formation of the mediaeval canon law. Others were added. Several had an immediate connection with the law of crimes and criminal procedure. One stated that a sin should not be forgiven unless the sinner made suitable restitution to the person injured (Reg. 4).

26 See e.g. Virginia Code Ann. § 18.2–388.

27 See, for example, Andreas von Hirsch, *Deserved Criminal Sentences: An Overview* (Oxford and Portland: Hart Publishing, 2017), 2: "the movement towards the modern proportionality-based conception of sentencing began in 1971".

28 See Laurent Mayali, "The Concept of Discretionary Punishment in Medieval Jurisprudence", in R. Castillo Lara, ed., *Studia in honorem eminentissimi Cardinalis Alphonsi M. Stickler* (Rome: Libreria Ateneo Salesiano, 1992), 299–315.

29 See R.H. Helmholz, *Natural Law in Court* (Cambridge, MA: Harvard University Press, 2015), 44–53.

Another held that there should be no exceptions for persons in courts of justice; all were entitled to equal treatment (Reg. 12). A third provided a statement of the obvious but important point at the time; no punishment should be meted out for conduct unless the law itself had declared that conduct criminal (Reg. 23). A fourth stated that within the Church's penal law, the more benign interpretation of texts and statutes should be preferred to harsh interpretations (Reg. 49). When Cesare Beccaria (d. 1794) wrote on the subject, in his *On Crimes and Punishments*, Chapter 27: "Leniency in Punishing", he was actually restating what was to be found in the canon law on the subject. Not that he cited it. He did not. But in assessing its transmission into legal practice, it is worth noting that all European students of law would have come into contact with the texts found within the *Regulae iuris* in either its Roman law or its canon law version. The rules found in these texts would have been brought to their attention in formal lectures at universities, including those at Oxford and Cambridge. To say more than this would be to go beyond the available evidence. Who knows what learning students actually absorb? To see and acknowledge the possibility, however, does not require a leap in the dark. For centuries it was the subject of regular discussion in legal treatises and would have been familiar to competent lawyers.[30] It would have played a role in their thinking, and it would likely have shaped their practice in court.

A third possible contribution to modern legal development growing out of canon law comes from the law of criminal sanctions. At first sight, the existence of any connection seems quite unlikely. A closer look reveals an interesting possibility. In strict legal terms, the mediaeval canon law knew only one sanction – excommunication.[31] There were different levels of excommunication, but all of them had the effect of separating a person from the sacraments and (with major excommunication) from the company of other Christians. Harsher corporal sanctions were regarded as inimical to the nature of an avowedly pacific Church, and when (as in the case of unrepentant heretics or scofflaws) the clergy felt obliged to admit that their powers of persuasion had been exhausted and their curses scorned, they called upon the power of "the secular arm" to carry out the sanctions from which they themselves were barred. Hypocrisy or not, this was the position taken in the mediaeval canon law. It was also an aspect of the laws that recognised and protected the special status of the clerical order. Men in holy orders were forbidden to be involved directly in blood sanctions. The resulting system of cooperation between Church and State was not followed to the letter in all European lands, but in England the notification (called a signification) to the King's government requiring that its officials imprison men and women who had

30 E.g. Andreas Fachinaeus, *Controversiarum iuris libri decem* (Venice, 1619), Lib. IX, c. 1 lit. B, citing the text and gloss of X 1.29.4.

31 See Elizabeth Vodola, *Excommunication in the Middle Ages* (Berkeley and Los Angeles: University of California Press, 1986).

remained excommunicated for more than 40 days became a matter of routine.[32] Sheriffs acted accordingly. They released the men they had imprisoned only upon their submission to ecclesiastical authority. This happened when sheriffs received an order based upon the diocesan bishop's certificate affirming that the excommunication had been lifted.

Without that tie between Church and State, one that was brought to a formal end in England only during the nineteenth century,[33] the courts of the Church were obliged to fall back on purely spiritual powers, and that meant excommunication. When one looks at the mediaeval and early modern records of the ecclesiastical courts in England, that is also mostly what one sees. The signification of excommunicates acted as a threat as often as it did a conclusion to a contested case. It was a matter of choice for the ecclesiastical courts, and normally the judges there must have decided that the sentence of excommunication itself was enough, at least if the person involved chose not to flee from the diocese. True, there were some men who scoffed at excommunication's supposed terrors, but their existence does not prove that their attitude was the norm.

There was one additional aspect of this subject. Any full account requires asking what persons subject to the Church's jurisdiction had to do to secure absolution from a sentence of excommunication. Herein lies the existence of possible ties to the development of our own criminal law. One instance grew out of the principle contained in Reg. 4 of the Sext just mentioned. Absolution could require making restitution to the party harmed by wrongful conduct. In the English ecclesiastical courts, this was put into practice where it was feasible. So, for example, manifest usurers were required to restore their ill-gotten gains wherever they had the ability to do so. Even in the exercise of its jurisdiction over defamation, the judges required defendants to do what they could to restore a slandered plaintiff's reputation, as by confessing before the congregation in the parish church where the plaintiff resided that the speaker had been mistaken or acted vindictively in speaking words that had caused harm. Of course, modern criminal law is not identical in this respect to that of the Church's courts of mediaeval and early modern England. Fines payable to the government or prison sentences are the normal penalties in use today. However, it is worthy of note that orders for restitution do play a part in some circumstances in modern criminal law.[34] They sometimes count in the severity of the sentence being imposed, and they might legitimately do so more often than they have in the immediate past.

Most intriguing of parallels and possible influences has been the rise of what are now called "shaming penalties" in modern criminal law. They run upon a parallel track with common practice in the courts of the mediaeval Church (and

32 See F.D. Logan, *Excommunication and the Secular Arm in Medieval England* (Toronto: Pontifical Institute of Mediaeval Studies, 1968).

33 50 Geo. III, c. 127 (1813) and 2 & 3 Wm. IV, c. 93 (1832).

34 See Sol Rubin, *The Law of Criminal Correction*, 2d ed. (St. Paul, MN: West Publishing Company, 1973), 295–7.

also some early American courts). Defendants in a sixteenth-century English ecclesiastical court who had been found guilty of a sexual offence such as fornication or of causing a public disturbance created by their open slander of another person could be required to appear on Sunday in their parish church, wearing penitential garb, carrying a candle in the parochial procession and then confessing their offence openly before the congregation.[35] Under the Church's law, wrongs that had become matters of public knowledge or that disturbed the peace of a community were thought to call for more than private confession. They called for open acknowledgement and public penance. The regularity of the resulting public humiliations found in the surviving court records does provide cause for wonder at their compatibility with the spiritual purposes of church services, but they were not rare occurrences in churches during the past centuries. Whether they actually succeeded in restoring parochial harmony and bringing offenders to contrition for their fault are difficult to determine. Even so, sincere or not, they represented an open acknowledgement of guilt. They might have brought some satisfaction to injured parties. They may also have promoted the healing of open sores in the parishes where their performance took place. Their existence for centuries in ecclesiastical court practice certainly suggests some recognition of their utility.

These penitential scenes could not occur today, at least in the same form, and certainly not often in our large and impersonal cities. But were they really any different in kind from a modern case in which a man convicted of stealing U.S. mail was required to spend a day standing outside the post office wearing a signboard stating "I stole mail. This is my punishment"?[36] Sentences like this have now passed beyond the realm of speculative possibilities of the sort that are occasionally raised in law school classrooms or in speculative academic literature. They have penetrated into our own law far enough to be described as acceptable options for American judges,[37] and the movement for restorative justice described in Daniel Philpott's chapter shows that the purposes of these ancient shaming punishments may serve some quite modern purposes where other forms of punishment prove impractical or self-defeating.

4.5 Conclusion

Modern scholarly literature on criminal law, of which there is a lot, has virtually nothing to say about the subject's pre-Enlightenment history. It contains even less about the place of Christian thought and practice within that history.[38] Most

35 Ingram, *Carnal Knowledge*, 108–15.

36 *U.S. v. Gementere*, 379 F.3d 596 (9th Cir. 2004), opinion of O'Scannlain, J.

37 See the many examples in Stephen P. Garvey, "Can Shaming Punishments Educate?", (1998) 65 *University of Chicago Law Review* 733–94.

38 See e.g. Michael Tonry, ed., *Handbook of Crime and Punishment* (New York and Oxford: Oxford University Press, 1998).

accounts of the history of modern criminal law appear to begin with Beccaria. The chapters in this book by Mathias Schmoeckel and Heikki Pihlajamäki provide cogent reasons for pause before accepting this approach to the history of criminal law. Many parts of the modern law of crime and criminal procedure had older antecedents. At the least, therefore, this chapter has called attention to one neglected aspect of the subject's history. Some of the concepts and procedural protections found in our own laws are also found within the classical law of the Church. It was more than a regime of rack and strappado. Whether canon law can be said to have directly influenced the course of secular law as was stated during the European Enlightenment is a more difficult question to answer. Causation is a hard thing to prove, one way or the other. But surely the possibility ought to be raised. The question ought to be asked. Study of criminal law will be enriched by taking account of the several examples of possible connections of our law with the religious law from the pre-Enlightenment period. Many of the principles found in legal thought that followed had older roots, and some of those roots are found within the canon law of the Church. For thoughtful students of modern criminal law, it is fair to conclude that their attention should include some understanding of possible connections between their subject and its antecedents in the law of the Church.

Further reading

Bradley, Gerard, ed. *Essays on Law, Morality and Religion* (South Bend, IN: Notre Dame University Press, 2014).

Deutscher, Thomas. *Punishment and Penance: Two Phases in the History of the Bishop's Tribunal of Novara* (Toronto: University of Toronto Press, 2013).

Dubber, Marcus and Lindsay Farmer, eds. *Modern Histories of Crime and Punishment* (Palo Alto: Stanford University Press, 2007).

Goebel, Julius. *Felony and Misdemeanor: Study in the History of Criminal Law* (Philadelphia: University of Pennsylvania Press, 1976).

Hale, William. *A Series of Precedents and Proceedings in Criminal Causes, 1475–1640* (Edinburgh: Bratton Publishing, 1973).

Kotiranta, M. and Norman Doe, eds. *Religion and Criminal Law* (Louvain: Peeters, 2013).

Maine, Henry Sumner. *Ancient Law: Its Connection with the Early History of Society and Its Relation to Modern Ideas* (London: John Murray, 1861; most recent ed. Cambridge: Cambridge University Press, 2012).

Sullivan, W.F. *Prison Religion: Faith-Based Reform and the Constitution* (Princeton: Princeton University Press, 2009).

Whitman, James Q. *The Origins of Reasonable Doubt: Theological Roots of the Criminal Trial* (New Haven: Yale University Press, 2008).

5 Retaliation

Christian reasons for punishment: an overview

Mathias Schmoeckel

5.1 Introduction

Does retaliation, contrary to the Christian obligation to charity, have any place in the Christian tradition of punishment? This reason for punishment will be singled out as a means to access a long and many-layered discussion of the reasons for punishment in the Christian tradition. The Church fathers discussed the nature of and reasons for punishment, questioning and mitigating the ancient traditions of retaliation as represented in the Old Testament and Roman law. In particular, Augustine of Hippo will serve as a paradigm whereby the thought of the Church fathers may be broadly sketched. As an example of the European reception of these ideas, some sources of Frankish law will be consulted, after which the position of Gratian and the canon law tradition will be explicated. This is followed by a survey of the Protestant Reformation, in order to explain how not only the great theologians but also the lawyers of the time thought about the function of punishment, which will lead us to the question of rehabilitation as well. The famous question of theodicy as developed by Gottfried Wilhelm Leibniz will conclude this survey.

5.2 Foundations in antiquity: the writings of Augustine

Retaliation appears to dominate the legal traditions of antiquity. The *Codex Hammurabi* asserts the emphasis put on retaliation in ancient laws, at least in cases in which free peoples are concerned. If a collapsing building kills its owner, the architect responsible has to be executed. If it is the owner's son who is killed, the architect's son must be put to death (§§229, 230). This is in accordance with the maxim "an eye for an eye". However, how typical such provisions were, and the question of how often they were carried out or whether punitive damages could be negotiated – in a manner akin to Roman law[1] – remains ambiguous.

1 Thus Guido Pfeiffer, "Die Gesetze des Königs Hammu-rapi von Babylon", in M. Schmoeckel and S. Stolte, eds., *Examinatorium Rechtsgeschichte* (Munich: Heymanns, 2008), 2.

Nearly identical questions can be raised with respect to the retaliation provisions in the Old Testament.[2] For example, in Genesis, Cain shall be avenged sevenfold and Lamech seventy and sevenfold (Gen. 4:24). Compared to this amplification, strict retaliation provisions such as are found in Ex. 21:22–25, Lev. 24:17–22 and Deut. 19:16–21 seem to be modifications of an older, harsher law. They are, in fact, regarded as a means of excluding an even cruder form of vengeance, a form which had been exercised in prior times.[3] Retaliatory provisions are, therefore, retained to deter the general public from committing other horrific deeds. It is tempting to assume an evolution from personal vendetta to retaliation and indemnification.

But retaliation as a principle of Jewish law in the Old Testament remains in question. In Deuteronomy, God himself is ready to punish his people when the priests fail to punish the guilty and condemn the innocent instead (Deut. 32). This punishment concerns the entire populace, and may even afflict the third or fourth generation (Ex. 20:5, 34:7). In these instances, God is not described as just and lenient, but as jealous and avenging.[4] If the country disregards God's commandments and laws, he will multiply the afflictions seven times over (Lev. 26:14 ff.). This punishment becomes necessary when the community is unwilling to render justice, becoming culpable itself. All of the people must endure God's vengeance and wrath,[5] as both the Noetic Flood and the destruction of Sodom and Gomorrah illustrate. God's punishment does not necessarily have measure and therefore vengeance is an inadequate term for that punishment. Consequently, retaliation remains a valid purpose of punishment in the Old Testament.

The New Testament, however, contains no direct provisions for the administration of punishment. On the one hand, God takes revenge into his own hands and away from humans (Rom. 12:19). Love for the neighbour excludes retaliation (Mt. 5:45). Repayment for evil done in response to another evil is prohibited (Rom. 12:17). The provision "an eye for an eye" is explicitly overruled in the Sermon on the Mount, where the call is to turn the other cheek (Mt. 5:38 ff).[6]

2 Jan Rothkamm, *Talio esto. Recherches sur les origines de la formule "oeil pour oeil, dent pour dent" dans les droits du Proche-Orient ancien, et sur son devenir dans le monde gréco-romain* (Berlin and New York: de Gruyter, 2011), 83.

3 Hartmut Schmökel, *Das angewandte Recht im Alten Testament* (Borna-Leipzig: Universitätsverlag von Robert Noske, 1930), 10; Hans Jochen Boecker, *Recht und Gesetz im Alten Testament und im Alten Orient*, 2d ed. (Neukirchen-Vluyn: Neukirchener Verlag, 1984), 152–3; Eckart Otto, *Altorientalische und biblische Rechtsgeschichte. Gesammelte Studien* (Wiesbaden: Harrassowitz, 2008), 32.

4 Ex. 20:5; Nahum 1:2: "The Lord is a jealous and avenging God; the Lord takes vengeance and is filled with wrath".

5 Peter Hoffmann, "Zum Verhältnis der Strafzwecke Vergeltung und Generalprävention in ihrer Entwicklung und im heutigen Strafrecht", Diss. Jur., University of Göttingen (1992), 18. For a detailed analysis of two different approaches in the New Testament, see Ingo Broer, "Das ius talionis im Neuen Testament", (1994) 40 *New Testament Studies* 1–21.

6 Fritz Stolz, "Rache", in *Theologische Realenzyklopädie*, vol. 28 (Berlin and New York: de Gruyter, 1997), 86.

And yet, vengeance did not vanish completely from the New Testament, as God's vengeance still plays an important role (e.g. 2 Tim. 4:14; Rev. 6:10, 19:2) in assuring ultimate justice. The balance between the wrong and the re-establishment of justice is maintained only at the level of the whole society,[7] if necessary by means of God's wrath by which all the people will suffer. Paul emphasises, however, that revenge can only be taken by God; for humans it is an evil thing to do (Rom. 12:19).

One of the first proven uses for the term *talio* is from around the year 450 BC, from table VIII.2 in the Law of the XII Tables: *Si membrum rupsit, ni cum eo pacit, talio esto* ("If someone maims another person the maimed person may retaliate"). This demonstrates Roman law's utilisation of the concept of retaliation. Mommsen suggested that this provided for a lasting influence on the developed form of Roman law, criminal law remaining *lex sacrata* and the verdict the *sanctio*, an opinion that finds support to this day. Yet, it is more likely that this provision did not endure longer than the republic, with only a few similarities found in the later law. Without a doubt, however, many reasons for punishment were discussed. But as used by the rhetors, the main function seems to have been the deterrence of future wrongdoing.

Aristotle seemed to value the idea of retaliation as a means of securing a standard of justice in society.[8] For this reason, he believed that punishment should be governed by the principle of the *iustitia commutativa* as a means of respecting the proportionality between a deed and its reward or a crime and its punishment. He argued for the importance of finding a just and fair measure by which to deal out punishment, the idea of retaliation thus being a means to secure a just punishment proportionate to the injustice committed. Because Aristotle was very brief when addressing this subject, his reasoning remains difficult to understand.

Later, when bishops began passing sentences, thereby acting in the role of judge, they had to surmount the conflict between the Old and New Testaments. Augustine of Hippo pointed to the contradiction between the notion of "an eye for an eye" as found in Ex. 21:24, and the Sermon on the Mount. He argued that in earlier times people were more prone to bloody vengeance and the Old Testament sought to deter them from blood feuds.[9] In the time of the New Testament, they had learned to react more compassionately. Retaliation, he concluded, is generally prohibited as being a sentence too cruel and severe. The standard of the new law therefore had to prevail. The notion of humankind's evolution into humanity obviously pre-dates, as well as prefigures, Norbert Elias' theory of civilisation. In this line of thought, it could very well be that the mod-

7 Gérard Guyon, *Justice de Dieu, justice des hommes. Christianisme et histoire du droit pénal* (Bouère: D.M. Morin, 2009), 84 ff.

8 Aristotle, *Nikomachische Ethik*, ed. R. Nickel (Düsseldorf and Zürich: Artemis & Winkler Verlag, 2001), 200, 1131b7.

9 Augustine, *Contra Adimantum Manichaei discipulum liber unus*, c.8, ed. J. Zycha, CSEL 25 (Prag: F. Tempsky, 1891), 115–90, 130, l.20 ff.

ern interpretation of retaliatory norms as a means of a civilisation progressing to a more humane standard is merely following this traditional notion.

For the Church fathers, the Last Judgment was a model for every secular judiciary. Just as God will take into account the good and bad deeds of each person, guilt should establish a more exact measure of human punishment.[10] The inner will alone determines the just verdict: good and bad intentions are then the sole criterion according to which all will be judged. Inner motivation affects culpability as well as punishment. Because of this, no harsh sentence can be passed on a subject who possesses only a small amount of culpability. Punishment, as Ambrose stated, can be regarded as medicine for the soul.[11] In this respect, it is conceived as a medicine for the cure of souls, and the improvement of humanity, that they may no longer walk in sin. This is not far from the idea of special prevention of crimes. A good, truly Christian judge should exercise mercy in order to avoid furthering more iniquity in society and promoting the perpetuation of atrocities and wrongdoing. This was all to be done in order to cure the sinners' wounds.

On the other hand, judges might tend to allow harsh sentences, and Augustine's argument in particular was understood in this way. For him, the salvation of the individual soul was paramount.[12] Harsh human sentences could therefore be used to prevent later divine punishment because, in the Last Judgment, God would respect the *ne bis in idem* principle, the principle of double jeopardy. Death sentences against a murder by a human court, according to Augustine, could spare the culprit a second and more horrible death ordered by the eternal court of the divine city. If one suffers in this world for wrongdoings, God will spare punishment for the same wrongs in the life to come. Punishment is not applied to aggravate wounds, but rather to heal the injured soul. The good judge is acting as a good doctor who applies what is necessary to remedy the sins committed, and the death provoked in the treatment will be rewarded by God in paradise.

Within the parameters of the reasoning presented above, retaliation was never considered to be a suitable reaction to a misdeed. The injured party is not served by a verdict inflicting the identical wound on the culprit. This is most likely why Augustine implores the emperor to avoid passing retaliatory sentences. Hence, it is imperative that punishment is a response to the specific needs of the culprit. Within this scheme, the just verdict might on occasion be harsh and at other times merciful – although retaliation is generally lacking as it is viewed as immoderate and excessively severe, which can lead to destabilising the peace of society.

10 Augustine, *Retractationum libri duo*, I.26, ed. A. Mutzenbecher, CCSL 57 (Turnhout: Brepols, 1984), 26, 1.50. For the new standard of culpability see Guyon, *Justice de Dieu*, 48 ff.

11 See Mathias Schmoeckel, *Jugend der Justitia* (Tübingen: Mohr Siebeck, 2013), 96 ff.

12 Augustine, *De civitate Dei*, ed. B. Dombart and A. Kalb, CCSL 48 (Turnhout: Brepols, 1955), 21.11, l.39.

For the reasons given above, vengeance is not a legitimate form of punishment to be enacted by Christians; furthermore, this form of punishment is sinful.

Augustine went even further, declaring that demanding more than what is due seems sinful for a Christian.[13] This model of morality may also be seen in the giving of oaths: though swearing itself is not a sin, it is better to avoid it in order to never commit the sin of perjury. With many similar analogies, he explicates his reasons for not taking revenge – for in revenge one risks taking more than what is due. In order to prevent unjust revenge, it is better to avoid taking revenge at all. Finally, all God asks of human jurisdictions are just rulings that prevent God's wrath and vengeance. Revenge is normally reserved for God alone.

Yet, some exceptions existed regarding the general prohibition of retaliation. In a few circumstances vindications remained legal. Judges who had passed an unjust sentence were to face punishments that were in accordance with what was ordered for the accused. This is an example of a retaliatory punishment commensurate with the offence committed. The justification for this exception is found in Jesus' declaration that a man will be judged as he himself has judged (Luke 6:38, see also Deut. 19:18). Consequently, the same logic applied for those who, through false accusation and perjury, caused false judgments. In this instance, the provision of Deuteronomy 19:15–21 (esp. 21) against false testimony remained valid. Because the bad inner will was the cause of punishment, the deed remained punishable even when the wrongly accused person did not suffer any consequences. Additionally, in cases of defamation, vindications were to remain legal.

Retaliation therefore remained applicable in a few cases. And yet, assuming the Sermon on the Mount as the rule and the provisions of the Old Testament as exceptions would be a false characterisation of Augustine's view. Instead, we see two suitable ways to react to sin and crime: the first way lenient, considerate and humane; the other marked by showing strength and determination in order to defend public values against perpetrators. The idea of God's wrath remained significant in the writing of Augustine.

These special cases, in which retaliation was legitimised, followed not only Deuteronomy 19:18–21, but also provisions present in late Roman law – for example, the new emphasis given to *talio* for the punishment of calumny. Such provisions can be found in the legislation of Christian emperors starting in the last third of the fourth century. Although it is possible that they also followed Christian theology, these ideas were clearly coined in older, non-Christian times. It no longer remains necessary to assume that they prove the long-lasting influence of the XII Tables, an opinion commonly held to this day.

The first of these cases concerns the unjust actions of a judge. Roman law determined the crime of *praevaricatio* (prevarication), which could potentially be committed by all parties in a lawsuit. In 371 (CTh 9.3.5 / C. 9.4.4 pr), a judge who helped the suspect to flee had to suffer the punishment for the crime of the perpetrator. The second case relates to false accusations, which at that time

13 Augustine, *Contra Faustum Manichaeum*, 19.25, 526 l.17.

came to be called calumny (*calumnia*). Calumny had long existed as a crime, its punishment depending on the arbitrary decision of the judge. But in the fourth century, the punishment was augmented. With Constantine, calumny received an automatic capital sentence in cases where a verdict of capital offence had been issued for someone falsely accused of the crime. Therefore, only with the dawn of Christian emperors did the crime of *calumnia* become connected with retaliation. An imperial constitution of 373 or earlier (CTh 9.1.11) tried to ensure that accusations were not made frivolously. The accuser had to give sureties (*vinculum inscriptionis*) with the knowledge that he would endure a *congruam poenam* (equivalent punishment) in the case that he could not prove the alleged deed.

A few years later, it was ordered that the accuser had to assent in advance to a punishment similar to the one intended for the accused. The norm speaks of a *poenam reciproci*.[14] Punishing the accuser with a corresponding punishment of one wrongly accused is a clear consequence. In the constitution of 423 (C. 9.46.10), this *similitudo supplicii* is stressed even more strongly. In this provision, an old tradition is invoked to legitimise the punishment. This state of affairs can also be found in earlier statutes.[15]

One can clearly see that Augustine knew how to defend leniency and restrain retaliation. Although punishment should try to correct the offender and thereby make society better, in some instances retaliation with harsh sentences was considered legal and necessary. Therefore, a certain ambivalence characterises the theory of Augustine in these matters.

5.3 Frankish law

In Frankish society there was a considerable risk of blood feuds.[16] Instead of a public prosecution of crimes, private individuals sought compensation for loss of men and money. Thus, the concept of retaliation appears to have been commonplace among the Franks. In order to eradicate these feuds, Frankish laws attempted to install a system of payments, which has been described as a system of "compositions" and which was intended to prevent families from resorting to violence. This system was undoubtedly also meant to function as a replacement for public punishments. But, on the whole, while such damages were intended to replace revenge, the Frankish criminal law was not characterised by retaliation.

On occasion, even the Frankish king recognised the need to condemn wrongdoers with harsh punishments.[17] The Frankish sources attest to a clear grasp of

14 CTh 9.2.3 (Gratian, Valentinian, Theodosius, a.380) = C. 9.3.2 – but this passage was omitted in Justinian's Code. It can be found again in C. Angilramni: see Karl-Georg Schon, ed., *Die Capitula Angilramni* (Hanover: Hahn, 2006), 147, c.XLVIII.

15 C. 9.39.2.3 (Marcian, a.451).

16 For the famous case of Sichar and its various interpretations, see Carsten Bernoth, *Die Fehde des Sichar* (Baden-Baden: Nomos, 2008).

17 Mathias Schmoeckel, "Germanic Period", in Brent A. Strawn, ed., *The Oxford Encyclopedia of the Bible and Law*, vol. 1 (Oxford: Oxford University Press, 2015), 343–50.

almost all the purposes of punishment: deterrence of other wrongdoers, betterment of the culprit and retaliation. In the Frankish context, the occasional harsh punishment was considered necessary for the community in order to make atonement for the offence, or else they had to risk the wrath and revenge of God. Heinrich Brunner, commenting in the nineteenth century on the Frankish system, did not denote a punishment that corresponded to the deed as retaliation to avoid acknowledging the influence of Christian theology.[18] He argued that the punishment was designed to remind the public of the crime committed and thereby strengthen the impact that the punishment would have on deterring further crime. In order not to confuse this idea with the Christian and Roman tradition, Brunner utilised the term *spiegelnde Strafen* ("mirror punishments")[19] only for the period after the Germanic kingdoms and would only admit the influence of the Mosaic law in that later period. His ideas had significant influence on legal historians of the twentieth century.

Consequently, researchers gathered cases in which retaliation took place, sometimes even where the sources merely used the term *talio*. These cases concern forgery, perjury, arson, calumny and unjust judges, who have to suffer the death penalty ("Decretio" of Childebert II, a.596),[20] particularly when the accused escapes (Chlotar II, after a.613, 616?).[21] Both of these provisions contain vivid elements of Roman law. In particular, the *praeceptio* mirrors the provision of CTh 9.3.5/ C. 9.4.4 pr. The offence of the unjust judge, however, has been amplified and generalised. Evidently, false condemnations are to be punished severely.

A "mirroring" punishment can be found in the Lex Ribuaria (LRib 59.3), the law of the Rhineland Franks, which commands the thumb of the culprit to be cut off in cases of forgery, and in many other texts. In the Visigothic realm (Lex Visigothorum 6.4.3), once again the law of retaliation concerning the unjust judge corresponds undeniably with such Frankish provisions.

5.4 Canon law

Augustine not only provides an important example of the position taken by the Church fathers, but his major statements can also be found in Gratian's Decretum. With astonishing accuracy, the author of this text inserted phrases which reveal a dimension of Augustine's theory: the correction of humankind is the most important aim of punishment. Although not all are destined for eternal

18 Thus, Heinrich Brunner and Claudius von Schwerin, *Deutsche Rechtsgeschichte*, vol. 2 (Munich and Leipzig: Duncker & Humblot, 1928), 763.

19 Ibid., 768.

20 Decretio Childebert, II 2 § 5 2nd sentence (a.596), in Karl August Eckhardt, ed., *Lex Salica. 100 Titel-Text* (Weimar: Böhlau, 1953), 252.

21 Chlotharii II praeceptio, c.6, in MGH Cap. I n.8, 19. On this law, see also Stefan Esders, *Römische Rechtstradition und merowingisches Königtum* (Göttingen: Vandenhoeck & Ruprecht, 1997), 107–8.

life, all wrongdoers must be corrected in the hope of God's mercy.[22] Gratian followed Augustine and Roman law with regard to calumny; it had to be punished by retaliation.[23] Punishment could be administered to avoid the wrath of God, yet personal revenge was considered as a vile reason for a verdict. Gratian also deliberated whether it was better to hold the public reaction in mind when passing sentence: the more public an offence, the greater the punishment.

A just punishment therefore required an arbitrary decision by the judges (*discretio*). The decision was only arbitrary to a certain extent: sometimes the personal qualities of the judge affected the ruling, or even a specific political issue – for example, a multitude of wrongdoers should not be harshly rebuked so as not to upset the people. Some punishments might be entirely superfluous. The ambiguity of punishment is characteristic of Gratian's theory of punishment, serving both to correct the individual and to protect society against malefactors. The human court might even help to reduce the culpability in the final judgment, while at other times unclear cases were to be left to God's judgment. Ambivalence was shown in the fact that humans were sometimes conceived as an object of misery, while at other times being in need of castigation and retribution.

The notion of ambiguity was contained in the later canon law. The judge was always to proceed *in humaniorem partem* ("humanely"),[24] while upholding the command that the severity of the sentence should deter others.[25] This situation allowed for the establishment of new forms of legal procedure as well as new definitions of criminal offences. Still, the theory of punishment required little adjustment.

The notions of prevention and the common good therefore prevail as purposes of punishment in the theory of Thomas Aquinas.[26] Punishment is permissible only for the benefit of the individual (amelioration) or society (tranquillity), and for the justice and honour of God. In any case, punishment belongs to Aristotle's *iustitia commutativa*, as he also values the relationship between the deed and the reward, or the crime and the punishment, and it is essential to find the just measure of punishment. Since chastisement is necessary (Prov. 13), sparing the rod

22 DG p. C. 23 q.4 c.24.

23 On Gratian's use of punishment, see René Pahud de Mortanges, "Strafzwecke bei Gratian und den Dekretisten", (1992) 78 *Zeitschrift der Savigny-Stiftung für Rechtsgeschichte: Kanonistische Abteilung* 121–58; René Pahud de Mortanges, *Zwischen Vergebung und Vergeltung. Eine Analyse des kirchlichen Straf- und Disziplinarrechts* (Baden-Baden: Nomos, 1992), 35 ff.; Lotte Kéry, *Gottesfurcht und irdische Strafe. Der Beitrag des mittelalterlichen Kirchenrechts zur Entstehung des öffentlichen Strafrechts* (Cologne: Böhlau, 2006), esp. 257 ff.

24 X 1.36.11 = 5Comp. 1.20.1, Honorius III, Po 5834, a.1218.

25 X 5.38.7 = 2Comp. 5.17.3, Clemens III, JL 16644, a.1188–91. See also Pahud de Mortanges, "Strafzwecke", 140.

26 Christiane Birr, "'Kriminalstrafe ist öffentliche Rache'. Beobachtungen zum Strafgedanken in der juristischen Literatur der Frühen Neuzeit", in Eric Hilgendorf and Jürgen Weitzel, eds., *Der Strafgedanke in seiner historischen Entwicklung. Ringvorlesung zur Strafrechtsgeschichte und Strafrechtsphilosophie* (Berlin: Duncker & Humblot, 2007), 63–4.

would be sinful; however, any excess of punishment would fall into a *peccatum crudelitatis vel saevitiae* ("sin of cruelty or brutality").

Nevertheless, retaliation remained a valid reason for punishment, especially in the writings of theologians. Some punishments prescribed by laws in the late Middle Ages even display an unusual brutality. In a case of a damaged tree, the intestines of the culprit were to be fixed at the point where the tree had been damaged and to be led around the tree as long as the intestines would permit. Dietmar Willoweit describes a tendency in the late Middle Ages, increasing towards the sixteenth century, of escalating brutal punishments and death sentences. But, while brutal executions might serve as a deterrent, they did not prove the case for retaliation.

In the thirteenth century, Albertus Gandinus stated that the *poena talionis* was no longer in use *per totam Italiam* (throughout Italy) for false accusation, because otherwise no-one would risk bringing an accusation forward.[27] Bartolus and Durantis confirmed this practice[28] just as Giulio Claro and Benedict Carpzov did later in regard to Italy and Germany, respectively.[29] Instead of the threat of corporal punishment, financial security (*satisdatio*) and bail were required. This was also upheld in Article 12 of the Carolina, though not entirely excluding retaliatory means of punishment.[30]

5.5 The Protestant Reformation and the purposes of punishment

5.5.1 Martin Luther

With Martin Luther, God's wrath regained authority as the principal reason for human government. Luther was well acquainted with the New Testament and the

27 Albertus Gandinus, *Tractatus de maleficiis*, in Ernst Kantorowicz, ed., *Albertus Gandinus und das Strafrecht der Scholastik*, vol. 2: *Die Theorie* (Berlin and Leipzig: de Gruyter, 1926), Qualiter fiat accusatio, n.5, 26.

28 Bartolus de Saxoferrato, *Commentaria at C. 9.2.17* in *Opera*, vol. 8 (Venice, 1528; repr. Rome: Il Cigno Galileo Galilei, 1996), fol. 124v; Guilelmus Durantis, *Speculum iuris* (Basel, 1584; repr. Frankfurt-am-Main: Vico, 2009), vol. 2, *De accusatione*, §1, qualiter, n.17, 6 (clearly only in rubric).

29 Julius Clarus, *Liber Quintus siue Practica criminalis* (Venice, 1640; repr. Goldbach: Keip, 1996), 124, q.12 n.17; Benedict Carpzov, *Practica nova Imperialis saxonica Rerum Criminalium* (Wittenberg, 1635; repr. Goldbach: Keip, 1996), 42, q.105 n.6, 60, q.166 n.40 ff.

30 In c.68 *von falschen Zeugen* ("of false witness"), the punishment for the crime continued to be the same which would have been due for the accused. In some translations this is correctly called a *talio*: see Georg Remus, *Nemesis Karulina* (Herborn, 1600; repr. Goldbach: Keip, 2000), 71, c.68. Louis Günther, *Die Idee der Wiedervergeltung in der Geschichte und Philosophie des Strafrechts. Ein Beitrag zur Universal-Historischen Entwicklung desselben*, vol. 2 (Erlangen: Bläsing, 1891), 15, lists laws that allowed private punishment when the adulterer was caught red-handed.

writings of Augustine, but focused more on the rulings of the Old Testament.[31] According to him, God gave humankind the power of cognition. But without faith, humanity is incapable of fulfilling God's commandments. Thus, the law merely serves to display all the provisions that humanity cannot obey in their totality. This state of affairs helps to demonstrate that humanity is hopelessly enslaved to sin,[32] whereas God ensures justice through his wrath in sending various pestilences upon the world: hail, thunder, fire, floods, monsters, hunger, wars and plagues.

According to Luther, another channel whereby God administered his wrath was that of human authority. Not only the law itself but also government required discipline in human society.[33] The magistracy should kill the people as long as they could move a limb, for it was the time of the sword and ire and not of mercy. This was written during the peasant's revolt of 1525. These peasants, guilty of treason, should be punished severely and without mercy. In Luther's view, all government was installed by God in order to prosecute criminals. Princes, as long as they were obedient to God, were a tool of God's ire and, as such, must punish the peasants harshly and without hesitation. Should they die in battle, they should be held as martyrs. By means of these severe sentences, the princes protected just and honest people. Evidently, in this interpretation, God's government does not act with mercy, or softness of any kind, but with the sword, signifying divine vengeance. But it is through this severity that God reveals his care for his people. For the sake of charity, the sword must be used without mercy. In this respect, government is divine service, carrying out God's will. This position is summarised in the short maxim "Frogs need storks", because men are nothing but frogs that croak and cannot be disciplined other than by the storks that eat them.[34]

Luther required retaliation in the sense of severe sentences. However, judges were not only to pass harsh sentences, but also to make sure that they were pragmatic. For example, when a spoon is dropped, one should not break the bowl; similarly criminal courts should not fill the country with widows and orphans. The government should be constantly aware that insufficient administration will provoke God's anger and revenge. In Luther's thought, God's judgment is considered as contemporaneous and concurrent with human jurisdiction. At any time, God might interfere just as described in the Old Testament. God's revenge, harsh punishments and retaliation therefore play a significant role in human society.

31 For the following, see Mathias Schmoeckel, "Fragen zur Konfession des Rechts im 16. Jahrhundert am Beispiel des Strafrechts", in Irene Dingel and Wolf Friedrich Schäufele, eds., *Kommunikation und Transfer im Christentum der Frühen Neuzeit* (Mainz: Von Zabern, 2007), 168–74.

32 See Lennart Pinomaa, *Der Zorn Gottes in der Theologie Luthers. Ein Beitrag zur Frage nach der Einheit des Gottesbildes bei Luther* (Helsinki: Suomalainen tiedeakatemia, 1938), 30–49.

33 Martin Luther, *Wider die räuberischen und mörderischen Rotten der Bauern* (1525), in *Werke*, vol. 18 (Weimar: Böhlau, 1964), 360, ll.1–27, "Widder die stürmenden bawren".

34 Martin Luther, *Von weltlicher Oberkeit, wie weit man ihr Gehorsam schuldig sei* (1523), in *Werke*, vol. 11 (Weimar: Böhlau, 1966), 268, l.18.

5.5.2 *Philipp Melanchthon*

After 1525, Melanchthon placed increasingly great value on the law. Generally speaking, even human laws are created as an expression of what is honest and good for society. Through the power of understanding and conscience, humanity has the ability to comply with human and divine laws.[35] Divine law, natural law and even human law help to improve humanity. One way to understand a code of law is as a treatise on the way to live a just and honest life.[36] With the aid of God-given abilities, an individual might seek to cultivate a disciplined life that helps that person to obey the law and find the way to a better life.

As an individual can improve, the betterment of the prince's subjects should be his primary aim.[37] In order to know God, a person requires good books to provide instruction in what is just and consolation given by faith. In this manner, one learns of God's desire that none should perish, and that faith is only achieved by repentance and a true change in one's life. This change is an inner renewal in the individual, whereby one learns new obedience to God. In cases where such a reversal is achieved, the death punishment is no longer necessary and the guilty may hope to find mercy. Grace thus overcomes the crime. God would not ask for excessive punishments when the sinner turns to him, but the sentence could become more lenient. From this vantage point, punishments are not hard and fast, but in each case the judges must investigate whether or not the guilty party still needs to receive the punishment.

5.5.3 *Jean Calvin*

For Jean Calvin, true penitence would lead to "mortification" and "vivification", an inner change (*metanoia*) and a turn to God[38] – a new birth as a true Christian. This new state has to be maintained afresh every day.[39] But, owing to humanity's inclination to sin, a perfectly just life is beyond a person's own capabilities. Calvin never developed a coherent theory of punishment. He stressed the princely obligation to fulfil God's will on earth. As *ministres de Dieu*, they are required to rule

35 Philipp Melanchthon, *De aequitate et iure stricto (Billigkeit und strenges Recht)* (1542), in *Corpus Reformatorum* vol. 11 (Halle: Schwetschke, 1843), 553–4.

36 For Melanchthon's reinvention of the pedagogical use of law, see Mathias Schmoeckel, "Recht durch Erziehung – Gesetz zur Bildung: usus legis Reformatorum", in Christoph Strohm, ed., *Martin Bucer und das Recht. Beiträge zum internationalen Symposium vom 1. bis 3. März 2001 in der Johannes a Lasco Bibliothek Emden Martin Bucer zum 450. Geburtstag* (Geneva: Librairie Droz, 2002), 245–70.

37 For the following, see Mathias Schmoeckel, "Metanoia: die Reformation und der Strafzweck der Besserung", in Reiner Schulze, Thomas Vormbaum, Chrstine Schmidt and Nicola Willenberg, eds., *Strafzweck und Strafform zwischen religiöser und weltlicher Wertevermittlung* (Münster: Rhema, 2008), 34–8.

38 Jean Calvin, *Institutio Christianae Religionis*, vol. 2, trans. O. Weber (Neukirchen: Erzichenverein, 1937), 79 ff., 3.3.6.

39 Ibid., 90, 3.3.14.

justly and to punish severely any offence.[40] If they neglect their duties, God will curse the land and pour out his wrath. In the case of the heretic Michel Servet, Calvin saw capital punishment as a necessity.

But in his lecture on Deuteronomy 19:21, he emphasised God's displeasure in killing and delight in the repentance of the criminal's soul. Therefore, the second generation of Calvinists slowly developed a new concept of punishment.[41] The death penalty would not only cost the culprit's life on earth, but also eternal life, as it deprived him or her of the possibility of showing repentance and improving his or her character. Temporal punishment combined with education in a profession would help the culprit to find a stable income for himself or herself and the family, changing the criminal into a valuable member of society. Capital sentence, in contrast, would eliminate the chance of rehabilitation.

In practice, in 1556 the old Bridewell palace in London (between Fleet Street and Watergate) was converted into a corrective facility. In 1596, in Amsterdam, the first penitentiary was established on the continent. Slowly, the critique of capital punishment grew: see, for instance, the writings of the seventeenth-century Saxonian theologian Valentin Weigel.

5.6 Reactions in the sixteenth and seventeenth centuries

5.6.1 Decline in practice

Undoubtedly, there were many reactions to the new theology in the legal writings of the time. The first reaction can be detected in severer and harsher criminal jurisdiction. One of the early commentators on the Carolina, Georg Remus, called his commentary the *Nemesis Karulina*. Therein, he stressed the importance of punishing the guilty and avenging crimes committed within the realm. In other texts, *talio* was interpreted as recompense and reparation of damages. Some authors attributed binding force to the precepts of the Old Testament and Mosaic law. Thus, retaliation was occasionally seen as the primary reason for punishment. Benedict Carpzov taught that the negligence of a prince or magistrate would bring about the wrath of God, and the land would be covered in his vengeance.[42] In this respect, he ascribed to the ideas of Martin Luther. But only

40 Jean Calvin, *Institution de la religion chrétienne* (Geneva, 1999), 202.

41 Christoph Strohm, *Ethik im frühen Calvinismus* (Berlin and New York: de Gruyter 1996), 68.

42 See Carpzov, *Practica*, 2, III q.101, n.8: *si Magistratus in poenis irrogandis negligens est, Deus ipsemet ad vindictam exsurgit*; 3, n.15: *Saepè enim ob unius delictum, dum non vindicatur, Deus in universum irascitur populum* (referring to Joshua 7:12 ff). See also Wolfgang Sellert, *Studien- und Quellenbuch zur Geschichte der deutschen Strafrechtspflege*, vol. 1 (Aalen: Scientia Verlag, 1990), 253. Similar arguments to those of Carpzov can be found in Adam Volckmann, *Tractatus criminalis* (Goslar, 1629), 24, III cons.4 n.8. J.-H. Zedler, *Großes vollständiges Universal-Lexikon aller Wissenschaften und Künste*, vol. 44 (Leipzig and Halle, 1745), 1471, "Tortur".

in general did Lutherans feel the requirement to emphasise the necessary harshness of human justice.

Many modern authors have described the increasing brutality of criminal prosecution in the sixteenth century. But the eighteenth-century Zedler's encyclopaedia states that retaliation was no longer in use in European courts – and was only continued in a small list of exceptions, all minor in and of themselves.[43] Altogether, retaliation was no longer considered an important factor in the judicial process.

5.6.2 Principle of common utility

A new line of reasoning was introduced by Hugo Grotius.[44] His statements on punishment had a large impact on the development of legal theory. He referred to a basic principle of *utilitas rei publicae*: all punishment should be useful for the State. According to Grotius, punishment is useful in hindering the wrongdoer from harming others by disposing of or incarcerating him or her, for corrective purposes. For example, public executions were a plausible means of deterrence.

Grotius believed that capital punishment should be avoided, with the exception of those rare cases in which leniency might cause greater harm than death. Vengeance should be permitted only as a means of self-defence, and therefore can only be applied when there is no law and no court to enforce it. The examples of retaliation found in the Old Testament and Greek history only remain valid in that they took place between nations at war.

Based on this principle of common utility, the Huguenot pastor Pierre Bayle developed a completely new theory of punishment. His reasoning followed early ideas such as the *De haereticis an sint persequendi* (*Should Heretics Be Persecuted?*) of Sebastian Castellio and the ideas of Montaigne.[45] For Bayle, the idea of common

43 J.-H. Zedler, *Großes vollständiges Universal-Lexikon aller Wissenschaften und Künste*, vol. 55 (Leipzig and Halle, 1748), 2326, "Wiedervergeltung".

44 See Hugo Grotius, *De iure belli ac pacis*, ed. B.J.A. de Kanter-van Hettinga Tromp and Robert Feenstra (Aalen: Scientia, 1993), 477, II.20 c.9 n.1, with reference to *utilitas*. For a classification of the reasons for punishment, see Hugo Grotius, *De jure praedae*, c.2 fols. 8v–9r (English translation by Gwladys Williams, *De iure praedae commentarius: Commentary on the Law of Prize and Booty* [Oxford and London: Clarendon Press 1950], 16–17; Latin text in H.G. Hamaker, ed., *De iure praedae commentarius, ex auctoris codice descripsit et vulgavit* [The Hague: Nijhoff, 1868]).

45 Thus, Charles de Secondat baron de la Brède et de Montesquieu, *De l'esprit des lois*, ed. Victor Goldschmidt (Paris: Garnier-Flammarion, 1979), 212, VI.12 and 218, VI.16; Cesare Beccaria, *Dei delitti e delle pene*, ed. Franco Venturi (Turin: Einaudi, 1999), 14–15, §3. See also Mario Alessandro Cattaneo, "Les fondements philosophiques de la fonction de la peine chez Beccaria", in Michel Porret, ed., *Beccaria et la culture juridique des Lumières* (Geneva: Librairie Droz, 1997), 83–8; Georg Ludolf Louis Günther, *Die Strafrechtsreform im Aufklärungszeitalter* (Leipzig: Vogel, 1907), 171 ff.

utility should govern the penal system.[46] The State should not punish according to the interest of the secular State. Every punishment should help to improve the culprit or to protect the public. For him, therefore, even a society of atheists was possible. In such a society, Bayle argued, the fear of the Last Judgment could no longer justify the criminal system, hence the division of State and religion.

For Frederick II of Prussia, *utilitas* became the leading principle for and purpose of punishment.[47] He was no longer afraid of the Last Judgment; instead, he was governed by his own obligation to provide a well-organised legal system. This new system, according to Frederick, had the responsibility to at least try to reduce delinquency and to prevent other crimes. Although in some cases harsh sentences remained necessary as a deterrent, generally speaking he sought a policy of leniency, as a means of educating his subjects to new righteousness. The contrast with his father could not have been starker.

5.7 Gottfried Wilhelm Leibniz and his *Essais de théodicée*

Gottfried Wilhelm Leibniz was probably the most powerful opponent of Pierre Bayle. In his *Essais de théodicée*, published in 1710, he defended the idea of a pre-established harmony of the world.[48] This invokes the theodicy question: how God could allow evil things in the world. According to Leibniz, God's harmonious organisation of the world does not exclude sin. One may opt for evil because humanity is entitled to exercise freedom. For this reason, the number of wrongs existing in the world is manifold; among them are sin and crime. Punishment is necessary, for God has given an order to the world because he wants people to use their free will for God's glorious purposes. Used as a guide for the individual, punishment helps to deter crime, just as rewards may induce righteous actions. Punishments and rewards therefore function as medicine. Normally, punishment is used for deterrence and for the improvement of the individual.

But sanctions are necessary, even when there is no possibility of the individual perpetrating the crime again. In such cases, punishment functions as revenge. Punishment may serve as recompense when other reasons for condemnation are lacking.[49] This idea is explained with the principle of convenience, which

46 Pierre Bayle, *Pensées diverses sur la comète*, ed. A. Prat (Paris: Cornély, 1911–12; repr. 1984 and 1994). For Bayle's theories in his *Lettres sur le comète*, see James Tully, *An Approach to Philosophy: Locke in Context* (Cambridge: Cambridge University Press, 1993), 208, n. 114.

47 Friedrich II, "Examen critique du système de la nature", in *Œuvres posthumes de Frédéric II* (Berlin: Voss & Decker, 1789), 9:162: *tout ce qu'on peut attendre d'un bon gouvernement, c'est que les grands crimes y soient plus rares que dans un mauvais.*

48 For Leibniz, see Vilem Mudroch, "Leibniz: §29. Leben", in Helmut Holzhey and Wilhelm Schmidt-Biggemann, eds., *Grundriss der Geschichte der Philosophie. Die Philosophie des 17. Jahrhunderts*, vol. 4.2: *Das heilige Römische Reich Deutscher Nation: Nord- und Ostmitteleuropa* (Basel: Schwabe & Co. 2001), 1008–22. For the *Théodicée*, see Wilhelm Schmidt-Biggemann and Helmut Holzhey in ibid., 1037–40.

49 On this aspect see in particular Gaston Grua, *La justice humaine selon Leibniz* (Paris: Presses universitaires de France, 1956), 321–2, who uncovers a law of recompense.

Leibniz later called "vindicatory". He is clearly referring to retaliation. With this argumentation, he legitimises retaliation as the purpose of punishment in general. Just as good actions require recompense, so also misdeeds must be answered proportionately.[50] This is the harmony that one also finds in music and architecture, wherein the proper proportion is not to be neglected. Harmonious justice, then, resembles these artistic forms, in so far as it represents proportionality.

For Leibniz, revenge is the retribution of crime by chastisement, but it is not necessarily cruel or bloody. Retaliation is justified as a necessary form of punishment but it is the modern State which – instead of God – is entitled and even obliged to utilise this authority to punish. Leibniz himself spoke of suitable and equitable punishments, calling only for castigation for crimes; he was not a proponent of capital punishment or severe verdicts. Nevertheless, the idea of equality that Kant later expressed in his *Metaphysische Anfangsgründe* is not to be found.[51]

5.8 Conclusion

Retaliation was most often perceived as a task reserved for God. Generally, neither society nor the individual, however, had a right to take revenge, revenge itself being an appalling sin. This concept is deeply rooted in our culture as well as our writing. When Brunner invented the term *spiegelnde Strafen*, he sought to clarify that Germanic laws did not refer to this tradition. However, the correspondence between Roman law, Augustine and Frankish law suggests that even the Franks, who were even more "Germanic" than the Visigoths, participated in this common tradition. In these instances, the Christian influence helped to propagate and enforce the old principle.

Within the influence of this tradition, however, the vocabulary encountered leaves one with an unclear mixing of terminology. Retaliation is nearly always mixed up with revenge and severe punishment, yet this connection is not compulsory. Revenge is not required to be bloody; retaliation can serve as a deterrent as well as vengeance. The question concerns the meaning of the word *talio*, which includes a number of possibilities:

50 For the equality of these reactions see Gaston Grua, *Jurisprudence universelle et théodicée selon Leibniz* (Paris: Presses universitaires de France, 1953), 509 ff.

51 Immanuel Kant, *Metaphysik der Sitten*, Rechtslehre, II.1 in *Werke*, vol. 4 (Darmstadt: Wissenschaftliche Buchgesellschaft, 1983), 454. For Kant's critique of Leibniz's *Théodicée*, see Klaus Fischer, *Schicksal in Theologie und Philosophie* (Darmstadt, Wissenschaftliche Buchgesellschaft, 2008),77 ff. Unfortunately, here as well as in the other writings on the *Théodicée*, the aspect of punishment is not mentioned. For Kant's doctrine on *ius talionis*, see Georg Steinberg, "Sittliche Strafwürdigkeit als Rechtfertigung staatlichen Strafens nach Kant", in Reiner Schulze *et al.*, eds., *Strafzweck und Strafform zwischen religiöser und weltlicher Wertevermittlung* (Münster: Rhema, 2008), 180. For the reception of Leibniz's *Théodicee*, especially in Germany, see Stefan Lorenz, *De mundo optimo. Studien zu Leibniz' Theodizee und ihrer Rezeption in Deutschland (1710–1791)* (Stuttgart: Steiner, 1997).

1. the *motif* of revenge;
2. the harshness of severe and bloody sanctions – that is the *character* of a punishment; and
3. the "mirroring" *form* of punishment, so that the punishment recalls the crime.

Or could *talio* indicate an equidistance between crime and punishment? Only the third option is an evaluation made by third parties.

These are three different topics, which would evoke different scientific subjects and analyses; they would also legitimise three completely different conclusions. As long as these topics remain convoluted, communication between their proponents is almost impossible. The confusion in this area has a long history. Some saw the "mirroring punishment" as something different vis-à-vis retaliation, while others believed there only to be different examples of the same principle. The "mirroring punishment" can be explained as an outdated expression, akin to magical convictions that the punishment is to be commensurate with the crime. But, in the Leibnizian sense, one can consider the "mirroring" options as an expression of harmonious proportion between offence and punishment. Retaliation cannot, therefore, necessarily be identified with the maxim "an eye for an eye", but might convey the notion of the improvement of the individual and hence a lesser punishment.

Owing to St Paul's verdict in Rom. 12:19, vengeance is generally perceived as evil. But Leibniz argued that the State might have a right to utilise vengeance. If this means only the right to punish in cases in which deterrence and correction are not attainable, it would be inconceivable that anyone would deny the State the right to enact such justice. Additionally, the term "vindication" can indicate not only both revenge and retaliation, but also merely harsh punishment. There are, in fact, times when it should be understood only as punishment, in others retaliation. Indisputably, there is a latent confusion of terminology here.

Perhaps thanks to the influence of tradition, any *lex talionis* is often understood as a means to overcome bloodier old customs. It seems that rules on retaliation can only be justified as a means of preventing something even worse. It is not uncommon to find nineteenth- and twentieth-century legal historians who praise the Germanic law for its boldness. Yet, this is only the same perspective with the opposite values, where not culture but rather a coercive spirit to overcome old standards receives praise. As seen above, retaliation as a means to limit feuds was a concept drawn up by Augustine; but it is unwise to presume this as a valid historical finding. Instead, this is a cultural explanation which does not necessarily have to do with history. If it is an explanation that has served for more than 15 centuries, we can hardly assume a single major shift from feuds to more civilised methods of punishment. These monocausal and homespun explanations should be avoided. And yet, even in the writings of Augustine, he allowed for several exceptions to the general ban on retaliation. Could it be that retaliation in some cases is necessary, and that this general condemnation of vengeance is not completely in accordance with the needed prerogatives of society?

One must be mindful that, historically, the "an eye for an eye" principle can be found in almost all cultures since the time of Hammurabi's code. Most of the other purposes of punishment are also present in the same periods and sources: deterrence for the sake of the general public and for the correction of the individual guilty of crime. The common contempt for revenge appears to be motivated by the Christian religion and thus rooted in Western culture.

The question remains, however, whether there is something in retaliation that cannot be dispensed with completely. Leibniz tried to legitimise retaliation from the perspective of harmony and proportionality. Indeed, if retaliation is just an expression of proportionality, it is the basic concept of any punishment. Consequently, in cases of severe crimes, harsh punishments re-establish the law which the crime violated. In this light, retaliation would be the essence of punishment and would indicate nothing more than the idea already expressed by Aristotle: that punishment is subject to the *iustitia commutativa*. If retaliation can be interpreted in this sense, revenge might be a prerequisite for all societies as the re-establishment of broken law. We should not forget that the ancient goddess Nemesis was not the goddess of revenge but of compensation, and thus of equalising retribution. The Greek term νέμειν (*némein*) means "to give what is due":[52]

> *Nemesis, winged balancer of life, dark-faced goddess, daughter of Justice ....*

Further reading

Bohatec, Josef. *Calvin und das Recht* (Graz: Böhlaus, 1934).

Günther, Louis. *Die Idee der Wiedervergeltung in der Geschichte und Philosophie des Strafrechts. Ein Beitrag zur Universal-Historischen Entwicklung desselben* (Erlangen: Bläsing, 1891).

Guyon, Gérard. *Justice de Dieu, justice des hommes. Christianisme et histoire du droit pénal* (Bouère: D.M. Morin, 2009).

Hoffmann, Peter. "Zum Verhältnis der Strafzwecke Vergeltung und Generalprävention in ihrer Entwicklung und im heutigen Strafrecht", Diss. jur., University of Göttingen (1992).

Kéry, Lotte. *Gottesfurcht und irdische Strafe. Der Beitrag des mittelalterlichen Kirchenrechts zur Entstehung des öffentlichen Strafrechts* (Cologne: Böhlau, 2006).

Pahud de Mortanges, René. "Strafzwecke bei Gratian und den Dekretisten", (1992) 78 *Zeitschrift der Savigny-Stiftung für Rechtsgeschichte: Kanonistische Abteilung* 121–58.

Pahud de Mortanges, René. *Zwischen Vergebung und Vergeltung. Eine Analyse des kirchlichen Straf- und Disziplinarrechts* (Baden-Baden: Nomos, 1992).

Puigelier, C. and F. Terré, eds. *La vengeance* (Paris: Éd Panthéon-Assas, 2011).

52 Mesomedes of Crete, *Hymn to Nemesis*, available at http://www.aoidoi.org/poets/mesomedes/meso-3.pdf (accessed 26 July 2011).

Rothkamm, Jan. *Talio esto. Recherches sur les origines de la formule "oeil pour oeil, dent pour dent" dans les droits du Proche-Orient ancien, et sur son devenir dans le monde gréco-romain* (Berlin/New York: de Gruyter, 2011).
Schmoeckel, Mathias. *Das Recht der Reformation. Die epistemologische Revolution der Wissenschaft und die Spaltung der Rechtsordnung in der Frühen Neuzeit* (Tübingen: Mohr Siebeck, 2014).
Strohm, Christoph. *Ethik im frühen Calvinismus* (Berlin/New York: de Gruyter, 1996).
Terradas Saborit, I. *Justicia vindicatoria* (Madrid: Consejo Superior de Investigaciones Cientificas, 2008).
Witte, John Jr. *Law and Protestantism: The Legal Teachings of the Lutheran Reformation* (Cambridge: Cambridge University Press, 2002).
Witte, John Jr. *The Reformation of Rights: Law, Religion, and Human Rights in Early Modern Calvinism* (Cambridge: Cambridge University Press, 2007).

6 Christianity and the liberal enlightenment reforms of criminal law

Heikki Pihlajamäki

6.1 Introduction

According to the traditional view, the Enlightenment brought with it a secularisation of philosophical and social thinking, contributing significantly to the process of modernisation in the West. Separation of Church and State and theoretical formulations of religious tolerance limited State control over religious compliance. At the same time, philosophical scepticism, atheism and influential critiques of the Church and clergy as institutions emerged.[1]

This view of the Enlightenment dominates histories of Western criminal justice, in both common law and civil law. Whereas *ancien régime* criminal justice essentially depended on a Christian worldview, the argument goes that first natural law theorists and then Enlightenment reformers delivered a decisive blow to Christianity as law's organising principle.[2] Particularly in criminal law, the late eighteenth- and early nineteenth-century Enlightenment caused an upheaval that brought humankind from pre-modernity to the modern era. This was the epoch of reforms that transformed European criminal justice, which had taken shape in the Middle Ages, into something more closely resembling the system we have today. Eberhard Schmidt connected the new criminal justice to "secularisation, rationalisation, humanisation and liberalisation".[3] As another prominent German legal historian described it, "punishment no longer means, as in the mediaeval theocratic system, God's revenge, but develops, following secular natural law, as a reaction to an earlier breach of the norm".[4] Punishments now needed to

1 One of the most influential modern works developing these themes is Peter Gay, *The Enlightenment* (New York: Knopf, 1966), 1–2. See also, e.g. Louis Dupré, *Religion and the Rise of Modern Culture* (Notre Dame, IN: University of Notre Dame Press, 2008); Margaret C. Jacob, *The Radical Enlightenment: Pantheists, Freemasons, and Republicans* (London: Allen & Unwin, 1981).

2 See Eberhardt Schmidt, *Einführung in die Geschichte der deutschen Strafrechtspflege* (Göttingen: Vandenhoeck & Ruprecht, 1983; first published 1947).

3 Eberhard Schmidt, "Die geistesgeschichtliche Bedeutung der Aufklärung für die Entwicklung der Strafjustiz aus der Sicht des 20. Jahrhunderts", (1958) 75 *Revue Pénale Suisse* 343.

4 Hinrich Rüping, *Grundriß der Strafrechtsgeschichte* (Munich: Beck, 1991), 59: "Strafe bedeutet nicht mehr wie im theokratischen System des Mittelalters, Gott zu rächen, sondern erschöpft sich für das profane Naturrecht in der Reaktion auf einen vorangegangenen Normverstoß".

match crimes – not, however, according to the mirroring logic of talion, but rather corresponding to the harm that the crime had caused the victim and society. This led, finally, to the abolition of torture and, if not the abolition of the death penalty everywhere, then at least to a considerable decrease in its use. Most breaches of Christian doctrine were no longer crimes at all, and crimes defined as such by Christian doctrine but which were not harmful to society (such as suicide) were decriminalised. Christian morality and the law parted ways, leading to lighter punishments for crimes such as blasphemy and sodomy, which were now punished only insofar as they threatened the public order. Many Enlightenment theorists now argued that all punishments were to be applied rationally, so that they would further *salus publica*, the common good, according to the principles of utilitarianism (propounded by Böhmer and Bentham). Rationalism and secularism also led to constructs such as P.J.A. Feuerbach's theory of "psychological compulsion".

Reformers considered *ancien régime* criminal justice cruel and arbitrary. This, combined with the religious notion of crime as conceptually connected to sin, as well as the haphazard nature of the inquisitorial procedure, coupled with judicial torture, made the old system intolerable for the reformers. The disproportionality and arbitrariness of the punishments did not improve matters. Consequently, the critique and demands for reform were directed at three different targets: the secularisation of criminal law by giving the State, with its utilitarian approach to punishment, the sole right to punish; the establishment of crimes and punishments through legislation only; and the application of the proportionality principle between crime and punishment. General leniency in sentencing could be added to these.[5]

For some decades, the traditional narrative of the Enlightenment as a secularisation procedure has become more nuanced, with the overarching theme being "restoring religion to the Enlightenment".[6] The scholarly consensus has significantly changed: scholars now generally agree that religion continued to play a decisive role in people's lives, as well as in politics and culture even during (and after) the Enlightenment.[7] The authority of the Bible all but waned,

5 Maximiliano Hernández Marcos, "Conceptual Aspects of Legal Enlightenment in Europe", in Damiano Canale, Paolo Grossi and Hasso Hoffmann, eds., *A Treatise of Legal Philosophy and General Jurisprudence*, vol. 9: *A History of the Philosophy of Law in the Civil Law World* (Dordrecht: Springer, 2009), 125–6.

6 See, for instance, Dale K. van Kley, *The Religious Origins of the French Revolution: From Calvin to the Civil Constitution, 1560–1791* (New Haven: Yale University Press, 1975); Simon Grote, "Review-Essay: Religion and Enlightenment", (2014) 75 *Journal of the History of Ideas* 137–61; Charly Coleman, "Resacralizing the World: The Fate of Secularization in Enlightenment Historiography", (2010) 82 *Journal of Modern History* 368–95.

7 Knut Haakonssen, "Enlightened Dissent: An Introduction", in Knut Haakonssen, ed., *Religion and Enlightenment: Rational Dissent in Eighteenth-Century Britain* (Cambridge: Cambridge University Press, 1996), 2–3; J.C.D. Clark, *English Society, 1688–1832: Religion, Ideology and Politics during the Ancien Régime* (Cambridge: Cambridge University Press, 2000).

as teaching changed to secure the Bible's position as a foundation of Western culture.[8] Enlightened theologians refashioned Christian teaching to suit modern natural science and promoted religious tolerance. Although sceptical towards religion and oriented towards solving social and scientific problems with the help of rationality, few *philosophes* were actually atheists. Voltaire, one of the biggest critics of the Church and Christianity, even said, "whatever the present-day scholars may say, one can be a very good philosopher and still believe in God. Atheists have never responded to the objection that a clock proves the existence of a clockmaker".[9]

This chapter provides a brief overview of the reformers' starting point, the criminal justice system of the *ancien régime*. I will then move on to a discussion of Enlightened criminal law thinkers and religion, and I will ask how religion featured in their writings and how it affected their theories. The final part will conclude and summarise the findings of the chapter.

6.2 The criminal justice system of the *ancien régime*

The criminal justice system, which the Enlightenment philosophers criticised, was firmly rooted in mediaeval canon law. Inquisitorial procedure emerged in the late eleventh century and became a general mode of procedure in canon law during the thirteenth century. In the late Middle Ages and the beginning of the early modern period, inquisitorial procedure spread to secular procedure and became the standard way of managing crime in most regions of Europe. Inquisitorial procedure, in fact, created criminal law in the modern sense, as separate from civil procedure. From the Middle Ages onwards, criminal procedure was divided into inquisitorial, adversarial and (sometimes) denunciatory procedures.[10]

The rise of the inquisitorial procedure brought with it tough penalties. When public powers – the Church, princes and cities – took over punishing, they used not only fines but also, increasingly, capital and corporal punishments. Part and parcel of this was the change in the law of evidence. Before the transformation of the thirteenth century, legal procedures relied on compurgators, oaths and ordeals. After the Fourth Lateran Council (1215), clerics could no longer participate in ordeals and, since the primary responsibility of their administration had

8 Jonathan Sheehan, *The Enlightenment Bible: Translation, Scholarship, Bible* (Princeton: Princeton University Press, 2005).

9 Voltaire to Jean-François Dufour, seigneur du Villevieille, 26 August 1768, in Richard A. Brooks, ed. and trans., *Voltaire: Selected Letters of Voltaire* (New York: New York University Press, 1973), 276; Ronald S. Love, *The Enlightenment* (Westport, CT: Greenwood Press, 2008), 57; S.J. Barnett, *The Enlightenment and Religion: the Myths of Modernity* (Manchester: Manchester University Press, 2003).

10 Heikki Pihlajamäki and Mia Korpiola, "Medieval Canon Law: The Origins of Modern Criminal Law", in Markus D. Dubber and Tatjana Hörnle, eds., *The Oxford Handbook of Criminal Law* (Oxford: Oxford University Press, 2014), 201–24.

been with the Church, the practice became extinct within a few decades.[11] Ordeals were replaced by a statutory theory of proof, a theory developed by legal scholars. According to the theory, in serious criminal cases "full proof" was needed for condemnation. Such proof consisted of the confession of two trustworthy eyewitnesses. An integral part of the theory was judicial torture, which helped to extract confessions in cases where some evidence existed but was insufficient.

Early modern criminal law scholars continued building on these mediaeval structures and the control of serious crime continued to be based on capital and corporal punishments. "Spectacles of suffering", as Pieter Spierenburg has called early modern executions, dominated the visual image of crime control,[12] even though in practice the number of capital punishment sentences put into effect decreased in most Western countries from the seventeenth century onwards.[13] Until its abolition, first by "Enlightened monarchs" such as Frederick the Great of Prussia, Catherine the Great of Russia and Charles III of Sweden, judicial torture continued to be formally in force as well. However, as John Langbein has demonstrated, the use of judicial torture and capital punishment diminished from the beginning of the early modern period.[14] The reason for their decline was the emergence of an alternative, the "extraordinary punishment", which had also formed part of mediaeval criminal law theory. The judge was to resort to "ordinary punishment" (*poena ordinaria*, typically capital punishment) if no alleviating or aggravating circumstances were present. Such circumstances would lead to an "extraordinary punishment" (*poena extraordinaria*) which could be, depending on the nature of the circumstances, either more lenient or more severe than the ordinary punishment. In practice, the extraordinary punishments most often served to alleviate harsh capital punishments. Extraordinary punishments also helped in cases in which full proof was lacking but the evidence was otherwise convincing.[15]

The rise of the modern State and its organised way of treating crime and convicted criminals favoured the extended use of extraordinary punishment. Viable alternatives to the death penalty emerged. Galley service and forced labour were typical examples of punishments whose organisation demanded State machinery unavailable to mediaeval polities but already within the reach of modern States.

11 Robert Bartlett, *Trial by Fire and Water: The Medieval Judicial Ordeal* (Oxford: Clarendon Press, 1986).

12 Peter Spierenburg, *The Spectacle of Suffering: Executions and the Evolution of Repression: From a Preindustrial Metropolis to the European Experience* (Cambridge: Cambridge University Press, 1984).

13 Richard Evans, *Rituals of Retribution: Capital Punishment in Germany, 1500–1987* (Harmondsworth: Penguin Books, 1996), 42.

14 John Langbein, *Torture and the Law of Proof: Europe and England in the Ancien Régime* (Chicago: University of Chicago Press, 1976).

15 On the early modern criminal justice system, see Massimo Meccarelli, "Criminal Law: Before a State Monopoly", in Heikki Pihlajamäki, Markus D. Dubber and Mark Godfrey, eds., *The Oxford Handbook of European Legal History* (Oxford: Oxford University Press, 2018), 632–54.

As a result, the use of the death penalty declined and, by extension, judicial torture became increasingly unnecessary. This much more gradual erosion of judicial torture led Langbein to call the narrative of Enlightenment reformers abolishing torture a "fairy tale": the decisive turn towards the demise of torture had occurred long before the Enlightenment.[16]

Nevertheless, at the end of the eighteenth century, the mediaeval core of Western criminal justice remained intact. Even though capital punishment and judicial torture were less frequent than they once had been, these gruesome institutions were still available and used. The case of the cruel execution of Damiens the regicide, which Foucault describes in *Discipline and Punish*,[17] may have been exceptional, but in eighteenth-century Europe it was still possible that the death penalty could follow from even a minor crime, such as stealing a handkerchief.[18] From the point of view of the reformers, the fact that capital punishment and torture were used less often than a couple of hundred years earlier (if the reformers were even aware of this) was probably just as irrelevant as it is for opponents of the death penalty in the United States or China today.

In theory, one of the main areas in which the death penalty and judicial torture were used was that of religious crimes and those connected to the Christian faith: blasphemy, witchcraft, sodomy and adultery. However, although the letter of the law remained unchanged, in the legal practice of many European regions these crimes no longer carried capital punishment. As for the organisation of the judicial system, the Church's influence had begun to wane as well. In Protestant regions, the State had taken over the courts of the Catholic *forum externum* as early as the sixteenth century, although Protestant Churches remained closely connected to the State and they jointly exercised social control.[19] Similarly, in Catholic areas of the West, the Church courts had lost much of their jurisdiction to secular courts long before the Enlightenment era.[20]

Despite these changes, the Christian faith still provided the main legitimation for the criminal system. Although general deterrence and betterment of the criminal already figured in the punishment theories of thinkers such as Antonius Matthaeus II (1601–54), retaliation or retribution remained an important justification for punishments.[21] Crime merited punishment because crime constituted

16 Langbein, *Torture and the Law of Proof.*

17 Michel Foucault, *Discipline and Punish: The Birth of the Prison* (New York: Random House, 1975).

18 See John Hostettler, *Cesare Beccaria: The Genius of "On Crimes and Punishments"* (Hook, Hampshire: Waterside Press, 2011).

19 Heikki Pihlajamäki, *Executor divinarum et suarum legum: Criminal Law and the Lutheran Reformation* (Leiden: Brill, 2006), 171–204.

20 Paolo Prodi, *Eine Geschichte der Gerechtigkeit. Vom Recht Gottes zum modernen Rechtsstaat* (Munich: Beck, 2003).

21 Jan-Willem Oosterhuis, "Grotius, Matthaeus and the Secularization of Early Modern Criminal Law in the Dutch Republic", paper presented at the Annual Meeting of American Society for Legal History, 8–11 November 2018.

a sin, which was harmful to society. If crimes went unpunished, not only did the individual criminal in question, but also the ruler and his or her realm risk perdition. A good example of Lutheran argument is Benedict Carpzov, whose thinking influenced many generations of European criminal law theorists.[22]

6.3 The reforms, reformers and religion

The concept of "Enlightenment" is notoriously challenging. Some scholars define it as the period typically ranging from the mid eighteenth to the early nineteenth centuries, whereas others prefer to define it as ways of thinking which originated in roughly that period. For the purposes of this chapter, it should suffice to assume a pragmatic approach and proceed from a conventional list of Enlightenment thinkers. My purpose is to look at their views on religion and to see how those views affected their teachings on criminal law. I will start with Christian Thomasius.

Christian Thomasius (1655–1728), the first representative of the German Enlightenment and a major reformer of criminal law, is considered an important seculariser of criminal law and is mainly known for his campaigns against inquisitorial procedure and judicial torture and for the decriminalisation of bigamy, witchcraft and heresy. However, as Thomas Ahnert has shown, none of Thomasius' key teachings can be understood without reference to his religious beliefs. His contemporaries considered them outrageous but none would have described him as anti-religious.[23] As Ian Hunter demonstrates, Thomasius effectively mobilised the Lutheran concept of Christians' inner freedom not only to shield Christian faith from interference by the State but also to protect religion from the secular systems of power – such as criminal justice.[24] Interestingly, later representatives of criminal law – such as Beccaria, Pagano and Feuerbach – adopted similar views with regard to the relationship between religion and the State.

Similarly, although Charles de Montesquieu (1689–1755) was critical of the Catholic Church and the clergy as institutions, he was not against religion as such. Montesquieu discusses religion in Books 24 to 26 of *De l'esprit des lois* (1748). For him, religion could be useful not only in strengthening morality, but also in undermining it (XXIV, 21). Religion did not necessarily contradict secular ends and Christians could also be good citizens (XXIV, 6). According to Montesquieu, "Religion may [even] support a State, when the laws themselves are incapable of doing it" (XXIV, 16). He suggests that both religion and civil

22 Rüping, *Grundriß der Strafrechtsgeschichte*, 43.

23 Thomas Ahnert, *Religion and the Origins of the German Enlightenment: Faith and the Reform of Learning in the Thought of Christian Thomasius* (Rochester, NY: University of Rochester Press, 2006).

24 See Ian Hunter, *The Secularisation of the Confessional State: the Political Thought of Christian Thomasius* (Cambridge: Cambridge University Press, 2007).

law are responsible for the forming of "good citizens"; when one of them fails in the task, the other one should step in (XXIV, 14).[25]

For many historians, Cesare Beccaria marked the decisive change from pre-modern to modern criminal law. His major work, the little book called *On Crimes and Punishments* (1764), was the big bang of criminal law reforms all over the Western hemisphere. This was not so much because of its originality – none of Beccaria's ideas were novel – but because he succeeded in presenting those ideas in an accessible form.[26] Translated into many languages, *On Crimes and Punishments* spread quickly around Europe and the Americas. It became known (and still is) mostly for its utilitarian and rationalist tone. For Beccaria, punishments were necessary and rational only insofar as they deterred people from committing crimes (general deterrence). Therefore, it is rational that punishments be proportionate to the crime. The famous legal principle – no crime without law, no punishment without law (*nullum crimen sine lege, nulla poena sine lege*) – flowed from the same idea of general deterrence: people should be able to know beforehand what deeds were criminal and which punishment would follow which crime. Furthermore, Beccaria was opposed to the death penalty and judicial torture.

It is also difficult to deny the general view according to which religion plays little role in Beccaria's work, although *On Crimes and Punishments* does not remain silent on the theme. Beccaria writes:

> But our religion is more holy than that of the Romans, and consequently impiety is a greater crime. Granted. God will punish it. The part of man is, to punish that which is criminal in the public disorder which the impiety hath occasioned. But if in the act of impiety the delinquent hath not even stolen a handkerchief; if the ceremonies of religion have been in no wise disturbed, shall we, as I said before, punish the impiety as we would punish parricide?
> (Chapter VI)

Beccaria does not forcefully deny the importance of religion; it just does not have a place in his system. It is up to humans to take care of discipline; God will punish crimes against religion: "Religion is of God to man; the civil law is of you to your people" (Chapter IV).

25 Rebecca Kingston, "Montesquieu on Religion and on the Question of Toleration", in David W. Carruthers, Michael A. Mosher and Paul Anthony Rahe, eds., *Montesquieu's Science of Politics: Essays on "The Spirit of Laws"* (Oxford: Rowman and Littlefield, 2001), 375–408.

26 For instance, many philosophers and jurists opposed judicial torture at least from the sixteenth century onwards: see Mathias Schmoeckel, *Humantität und Staatsräson. Die Abschaffung der Folter in Europa und die Entwicklung des gemainen Straf- und Beweisrechts seit dem hohen Mittelalter* (Cologne: Böhlau, 2000), 93–186. In legal practice, judicial torture had been on the decline long before the Enlightenment reformers' criticism: see, for instance, on legal practice in Toulouse, Lisa Silverman, *Tortured Subjects: Pain, Truth, and the Body in Early Modern France* (Chicago: University of Chicago Press, 2001), 71–84.

Nor does a human judge have access to the mysteries of sin. Therefore, comparing crime to sin is beyond human capacity and humans should not engage themselves in such activity:

> In short, others have imagined, that the greatness of the sin should aggravate the crime. But the fallacy of this opinion will appear on the slightest consideration of the relations between man and man, and between God and man. The relations between man and man are relations of equality. Necessity alone hath produced, from the opposition of private passions and interests, the idea of public utility, which is the foundation of human justice. The other are relations of dependence, between an imperfect creature and his Creator, the most perfect of beings, who has reserved to himself the sole right of being both lawgiver and judge; for he alone can, without injustice, be, at the same time, both one and the other. If he hath decreed eternal punishments for those who disobey his will, shall an insect dare to put himself in the place of divine justice, to pretend to punish for the Almighty, who is himself all-sufficient; who cannot receive impressions of pleasure or pain, and who alone, of all other beings, acts without being acted upon? The degree of sin depends on the malignity of the heart, which is impenetrable to finite being. How then can the degree of sin serve as a standard to determine the degree of crimes? If that were admitted, men may punish when God pardons, and pardon when God condemns; and thus act in opposition to the Supreme Being.
> (Chapter VII)

Beccaria also comments on the relationship between canon law and secular law when he discusses judicial torture and confession. According to him, the sacrament of confession had been misused on several occasions when penitents sought absolution in advance, before committing a serious crime. For instance, "Jaurigny and Balthazar Gerard, who assassinated William I, Prince of Orange; Clement the Dominican, Chatel, Ravaillac, and all the other parricides of those times, went to confession before they committed their crimes" (Chapter XVI). Therefore, "Confession, which was intended as a curb to iniquity, hath frequently, in times of confusion and seduction, become an incentive to wickedness" and "Probably it was for this reason, that so many Christian states have abolished a holy institution, which appeared to be as dangerous as useful".

In the chapter on torture, Beccaria speculates that it is probably a human application of purgatory: "Now infamy is a stain, and if the punishments and fire of purgatory can take away all spiritual stains, why should not the pain of torture take away those of a civil nature?" (Chapter XVI). If torture was akin to purgatory, then confession of a crime was related to a confession of sin:

> I imagine that the confession of a criminal, which in some tribunals is required, as being essential to his condemnation, has a similar origin, and has been taken from the mysterious tribunal of penitence, where the confession of sins is a necessary part of the sacrament. Thus have men abused the

> unerring light of revelation; and in the times of tractable ignorance, having no other, they naturally had recourse to it on every occasion, making the most remote and absurd applications.
>
> (Chapter XVI)

Beccaria was thus not opposed to the Christian faith but removed it from the secular system. The secular system was for human beings to operate. This was not, however, the view of all who supported his reformist views and developed them further. I will take two examples of such scholars, both of the Italian school: Gaetano Filangieri and Francesco Mario Pagano.

Besides Beccaria, Gaetano Filangieri is the best known internationally of the early Italian criminal law scholars. His main work, *The Science of Legislation* (*La scienza della legislazione*), appeared between 1780 and 1791 in five volumes, of which the third was devoted to criminal law and procedure. His critical points largely followed those of Beccaria. According to Filangieri, judicial torture was not only inhumanely cruel but also produced uncertain results (3:147–8). He advocated for the limitation of the death penalty, but accepted it in certain serious cases. His reform philosophy thus followed that of Beccaria.

However, and unlike Beccaria, Filangieri discussed religion at length. Like many of his intellectual contemporaries, he was a Freemason and a deist. He did not consider religion necessarily a superstitious fraud, but thought that it could play an important role in the construction and maintenance of the social order. Religion was "so inherent to the nature of man, so necessary to the formation, perfection and preservation of society, and so terrible in its degeneration". Religion belonged, however, to the "internal forum", whereas politics was a matter for the outer forum. Freemasons' lodges could be an excellent tool in developing Christianity into a civil religion which would be spread to the masses and which could help combat the traditional power of the Church and the privileges of the clergy. In the way that Filangieri envisaged it, civil religion had nothing to do with the Church as a separate power competing with the secular power, and nothing to do with what he and other deists considered to be superstitious beliefs. His vision of a civil religion was, however, in complete disagreement with the Jacobin idea of uprooting the existing religions altogether and founding a completely new one.[27]

Filangieri thus thought that religious sentiments were unavoidable for humans and, in fact, religion could be used as a social glue. His reference to the canon law institutions of internal and external fora which had their origins in the mediaeval period is revealing: since the canon *omniusque sexus* had been issued in 1215, the two fora had formed the branches of ecclesiastical social control. In Filangieri's thinking, an external forum of the Church had, of course, no place. Instead, the

27 Maurizio Viroli, *Machiavelli's God* (Princeton: Princeton University Press, 2010), 249–51; Gaetano Filangieri, *La scienza della legislazione* 1:57–8 (as cited in Viroli, *Machiavelli's God*, 250).

external forum was wholly reserved for the secular power, which did not have to compete with the Church.

Francesco Mario Pagano (1748–99) was a contemporary of Filangieri and a well-known international figure, despite the fact that standard lists of Enlightenment criminal justice reformers now seldom include his name. He studied law at Naples and later became professor of moral philosophy and jurisprudence. His *Saggi politici* (*Political Essays*, 1783–5) is a philosophical history of the Kingdom of Naples. Like Beccaria's and Filangieri's works, the *Saggi* argues for more lenient criminal justice, and against torture and capital punishment.[28] Pagano authored a republican constitution for Naples and was executed when the short-lived republic fell in 1799.[29]

From the point of view of this chapter, Pagano's *Considerations on Criminal Procedure* (*Considerazioni sul processo criminale*) (1787) is pivotal. Unlike Beccaria, Pagano departed from the principle of talion: not, however, in the draconic sense of the term – an eye for an eye – but rather meaning that every violation of a right had to be paid back by the loss of a right.[30] His attitude towards religion was much closer to Beccaria's than Filangieri's. He was critical of the Church and blamed past canon lawyers for the degeneration of the inquisitorial procedure – inherited, as he saw it, from the ancient Romans – into a secretive and arbitrary business. The inquisitorial procedure as the Roman emperors had introduced it had been a transparent process, but decretals of mediaeval popes such as Innocent III (*de accusationibus, de judiciis*) had transformed it. Emperor Frederick the Great of Prussia had adopted the inquisitorial mode of procedure in his constitution *Inquisitiones generales*, "but not with its ancient methods, but rather with that terrible and ferocious one introduced by the churchmen". That had been "one step too far" ("un passo di più") from the ecclesiastics.[31]

Pagano wrote little about the Church, but his main idea was clear. The Catholic Church was, historically and in Pagano's time, connected to the feudal structures that supported the early modern State. This position needed to be eradicated to make way for a liberal State. This basic position formulated in the *Saggi* is reformulated in the *Considerazioni* when he discusses the institution of the oath. Religious oaths needed to be abolished from legal proceedings. For Pagano, an oath was "moral violence" (*violenza morale*) just as judicial torture was physical violence (*violenza fisica*). An oath did not constitute moral violence because of its

28 Francesco Mario Pagano, *Considerazioni sul processo criminale*, 150–3, 184.

29 Mark Goldie and Robert Wokler, eds., *The Cambridge History of Eighteenth-century Political Thought* (Cambridge: Cambridge University Press, 2008), 765.

30 Omid Shahibzadeh, "Penal Philosophy in 18th Century Italy: A Historical Enquiry into the Ideas of Francesco Mario Pagano", unpublished master's thesis, University of Oslo (2016), 3. Pagano, *Considerazioni sul processo criminale*, 33: "L'arbitrario procedimento senza formalità e senza processo è l'indice, e l'istrumento insime di un fateale illimitato dispotismo".

31 Pagano, *Considerazioni sul processo criminale*, 70–1. Shahibzadeh, "Penal Philosophy in 18th Century Italy", 88. See also Paolo de Angelis, *Politica e giurisdizione nel pensiero di Francisco Mario Pagano* (Naples: Istituto italiano per gli studi filosofici, 2006).

connection to sin but because it violated the human dignity of the one giving the oath. The institution of the oath represented, as de Angelis puts it, a compromise between Church and State, a concession that had been made to fit ecclesiastical and religious interests into a procedure that now needed to be essentially secular. In Pagano's time, better truth-finding mechanisms than the oath already existed as forensic techniques had begun to advance.[32]

Similarly, as regards the theory of evidence, the elevated position of confession (*regina probationum* since the Middle Ages) needed to be changed. Confession had to be relegated to the same level as all other instruments of evidence: "La confessione dev'essere sostenuta dalla prova del delitto". Obviously, Pagano's thinking ran along the same lines as the general European reform ideas of the late eighteenth and early nineteenth centuries, which emphasised the importance of ridding the system of proofs of the remaining vestiges of the Roman canon law theory of proof. Since the thirteenth and fourteenth centuries, the concept of full proof had played a major role. It consisted of what Pagano called "natural proofs" ("prova naturale"), confession and eyewitnesses, as opposed to other, "indirect" proofs. A prominent position given to natural proofs was, according to Pagano, a mark of an underdeveloped, barbaric legal order: "le barbare nazioni amano una pronta giustizia, ed alle loro semplici idee conforme; attendono solo alla realità del fatto, ed alla naturale pruova" (*Considerazioni*, VI).

The secular nature of the Enlightenment reforms lay in the fact that the right to punish (*ius puniendi*) now became the sole prerogative of the State. Crime was no longer derived from sin; instead, it was defined through the social harm it produced. Contrary to earlier thinking, crimes pertaining to conscience or private morals were not, in fact, crimes at all. This is what Beccaria, Filangieri and Pagano – and the great majority of nineteenth-century criminal law thinkers – had in common.

Not all of them, however, held this view. Interestingly, William Blackstone, although greatly influenced by Beccaria,[33] still retained God in his theory of punishment:

> To shed the blood of our fellow creature is a matter that requires the greatest deliberation, and the fullest conviction of our own authority: for life is the immediate gift of God to man; which neither he can resign, nor can it be taken from him, unless by the command or permission of him who gave it;

32 De Angelis, *Politica e giurisdizione*, 70–1. Beccaria, *On Crimes and Punishments*, had touched on the subject of the oath as well, stating that it was becoming a mere formality: Chapter XI, "Dei delittie delle pene": "Il giuramento a poco a poco diviene una semplice formalità, distruggendosi in questa maniera la forza dei sentimentidi Religione, unico pegno dell'onestà della maggior parte degli Uomini".

33 Bernard E. Harcourt, "Beccaria's 'On Crimes and Punishments': A Mirror on the History of the Foundations of Modern Criminal Law", (2003), 6.2 *Buffalo Criminal Law Review* 691–83.

> either expressly revealed, or collected from the laws of nature or society by clear and indisputable demonstration.

On the other hand, "punishments are … only inflicted for abuse of that free will, which God has given to man".[34]

In one area of criminal justice – the execution of punishments – the effects of secularisation remained particularly modest. One of the effects of the modernisation of criminal law was that it brought with it a thorough change in the system of punishment. When punishments were to be meted out according to the principle of proportionality, capital and corporal punishments could no longer serve as part of the backbone of the punishment system. Fines did not serve this purpose very well either, because most convicted criminals did not have the means to pay. Imprisonment, however, had its benefits. It became, as Michael Ignatieff put it, "a just measure of pain": long sentences for serious crimes, shorter sentences for less serious crimes.[35] Imprisonment was also flexible in the sense that it could be made to meet several other objectives. During their prison term, inmates could be resocialised to help them return to society as useful citizens.

Prison reform was thus an integral part of the transformation of criminal justice in the late eighteenth and early nineteenth centuries. John Howard's famous account of British prisons in the 1770s gives a vivid description of the problems that needed to be addressed. The old prisons were overcrowded and difficult to supervise. Diseases and violence spread easily, and hardened criminals were housed together with first-timers.[36] Prison doctors and infirmaries were on the list of demands made by the reformers, many of whom were devout Christians, such as Quakers and Evangelicals. To combat disease, prisons were to be dry, heated, clean and hygienic.[37] Even Jeremy Bentham, a well-known opponent of religions, envisaged a chapel as a necessary part of his Panopticon. In an early draft for the frontispiece of a planned book on the Panopticon, he sketched the words from the 139th psalm: "Thou art about my path, and about my bed: and spiest out all my ways". Chapels were then built in prisons following (albeit otherwise loosely) the Panopticon model, such as Pentonville prison in London.[38]

The Auburn model – daytime labour, night-time solitude – dominated early nineteenth-century American disciplinary institutions. U.S. Protestant reformers also made religion an integral part of everyday life in prisons. It was hoped –

34 William Blackstone, *Commentaries on the Laws of England*, 4 vols. (Oxford: Clarendon Press, 1765–9), Book 4, Chapter 1, "Of the Nature of Crimes; and Their Punishment".

35 Michael Ignatieff, *A Just Measure of Pain: The Penitentiary in the Industrial Revolution 1750–1850* (New York: Pantheon Books, 1978).

36 John Howard, *The State of the Prisons in England and Wales, with Preliminary Observations, and an Account of Some Foreign Prisons* (Warrington, 1777).

37 Philip Steadman, "The Contradictions of Jeremy Bentham's Panopticon Penitentiary", (2007) 9 *Journal of Bentham Studies* 5; Robin Evans, *The Fabrication of Virtue: English Prison Architecture, 1750–1840* (Cambridge: Cambridge University Press, 1982), 354–7.

38 Steadman, "Contradictions", 7, 9.

as many, contrary to criminological studies, still do hope – that prison could and should do something to reform criminals. In American prisons, as Jennifer Graber has shown, the prison chaplain became one of the key administrative figures. Chaplains continuously reminded inmates of suffering and redemption, and religious ideology was an important part of prison discipline, continuing to be so even after the Civil War.[39] The same was true for France after 1816, when all prisoners were obliged to attend services every Sunday and on religious holidays. In 1868, French prisons counted approximately 800 priests among their staff. Inmates were placed in disciplinary institutions according to their faith, so that those representing "dissident faiths" – Protestants and Jews – served mainly in Ensisheim, Nîmes and Haguenau.[40]

One more point deserves a mention. A few features of modern criminal law, which during the nineteenth century became the rule rather than the exception, had their roots in the Middle Ages. Paradoxically, the "secularising" Enlightenment reforms, rather than rooting them out, reinforced them. Imprisonment, as Michel Foucault informs us in *Discipline and Punish*, was not a modern innovation but, instead, had been part of the Catholic Church's tradition since the early Middle Ages.[41] Solitary confinement was part of penitential practice and, especially after the 1215 Fourth Lateran Council prohibited churchmen from shedding blood, the penitentiary's use as an ecclesiastical punishment widened. In the early modern period, different forms of imprisonment were brought into use in England and the Netherlands. In the nineteenth century, imprisonment became the major punishment for serious crime in modern criminal justice systems.[42]

Another central component of modern criminal justice systems is the notion of individual culpability. The significance of this idea emerged as a product of twelfth- and thirteenth-century canon law at its most innovative. Canonists such as Raymundus de Penyafort developed and refined the jurisprudence of penance, stressing the individual nature of sin. The assessment of the sin's harmfulness belonged to the jurisdiction of the priest (*forum internum*). The penitential literature and practice were pivotally influential on secular criminal law as well. Although sin and crime were not the same, the two concepts were closely related. Not all sins were crimes, but all crimes were sins. According to a common understanding, all sins that found an expression in observable deeds and were serious

39 Jennifer Graber, *The Furnace of Affliction: Prisons and Religion in Antebellum America* (Chapel Hill: University of North Carolina Press, 2011).

40 Jacques-Guy Petit, Claude Faugeron and Michel Pierre, *Histoire des prisons en France (1789–2000)* (Toulouse: Editions Privat, 2002), 86–7.

41 See Spierenburg, *Spectacle of Suffering*, viii–ix.

42 Thorsten Sellin, *Pioneering in Penology: The Amsterdam Houses of Correction in the Sixteenth and Seventeenth Centuries* (Philadelphia: The University of Pennsylvania Press, 1944); James Q. Whitman, "The Transition to Modernity", in Dubber and Hörnle, *Oxford Handbook of Criminal Law*, 84–110. On mediaeval Italian prisons, see Guy Geltner, *The Medieval Prison: A Social History* (Princeton and Oxford: Princeton University Press, 2008).

enough to "scandalise" society were also crimes. The decretists of the late twelfth century developed teachings on necessity, duress and self-defence, which were then, in the nineteenth century, systematically worked into the "general part" (*allgemeine Lehren*) of modern continental criminal law.[43]

Even though some Enlightenment reformers were eager to rid criminal justice of its Christian underpinnings, it was impossible to do so without demolishing the whole system. In fact, the two central mediaeval inventions which survived the early modern period – incarceration and individualised punishment – were useful enough to be included as fundamental parts of the transformed criminal justice system of the modern era.

6.4 Conclusions

The traditional view of the Enlightenment as a secularisation process has greatly changed during the last few decades. Most experts now agree that religion survived the Enlightenment better than previously assumed. It would be difficult to make a similarly bold statement as regards criminal law to claim that, after the major Enlightenment critique of the late eighteenth and early nineteenth centuries, Christianity remained an important part of criminal law. This was simply not the case. In many ways, the tide did indeed turn. Modern criminal law emerged and its relationship with Christianity changed in important ways. The attacks on Christianity and the clergy as institutions removed many institutional barriers that had emanated from rigid Christian ideology. The decriminalisation of witchcraft is perhaps not the best of examples because, by the time the Enlightenment critique against witchcraft trials had started, they were mostly over. After the late eighteenth-century radical scholars had delivered their input, Christianity no longer served as the background ideology, "punishment theory", of criminal law. Few criminal law theorists believed any more that criminal law was necessary to channel God's retribution on sinners. Instead, most thought that, at its best, criminal law could affect potential wrongdoers through either general deterrence (Beccaria) or individual psychology (Feuerbach). Regarding the elements of crime, religious arguments no longer played a role, and it is difficult to find religion in nineteenth-century presentations of criminal law, such as Paul Johann Anselm Feuerbach's seminal *Lehrbuch des gemeinen in Deutschland gültigen peinlichen Rechts* (1801). Crimes against religion did not disappear completely, but their importance diminished. Offences which originated in religious morality, such as suicide, were decriminalised. The role of confession in evidence law as

43 See Stephan Kuttner, *Kanonistische Schuldlehre von Gratian bis auf die Dekretalen Gregors IX systematisch auf Grund der handschriftlichen Quellen dargestellt* (Vatican City: Biblioteca Apostolica Vaticana, 1935); Woldemar Engelmann, *Die Schuldlehre der Postglossatoren und ihre Fortentwicklung. Eine historisch-dogmatische Darstellung der kriminellen Schuldlehre der italianischen Juristen des Mittelalters seit Accursius* (Aalen: Scientia Verlag, 1965; first published 1895).

a corollary to confession in penitence finally disappeared as free evaluation of evidence (*freie Beweiswürdigung*, *l'intime conviction*) gained ground and placed all instruments of proof in the same position. The different kinds of evidence had no intrinsic value as such; instead, their worth was to be evaluated separately in each case.

Nevertheless, the traditional picture of the secularisation of criminal law still requires revision. I hope that this chapter has been able to highlight five points. First, Enlightenment reformers did not invent all the novelties that have traditionally been attached to their names. Religious theories of punishment were already being replaced by those stemming from general and individual deterrence much earlier, in the seventeenth and eighteenth centuries. Although not formally abolished, the death penalty and judicial torture were much less used in practically all parts of Europe by the time the Enlightenment launched its attack on these institutions.

Secondly, it is important to emphasise that scholars such as Beccaria, Filangieri and Pagano were not themselves atheists or even anti-religious. Most of the radical, "enlightened" criminal law theorists of the late eighteenth century were, however, anti-Church and anti-clergy – against the prevailing prerogatives of the Church and its representatives. Here, the criminal law theories of the Enlightenment did not differ from Enlightenment philosophy and political thinking in general. Many of the criminal law reformers were free-thinking Christians or deists. Some, such as Thomasius and Feuerbach, were Protestants, and it was logical for them to accord the Church a minimal role in criminal law, which was the domain of the State.

Thirdly, it is worth noting that Enlightenment criminal law did not completely purge criminal law of Christianity. In some cases, religion could still serve as the background ideology of criminal law. Although Beccaria is not an example of this, Filangieri certainly is. As late as the nineteenth century, some criminal law theorists endorsed Christian betterment as a means of individual deterrence and therefore an important goal of imprisonment. Others accorded Christianity a place in the theory of retribution.

Fourthly, it is important not to forget that, although modern criminal law was in many ways a product of the Enlightenment, many of the basic precepts of modern criminal law emerged much earlier, in mediaeval canon law. The mediaeval canonists were the first to stress the importance of individual responsibility and its different degrees not only for sins but also for crime, and the same canonists came up with most of the justifications and excuses of modern criminal law. These innovations survived the Enlightenment attack on religion.

Finally, in most Western countries, active prison reformers were often themselves oriented towards the Christian faith. Alongside labour, religion was, far into the nineteenth century, considered one of the primary tools for resocialising and disciplining inmates.

Despite these observations, the fact remains that religion plays little if any role in the criminal law system of the West today. When, then, did the final decisive turn to secularisation take place? That discussion is beyond the confines of this chapter. However, it seems clear that, towards the end of the nineteenth century, positivist criminal law and criminology no longer left any space for religious arguments in the theory of criminal law, at least not in approaches to imprisonment.

Further reading

Ahnert, Thomas. *Religion and the Origins of the German Enlightenment: Faith and the Reform of Learning in the Thought of Christian Thomasius* (Rochester, NY: University of Rochester Press, 2006).

Graber, Jennifer. *The Furnace of Affliction: Prisons and Religion in Antebellum America* (Chapel Hill: University of North Carolina Press, 2011).

Hostettler, John. *Cesare Beccaria: The Genius of "On Crimes and Punishments"* (Hook, Hampshire: Waterside Press, 2011).

Hunter, Ian. *The Secularisation of the Confessional State: The Political Thought of Christian Thomasius* (Cambridge: Cambridge University Press, 2007).

Ignatieff, Michael. *A Just Measure of Pain: The Penitentiary in the Industrial Revolution 1750–1850* (New York: Pantheon Books, 1978).

Kuttner, Stephan. *Kanonistische Schuldlehre von Gratian bis auf die Dekretalen Gregors IX systematisch auf Grund der handschriftlichen Quellen dargestellt* (Vatican City: Biblioteca Apostolica Vaticana, 1935).

Langbein, John. *Torture and the Law of Proof: Europe and England in the Ancien Régime* (Chicago: University of Chicago Press, 1976).

Schmoeckel, Mathias. *Humanität und Staatsräson. Die Abschaffung der Folter in Europa und die Entwicklung des gemeinen Straf- und Beweisrechts seit dem hohen Mittelalter* (Cologne: Böhlau, 2000).

Whitman, James Q. "The Transition to Modernity", in Markus D. Dubber and Tatjana Hörnle, eds., *The Oxford Handbook of Criminal Law* (Oxford: Oxford University Press, 2013), 84–110.

Part II

Christianity and the principles of criminal law

7 The nature of sin and crime

Spiritual and civil jurisdictions compared

Norman Doe

Theological discussion among Christians about the nature of sin has traditionally focused on the category of "original sin" and the causal link between the first sin of Adam and the subsequent sins of humankind. As a result, sin is broader than immorality and embraces violations against the will of God and righteousness, so that it may be defined as "any word or deed or thought against the eternal law" of God (Augustine). While the classical focus of Roman Catholic moral theology has been "sins" (and their categories, mortal and venial), Protestant ethics addresses "sin" as the broken relationship with God, lack of faith rather than of virtue. In turn, theology discusses sin in the context of, variously: the exercise of free will, responsibility and agency; its consequences for the salvation of souls; and its eradication through repentance, forgiveness, atonement, divine grace and mercy. By way of contrast, in the common law tradition, "crime" is narrower: it is classically understood as the violation of the humanly made criminal law, an act (or omission) which tends to the prejudice of the State or of society (which the criminal law seeks to protect) and an act forbidden by law on pain of punishment inflicted at the instance of the State – thus, a crime is an illegal act, whose elements are defined by statute as interpreted judicially, which is capable of being prosecuted in criminal proceedings in State courts, on the basis of due process and requisite standards of proof and liability (including causation, capacity and voluntariness), and which may result in punishment.[1] This study connects what the laws of churches have to say about these basic elements within the theological category of sin and the civil category of crime by exploring: the purposes of penal law; classifying and defining penal offences; courts and their penal jurisdiction; due process in penal cases; and penal sanctions. It examines the laws and other norms on the Christian discipline of eight historic churches. It does so in the context of common principles recently articulated by a panel (meeting in Rome in 2013–2016, and in Geneva in 2017) in A Statement of the Principles of Christian Law (Rome, 2016; henceforth Principles of Christian Law) and induced from

1 See e.g. *Proprietary Articles Trade Association v Attorney-General for Canada* [1931] AC 310 at 324 *per* Lord Atkin: "The domain of criminal jurisprudence [is] what acts … are declared by the State to be crimes, and the only common nature they will be found to possess is that they are prohibited by the State and that those who commit them are punished"; and so, at its core, a crime is an "act prohibited with penal consequences".

the profound similarities between the laws of these churches.[2] It concludes with a general comparison of the key elements of spiritual and civil jurisdictions relating to sin and crime.[3]

7.1 The purposes of penal law

While the topic is much debated, it is generally agreed that the core purposes of secular criminal law are to forbid and penalise conduct which is harmful to or otherwise endangers the property, health, safety and moral welfare of people in society. It serves these purposes by seeking, for example, to maintain order; to provide predictability as to expectations of conduct; to resolve disputes peacefully; to protect persons and their property; to provide for the smooth functioning of society; and to safeguard civil liberties and human rights. In turn, a criminal justice system seeks, typically, to deliver justice for all, by convicting and punishing the guilty and helping them stop offending, while protecting the innocent; to detect and bring crime to justice; and to carry out court orders, such as collecting fines and supervising the punishment of offenders. The criminal law also limits and controls the State in its use of coercive powers to investigate and prosecute crime, and convict and punish offenders for social (and perhaps moral) ends. There are both similarities and differences between these secular ideas and approaches of the churches to the discipline of the faithful.

Today, all the historic churches recognise both the need and their own right to enforce ecclesial discipline – and they commonly weave theological justifications for discipline into their laws. For the Roman Catholic Church "the integral development of the human and Christian person ... positively includes penal discipline" as a means of "fostering communion" in the Church;[4] "judicial power" is fundamental to sustaining ecclesial discipline – the Church has "its own and exclusive right to judge" in cases of "the violation of ecclesiastical law and whatever contains an element of sin", and "to determine guilt and impose ecclesiastical penalties"; and this belongs to the Church by divine institution. But "penal process" is a last resort – disputants must seek to settle amicably, promptly and equitably out of court.[5] Similar ideas appear in Orthodox canon law and in the laws of Anglican churches worldwide.[6]

2 M. Hill and N. Doe, "Principles of Christian Law", (2017) 19 *Ecclesiastical Law Journal* 138–55.

3 This study does not examine juridical treatment of sin in the internal forum, e.g. public or private confession.

4 Pope John Paul II, First Address to the Roman Rota, "The Church and Protection of Fundamental Human Rights", in W.H. Woestman, ed., *Papal Allocutions to the Roman Rota (1939–1994)* (Ottawa: Faculty of Canon Law, Saint Paul University, 1994), 153–8.

5 Code of Canon Law 1983 (*Codex Iuris Canonici*, henceforth CIC), cc. 129, 135, 1401, 1446.

6 See e.g. Russian Orthodox Church: Statutes X.18: "canonical order and church discipline"; and *The Principles of Canon Law Common to the Churches of the Anglican Communion* (London: Anglican Communion Office, 2008) (henceforth PCLCCAC), Principles 6, 24.1–6.

By way of contrast, the juridical instruments of Protestant churches contain far richer statements about ecclesial discipline in terms of its importance, underlying authority and purpose. First, some Protestant churches across the traditions assert their own right to "apply discipline", as well as their own authority to adjudicate on disputes among their members.[7] The competence to discipline is based on the idea that the Church is under the "rule and authority" of Christ or "the discipline of the Holy Spirit".[8] Secondly, therefore, for many churches, disciplinary competence is based on scriptural, or divine, authority; typically:

> Discipline is an ordinance appointed by the Lord Jesus Christ as King and head of the Church, to be administered by the Church in His name and under His authority by methods in harmony with the constitution of the Church as a spiritual community.

Discipline may also be seen as "the process by which the Church seeks to exercise the authority given by Christ, both in the guidance, control and nurture of its members, and [the] correction of offenders".[9]

Thirdly, the aims of discipline are divine, corporate and personal: discipline is "directed to the glory of God, the purity of the Church and the spiritual benefit of members".[10] For some churches, discipline is an aspect of individual discipleship – "to sustain and strengthen the members to obey the word of God, to protect them from sin, to uplift those who have fallen and guide them back into the fellowship of the congregation". As such, it is restorative:

> Ecclesiastical discipline shall be carried out in an evangelical manner in accordance with scriptural principles and upholding the rules of natural justice. At all stages of the procedure the purpose of all ecclesiastical discipline, to gain a member, is to be observed.[11]

Again:

> The objectives of church discipline are to sustain the integrity of the church, to protect the innocent from harm, to protect the effectiveness of the witness

7 Lutheran Church of Australia: Constitution, Art. VI.7 and X.1–3; Constitution of the Districts, X; Bylaws, X.A.1–3: "The Church shall establish a judicial system to deal with discipline" as to e.g. "ungodly life".

8 Evangelical Lutheran Church in America: Constitution, Ch. 4.03 and Ch. 5.01ff. United Methodist Church in Northern Europe and Eurasia: Book of Discipline, para. 201.

9 United Free Church of Scotland: Manual of Practice and Procedure, VI.I–VI, I: discipline is for "the maintenance of the Church's purity, the spiritual benefit of her members, and the glory of the Redeemer". Presbyterian Church of Aotearoa New Zealand: Book of Order, 15.1.

10 Presbyterian Church in Ireland: Code, para. 131.

11 Evangelical Lutheran Church of Southern Africa: Guidelines, 5. Lutheran Church of Australia: Constitution, Art. X.1–3; and Bylaws, X.A.1–3.

> of the church, to warn and correct the careless, to bring the guilty to salvation, to restore to effective service those who are rehabilitated, and to protect the reputation and resources of the church.[12]

For the Methodist Church in Great Britain, discipline "stems from the imperfect nature of human beings", from the fact that "The Church is a fallible community" and because members' acts may not only be "damaging to themselves and others" but also "undermine the credibility of the Church's witness"; in short, discipline seeks "to enable healing and reconciliation to take place through ... accountability", so as to respond to "the call through Christ for justice, openness and honesty, and the need for each of us to accept responsibility for our own acts".[13]

Fourthly, "ecclesiastical discipline must be purely moral or spiritual in its object, and not attended with any civil effects" and "can derive no force whatever, but from its own justice, the approbation of an impartial public and the countenance and blessing of the great Head of the Church". Consequently, discipline is to be administered with mercy and gentleness: it is to be exercised under "the dispensation of mercy" and in faithfulness, meekness, love and tenderness for "the condemnation of offences and the recovery of offenders".[14] Lastly, all the faithful – ministers and laity – are subject to Church discipline.[15] The Methodist Church in Ireland captures these themes; it provides:

> Discipline in the Church is an exercise of that spiritual authority which the Lord Jesus has appointed in His Church. The ends contemplated by discipline are the maintenance of the purity of the Church, the spiritual benefit of the members and the honour of our Lord.

Moreover:

> All Members and Ministers of the Church are subject to its government and discipline, and are under the jurisdiction and care of the appropriate Courts of the Church in all matters of Doctrine, Worship, Discipline, and Order in

12 Church of the Nazarene: Manual, Part VI.I: Judicial Administration.

13 Methodist Church in Great Britain: Constitutional Practice and Discipline, Standing Orders 1100–56.

14 Presbyterian Church in America: Book of Church Order, Preface, II.8. Presbyterian Church in Ireland: Code, para. 131. Presbyterian Church of Aotearoa New Zealand: Book of Order, 15.1: "gentleness, impartiality and faithfulness". Methodist Church of New Zealand: Laws and Regulations, 8.1: "grace, forgiveness and reconciliation". Lutheran Church of Australia: Constitution, Art. X.1 and Bylaws, X.C: "prerogative of mercy".

15 See e.g. Bethel Baptist Church (Choctaw): Constitution, Art. VII: a member who ceases to meet the standards of the New Testament "will be subject to the discipline of the church".

accordance with the Rules and Regulations from time to time made by the Conference.[16]

There are similarities and differences in ideas about the purposes of civil and ecclesial penal law. On the one hand, both seek to express a right to penalise; to maintain order; to protect the vulnerable; to forbid harmful acts; and to penalise for the reform of the offender. On the other hand, the objects of and reasons for these purposes differ: in criminal law, the right to penalise comes from the State – in church law, from God; in the temporal sphere, the order maintained is that of society in general – in church law, it is communion between the faithful and with God; criminal law protects physical persons and property – church law, the spiritual welfare of the faithful; criminal law forbids harm for society to function cohesively – church law forbids harm (and, sometimes, "sin") to foster Christian discipleship and church integrity; and criminal law seeks punishment and, *inter alia*, retribution – church law, gentleness, reconciliation and restoration of the offender. The aims of church penal law are summed up in the Principles of Christian Law. All the churches have a system of discipline, the administration of which is regulated by norms dealing with the purposes of discipline and the processes to enforce it. A church as an institution has the right to enforce discipline among the faithful. This right has various foundations including divine and spiritual authority. A church may exercise discipline over both lay and ordained persons to the extent provided by its own law. The purpose of discipline is to glorify God, to protect the integrity and mission of the Church, to safeguard the vulnerable from harm and to promote the spiritual benefit of its members. Church discipline is exercised by competent authority in accordance with law.[17]

7.2 The classification and definition of penal offences

In the civil sphere, determining which conduct is to be criminalised is shaped in part by ideas about the purposes of criminal law itself as well as actual social mischiefs – and there is much debate about, for example, the criteria to determine what concepts of harm, and even of social morality, criminal law should reflect, including one common law view that "there remains in the courts a residual power to enforce the supreme and fundamental purpose of the law, to conserve not only the safety and order but also the moral welfare of the State".[18] In any event, crimes are generally classified in five ways, namely: offences against the person (fatal and non-fatal offences, including sexual offences) and offences which involve property (such as theft and damage to property); offences of proscribed acts which require proof of a prescribed mental element (such as intention, reck-

16 Methodist Church in Ireland: Constitution, s. 5.

17 Principles of Christian Law (Rome, 2016) V.1.1–2. The right to discipline is one which a church may assert, variously, against the State, the faithful and sometimes other churches.

18 *Shaw v DPP* [1962] AC 220 at 267 *per* Viscount Simmonds.

lessness or negligence); choate and inchoate offences as well as those of strict liability, vicarious liability, complicity and public office; offences classified according to the defences available; and offences classified according to the mode of trial e.g. summary and indictable. Most crimes are established by statute which defines their elements – and it is a principle of law that offences should not be retroactive. The laws of Christians mirror, to some extent, these features of secular crimes.

The churches studied here generally agree about the nature of an ecclesiastical offence, the requirement that an offence must be set out in legislation enacted by competent ecclesial authority, the definitional elements of the offence and the classes within the church who may be liable to penal process. However, there is diversity as to defences available to excuse or justify conduct. For the Roman Catholic Church, a canonical offence is an external violation, gravely imputable to the person by reason of deliberate intent or culpable negligence, of a law or precept to which a penalty attaches; it is committed in the public life of the Church and not in the forum of conscience; penal laws must be interpreted strictly. These include offences against religion and Church unity (e.g. apostasy, heresy, schism, blasphemy, perjury and harm to public morals); those against Church authorities (e.g. the use of physical force against the Pontiff, teaching doctrine condemned by him, incitement to hatred against the Apostolic See and profaning a sacred object); usurpation of ecclesial offices (e.g. seeking to celebrate Mass when not a priest, simony and the unlawful exercise of sacred ministry); falsehood (e.g. falsely denouncing an offence to a confessor); offences against special obligations (e.g. unlawful clerical engagement in a trade); and offences against human life and liberty (e.g. murder, inflicting bodily harm and procuring abortion). When an external violation occurs, imputability is presumed – but this may be rebutted; however, an external violation will not be penalised if the person has a recognised defence – for example, the person is under 16 years of age, is unaware that the action was a violation of law, acted accidentally, lacked the use of reason, acted under duress or acted in self-defence or in the defence of another.[19]

Orthodox, Anglican and Lutheran laws contain fewer offences than Roman Catholic law – and offences listed are spelt out with a far higher level of generality not least in terms of the *mens rea* required. One Orthodox definition of an ecclesiastical offence is "any transgression by an external action or omission against the ecclesiastical law"; offences include apostasy, heresy, schism, simony, sacrilege, violation of graves and perjury; those for which only the clergy may be liable include: repetition of a valid ordination, the performance of priestly actions by a deposed cleric, the exercise of ministry outside the jurisdiction and conspiracy against canonical authorities; and those for which both clergy and laity may be liable include: apostasy, heresy, schism, simony and sacrilege.[20] With regard to the regulatory instruments of Orthodox churches, therefore, offences for which the

19 CIC, cc. 18, 1311–30, 1364–99.

20 P. Rodopoulos, *Overview of Orthodox Canon Law* (Rollinsford, NH: Orthodox Research Institute, 2007), 173–8.

faithful may be liable include: "infringing the church discipline and teaching"; violation of "the doctrinal, canonical or moral norms of the Orthodox Church"; "unorthodox belief, [and] breaches of canonical or moral discipline"; and violation of moral standards and the commission of more specified actions.[21]

Anglicanism too is notable for the lack of juridical precision in the definitional elements of its ecclesiastical offences – though the Principles of Canon Law Common to the Churches of the Anglican Communion provide: "In disciplinary cases, ecclesiastical offences and defences to them are to be clearly defined and set out in writing". Thus, under the laws of churches, bishops, clergy and (in some churches) the laity may be tried for, typically: the commission of a crime under State law; "immorality" or immoral conduct; teaching doctrines contrary to those of the Church; violation of church law or of ordination vows; habitual or wilful neglect of duty; conduct unbecoming the office and work of an ordained minister; and disobedience to the lawful directions of a diocesan bishop.[22] These are mirrored, broadly, in some Lutheran lists of ecclesiastical offences for which pastors may be disciplined: preaching or teaching contrary to the faith confessed by the Church; conduct incompatible with the character of ministerial office; wilful disregard or violation of church law; wilful disregard or violation of ministerial standards; unlawful disclosure of confidential communications; sexual misconduct; fiscal mismanagement; and divorce and re-marriage. Moreover, lay persons may be disciplined for prescribed offences to the extent that is authorised by law.[23]

The concept of "sin" is more prominent in Reformed and Presbyterian penal laws: again, generally, the elements are not closely defined and explicit defences not spelt out. The Book of Church Order of the Presbyterian Church in America has a well-developed definition of an "offence" as "anything in the doctrines or practice of a Church member professing faith in Christ which is contrary to the Word of God"; offences are personal or general, private or public; being "sins" against God their commission is a ground for discipline; personal offences are violations of divine law involving wrongs to particular individuals, and general offences are heresies or immoralities; private offences are those known to a few people, and public ones those which are notorious (par. 29). By way of contrast, the Presbyterian Church of Wales provides:

> It is not practicable to draw up a list of transgressions and specify the appropriate discipline for each one. This must be left to the conscience and

21 See, respectively, Romanian Orthodox Church: Statutes, Art. 14, 148–60; Russian Orthodox Church: Statute, X.35; Ukrainian Orthodox Church in America: Statutes, Arts. VIII and XII.

22 PCLCCAC, Principle 24.9. For the laws themselves, see N. Doe, *Canon Law in the Anglican Communion* (Oxford: Clarendon Press, 1998), 83–5.

23 See e.g. Lutheran Church in Great Britain: Rules and Regulations, Disciplinary Procedure for Pastors of the Church: failure to observe the rules "in a serious and persistent manner"; and Evangelical Lutheran Church in America: Constitution, Ch. 20.21.

> judgement of the church and it must administer judgement in accordance with the nature of the transgression, taking into consideration ... the age, experience, history and circumstances of the transgressor, and ... the discipline which would be appropriate. Every act of discipline should be an opportunity for the church to examine itself, to bring its conscience to the light and to strengthen its life and unity.
>
> (Handbook of Order and Rules, 2.5.2)

Nevertheless, Presbyterian offences may include: teaching or conduct of a person under its jurisdiction which has been declared censurable by the word of God or the law and practice of the Church; anything among members which gives rise to "scandal injurious to the purity or peace of the Church" (e.g. disobedience to the church courts); "conduct unbecoming a minister"; "gross crime or heresy"; prolonged absence from the gospel ordinances and a sin/offence of "doctrinal error or grave impropriety of conduct" especially on account of its public and scandalous nature; and the conviction of a minister in a secular criminal court for "any grave criminal charge".[24]

Methodist lists of offences are generally more extensive; for instance: neglect of the vows of the baptismal covenant and regular absence from worship without valid reason; immorality including not being celibate in singleness or faithful in a heterosexual marriage; practices declared incompatible with Christian teaching (e.g. practising homosexuality, conducting ceremonies which celebrate homosexual unions or performing same-sex weddings); the breach of the secular criminal law; failure to perform ministry; disobedience to the order and discipline of the Church; dissemination of doctrines contrary to the established standards of Church doctrine; relationships and/or behaviour that undermine the ministry of another pastor; child abuse; sexual abuse; sexual misconduct or harassment; racial and/or sexual harassment; gender discrimination – and any professing members may be charged with the same offences or if they undermine the ministry of those serving in a Church appointment.[25]

The secular classification and definition of crimes are broadly mirrored conceptually in Church penal laws; for example: offences must in both the State and in churches be set out in enacted law; negligence may generate liability; not all harmful conduct is subject to secular criminal proceedings (only that which is proscribed by law) in the same way that not all sin is subject to ecclesial penal process (only that which is listed in church laws for which disciplinary process is available); and private individuals and those in public office may be liable to penal

24 See, respectively, Presbyterian Church in Ireland: Code, paras 131–2: (e.g. I Cor. V.9–11); Presbyterian Church of Aotearoa New Zealand: Book of Order, 15.2; Presbyterian Church in America: Book of Church Order, 30.1–5; United Free Church of Scotland: Manual of Practice and Procedure, VI.I–VI, I; United Congregational Church of Southern Africa: Procedure 13 and 15.

25 United Methodist Church in Northern Europe and Eurasia: Book of Discipline, paras 228(b) and 2702.

process – and ecclesial discipline may be pursued when the faithful have committed secular crimes. However, ecclesiastical offences are defined with far less precision than secular crimes: defences in church laws are generally less well developed than in the secular law; church doctrinal offences applicable to erroneous belief have no obvious secular equivalent; and the category of "sin" in ecclesiastical offences is absent, unsurprisingly, from the secular criminal law – and "sin" is most explicit in laws of non-episcopal churches. Ideas about the classification and definition of penal offences are summed up in the Principles of Christian Law. A church may institute a system of ecclesiastical offences. Ecclesiastical offences and defences to them are to be clearly defined in writing and a court, tribunal or other judicial body must give reasons for its finding of breach of discipline (Principles V.5.1–2). Beyond these, however, the Principles of Christian Law do not offer a compendium of ecclesiastical offences; but specific offences are included in relation to particular areas of church life – for example: "Any person who offends church doctrine may be subject to disciplinary process" (Principle VI.3.5).

7.3 Courts and their penal jurisdiction

In the sphere of the State, generally, it is the constitutional law which provides for the establishment, composition and jurisdiction of criminal courts – and, in the common law, for the division of trials between distinct courts in relation to different classes of offence. These matters are in the keeping of the legislature but oversight of the administration of the criminal justice system vests in the executive. Yet, judicial independence is fundamental and applies equally to the criminal courts, the function of which is to establish guilt, enforce the criminal law and impose lawful punishments. Likewise, the historic churches have mechanisms to enforce discipline through the judicial resolution of penal cases in a system of courts or tribunals usually ordered hierarchically – and often, they are styled as "disciplinary tribunals".

Roman Catholic tribunals are established on the basis of canon law, are ordered hierarchically and have jurisdiction over cases concerning spiritual matters, the violation of ecclesiastical laws and all those cases in which there is a question of sin as to the determination of culpability and the imposition of ecclesial penalties. In the diocese, the forum of first instance is the diocesan tribunal, presided over by the bishop exercising judicial power personally or through a judicial vicar who may be assisted by adjutant judicial vicars who are priests, but lay judges may be appointed to assist. Disciplinary matters dealt with by the tribunal include cases concerning dismissal from the clerical state. The tribunal of second instance is the metropolitan tribunal (of a province) or a regional tribunal hearing appeals from the diocesan tribunal. The Pontiff is supreme judge for the universal Church and may judge personally or through tribunals of the Apostolic See. The Roman Rota is the ordinary tribunal constituted by the Roman Pontiff to receive appeals (e.g. third instance) and the Apostolic Signatura is "the supreme tribunal" for e.g. appeals against Rotal judgments – it also functions as the supreme administrative tribunal in disputes about administrative acts and the competence of the inferior tribunals. All the faithful may refer a case directly to the Pontiff – but: "There is neither appeal nor recourse against a judgment or decree of the Roman Pontiff".[26] Orthodox courts are also ordered hierarchically and there are rules on their establishment, composition (which may include laity) and original and appellate jurisdiction (over clergy and/or laity).[27]

In Anglicanism, the relation between courts or tribunals of original and appellate jurisdiction in the judicial hierarchy is to be prescribed by law as is their subject-matter jurisdiction in disciplinary and other causes. Judges are to be duly qualified, selected and appointed by a designated Church authority in accordance with a prescribed procedure, and must adjudicate impartially, without fear or favour. Courts and tribunals are independent from external interference and must uphold the rule of law in the Church.[28] The power to establish courts and tribunals is generally reserved to the central assembly of a church, but that assembly itself exercises no judicial power (unless the law allows this). A diocesan tribunal, presided over by a judge appointed by the bishop, has original jurisdiction over the discipline of clergy and in some cases over the laity (and the commission of ecclesiastical offences by them). As to appeals, laws provide for: limitation periods; grounds of appeal; leave to appeal; and powers of the appellate tribunal – superior tribunals may also have an original jurisdiction over, for instance, the trial of bishops, and matters relating to doctrinal and liturgical discipline.[29]

The judicial bodies of Protestant churches are ordered similarly. However, the court of first instance is generally at the local rather than regional level. For example, in the Lutheran Church in Australia: "The Church shall establish a judicial system to deal with discipline and adjudication. The rules governing such judicial system shall be laid down in the By-laws"; in turn, the district must establish a judicial procedure to deal with discipline, adjudication and appeals.[30] Presbyterian churches have three tiers: Kirk Session (to adjudicate on disciplinary charges against members); Presbytery (with authority over ministers and elders and appeals in cases of lay members); and General Assembly (which may adjudicate through a judicial commission), the decisions of which are "final and binding".[31] In the Methodist Church in Ireland, members are under the disciplinary authority

26 CIC, cc. 391, 469, cc. 1401–57; c. 1405: contentious cases reserved to the pope e.g. judging cardinals and bishops; c. 1417: referral to the pope; c. 333: no appeal against a papal judgment.

27 Rodopoulos, *Orthodox Canon Law*, 170ff; and N. Doe, *Christian Law: Contemporary Principles* (Cambridge: Cambridge University Press, 2013), 166–7.

28 PCLCCAC, Principle 24: church courts/tribunals should be available as needed to resolve disputes.

29 See e.g. Scottish Episcopal Church: Canons 52 and 54; Church of Ireland: Constitution, VIII.5–6; Church of England: Ecclesiastical Jurisdiction Measure 1963 and Clergy Discipline Measure 2008.

30 Lutheran Church of Australia: Constitution, Art. X.1–3.

31 Presbyterian Church in Ireland: Code, paras 34–44: Kirk Session; Presbyterian Church of Wales: Handbook of Order and Rules, 2.5.1: Presbytery; Presbyterian Church in Ireland: Code, paras 104–9: General Assembly.

of the Church Council. Cases about local preachers are heard by the Circuit Executive (the District Superintendent presides), with appeal to the District Disciplinary Committee (with seven members from the district) and further appeal to the Conference which must appoint a committee to hear the appeal – the President of the Methodist Conference presides at the committee and only the Conference Ministerial Session may make the final decision on "Discipline and Expulsion of Ministers".[32]

There seems to be far greater convergence between the secular law on criminal courts, their establishment, composition and jurisdiction, and the penal laws of churches than as to the purposes of penal law and the classification and definition of penal offences. Secular criminal courts exercise a coercive jurisdiction over citizens – church courts and tribunals have a coercive jurisdiction over the faithful in disciplinary matters to the extent that members of a church voluntarily submit to its disciplinary norms. Like the State and its criminal courts – as summed up in the Principles of Christian Law: a church may have a system of courts, tribunals or other such bodies to provide for the enforcement of discipline and the formal and judicial resolution of ecclesial disputes. Such bodies may exist at international, national, regional and/or local level to the extent permitted by the relevant law. Their establishment, composition and jurisdiction are determined by the law applicable to them. Church courts and tribunals are established by competent authority, administered by qualified personnel and may be tiered as to their original and appellate jurisdiction. They exercise such authority over the laity and ordained ministers as is conferred on them by law (Principles V. 3.1–5).

7.4 Due process in penal cases

For the secular world, in the determination of any criminal charge, everyone is entitled to a fair and public hearing within a reasonable time by an independent and impartial tribunal established by law. Judgment must be pronounced publicly but the press and public may be excluded from all or part of the trial in the interests of morals, public order or national security. Everyone charged with a criminal offence must be presumed innocent until proven guilty according to law. Such people have the right, for example, to be informed promptly of the nature and cause of the accusation, adequate time and facilities to prepare their defence, to defend themselves in person or through legal assistance, to examine witnesses against them and to the attendance of their own witnesses.[33] These principles are also found, to varying extents, in church laws – and many expressly invoke the processes set out in Matthew 18.[34]

In Roman Catholic canon law, trial is a last resort: disputants must settle amicably, promptly and equitably out of court – the Episcopal Conference is

32 Methodist Church in Ireland: Regulations, Discipline and Government, 5, 6.4, 10.0.1.

33 ECHR, Art. 6, which is incorporated into UK law by means of the Human Rights Act 1998.

34 See Doe, *Christian Law*, 171.

encouraged to establish permanent offices in every diocese to resolve disputes without going to trial.[35] The object of a trial is to prosecute or vindicate the rights of physical or juridical persons, declare juridical facts and pronounce penalties; judicial power must be exercised lawfully. Anyone (whether baptised or not) may bring an action. The faithful have access to the tribunals to vindicate or defend their rights and there is an action to defend every right. Provision is made for oral hearings but proceedings are generally in writing; cases must be concluded within a year.[36] There are special norms on penal cases.[37] The ordinary (e.g. bishop) initiates penal processes when all other pastoral means have failed – the accused must be given the opportunity to be heard and be given canonical counsel; if a violation is established, but the person is truly sorry for the offence and promises to make amends, there is no penalty.[38] Anglicanism is not dissimilar.[39]

Among Protestant churches, for process against ministers, the Lutheran Church in Great Britain, for instance, has three stages. First, informal settlement: the bishop (with others) determines whether a pastor's performance, behaviour, practices or beliefs are of sufficient concern as to merit discussion with the pastor; an informal meeting with the pastor follows. If concerns remain, an action plan may be instituted to resolve the issue. If unsuccessful, the bishop recommends to the Council withdrawal of the pastor's authority to minister and an interim suspension may be imposed pending investigation by the bishop: reasons must be given. Secondly, there is an investigation. Thirdly, if formal discipline is decided upon there is a hearing before a panel of Council members chosen by the bishop – the pastor is given notice and a right to a hearing (which may be in private). If the bishop and Council decide to withdraw the pastor's authority to minister, there is a right of appeal to a Board of Appeal appointed by Council.[40] Similarly, in the Presbyterian Church in America, if pastoral measures fail, an investigation follows and, if this results in "a strong presumption of guilt", there is a trial – of ministers by the Presbytery and of laity by the Session. An appeal lies to the General Assembly, a judicial commission of which deals with the matter – it must deliver a summary of the facts, a statement of the issues and a judgment which affirms/reverses the decision or orders a re-trial – this must include the reasoning upon which the decision is based. At trial, the accuser is always the Church and the court may appoint a committee to converse privately with the offender to establish guilt before instituting full process by means of an indictment. At trial, the accused may be represented by a communing church member, the moderator

35 CIC, c. 1446: mediation or arbitration; cc. 1717–20; c. 1733: the Episcopal Conference.
36 CIC, cc. 135, 221, 1400; c. 1476: right to an action; c. 1453: delays; c. 1455: confidentiality; cc. 1456–7: impartiality; cc. 1458–75: hearing; cc. 1465–7: time limits; cc. 1468–9: place; cc. 1491–1500: actions.
37 CIC, cc. 1717–19: investigation; cc. 1720–8: process; cc. 1729–31: compensation for harm.
38 CIC, cc. 1341–9, 1717–32.
39 PCLCCAC, Principle 24: due judicial process.
40 Lutheran Church in Great Britain: Rules and Regulations, Disciplinary Procedure for Pastors of the Church.

charges the court, the indictment is read, witnesses and the accused are examined and parties must be heard; court members express their opinion and vote, and the verdict is announced and recorded – it must be "equitable" and promote "the welfare of the church".[41]

The Methodist Church in Great Britain is similar. A respondent should have an adequate opportunity to respond to the complaint, to meet any charge and deal with the evidence, be treated fairly by the complaints team and receive "a fair hearing from any church court which is to decide whether any charge is established". Provision exists for Local Complaints Officers and Support Groups, District Reconciliation Groups, Connexional Complaints Panels and Advocates, and for interim suspension. If, at district level, a reconciliation fails, the complaint is investigated at connexional level; if a case exists, a charge is issued for a hearing by the Connexional Discipline Committee which may find that the charge is established on the balance of probabilities, and a penalty is imposed. There is an appeal to the Connexional Appeal Committee and further appeal to Conference (Ministerial Session).[42]

There are direct parallels between the procedural standards of the secular criminal process and those applicable to ecclesial penal processes. The latter are summed up in the Principles of Christian Law. Every effort must be made by the faithful to settle their disputes amicably, lawfully, justly and equitably, without recourse in the first instance to church courts/tribunals. Formal process is mandatory if church law or civil law requires it. Judicial process may be composed of informal resolution, investigation, a hearing and/or such other elements as may be prescribed by law including an appeal. Christians must be judged in church according to law applied with equity, and disciplinary procedures must secure fair, impartial and due process. The parties, particularly the accused, have the right to notice, to be heard, to question evidence, to an unbiased hearing and, where appropriate, to an appeal (Principles V.4.1–5).

7.5 Penal sanctions

In secular criminal law, there shall be no punishment without law: no-one is to be held guilty of any criminal offence on account of any act or omission which did not constitute a criminal offence under national or international law at the time it was committed. Nor may a heavier penalty be imposed than the one that was applicable at the time the offence was committed – unless it was contrary to the general principles of law recognised by civilised nations.[43] *Mutatis mutandis*, there are obvious juristic equivalents in the laws of churches studied here.

41 Presbyterian Church in America: Book of Church Order, 15, 31–42.

42 Methodist Church in Great Britain: Constitutional Practice and Discipline, Standing Order 1100–55.

43 ECHR, Art. 6, which is incorporated into UK law by means of the Human Rights Act 1998.

Ecclesial sanctions are medicinal. Roman Catholic penalties are designed to repair scandal, to restore justice and to reform the offender; however, if a violation of the law is established, a person truly sorry for the offence who seriously promises to make amends cannot be penalised. Penalties may be imposed by a formal sentence (*ferendae sententiae*) or they may be incurred automatically (*latae sententiae*). They include penal remedies (used to prevent future violations, such as admonition and rebuke); penances (such as a retreat, alms or fast); expiatory penalties which may be permanent or for a determinate period (to make satisfaction, such as deprivation of office); and medicinal penalties or censures (such as excommunication); provision also exists for the cessation of penalties. Different penalties apply to different offences, e.g. apostasy, heresy and schism attract *latae sententiae* excommunication; participation in prohibited rites attracts a "just penalty"; simony attracts suspension; and clerics engaging in unlawful trading are "punished according to the gravity of the offence".[44] Orthodox sanctions are similar; and in Anglican law the penalties imposed following judicial proceedings are to be clearly set out in written law – and: "Customary censures include deposition, deprivation, suspension, inhibition, admonition and rebuke".[45]

Protestant juridical instruments provide a similar wide range of sanctions. For example, in the Lutheran Church in Australia, a complainant may issue a "personal admonition" when alleging "fault against a member" or (if this fails) the congregation may admonish that member; if the member remains impenitent the pastor may pronounce excommunication; and if the errant member fails to submit to this, the congregation may declare such person to be no longer a member (Constitution, Art. X.1: e.g. for departure from the confession and leading an ungodly life). Similarly in the Evangelical Lutheran Church in Southern Africa, if "a brotherly consultation" with the minister fails, the church committee may require the person to render an account and if this is unsatisfactory the congregation may deny "some or all church rights", such as deprivation of admission to office, rights to vote or church burial, postponing the baptism of children and denial of the Lord's Supper (Guidelines, 5). As to pastors, in the Evangelical Lutheran Church in America, as well as suspension pending a formal investigation or disciplinary hearing, the bishop may impose private censure and admonition, or suspension from office, and ultimately removal from the ordained ministry.[46]

Equivalent arrangements are found in Presbyterian churches. In the United Free Church of Scotland: "censures are not in the nature of penance or satisfaction ... [nor] punishments or the exercise of retributive justice" but are "the means of grace used for the recovery of the erring from sin and peril, for the

44 CIC, cc. 1341–9, 1717–32: sanctions; c. 1314: automatic excommunication (e.g. for procuring an abortion); cc. 1331–98: types of penalties; cc. 1364, 1365, 1380 and 1392: penalties for specific offences.

45 Rodopoulos, *Orthodox Canon Law*, 176–8; and PCLCCAC, Principle 24.9, 11 and 15.

46 Evangelical Lutheran Church in America: Constitution, Ch. 20.

protection of Christ's people from occasions of stumbling, and for the edification of the Church" – and the church should seek to manifest "a forgiving spirit in its own community"; moreover, sins or offences not publicly known may be addressed by private admonition, counsel and reproof, and the public censures are admonition, rebuke, suspension, deposition from office and excommunication – similarly, the Presbyterian Church in America also provides a detailed list of censures with definitions of each of them.[47]

Needless to say, these penal sanctions are very different from those in secular criminal law with its fines and imprisonment. Ecclesial approaches are summed up in the Principles of Christian Law. A church has a right to impose spiritual and other lawful censures, penalties and sanctions on the faithful provided a breach of ecclesiastical discipline has been established. Sanctions should be lawful and just. They may include admonition, rebuke, removal from office and excommunication. They may be applied to the laity, clergy and office holders to the extent provided by law. Their effect is withdrawal from some benefits of ecclesial life. Sanctions are remedial or medicinal. A church may enable the removal of sanctions (Principles V.5.3–5). The principles do not deal with the role of forgiveness.[48]

In English common law, the civil process of judicial review is not available to challenge disciplinary process within those churches which have the civil status of voluntary religious associations: they do not perform public functions and are not entangled in the fabric of the State. However, it may be possible that judicial review is available to challenge decisions of the disciplinary tribunals of the established Church of England in so far as they are creatures of statute. Nevertheless, it has not been tested in civil courts whether the disciplinary norms of a church which is a voluntary association may be enforced or challenged on the basis that the internal norms of such associations have been classified by secular courts as the terms of a contract entered into by the members (the doctrine of consensual compact) – yet, the failure of a church to comply with its disciplinary norms in relation to ministers of religion may be the subject of challenge in the civil courts provided that the minister of religion has a contract of employment with the minister in question – this matter is much debated at the moment.[49]

47 United Free Church of Scotland: Manual of Practice and Procedure, V.II: censures generally; VI: private reproof etc. Presbyterian Church in America: Book of Church Order, 30.1–5; 36: infliction of censures; 37.

48 See N. Doe, "A Facilitative Canon Law: The Problem of Sanctions and Forgiveness", in N. Doe, ed., *Essays in Canon Law: A Study of the Law of the Church in Wales* (Cardiff: University of Wales Press, 1992), 80–7.

49 M. Hill, R. Sandberg and N. Doe, *Religion and Law in the United Kingdom*, 2d ed. (Aalphen an den Rijn: Walter Kluwer, 2014), 29–39, 76–80, 117–26. Religious freedom is the civil basis of a church right to discipline; in the UK, the importance of this right is recognised by (the little-cited) section 13 of the Human Rights Act 1998.

7.6 Conclusion

There is profound juridical unity between the Christian traditions studied here with regard to ecclesial discipline and penal law. It is in the study of these, and the Principles of Christian Law induced from them, that we are able to compare the spiritual and temporal jurisdictions in terms of their respective treatments of sin and crime. First, all the Christian traditions accept and justify theologically the need and the right of churches to enforce discipline among the faithful – its purpose is to glorify God, to protect the integrity of the Church, to safeguard the vulnerable from harm and to promote the spiritual benefit of its members through just structures. The purposes of secular criminal law are based on similar concepts of order and protection from harm – but unlike spiritual jurisdictions, these protect social cohesion and human dignity. Secondly, penal offences are employed in all the historic churches, but generally offences are expressed with a higher degree of generality than those in secular criminal law, defences are not generally spelt out and the dominant object of protection is persons and the integrity of the Church, not its property, unlike in secular criminal law. Thirdly, all the Christian traditions have a hierarchical system of courts/tribunals to enforce their penal laws: there are norms on the establishment, composition and jurisdiction of these, as is the case in secular law. Fourthly, both secular law and church law provide for standards of due process with norms on formal investigation, an impartial hearing and rights to notice, to be heard, to question evidence and to silence. There is an obvious need for empirical research into how Church penal norms work in practice, and whether retribution, desert, forgiveness and proportionality are features of the administration and enforcement of Church penal law in particular cases determined within churches. In sum, the theological category of "sin" as violation of divine law is wider than "crime" in secular law and it rarely appears in church law lists of penal offences. However, on balance, ecclesiastical offences and secular crimes share much – but differ somewhat as to the ends they each serve. Finally, church laws provide for disciplinary sanctions, censures or penalties which include withdrawal from spiritual benefits for the remedial or medicinal purpose of the reform of the offender and the welfare of the Church. Secular criminal law is very different with its fines and imprisonment.

Further reading

Beck, Brian. "Ministerial Discipline in the Methodist Church in Great Britain", (1993) 3 *Ecclesiastical Law Journal* 36–40.

Doe, Norman. *Canon Law in the Anglican Communion: A Worldwide Perspective* (Oxford: Clarendon Press, 1998), 80–102.

Doe, Norman. *Christian Law: Contemporary Principles* (Cambridge: Cambridge University Press, 2013), 154–87.

Domingo, Rafael. "Penal Law in the Roman Catholic Church", (2018) 20 *Ecclesiastical Law Journal* 158–72.

Duncan, Graham A. "Church Discipline: *semper reformanda* in Reformation Perspective", (2010) 66 *HTS Theological Studies* 789–95.

Foster, Richard J. *Celebration of Discipline: The Path to Spiritual Growth* (London: Hodder and Stoughton, 1980).

Herron, Andrew. *The Law and Practice of the Kirk* (Glasgow: Chapter House, 1995), 237–47.

Hill, Mark, ed. *Faithful Discipleship: Clergy Discipline in Anglican and Roman Catholic Canon Law* (Cardiff: Centre for Law and Religion, 2001).

Koffeman, Leo. *In Order to Serve: An Ecumenical Introduction to Church Polity* (Zurich: LIT, 2014).

Panteleimon, Rodopoulos. *Overview of Orthodox Canon Law* (Rollinsford, NH: Orthodox Research Institute, 2007), 166–78.

Weatherhead, James L., ed. *The Constitution and Laws of the Church of Scotland* (Edinburgh: Board of Practice and Procedure, Church of Scotland, 1997), 62–77.

Winger, Thomas M. "Ruminations on Church Discipline", (2006–7) 19 *Lutheran Theological Review* 107–23.

8 Christianity, *mens rea* and the boundaries of criminal liability

David McIlroy[1]

8.1 Introduction

Christian natural law theory asserts that Christian principles of morality and social organisation are reasonable, and conversely that human beings and societies are able to reason towards principles of morality and social organisation which are compatible with Christianity. To trace the historical influence of Christianity on the idea of *mens rea* is not to assert that it was a unique achievement of Christian civilisation. It is, however, to challenge a persistent view, expressed by those whose enquiries into criminal liability start from the Enlightenment presupposition that the Middle Ages was a time of superstition and ignorance and begin with the time of the Bloody Code (1723–1823, ironically in place at the time of the Enlightenment!),[2] that it was only when criminal law was released from the baleful influence of religion that proper attention was paid to the mental element in criminal liability. Heikki Pihlajamäki's chapter exposes some of the errors in that view.[3]

This chapter does not seek to show that either the common law or civil law systems in general, or the criminal law of any particular jurisdiction, was ever wholly or predominantly Christian in its doctrine or operations. It is no more possible to establish that historical criminal law was consistent with the insights of Christian theology than it would be credible to suggest that all priests, bishops or even popes lived lives in accordance with the faith they professed.

If a generalisation may be ventured, it is that criminal law has always been a mix of the stabilisation of the powers of regimes, the delivery of peace for all within society and the repression of the underclasses. Christian theology has been both an influence on criminal law in common law and civil law systems and a critique of those systems.

1 I am grateful to my research assistants Robin Younghusband and Annie Evans for their work on criminal law in Roman law and Islamic law, respectively. All errors are my sole responsibility.

2 The number of crimes carrying the death penalty rose from 50 in 1688 to more than 220 by 1815. On the effect of the Bloody Code on the development of English criminal law, including fault and *mens rea*, see K.J.M. Smith, *Lawyers, Legislators and Theorists: Developments in English Criminal Jurisprudence 1800–1957* (Oxford: Clarendon Press, 1998), 369–70.

3 See pages 80–95 of this volume.

What Christian theology offered the civil law systems and the common law systems of the West was a grammar for criminal law built around the idea of criminal responsibility for personal, voluntary, culpable acts. The influence of Christian doctrine on those legal systems was a sufficient but not a necessary condition for the development of such a conception.

In canon law, the connection between sin, guilt and crime is obvious because the same word *culpa* is used to cover all three. In mediaeval civil law systems, *mens rea* was inherent in the linguistics of culpability. This is reflected in the German language's use of the word *Schuld* which includes ideas of debt, blame, fault, guilt, liability and trespass. What requires a greater explanation is how Christian ideas about criminal responsibility came to influence the common law.

8.2 The distinction between criminal law and civil law

The boundary between criminal law and civil law is not fixed. The fields of criminal law and civil law were not clearly distinguished in ancient legal systems. In ancient Egypt, although "Criminal law was … not a separate and clearly defined discipline",[4] there were cases which were characteristically resolved by the imposition of economic sanctions (compensation and exemplary damages) while in other cases the punishment could include corporal punishment, forced labour, banishment and the death penalty. Aristotle does not discuss the distinction between criminal liability and civil liability in his notoriously unsatisfactory account of justice in *Nicomachean Ethics* V. In Roman law, the word *crimen* could be used to describe a claim for lost profits: Cicero, *pro Roscio comoedo 25* (in the context of a suit over damages from the death of a slave).

In contemporary societies, there are three partially overlapping distinctions, each of which is a candidate for identifying the dividing line between criminal cases and civil cases. The first distinction is a distinction between cases leading to punishment and cases leading to compensation. The second distinction is a distinction between cases in which the State is an actor as prosecutor and cases in which the State merely provides a forum for adjudication between two competing parties. The third distinction is a distinction between criminal tribunals and civil tribunals. The second and third distinctions depend upon and partially reflect the first.

8.2.1 Wrongs committed by offenders which are punished and harms suffered by victims who are compensated

The focus of criminal liability is the idea of punishment whereas compensation is the focus of civil liability.[5] This centres criminal liability around the idea of

4 A.J. van Loon, "Law and Order in Ancient Egypt: The Development of Criminal Justice from the Pharaonic New Kingdom until the Roman Dominate", unpublished MA thesis, Leiden University (2014), 9.

5 M.E. Badar, *The Concept of Mens Rea in International Criminal Law: The Case for a Unified Approach* (Oxford: Hart, 2015), 13; J.H. Wigmore, "Responsibility for Tortious Acts: Its History", (1894) 7 *Harvard Law Review* 315–37, 383–405, 441–63.

Table 8.1 Differences between civil and criminal liability

Type of liability	*Focus of the enquiry*	*Penalty imposed*
Civil	The harm to the victim	Compensation to the victim
Criminal	The guilt of the offender	Punishment of the offender

wrongdoing whereas once liability has been established in a civil case the question of harm determines the award against the defendant (Table 8.1).

This distinction can be seen in some ancient laws, even though the conception of criminal liability and civil liability as distinct spheres had not yet emerged.[6] Possibly the most famous ancient legal text of all is the *lex talionis* which prescribes the punishment of "life for life, eye for eye, … wound for wound" (Exodus 21:24–25, NIV). The *lex talionis* is a limiting principle: the punishment that may be inflicted for a physical injury is to be no more than the injury that was inflicted. If, as Jonathan Burnside argues, most of the punishments could be commutated upon payment of a financial penalty, then the offender could pay compensation to the victim in lieu of being mutilated in turn.[7]

By contrast to the equation of reparation with the harm caused specified in the *lex talionis*, Exodus 22:1 states: "Whoever steals an ox or a sheep and slaughters it or sells it must pay back five head of cattle for the ox and four sheep for the sheep". Exemplary damages, punitive in their effect, are awarded in the case of sheep stealing. Already, therefore, in ancient Israel's laws, two principles are at work: a principle of equivalence in respect of bodily harm caused and a principle of punishment in respect of deliberate financial losses.

At the dawn of the Dark Ages, Christian thinkers had already identified the basis for distinguishing between punishment and compensation. Isidore (560–636) catalogued two different kinds of evils: those that a man does and those he suffers (*Etmyologiae*, 5.27). Criminal liability is imposed on those whose state of mind is adjudged to make them guilty for the wrongs they have done to others. Civil liability arises when it is adjudged that it is right that one person should compensate another for the harm their actions have caused.[8] Thus, criminal and civil proceedings have different purposes: the purpose of civil claims is to award compensation for the harms a person suffers whereas the purpose of criminal proceedings is to punish the wrongs a person does.

6 See the survey in Badar, *The Concept of Mens Rea*, 15–22.

7 See the discussion in J. Burnside, *God, Justice and Society: Aspects of Law and Legality in the Bible* (Oxford: Oxford University Press, 2011), 275–82, about the possibility of live substitution.

8 Thus, a legal system can provide for no-fault compensation for accidents if all participants in certain activities are required to carry insurance, as has been the case in New Zealand since 1974.

To be convicted as a criminal, one has to have done something deserving of punishment. This is fundamental. The punishment of wrongdoing is the primary purpose of the criminal law. The verdict in a criminal trial is a public declaration of wrongdoing which is worthy of the punishment that is meted out as a sentence. Other objectives, such as the vindication of victims, the protection of the community whose peace the offence has disturbed and the stabilisation and exertion of power by a political regime, ought not to go beyond or be pursued in ways which are contrary to that primary purpose.

8.2.2 Crimes which the State will prosecute and civil claims where the State merely provides a forum for adjudication

The distinction drawn in common law systems between crime and tort suggests a neat distinction between cases which are brought by the State because there is some public interest at stake and cases which are brought by private individuals because there are only private interests at stake. The distinction is not absolute: even today, private prosecutions are possible while government agencies pursue claims in tort. It is also recent. For much of English legal history, trespasses of various kinds were both crimes and torts.[9]

Civil law systems are closer to the Roman law, in which the distinction between *crimina* and *delicta* was a distinction between those wrongs which would be prosecuted by the State or only with the State's permission and those wrongs which the State had no interest in prosecuting. Victims of theft were, in most cases, left to bring a claim in delict until the time of Diocletian.[10]

As the example of Roman law shows, criminal liability is imposed because of the implications for the State. The State's interest can be conceived of narrowly, as concerned only with offences against the ruling regime. Thus, in Greek law before Solon,[11] crimes such as theft of public money or sedition were public wrongs, but crimes against individuals were matters which had to be pursued privately. The State's interest can also be understood more broadly as anything which would jeopardise the safety and security of its citizens (as in the idea of a breach of the peace which is the unifying idea underlying the common law conception of the scope of criminal liability). In between is the approach of Cnut's Danelaw in England, under which the king's peace "only covered deeds of violence done to persons, or at places, or in short seasons that were specially protected by royal power".[12]

9 F. Pollock and F.W. Maitland, *The History of English Law before the Time of Edward I*, 2d ed., 2 vols. (Cambridge: Cambridge University Press, 1898, reissued 1968), 2:511–43.
10 O.F. Robinson, *The Criminal Law of Ancient Rome* (London: Duckworth, 1995), 10.
11 G.M. Calhoun, *The Growth of Criminal Law in Ancient Greece* (Berkeley: University of California Press, 1927), 56; Plutarch, *Solon*, 18.
12 Pollock and Maitland, *History of English Law*, 2:453–4.

The crimes which a State will prosecute depend on two factors: (1) the resources of the State to bring prosecutions and (2) the regime's conception of its role vis-à-vis the society it governs. A regime which is exploiting its subjects will have little interest in prosecuting the crimes which they commit against one another, and will concentrate its attention on those crimes committed against its interests. By contrast, a regime which regards its purpose as serving the interests of its subjects will aspire to use the criminal law to provide them with effective security and protection.

The rise of Christianity confirmed the tendency of the later Roman Empire to act as the prosecutor for crimes affecting the security of its subjects and the call on rulers to defend the victims of violence and oppression was maintained by the Church through the Dark Ages and the Middle Ages.

Despite the focus of criminal liability being on the offender, and the tendency of criminal proceedings to sideline the victim, Christian theology's concern for the individual whatever their station in society expanded the scope of criminal law from protection of the interests of the regime to the security of all in society.

Augustine (*City of God*, 19.6) and Aquinas insisted that rulers are the servants of the people they govern, obliged to act for the good of their subjects. Thus, crimes are conceptualised as offences against society, "actions which harm or put at risk the community of its members in ways that cannot be remedied by compensation in the form of money or replacement property".[13]

8.2.3 Criminal courts and civil courts

The distinction between criminal liability and civil liability has led to the development of separate courts in many countries. The primary distinctions between these courts relate to the procedures they employ, the verdicts they can impose and the social opprobrium which attaches to those found guilty of a crime. Nonetheless, it is not the case that the guilty are only pursued in criminal cases, or that compensation is only awarded to victims in civil cases, or that punishment is only meted out in criminal cases.

Because of the heavy requirements of the burden of proof in criminal cases, many legal systems have found it expedient to use the civil courts to impose monetary penalties. The modern equivalent of provisions imposing multiple damages for theft are civil recovery schemes for shop-lifting in England and the United States, where instead of a prosecution for theft, the shop owner brings a civil claim which results in a payment by the wrong-doer which is equivalent to a multiple of the value of the goods stolen.

The French legal system reasons that if a criminal court has already found someone guilty of an offence, why should the victims have to bring a civil claim in order to receive compensation? Why should the same incident have to be

13 R.H. Hiers, *Justice and Compassion in Biblical Law* (New York: Bloomsbury, 2014), 61.

considered twice, once through the criminal courts and then again through the civil courts? The French legal system therefore allows victims to participate in criminal cases as a *partie civile*.

Finally, if a civil action leads to a court finding that someone is guilty of deliberate wrongdoing, why should the court not have the power to award exemplary damages to mark that fact rather than the State having to bring a separate claim? So reasons the American legal system and, to a far lesser extent, the English.[14] The scope of liability for criminal activity is wider than the jurisdiction of the criminal courts.

8.3 The historical importance of Christianity on the idea of *mens rea*

The United States Supreme Court proclaimed in *Morissette v. United States* 342 U.S. 246, 251 (1952):

> The contention that an injury can amount to a crime only when inflicted by intention is … universal and persistent in mature systems of law as belief in freedom of the human will and a consequent ability and duty of the normal individual to choose between good and evil.

That assessment, delivered by Mr Justice Jackson, identifies two key foundations for criminal law: a belief in free will and a correlation between punishment and intention. These were two of the ideas which Christian theology gave both common law and civil law systems, for it was from Christian theologians that those systems derived their concept of criminal responsibility as requiring a personal, voluntary, culpable act.

8.3.1 The idea of mens rea *in the thought of Augustine of Hippo*

The idea of *mens rea* can be traced back to a sermon of Augustine of Hippo,[15] not on the texts in the Pentateuch discussing homicide nor on Jesus' reflections on the Ten Commandments in the Sermon on the Mount (though Augustine did

14 For a discussion of exemplary damages in English law, see *McGregor on Damages*, 20th ed. (London: Sweet & Maxwell, 2018), §13-001. Exemplary damages are not available in civil cases in Scots law.

15 Demetrios Agretelis argues in "'Mens Rea' in Plato and Aristotle", (1965) 1 *Issues in Criminology* 19–33, that Augustine was drawing on ideas in Platonic and Aristotelian moral philosophy. J.M.B. Crawford and J.F. Quinn cite the influence of Cicero: *The Christian Foundations of Criminal Responsibility: A Philosophical Study of Legal Reasoning* (Lewiston: Edwin Mellen, 1991), 63–76.

deliver homilies on the Sermon on the Mount), but on James 5:12, a text which is, on its face, about whether or not to swear oaths.[16]

Addressing the question of perjury, Augustine says: "*Ream linguam non facit, nisi mens rea*" ("The tongue is not a liar, unless the mind is guilty"). This comment specific to perjury was generalised as the aphorism "*Reum non facit nisi mens rea*" ("A person is not to be considered guilty until he has a guilty intention").[17] Henceforth, "a guilty mind" was required before criminal penalties could be imposed, though it has not proved easy to determine what a guilty mind consists of.

8.3.2 Mens rea *as a concept common to civil law systems and common law systems*

Augustine's idea of *mens rea* was quoted by Ivo of Chartres in his *Panormia*, 8.111 and 116. Ivo of Chartres' work prepared the ground for Gratian's *Decretum* (discussed in Richard Helmholz's chapter) and the re-establishment of a unified system of canon law for the Western Church throughout the different secular jurisdictions of Europe, "not merely by cultivating the idea of the rule of law but also by stressing the kind of society that could call itself Christian and the role of law within it".[18]

Mens rea was therefore a key organising concept in canon law. It was also, along with the idea of *aequitas*, one of the few ideas which the English common lawyers borrowed from the canon lawyers.[19] *Mens rea* became a feature of criminal law shared by the legal systems of both continental and insular Europe.

8.3.3 The development of mens rea *in the common law*

However, the history of *mens rea* is controversial. Nicola Lacey has argued that English law has moved from a criminal law dominated by character and outcome responsibility in the eighteenth century, through a period in which capacity responsibility was gradually established at the core of criminal law, with outcome responsibility widespread but ideologically marginal.

The *mens rea* for crimes of violence was often identified as malice in English criminal law. Lacey suggests that early references to malice are to "meanness of

16 The Latin text of the sermon may be found at http://www.augustinus.it/latino/discorsi/discorso_233_testo.htm (accessed 30 May 2018).

17 The aphorism is to be found before the official dawn of legal memory in the common law, in L.J. Downer, ed. and trans., *Leges Henrici Primi* (Oxford: Clarendon Press, 1972).

18 William W. Bassett, "Canon Law and the Common Law", (1978) 29 *Hastings Law Journal* 1391.

19 John Baker, *The Reinvention of Magna Carta 1216–1616* (Cambridge: Cambridge University Press, 2017), 113.

status" rather than to "substantive evil or wickedness",[20] but Kamali contends that this is to reject what is their plain meaning.[21]

The editor of Kenny's *Outlines of Criminal Law* maintained that originally in English law, *malitia* described the circumstances of the killing (secretly rather than in an open and fair fight) rather than the mind-set of the killer (though the secret nature of the killing was taken to establish the malice of the killer). Killing openly, i.e. in a fair fight, was something for which monetary compensation (*wergeld* and *wite*) could be paid,[22] but a secret killing involved premeditation.[23]

However, Kamali has argued that interpretations of mediaeval English criminal law which regarded it as deaf "toward such nuanced subjects as intentionality and motive" were based on presuppositions that the Middle Ages were a time of superstition, emotionality and immature reasoning.[24] In reality, "The thirteenth and fourteen centuries were the centuries of ... theological debates about intentionality, sophisticated literary personifications of the emotions, and texts designed to aid with the examination of conscience in preparation for confession".[25] The word "felony" both within mediaeval legal texts and within religious and literary sources of the period is consistently associated with a guilty mind.

Bracton states that "it is will and purpose which mark *maleficia* (crimes)" and that "a crime is not committed unless the intention to injure exists".[26] In Bracton, one sees the distinction between criminal liability and civil liability in his discussion of arson. Capital punishment is the penalty for arson committed "wickedly and feloniously, either through enmity or for the sake of spoil".[27] By contrast, "accidental fires or those caused negligently and without evil intent (*per negligentiam facta et non mala conscientia*)" gave rise to civil liability only.

In England, the necessity for the guilty mind as a requirement of English criminal law is a constant from Bracton, writing in the thirteen century, to Coke, whose *Third Institutes* in 1644 were the first major study of English criminal law.

20 Nicola Lacey, "Character, Capacity, Outcome: Toward a Framework for Assessing the Shifting Pattern of Criminal Responsibility in Modern English Law", in Markus Dirk Dubber and Lindsay Farmer, eds., *Modern Histories of Crime and Punishment* (Stanford: Stanford University Press, 2007), 21.

21 Elizabeth Papp Kamali, "A Felonious State of Mind: *Mens Rea* in Thirteenth- and Fourteenth-Century England", unpublished PhD thesis, University of Michigan (2015), 55. Available online at https://deepblue.lib.umich.edu/handle/2027.42/113574 (accessed 7 January 2019).

22 The notion of a "man-price" provides a self-executing rule which can bring blood feuds to an end and which is capable, in principle, of valuing the life of all people equally.

23 J.W. Cecil Turner, *Kenny's Outlines of Criminal Law*, 17th ed. (Cambridge: Cambridge University Press, 1958), §103; Pollock and Maitland, *History of English Law*, 2:468–9.

24 Kamali, "A Felonious State of Mind", 50.

25 Ibid., 458.

26 S.E. Thorne, ed. and trans., *Bracton: On the Laws and Customs of England* (Cambridge, MA: Belknap Press, 1968), vol. 2; Martin R. Gardner, "The *Mens Rea* Enigma: Observations on the Role of Motive in the Criminal Law Past and Present", (1993) *Utah Law Review* 655–6.

27 Thorne, *Bracton*, 2:414.

8.4 The principal contributions of Christianity to the requirement for a mental element in crime

Nonetheless, "*Mens rea*, the most significant factor in determining criminal responsibility, is still one of the most complex areas of criminal law".[28] What Christian theology has contributed to its core are that ideas that criminal acts are those which are committed personally, voluntarily and culpably.

8.4.1 The insistence that criminal liability is personal

Scholarly consensus has moved away from the idea that ancient Judaism originally held to notions of collective responsibility and only slowly focused on the idea of personal accountability. Christopher Wright argues that the stories of Adam and Eve and of Cain and Abel turn on the issue of personal accountability: "Where are you?", "Who told you?", "What have you done?" (Gen. 3:9–13), "Where is your brother?" (Gen. 4:9).[29]

Notwithstanding the declarations in the Decalogue that the effects of divine punishment may last three or four generations (Deut. 5:9), collective punishment is excluded by Deuteronomy 24:16: "Parents are not to be put to death for their children, nor children put to death for their parents; each will die for their own sin". By the time of the exile, the prophet Ezekiel is insistent that "the one who sins is the one who will die" (Ezek. 18:4), definitively setting his face against notions of inherited liability without personal guilt.

Christianity, in common with Second Temple Judaism, emphasises personal responsibility for one's actions. Crawford and Quinn's study of the Christian foundations of criminal responsibility says that personal responsibility was key to Christian thinking.[30] A person who has committed a crime is liable to punishment; an innocent person who simply happens to be the close relative of a criminal is not. This both protects the individual from punishment based on scapegoating or stereotyping and dignifies the individual as an agent capable of responsible choice.

8.4.2 The requirement that criminal acts are voluntary

Aristotle required the unjust action to be done voluntarily as "that which is done involuntarily is not unjust": *Nicomachean Ethics* V.8. Christian theology agrees with this insight; we are not guilty for those acts which we could not have controlled.[31] *Mens rea* requires that the criminal act has been committed voluntarily, that it was chosen and not a matter of necessity. "Felony required a freely made

28 Badar, *The Concept of Mens Rea*, 1.

29 C.J.H. Wright, *Old Testament Ethics for the People of God* (Leicester: IVP, 2004), 365–7.

30 Crawford and Quinn, *Christian Foundations of Criminal Responsibility*, i.

31 Ibid., 30. Though we are guilty for failing to resist the development of habits which lead us to act wrongly: Augustine, *Confessions*, Book 8.

choice, and it connoted an action that in its very essence was wicked and evil, frequently described in legal terms by references to premeditation, malice, or deliberation".[32]

From its very beginning, Christianity was a religion concerned with the inner life. Jesus' Sermon on the Mount condemned as sinful not just the acts of murder and adultery but the thoughts that could lead to them, even if never acted upon (as does the prohibition in the Ten Commandments on coveting). This concern was given its definitive stamp by Augustine, whose *Confessions* vividly describe the struggle between that which is known to be good and one's own desires.

The importance of the will to the status of an action was discussed by Augustine in connection with the anguished question of the status of women (including nuns) who had been raped during the Visigoth sack of Rome in AD 410. Augustine affirmed that the dignity, status and vows of the women raped during the sack of Rome were intact because their wills had not consented to the violation which had been done to their bodies.[33]

Precisely what Augustine taught regarding the relationship between free will and grace with regard to salvation has been the cause of great historical controversies within the Western Church. What is clear, however, is that Augustine insisted that human beings were created by God with free will and that, despite sin's impairment of human desires and human reasoning, human beings nonetheless remain free to choose and therefore are responsible for their choices.[34] Notwithstanding his stance against the self-righteousness of Pelagianism, Augustine insisted on the compatibility of human free will with the practical inevitability of sin and the consequent need for redemption which only the incarnation, death and resurrection of Jesus Christ could achieve. God's punishment of human sin was just because "evil people are the authors of their evildoing". It would be unjust for God to punish evil deeds "unless they come about through the will".[35]

The combination of the doctrines of free will and liability only for one's voluntary actions is the justification of the presumption of innocence. Because all have sinned and fall short of the glory of God, there is no distinct category of persons who are to be identified by class, upbringing, genetics or disposition as being "criminal types". Incorrigibility is not to be presumed against anyone. The category of those who are not capable of criminal responsibility because of mental illness is a limited one. Treatment is not the dominant paradigm for criminal punishment because those who commit crimes are not to be regarded primarily as patients but as actors, responsible for their actions.

32 Kamali, "A Felonious State of Mind", 135.
33 Augustine, *The City of God*, 1.18–19.
34 Augustine, "On Grace and Free Choice", §2.2, in Peter King, ed., *Augustine: On the Free Choice of the Will, on Grace and Free Choice, and Other Writings* (Cambridge: Cambridge University Press, 2010), 142.
35 King, *Augustine: On the Free Choice of the Will*, 3.

8.4.3 The requirement that criminal acts are culpable

As C.S. Lewis stressed in "The Humanitarian Theory of Punishment",[36] Christian doctrine makes guilt in respect of *this crime* the *sine qua non* before the coercive power of the State may be used against someone's life or liberty. Christian doctrine affirms that all human beings were created good, that all human beings are tainted by original sin, that God's grace is at work in the world so that co-operative human life is not wholly impossible notwithstanding the Fall.

8.4.3.1 The central case of intention

The requirement of culpability has proved to be the most troublesome of the components of *mens rea*. The central case of culpability is intention. A person commits a crime if they intended to carry out the criminal act. So, a person intends to steal from a shop if they deliberately leave without paying for the items they have taken whereas they do not if they absent-mindedly forget that they have not done so.

However, many offences against the person are defined in terms not only of the acts carried out by the offender but also by the harm suffered by the victim. If the offender strikes the victim, whether the crime is common assault, assault occasioning actual bodily harm, assault occasioning grievous bodily harm or homicide depends on the severity of the harm caused to the victim. This then raises the question: what must the agent have intended – the action or the harm which resulted from it?[37]

8.4.3.2 The biblical classification of homicides

Brent Strawn's chapter looks in detail at the Old Testament laws dealing with homicide.[38] The most influential of these is the priestly law set out in Numbers 35. The Book of Numbers establishes cities of refuge to which "a person who has killed someone accidentally may flee" (Numbers 35:11). It identifies certain forms of assault occasioning death which are to be regarded as murder (striking someone with an iron object, or with a stone or a wooden object held in the hand; vv. 16–19). It then distinguishes between someone who "*with malice aforethought* shoves another or throws something at them intentionally so that they die or … *out of enmity* one person hits another with their fist so that the other dies" (vv. 20–21) and the person who "*without enmity* … suddenly pushes another or throws something at them unintentionally or, *without seeing them*,

36 C.S. Lewis, "The Humanitarian Theory of Punishment", in W. Hooper, ed., *God in the Dock* (Grand Rapids: Eerdmans, 1970), 287–94.

37 Badar, *The Concept of Mens Rea*, 162–3.

38 See Chapter 2 of this volume, Brent Strawn, "Criminal Law in the Old Testament: Homicide, the Problem of *Mens Rea* and God", pp. 13–30.

drops on them a stone" (v. 22).[39] The murderer must be put to death (v. 31) while the accidental killer must remain in the city of refuge until the death of the high priest (v. 25).[40]

What is not immediately obvious from the text is how many different categories are being distinguished. Jonathan Burnside argues that the parallel but earlier text in Exodus 21:12–14 distinguishes between three kinds of killing: those which occur by accident (v. 13b), those which are the result of a spur of the moment decision (v. 13a) and those which are premeditated.[41] This is the same distinction that is to be found in Roman law, where there is a threefold classification of crimes committed "from forethought, on impulse or by accident (*aut proposito, aut impetus, aut casu*)".[42]

Burnside sees the same distinction in Numbers 35:16–24; however, when we put this categorisation alongside other distinctions, we see that it omits the category of the negligent killing (which is culpable because the killing could have been avoided but not intentional) and it does not recognise a difference between the killing that was directly intended and the one which was foreseen but not directly intended (which the U.S. Model Penal Code refers to as "knowingly").

Table 8.2 shows how difficult it is to arrive at a coherent set of terms which reflect intuitions regarding comparative culpability.

Numbers 35 was to have an enduring influence on the common law. "Malice aforethought" came, over a long history and never entirely satisfactorily, to describe the intention to kill (*mens rea*) required in the case of murder.[43] In mediaeval English law, a murderer faced death or mutilation while the man who killed another by misadventure had to pay a fine, could be sued for compensation by the family of the deceased and could suffer forfeiture of his assets by the king unless pardoned.[44]

It might be thought that the distinction between intentional and unintentional killing to be found in Numbers 35 would have been the origin of a generalised distinction between crimes which were punished because a wrongdoer had put a premeditated evil intention into effect and civil cases where compensation was awarded because unpremeditated or accidental harm had been caused. That would be wrong. Across wide distances of time and geography, instances causing

39 In *R. v. Grey* (1666) Kelyng 64, a blacksmith who had hit his apprentice on the head with a bar of iron was convicted of murder, as was a mother who had punished her child by stamping on its body: *Kenny's Outlines of Criminal Law*, §107.

40 The logic of this provision is that, since the death caused by the accidental killer was essentially random, so the accidental killer's punishment lasts till the occurrence of another random event, viz. the death of the high priest: Burnside, *God, Justice and Society*, 265.

41 Burnside, *God, Justice and Society*, 257, 261.

42 *Digest*, 48.19.11.2.

43 See Smith, *Lawyers, Legislators and Theorists*, 370–1, for changes in the meaning of malice aforethought in the first half of the twentieth century.

44 *Kenny's Outlines of Criminal Law*, §98, §101; Pollock and Maitland, *History of English Law*, 2:480. The law of murder was reformed in England by the Homicide Act 1957.

Table 8.2 Gradations of criminal intent

	Numbers 35:16–24 (Burnside)	*The Book of Common Prayer*	*Burnside's examples from modern law (**God, Justice and Society**, 254)*	*U.S. Model Penal Code*
Premeditated	Killing with malice aforethought (v. 20a) Throwing something or hitting someone intentionally (vv. 20b–21) Striking with an iron object, a stone, a wooden object (vv. 16–18)	Deliberate Fault	Case (1): A man lies in wait on a walkway and drops a concrete block onto his chosen victim	Purposely
Knowingly		Deliberate Fault	Case (2): A terrorist blows up a shopping centre in order to make a political statement	Knowingly
Deliberate but spur of the moment	Suddenly pushing someone or throwing something unintentionally (v. 22)	Weakness	Case (3): A man taunted by his sexual abuser, loses his self-control and kills his tormentor	Purposely
Recklessly		Ignorance	Case (4): A patient dies because the anaesthetist is out of the room for too long	Recklessly
Negligently	Dropping a stone without seeing them (v. 23)	Ignorance	Case (5): A pedestrian is killed because the road signs have been put in the wrong place by the council	Negligently
Accidentally			Case (6): A driver loses control on an icy road and collides with some cyclists	No criminal liability

death were regarded as anomalous because of the finality of the harm which had been caused.

8.4.3.3 Classification of wrongs in Christian theology

Unlike Numbers 35, Christian thought did distinguish between unavoidable accident and harm caused by negligence. Aquinas argued that injury could be done in three ways: "through ignorance, through passion, and through choice" (*ST* I-II.47.2), a distinction which Kamali maps onto "the categories of misadventure, acts committed upon provocation, and intentional (in the stronger sense of premeditated) wrongdoing".[45]

The Book of Common Prayer of the Church of England says, as part of its general confession, "we have sinned against you and against our fellow men, in thought and word and deed, through negligence, through weakness, through our own deliberate fault".[46]

Christian theology, in dialogue with the Hebrew Scriptures and especially Numbers 35, recognises graduations in volition, which are properly acknowledged through distinctions in the penalties paid by the offender and/or the compensation received by the victims.

8.4.3.4 Guilty minds without intention?

As we have seen, if deliberate intent is the central case of criminal liability, it is not the only form of guilty mind for which it is permissible to impose punishment. Nonetheless, in his *Commentary on Thomas Aquinas' Treatise on Law* I-II.91.4, Budziszewksi complains, in a footnote at 105, that "Shamefully, in contemporary criminal regulatory law, the element of *mens rea*, guilty mind, is often violated. A person may be convicted of a regulatory offense even if it is conceded that he had no intention of doing wrong".[47]

Budziszewksi's footnote is too hasty and is inconsistent with passages in Aquinas that he himself cites. He quotes Aquinas saying: "what a man does in ignorance, he does accidentally. Hence according to both human and Divine law, certain things are judged in respect of ignorance to be punishable or pardonable" (*ST* I-II.100.9) but

> according to jurists, if a man pursue a lawful occupation and take due care, the result being that a person loses his life, he is not guilty of that person's

45 Kamali, "A Felonious State of Mind", 221.

46 Morris cites a twelfth-century homily in which the preacher drew a fourfold distinction between sins committed through ignorance, through weakness, through recklessness or through evil thought: Richard Morris, ed. and trans., *Old English Homilies of the Twelfth Century* (London: N. Trübner & Co, 1873), 63.

47 J. Budziszewski, *Commentary on Thomas Aquinas's Treatise on Law* (Cambridge: Cambridge University Press, 2014).

> death: whereas if he be occupied with something unlawful, or even with something lawful, but without due care, he does not escape being guilty of murder, if his action results in someone's death.
>
> (*ST* II-II.64.8 ad.1)

The thirteenth-century scholastics distinguished between excusable and culpable ignorance, between the unavoidable accident and the one which could have been prevented had sufficient care been taken.[48] In *ST* II-II.64.8 ad.1, Aquinas discusses the case of Lamech in Genesis 4. According to one Jewish tradition, Lamech, when out hunting, mistook a man for a wild beast and killed him. Aquinas' assessment is that, in such a case, Lamech was culpable for the homicide because he did not take sufficient care to avoid taking a man's life.

Criminal liability may be properly imposed for negligence where a person is engaged in a profit-making activity or some other form of action which carries risks to others against which he ought to be taking precautions. To wield an axe in an area where there is an obvious risk to others is not as serious as deliberately plunging it into someone's chest, but it is nonetheless a culpable act if someone is injured as a result.

The boundary of criminal liability is not between directly intended acts and unintended accidents. Accidents are of different types: some are unavoidable or result from excusable ignorance; others are caused by want of due care. A person's ignorance of the law amounts to a want of due care if it can reasonably be said that it is their business to know the law. Stroud was right to describe culpable states of mind as "all blameworthy forms of intentionality, consisting either of intent to break the law, or of inattention to a matter where the law requires attention thereto".[49]

A person's ignorance of the law is excusable if it is impossible or impracticable for them to know what the law requires of them. It is unjust to impose criminal penalties in the latter situation but not the former.

Even strict liability offences may be appropriate where the circumstances are such that ignorance is inexcusable. One such example is section 53A of the United Kingdom's Modern Slavery Act 2015 which makes it a criminal offence to buy sexual services from someone who has been the victim of trafficking. The person paying for sex is supposed to make sure that the person prostituting themselves is doing so voluntarily and not because they have been subject to deception or coercion.

Another strict liability offence is section 330(1) of the United Kingdom's Proceeds of Crime Act 2002 which imposes on lawyers and bankers strict liability for failing to disclose knowledge or suspicions of money laundering. Under

48 Crawford and Quinn, *Christian Foundations of Criminal Responsibility*, 19.

49 Douglas Stroud, *Mens Rea or Imputability under the Law of England* (London: Sweet & Maxwell, 1914), 14–15; Crawford and Quinn, *Christian Foundations of Moral Responsibility*, 19–22.

this section, criminal liability is incurred not just on those who know or suspect money laundering is occurring but do not report it but also on those who did not know or suspect that money laundering was occurring but ought to have done. Section 330(1) therefore creates a crime which one can commit unconsciously. However, criminal liability is imposed because the law has made it the business of bankers and lawyers to be alert to signs of money laundering. A banker or lawyer who does not display the necessary alertness to the possibility of money laundering is guilty of a want of due care. It is for that want of due care that he or she is exposed to the risk of punishment.

Nonetheless, Budziszewski is right to highlight an unease which Christian teaching has with the idea of strict liability offences. From the point of view of legislators and prosecutors, strict liability offences are attractive because they make it much easier to obtain a conviction. Strict liability offences operate similarly to the self-executing rules in the Hebrew Scriptures (e.g. Exodus 22:2–4) which could be easily applied without complex adjudication. However, whereas the biblical rules were clear, publicly accessible and widely known, too many strict liability offences turn on details of regulation which are poorly drafted or difficult to interpret, and which only experts in compliance are able to understand.

8.4.4 The requirement that the intention results in an act

The distinction between crime and sin was clear in Christianity from the moment Jesus delivered his Sermon on the Mount. Adultery was, in his day, a crime punishable by the religious authorities. In making his point that "anyone who looks at a woman lustfully has already committed adultery with her in his heart" (Matt. 5:28), Jesus was not only condemning those authorities for their double standards, but he was also pointing out how guilty thoughts can (though not always) lead to wrongful acts.

Augustine's sermon on James 5:12 establishes not only the importance of *mens rea* (the guilty mind) but also the need for *mens rea* to be combined with an *actus reus* in order to constitute a crime. In his homily, Augustine drew a distinction between the person who intends to swear truly but because of his ignorance of the facts swears falsely by mistake ("the accidental false swearer"), the person who intends to swear falsely but because of his ignorance of the facts swears truly by mistake ("the accidental true swearer") and the person who intends to swear falsely and does so ("the perjurer").

The accidental false swearer has made a mistake. Both the accidental true swearer and the perjurer intended to lie. Both had a guilty mind. But (outside of a confession by the accidental true swearer of their intention or a set of facts designed to test philosophy students), the intention of the accidental true swearer would never come to light.

Similarly, Aquinas: "For human law does not punish the man who wishes to slay, and slays not: whereas the Divine law does, according to Matthew 5:22 'Whosoever is angry with his brother, shall be in danger of the judgment'" (*ST* I-II.100.9). So the Puritan judge Sir Matthew Hale, speaking in the case of a woman accused of witchcraft, held "it cannot come under the judgment of felony, because no external violence was offered whereof the common law can take notice, and secret things belong to God".[50]

8.5 Conclusion

Christianity's influence on the development of criminal liability in civil law and common law systems was mainly in terms of negations. Criminal liability was personal; acts of collective punishment were prohibited. There was no criminal liability for thought crimes; they were to be dealt with in another tribunal. Punishment was only for those voluntary acts committed with a guilty mind. The central case of the guilty mind was the deliberate intent to harm but, in principle, criminal liability was justly imposed whenever one was culpable for causing harm to others which one ought to have avoided.

Badar has shown that the necessity for *mens rea* as well as *actus reus* is common to Christian theology and the Islamic legal tradition (influenced by Mosaic rather than Roman law),[51] and the concept is capable in principle of being systematised and universalised.[52] *Mens rea* is a part of the natural criminal law. Criminal liability may justly be imposed on those who show culpable disregard for the interests of their neighbour. Criminal conduct is conduct which deserves such punishment, whether it is administered by a criminal or a civil trial.

Further reading

Badar, M.E. *The Concept of Mens Rea in International Criminal Law: The Case for a Unified Approach* (Oxford: Hart, 2015).

Budziszewski, J. *Commentary on Thomas Aquinas's Treatise on Law* (Cambridge: Cambridge University Press, 2014).

Burnside, J. *God, Justice and Society: Aspects of Law and Legality in the Bible* (Oxford: Oxford University Press, 2011).

Crawford, J.M.B. and, J.F. Quinn. *The Christian Foundations of Criminal Responsibility: A Philosophical Study of Legal Reasoning* (Lewiston: Edwin Mellen, 1991).

Kamali, E.P. "A Felonious State of Mind: Mens Rea in Thirteenth- and Fourteenth-Century England", Unpublished PhD thesis, University of Michigan (2015). Available at https://deepblue.lib.umich.edu/handle/2027.42/113574 (accessed 7 January 2019).

Lewis, C.S. "The Humanitarian Theory of Punishment", in W. Hooper, ed., *God in the Dock* (Grand Rapids: Eerdmans, 1970), 287–94.

50 M. Hale, *Historia Placitorum Coronae*, 1.429, cited in Pollock and Maitland, *History of English Law*, 2:475.

51 Patricia Crone, *Roman, Provincial and Islamic Law* (Cambridge: Cambridge University Press, 1987).

52 Badar, *The Concept of Mens Rea*, ch. 12.

9 Christianity, human dignity and due process

Peter Collier QC

9.1 Introduction

This chapter surveys in broad terms the concepts of human dignity and due process in the context of the criminal law and examines what part the Christian Church may have played in the development of those concepts. It comes from the perspective of a former English criminal practitioner and judge.

In any such consideration of the criminal law, whether considering its basis or particular examples of criminal laws in different jurisdictions, it is important to remember that everything to do with criminal justice has to do with its many different participants. Those participants include the law makers; the victims of crime; the perpetrators of crime; those who witness crime and become caught up in the criminal justice process; those who investigate crime: the police and the other agencies, such as professional regulators, dealing with particular types of criminality; those who are the professional players in the process whether as prosecutors, defenders or judges; those who deal with the convicted perpetrators: probation officers and prison officers; and those who make the system work: the staff in many of the organisations that are necessary for the various criminal justice processes to happen. A given individual could play any of these roles, and some people play different roles at different times. Many will become victims of crime and more of us than we might expect may become perpetrators of crime.[1] Each person playing any of these roles is a member of the human race.

What is the connection between our common humanity and our understanding of the criminal law and its operation? What does our humanity have to do with the whole concept of justice and criminal justice? In recent years, references to human dignity suggest that there is such a connection.

1 Of men born in 1953, 33% had at least one conviction for a "standard list" offence before the age of 46: J. Prime, S. White, S. Liriano and K. Patel, "Criminal Careers of Those Born Between 1953 and 1978", England and Wales Home Office Research Paper 4/01, 12 March 2001, https://webarchive.nationalarchives.gov.uk/20110218145340/http://rds.homeoffice.gov.uk/rds/pdfs/hosb401.pdf (accessed 21 January 2019).

9.2 Human dignity: its place in modern legal systems

The phrase "human dignity" has been associated with the human rights movement since the UN Charter was adopted on 26 June 1945. The preamble to the Articles begins by expressing a determination "to save succeeding generations from the scourge of war, which twice in our life-time has brought untold sorrow to mankind", and then reaffirms "faith in fundamental human rights, in the dignity and worth of every human person, in the equal rights of men and women and of nations large and small". The words dignity and worth do not occur again in the Charter, which is principally concerned with the establishment of the UN and the relationships between nations.

The word "dignity" was, however, picked up in 1948 and used in the Universal Declaration of Human Rights. The first phrase of the preamble to the Declaration reads: "Whereas recognition of the inherent dignity and of the equal and inalienable rights of all the members of the human family is the foundation of freedom, justice and peace in the world". Dignity reoccurs in Article 1: "All human beings are born free and equal in dignity and rights. They are endowed with reason and conscience and should act towards one another in a spirit of brotherhood". And also in Articles 22 and 23.3: "Everyone, as a member of society, has the right to social security and is entitled to realization ... of the economic, social and cultural rights indispensable for his dignity and the free development of his personality" and "Everyone who works has the right to just and favourable remuneration ensuring for himself and his family an existence worthy of human dignity".

The word "dignity" did not appear in the European Convention on Human Rights (ECHR) as adopted on 4 November 1950, although the word was used in the 13th Protocol, adopted on 3 May 2002, concerning the abolition of the death penalty in all circumstances. The preamble to that Protocol reads:

> Convinced that everyone's right to life is a basic value in a democratic society and that the abolition of the death penalty is essential for the protection of this right and for the full recognition of the inherent dignity of all human beings.

A number of countries have referred to human dignity in their constitutions. A typical example is that of the Federal Republic of Germany for which the Basic Law (*Grundgesetz*) opens with terms almost as ringing as the prologue to John's gospel:

> Article 1 [Human dignity – Human rights – Legally binding force of basic rights]
>
> (1) Human dignity shall be inviolable. To respect and protect it shall be the duty of all state authority.

(2) The German people therefore acknowledge inviolable and inalienable human rights as the basis of every community, of peace and of justice in the world.
(3) The following basic rights shall bind the legislature, the executive and the judiciary as directly applicable law.

How did the phrase "human dignity" come to have such a significant place in these and other legal instruments? There has been some discussion about the reference to dignity and human dignity in the Charter and Declaration. In his article "Human Dignity and Judicial Interpretation of Human Rights", Christopher McCrudden says that although there is a dearth of evidence of how the reference to inherent dignity came to be incorporated into the Charter, we know that the first draft of the Declaration was much influenced by John Humphrey and did not include the phrase which was added at the insistence of Rene Cassin.[2]

The advantage of the phrase "human dignity", whether or not more than "mere rhetoric" (*per* Humphrey), was that it did provide a reason for asserting that people should be treated equally without the need to appeal to a religious creed. It was a phrase that because of its usage by people with different religious and philosophical beliefs over a long period of time would be acceptable to those with faith and those without. Those with faith in a creator would see the phrase as being fully consistent with and justified by their belief that all people were created by God and therefore equal. Those from a Judaeo-Christian tradition would not find the phrase in their scriptures and even references to "dignity" are few and far between,[3] but it would clearly resonate with their worldview. Those without such a belief in a creator could accept that it was self-evident in the current world that all people must be treated as equal in order to avoid the "untold sorrow" so recently twice experienced.

9.3 Human dignity: its deeper roots

The developing ideas about dignity which led to the use of the word in 1945 and thereafter had a history that is well rehearsed. It is a concept that had been used as men – and it was usually men – attempted to understand and explain what it is that is the distinctive mark of being human, what it is that distinguishes humanity

2 Christopher McCrudden, "Human Dignity and Judicial Interpretation of Human Rights", (2008) 19.4 *European Journal of International Law* 676.

3 A search of an online analytical Bible concordance across multiple translations shows the word "dignity" occurring a total of 17 times in the Old and New Testaments in a combination of 13 different translations: Gen. 49:3; Ex. 28:2, 40; Esther 6:3, 10:2; Job 30:15, 40:10; Ps. 62:4; Prov. 5:9, 30:29, 31:25; Eccl. 10:6; Hab 1:7; 1 Cor 12:24; 1 Tim 2:2, 3:4; Tit 2:7. The usage of the word in translations of the Bible may tell us more about the worldview of the translators than about the original meaning of the several words translated as "dignity", which are mostly associated with high position or strength or power.

from the animal kingdom. Cicero, Aquinas and Kant have been identified as three of the more influential writers on the subject.

Cicero (106–43 BC) spoke of humankind as a whole being treated with dignity by virtue of being human as against being one of the animals.[4] He describes

> how far superior man is by nature to cattle and other beasts; they have no thought but for sensual pleasure and this they are impelled by every instinct to seek; but man's mind is nurtured by study and meditation; he is always either investigating or doing and he is captivated by the pleasure of seeing and hearing.

So, Cicero concludes, "From this we see that sensual pleasure is quite unworthy of the dignity of man and that we ought to despise it and cast it from us ...". In his thinking, it is reason that sets humans apart from the animals. Human beings share the ability to reason with the gods. Because they can reason, they can understand the natural law which arises from reason. Since all people share reason and natural law, they belong to a community and have duties to one another.

Thomas Aquinas (1225–74) only used the phrase "dignity of his manhood" when discussing whether it is appropriate to kill sinners. He said

> By sinning man departs from the order of reason, and consequently falls away from the dignity of his manhood, ... Hence, although it be evil in itself to kill a man so long as he preserve his dignity, yet it may be good to kill a man who has sinned, even as it is to kill a beast. For a bad man is worse than a beast, and is more harmful, as the Philosopher states. (Polit. i, 1 and Ethic. vii, 6)[5]

All of this is premised on his understanding of what it is that gives someone their dignity, namely their personhood. Aquinas goes beyond the fact that the human is a rational being as the classical authors had taught and brings in the fact that humans are created in the image of God. As a result, they have not only intellect, but also the capacity of choice and movement towards the ultimate goal of union with God. It is in that union with the source of all that is good that the human being finds his or her ultimate fulfilment.

The third major thread comes from Immanuel Kant (1724–1804). His belief was that human beings have an intrinsic worth (the German word he uses which is often translated as "dignity" is *Würde*[6]):

4 Cicero, *De Officiis*, trans. Walter Miller (Cambridge, MA: Harvard University Press, 1990), 1.30.

5 Thomas Aquinas, *Summa Theologiae*, II-II q. 64 a. 3.

6 The first thing to say about this definition is that "dignity" is the English translator's term, not Kant's. Kant uses the German word *Würde*. There is a well-established practice of translating *Würde* as "dignity", but the two words have slightly different connotations. Jeremy Waldron, *Dignity, Rank and Rights: The Tanner Lectures on Human Values* (New York: Oxford University Press, 2012), 24, remarks: "*Würde* is certainly much closer to 'worth' than our term

> In the kingdom of ends everything has a price or a dignity. If it has a price, something else can be put in its place as an equivalent; if it is exalted above all price and so admits of no equivalent, then it has a dignity. What is relative to universal human inclinations and needs has a market price; what, even without presupposing a need, accords with a certain taste – that is, satisfaction in the mere purposeless play of our mental powers – has a fancy price but that which constitutes the sole condition under which anything can be an end in itself has not merely a relative value – that is, a price – it has an intrinsic value that is, dignity.

Thomas Hobbes had spoken about price and dignity in *Leviathan* in 1651.[7] For Kant, such relative and conditional assessments of worth and dignity were anathema. Dignity flows from acceptance of and obedience to the categoric imperative.

9.4 Human dignity and human equality

Each of these writers gave to humanity a uniqueness and distinctiveness. Each referred to dignity at some point. Each had a different reason for assigning dignity as something that gives distinctiveness to humankind. But in each of their times there were real inequalities between the members of the human race who shared in that distinctiveness. In Rome there was slavery, but Cicero saw no problem with that; he considered that social distinctions were necessary for the proper functioning of the state.[8] In the mediaeval Church, not only were there clear ranks and distinctions of status within the clergy but also a recognition that God had ordered humankind and assigned to each person their status. In eighteenth-

---

'dignity' is". In a footnote to the published text he adds: "For a suggestive discussion of some differences, see Kolnai, 'Dignity', 251–52. See also the comment in *Dignity: Ethics and Law—Bibliography* (Copenhagen: Centre for Ethics and Law, 1999), 9: The Scandinavian and German nouns *værdighed* and *Wurde* are derived from the germanic *werpa- (werd, wert) which means that these languages point to worth and value more than to dignity" (ibid., 40).

7 Thomas Hobbes, *Leviathan* (London, 1651), Chapter 10: "The value or WORTH of a man is like the value of anything – his *price*; that is to say, the amount that would be given for the use of his power. So it is not absolute but conditional, because it depends on someone else's need and judgment. … A man may rate himself at the highest value he can (as most men do); but his true value is no more than others reckon it to be. … The public worth of a man, which is the value set on him by the commonwealth, is what men commonly call DIGNITY. And this value that the commonwealth assigns to him is shown by offices of command, judicature, or other public employment, or by names and titles that are introduced to mark out such value".

8 Cicero, *Republic*, 27, in G.W. Featherstonehaugh, trans., *The Republic of Cicero* (New York, 1829), 58: "In kingdoms however, the governed are too much deprived of common rights, and of power. Under the better class, the multitude can scarcely be partakers of liberty, as they are not admitted either to the public councils or offices: and when the government is conducted by the people, although it be justly and moderately administered, yet equality itself becomes injustice, seeing that it admits of no degrees of rank. … And the Athenians at a certain period having abolished the Areopagus, conducted everything by ordinances, and decrees of the people; yet as they had no distinctions in dignity, their state was without its ornament".

century Europe, Kant did not see his understanding as leading to a conclusion that all must be treated equally. Not only was dignity considered consistent with inequality, but the word "dignity" has often been used to give a recognition to differences of status. People should be treated with the dignity that was due to the status they held.

Even today in cathedral churches the various offices held are referred to as "dignities". The current Statutes of York Minster say that "The Archbishop shall have the principal seat and dignity in the Cathedral Church", that "The Dean shall be the principal dignitary of the Cathedral Church next after the Archbishop" and that "Four of the Residentiary Canons shall be appointed by the Archbishop to hold the Major Dignities" and "each holder of a Major Dignity shall be entitled to have a house".[9] These are clear references to relative ranks of seniority.

In the French Declaration of the Rights of Man and of the Citizen (1789), Article 6 said that "all citizens, being equal in the eyes of the law, are equally eligible to all dignities and to all public positions and occupations according to their abilities and without distinction except that of their virtues and talents".

It was such distinctions of status and the resultant discrimination that led to calls for equality in the late eighteenth and nineteenth centuries. The rise of socialism, the labour movement, the drive to abolish slavery and other similar campaigns often spoke of human dignity. Slowly, dignity came to be seen not just as something that belonged to humankind, but something to which everyone was entitled by way of equal treatment in relation to education along with their economic and social lives.

During the nineteenth century, the Catholic Church was also developing its social doctrine based on human dignity. The Church regarded some of the secular socialist writing, which called for equality, as a threat to its doctrine of a society ordered by God. In 1891, Pope Leo XIII issued *Rerum Novarum*. It dealt with the problems of unfair wages and working conditions. It called upon employers to respect the dignity of workers and not regard them as bondsmen. That dignity arose from the fact that a person is created in the image of God, endowed with free will and an immortal soul. Respecting the dignity of the person in the workplace required time off work to worship God and fulfil family obligations, periods of rest and adequate sleep, safe working conditions and fair wages. In 1931, Leo XIII issued *Quadragesimo Anno*. He was concerned to address any unrestrained form of capitalism as well as totalitarian socialism and communism. Human dignity was a significant part of his argument. In 1965, following the Second Vatican Council, Paul VI issued *Gaudium et Spes*. It began by addressing "The Church and Man's Calling" and the first section dealt with "The Dignity of the Human Person". The human's true dignity rests in observing the law that their moral conscience calls them to obey. If conscience goes astray then humans lose that dignity. But that same dignity requires that such obedience comes from freely choosing what is good. In an attack upon atheism, Paul VI argued that the

9 York Minster Statutes III 1, IV 1, V 5, V 7.

Church which champions the dignity of humanity's calling was the best protector of such dignity. In 1991, on the hundredth anniversary of *Rerum Novarum*, John Paul II issued *Centesimus Annus*. It reviewed and celebrated *Rerum Novarum*, drawing attention to its guiding light being human dignity.

Much of the secular movement towards equalisation of status had not felt the need for a philosophical anchor. Indeed, the work of Kant, influential as it was, was much criticised by those committed to equal rights causes. In 1840, Arthur Schopenhauer wrote a critique of Kant in which he described the concept of the dignity of man as developed by Kant as "the shibboleth of all the perplexed and empty-headed moralists who concealed behind that imposing expression their lack of any real basis of morals, or, at any rate one that had any meaning".[10] It was further criticised because placing emphasis on a person's dignity as being what mattered and calling upon them to maintain their dignity even in adverse circumstances would inevitably lead to people remaining enslaved, or trapped in demeaning work.

9.5 Human dignity: where we are now

In countries that have put human dignity into their constitutions or statutes, their courts interpret and apply the concept.[11] An example would be the German approach to digital data. That approach is based on Article 1. The Constitutional Court has required the State to take positive action to protect human dignity, resulting in a "right of personality" and in relation to digital data "the right of informational self-determination". However, the concept has been the subject of judicial criticism. In the Canadian case of *R v Kapp*, the Supreme Court said

> Human dignity is an abstract and subjective notion that, even with the guidance of the four contextual factors, cannot only become confusing and difficult to apply; it has also proven to be an *additional* burden on equality claimants, rather than the philosophical enhancement it was intended to be.[12]

That confusion can also be seen in how countries where human dignity is recognised as giving a constitutional basis for rights have interpreted it very differently. Michael Rosen cites two cases (the French dwarf-throwing case and the German case of shooting down hijacked aeroplanes) as examples of how widely differing conclusions can be arrived at when courts address the issue of human dignity.[13] In England and Wales there have been no such headline criminal cases. Human dignity has certainly figured in many cases in the UK, but it is remarkably absent

10 Arthur Schopenhauer, *On the Basis of Morality*, trans. E.F.J. Payne (Indianapolis: Hackett, 1998; first published 1840), 100.

11 For a recent global initiative on this subject, see the Punta del Este Declaration on *Human Dignity for Everyone Everywhere* (2018): https://www.dignityforeveryone.org/.

12 [2008] SCR 41 at para 22.

13 Michael Rosen, *Dignity: Its History and Meaning* (Cambridge, MA: Harvard University Press, 2012).

in the area of crime. A search of BAILLI for cases where human dignity has been mentioned in the Court of Appeal Criminal Division produced a total of six cases where the phrase was mentioned in the judgment.[14] In none of the cases was there any discussion about what human dignity meant or any reliance placed on human dignity as a factor in the decision. In *Perrin*, the *Marines* and *N and LE*, the references to human dignity were just in passing. In *Bieber*, *Altham* and *Qazi*, although arguments had been advanced in relation to human dignity, the court in each case based its decision on an analysis of Article 3 and in each case decided that Article 3 rights were not engaged on its facts.

So, the evidence suggests that in the criminal courts of England and Wales the concept of human dignity as a free-standing legal concept or as a right to which any individual can lay claim when pressing his or her cause barely exists. The courts are concerned to interpret the statutes of England and Wales and human dignity is not a concept that occurs in a criminal statute. The Human Rights Act 1998 incorporated the European Convention on Human Rights into English law and so its Articles are applied by the courts, but as the ECHR does not itself refer to human dignity, it is a phrase that is rarely used in the courts and has not been decisive in English criminal law.

The position is necessarily different in countries which have put human dignity into their written constitutions. If there was such a written statute in England as the German Basic Law, then the criminal courts would be bound to interpret and apply it, but the absence of such a written code means that the criminal courts are left to apply the specifics without being required to look at the underlying basis. For the most part, those specific particular convention rights are to do with the right to a fair trial which leads us to a consideration of due process.

9.6 Due process: what does it mean?

"Due process" is common shorthand for the phrase "without due process of law". That phrase in a criminal context is generally understood as meaning that the law must be applied fairly and equally to all people, especially to a citizen accused of crime, and that such fairness has a number of minimum requirements.

9.6.1 Due process: its roots

It is often said that the root of due process is to be found in Magna Carta. The phrase, however, is not used in Magna Carta. The relevant article is 39

14 *R. v. Bieber (Aka Coleman)* [2008] EWCA Crim 1601 (23 July 2008) [2008] HRLR 43; *R. v. Perrin* [2002] EWCA Crim 747 (22 March 2002); *R. v. Altham* [2006] EWCA Crim 7 (24 January 2006) [2006] 1 WLR 3287; *R. v. Qazi & Anor* [2010] EWCA Crim 2579 (4 November 2010) [2011] 2 Cr App R (S) 8; *Marines A & Ors v. Guardian News and Media & Other Media* [2013] EWCA Crim 2367 (17 December 2013) [2014] 1 Cr App R 26; *R. v. N.* (Rev 1) [2012] EWCA Crim 189 (20 February 2012) [2012] 1 Cr App R 35.

of the 1215 version and 29 of the 1225 version. The wording is not identical. Article 39 states:

> No free man shall be taken or imprisoned or disseised or outlawed or exiled or in any way ruined, nor will we go or send against him, except by the lawful judgement of his peers or by the law of the land.

The later version in Article 29 added the words "of any free tenement of his or of his liberties or free customs" after "disseised".

It was in the reign of Edward III in 1354 that the Liberty of the Subject Act was passed.[15] It appears on the legislation.gov.uk website as still being in force. It reads:

> ITEM all, That no Man of what Estate or Condition that he be, shall be put out of Land or Tenement, nor taken, nor imprisoned, nor disinherited, nor put to Death, without being brought in Answer by due Process of the Law.[16]

It is sometimes said that due process is tautologous in that it simply provides that legal proceedings must follow their prescribed course whatever that may be. It may be a process that is protected by any number of procedural safeguards of the sort that we would recognise today as being necessary for a fair trial. But equally, if the law provides for trial by ordeal, then provided that the rules recognised as applicable to that form of trial are followed, there will have been due process.

Consider the options for determining the facts when charged with crime in early English law. There was the choice of compurgation if you could find sufficient people who would swear on oath to your trustworthiness in support of your own oath. In some instances, compurgation was not allowed. If you were caught red-handed or were unable to find sufficient compurgators or were not a free man, then the alternative of ordeal was required. The ordeal was either hot iron, hot or cold water or the corsnaed (accursed morsel). Apart from cold water, the ordeals took place in church and under the supervision of a priest. The underlying belief was that God would make the truth plain to all.[17] Provided all proper procedures were followed, it could be argued that due process had been followed.

The language of Magna Carta spoke about four things: (i) lawful judgment, (ii) by peers, (iii) according to the law of the land and those three things being (iv) applicable to free men and the king. These principles can be seen in antiquity. In Aeschylus' *The Eumenides*, Athena in a soliloquy says:

15 1354 28 Edw. 3, c. 3.

16 http://www.legislation.gov.uk/aep/Edw3/28/3 (accessed 21 January 2019).

17 T.F.T. Plucknett, *Taswell-Langmead's Constitutional History*, 11th ed. (London: Sweet & Maxwell, 1960), 23.

> So you, you Furies, bring your case on here;
> call witnesses and arguments to your aid,
> evidence that will support your plea;
> and I'll return when I have found the best
> within my Athens to be jurors here.
> They will swear an oath to hear this duly;
> and I will swear that they will judge it truly.[18]

The basic principles of a clear allegation, the opportunity to examine and test the evidence said to support it, the chance to give an answer and a decision by an impartial tribunal lie at the heart of a modern understanding of due process and they were all spoken of by Athena.

9.6.2 Due process: two systems

Just as the common law was developing in England with a strong emphasis on judgment in accordance with the law of the land, a parallel judicial process was developing in the canon law tradition. In his chapter on "Due Process in Magna Carta", John Baldwin describes that development.[19] He discusses its origins in classical Roman law with its development initially in Bologna and then Paris. He refers to the biblical justification said to be derived from the garden of Eden when God brought suit against Adam for his disobedience. The essence was that sentence required a preceding conviction or confession. However, the difficulties of providing satisfactory evidence of the alleged crime or sin, particularly when it was of a sexual nature or was an allegation of simony, led to the development of procedures such as the *inquisitio*. Summary justice was introduced where secret accusations, an inquisitorial procedure requiring testimony under oath and sometimes the use of torture, became the order of the day, then described as the *ordo iudicarius*. The authority under which this developed was the authority of the Pope and of the Emperor, neither of whom were subject to it.

In his essay for *Magna Carta, Religion and the Rule of Law*, Sir John Baker contrasts the procedures of the church courts with those of the common law courts in the fourteenth and fifteenth centuries.[20] The common law

> was nurtured in the courts of law and in the Inns of Court by men of common sense, men who listened to both sides, men of the world who married

18 Sophie Grace and Tim Chappell, *Aeschylus: Eumenides. A New Translation*, http://www.open.ac.uk/people/sites/www.open.ac.uk.people/files/files/eumenides-definitive.pdf (accessed 21 January 2019), lines 485–9.

19 John Baldwin, "Due Process in Magna Carta", in Robin Griffith-Jones and Mark Hill, eds., *Magna Carta, Religion and the Rule of Law* (Cambridge: Cambridge University Press, 2015), 36–40.

20 Sir John Baker, "Magna Carta and Personal Liberty", in Griffith-Jones and Hill, *Magna Carta, Religion and the Rule of Law*, 87–91.

> and had children and learned about human nature from people rather than scholastic books.[21]

On the other hand, someone suspected of heresy would be cited to appear before a court, and if he failed to do so could be tried for his life in his absence; he was not entitled to know the names of his accusers; there was no indictment specifying what particular heretical beliefs he was alleged to hold; the trial could be in secret; he would be interrogated at length; and torture could be used.[22]

Baker then describes the establishment of the High Commission. The Commission which followed on earlier Ecclesiastical Commissions established under the prerogative powers of the Crown was put on a statutory footing in 1559. It followed on the Acts of Uniformity and Supremacy and was used to enforce the Reformation settlement. Being an ecclesiastical court it used the *ordo*. People would be summoned before it and required to take the oath *ex officio*; if they refused they were imprisoned indefinitely for contempt, if they took it they were then examined as to their beliefs. The Commission remained effective for almost one hundred years.

9.6.3 Due process: back to the judges in England and Wales

As time passed, the common law courts from time to time were asked to give relief against the Commission. On occasions, actions for habeas corpus were brought against the Commission. Baker describes a number of these instances and the development of a school of thought in the Inns of Court that these practices were contrary to the right not to be disseised of one's liberty, which, it was asserted, included religious liberty.[23]

The significance of this period of history is that the matters that we would now say were necessary for there to be due process: the requirement that there be specific prohibition in law before an accusation could be made that might result in punishment; the right to know specifically what you are alleged to have done that infringes that law; the right to see and test the evidence that is said to show that the law has been infringed and by you; the right to be able to explain yourself and your case; the right to be judged by an impartial tribunal; and the requirement that such a judgment be arrived at before sentence is pronounced, were all promoted and protected by the English common lawyers and not those trained in the law as promoted by the Christian Church.

The law of those common lawyers was law that they would have said was long known and was derived from natural law. In 1689, when the English had their

21 Ibid., 88.
22 Ibid., 91.
23 Ibid., 100.

Glorious Revolution, they spoke not of "self-evident … unalienable rights"[24] nor of "the natural unalienable and sacred rights of man",[25] but of the "knowne Lawes and Statutes and Freedome of this Realme".[26] These ancient laws, statutes and liberty had always been there, even if in recent times they had been denied and overridden. Natural law expressed in local law was the historic understanding of where due process came from in England and Wales. Often, that local law would be in the form of statute, but sometimes it was "declared" by the judges.

In England and Wales that continues to be the position, although in doing so the judges are very anxious to say that they are not making the law, only declaring it. In the case of *Gouriet v Union of Post Office Workers and Others*, Lord Denning famously said:

> In another sense the proposition put forward by the Attorney-General is not true. It is not true when we are considering the powers of the Attorney-General and the prerogative which he claims. Parliament has passed no enactment upon it. There is no binding precedent in our books upon it. It is a new thing. Whenever a new situation arises which has not been considered before, the judges have to say what the law is. In so doing, we do not change the law. We declare it. We consider it on principle: and then pronounce upon it. As the old writers quaintly put it, the law lies "in the breast of the judges" … We have but one prejudice. That is to uphold the law. and that we will do, whatever befall. Nothing shall deter us from doing our duty.[27]

It is in this way that judges have developed the law so as to protect the interests of those accused of crime.

The question of the fairness of the trial procedure has often occupied the attention of the judges in England and Wales. They have developed practices and procedures to ensure that a trial is fair not only to the defendant but also to the prosecutor and others engaged in the process as complainants or witnesses. Examples of this are seen in relation to the requirement for corroboration, the admission of confession evidence and how courts deal with eyewitness identification. It is also significant to see that Parliament sometimes intervenes in relation to these judge-created provisions.

It was judges who introduced the requirement that juries should be warned of the danger of convicting in the absence of corroboration in cases involving the evidence of children and in cases of sexual assault. Changed understanding of the dangers of stereotyping in sexual crime and a change in understanding about

24 U.S. Declaration of Independence 1776.

25 The Declaration of the Rights of Man and of a Citizen (France, 1789).

26 1 Will and Mar (Sess 2) c. 2 (1688). The Bill received Royal Assent on 16 December 1689 but was assigned to 1688 using the old method of reckoning, according to which, until 1793, all Acts passed in a session of Parliament with no specified commencement date were deemed to be passed in the year in which that session began.

27 [1977] QB 729.

children's evidence led Parliament to intervene and abolish the judge-made rules. On the other hand, initially the executive[28] and then Parliament put on a statutory footing what had been known as the "Judges' Rules"[29] in relation to the admission of evidence of confessions.[30] In relation to evidence of identification in *R v Turnbull*,[31] the Court of Appeal dealt with four cases in which evidence of identification had been unsuccessfully challenged at trial. In the course of giving judgment, Widgery LCJ said:

> Each of these appeals raises problems relating to evidence of visual identification in criminal cases. Such evidence can bring about miscarriages of justice and has done so in a few cases in recent years ... In our judgment the danger of miscarriages of justice occurring can be much reduced if trial judges sum up to juries in the way indicated in this judgment.

The court then went on to give guidance as to what should be said to juries in such cases to draw their attention to the risk of a miscarriage of justice and what they should look at and have in mind in order to test the reliability of the identification. So far, that has not attracted any statutory intervention.

A case which illustrates the relationship between fairness and due process is that of *R. v Hanif and Khan*. The issue was what should be done about a member of the jury who revealed in the course of the trial that he was a police officer. The trial judge asked some questions of the officer and declared himself satisfied as to the juror's impartiality. The Court of Appeal decided that given the issues in the case there was no risk of bias.[32] However, the European Court of Human Rights concluded that there had been a violation of Article 6.1.[33] The case was sent back to the Court of Appeal which allowed the appeal against conviction and directed a re-trial. Subsequently, the Lord Chief Justice has issued a Practice Direction setting out how courts should deal with the issues that arise when a police officer is summoned for jury service.[34]

In England and Wales, the right that is guaranteed to a defendant is that of a fair trial. Ensuring that right is delivered is in the hands of the trial judge. The starting point for assessing fairness is found in the laws and the liberties of the kingdom as set out in primary and secondary legislation[35] and in the procedural

28 Home Office Circular 31/1964.

29 Introduced by Lord Alverstone in 1912: see *R. v. Voisin* [1918] 1 KB 531; (1919) 13 Cr App R 89.

30 Police and Criminal Evidence Act 1984, s. 78, and Code C.

31 (1976) 63 Cr App R 132.

32 [2008] EWCA Crim 531; [2008] 2 Cr App Rep 13.

33 *Hanif and Khan v. UK* App. Nos. 52999/08, 61779/08 (ECtHR, 20 December 2011).

34 Criminal Practice Direction 26C.7.

35 The making of Criminal Procedure Rules was codified by sections 69–73 of the Courts Act 2003, which established a Criminal Procedure Rules Committee to draft the original Rules and propose amendments from time to time. The Rules come into operation by being

practices set out in Practice Directions[36] and in guidance from the courts through its judgments in cases concerning particular issues.

Such is the growth of the guidance in the form of Practice Directions which are linked to the Rules that Her Majesty's Courts and Tribunals Service now provides online access to a consolidated document in which the various Practice Directions are interspersed into the Criminal Procedure Rules.[37] The two text books on Criminal Law and Practice (Archbold and Blackstone) each produce supplements setting out those consolidated Rules and Practice Directions.

Beyond such rules and directions it is still possible in England and Wales to appeal to a judge to stop a trial on the ground of inherent unfairness, see *R. v Horseferry Road Magistrates' Court, ex parte Bennett.*[38] But that apart, the courts in England and Wales will now rarely look beyond the question of whether the laws, the rules or the directions have been complied with to decide whether a case is being dealt with in accordance with due process.

9.6.4 Due process elsewhere

In other places, due process has developed differently. In the United States, there has been a divergence between substantive due process, whereby the substantive rights of a citizen are protected by the courts that will declare legislation or executive requirements to be in breach of those rights, and procedural due process, whereby the courts will require that fair procedures are followed before anyone is deprived of life, liberty or property. The development of substantive due process has been significant and far-reaching. An example of procedural due process is the case of *Miranda v Arizona*,[39] in which the judges of the U.S. Supreme Court spelled out the right of a suspect to remain silent when questioned. This was based on the fifth amendment, which guarantees a suspect's right not to be a witness against him- or herself.

In contrast, the concept of procedural due process is not known on the European continent. However, the German *Rechtsstaatsprinzip* (the principle of the State being grounded in law and acting according to law) comes close.[40]

---

submitted to the Lord Chancellor and if he or she "allows" them they are then put into a Statutory Instrument which comes into effect subject to a negative resolution of either House of Parliament.

36 Criminal Practice Directions are now given by the Lord Chief Justice by virtue of section 74 of the Courts Act 2003. Some require the approval of the Lord Chancellor. They are "handed down" by the Lord Chief Justice from time to time.

37 http://www.justice.gov.uk/courts/procedure-rules/criminal/rulesmenu-2015 (accessed 21 January 2019).

38 [1993] UKHL 10.

39 384 U.S. 436 (1966).

40 In correspondence, Professor Mathias Schmoeckel has said: "This term was coined around 1800 by a lawyer called Peterson, who used this term to describe the followers of Kant. It means that the State is obliged to obey the law, and no property can be taken away without a proper law or judgment. This is based on the same Calvinist tradition as the U.S.-American

9.7 Conclusions

This review of human dignity and due process has shown the involvement of the Church in the development of these matters. Sometimes, from our modern perspective, the Church comes out well and sometimes not so well. Archbishop Langton played a significant role in the signing of Magna Carta.[41] At the same time in 1215, the Church officially sought to end trial by ordeal.[42] However, the church courts in the following centuries developed practices that were inimical to what we would today regard as being consistent with human dignity or due process. Latterly, the Church played a significant role in the overall shaping of the UN Declaration of Human Rights, which in turn has put a focus on the need for states to have due regard to human dignity in the shaping of their justice systems. John Nurser has written extensively on the initial role of the Church in that in *For All People and All Nations*.[43]

In the meantime, the English common law had been developing its ancient customs, some of which were put onto a statutory basis. Many of those customs could be traced back to Saxon England and many were familiar to other northern (Teutonic and Scandinavian) territories. The tradition of 12 lawmen which would eventually evolve into the jury of today has a history that has been written about on several occasions.[44] The English common law judges played a significant role in developing principles and practices to ensure that trials were fair. Many of these principles have been adopted into such documents as the European Convention on Human Rights.

However, at times, those same common law judges had a reputation for anything but fairness. In the Bloody Assizes of 1685, Lord Chief Justice George Jeffreys and four other judges presided over the trials of those accused of crime following the Monmouth Rebellion. Their disregard for what would now be considered proper due process was matched by the judges who imprisoned jurors who did not return verdicts they approved of in Bushell's case.[45]

'pursuit of happiness'. While Beza defended the individual *beatitudo* as the right to use all individual rights and assets, Kant reflected this issue in the perspective of the State. Both stand in the tradition of Calvin, who considered it illicit to take one's property away, because everybody had to prove by the management of his assets if he deserved salvation". See also his article "Die Gewährleistung der Freiheit des Einzelnen als Staatszweck nach Calvin", in H. de Wall, ed., *Reformierte Staatslehre in der frühen Neuzeit* (Berlin: Duncker & Humblot, 2014), 21–50.

41 Baldwin, "Due Process in Magna Carta", 40.

42 At the Fourth Lateran Council, Pope Innocent III promulgated Canon 18 forbidding the blessing of the participants in ordeals by iron or water and continuing the earlier prohibitions regarding duelling.

43 John Nurser, *For All People and All Nations* (Washington, D.C.: Georgetown University Press, 2005).

44 William Blackstone, *Commentaries on the Laws of England*, 4 vols. (Oxford: Clarendon Press, 1765–9), Bk III, ch. 23 on "Jury Trial Generally", and Bk IV, ch. 27 on "Criminal Juries"; William Forsyth, *History of Trial by Jury* (n.p., 1875).

45 *The King v. Penn and Mead* 6 How 951.

But over the longer term, the principles that have emerged through the common law tradition have become the principles which are now said to provide due process and which are said to be universally applicable as they are necessary to ensure that everyone is treated with the dignity that they deserve as members of the human race. Lord Justice Judge, as he then was,[46] remarked in one judgment:

> Our attention was drawn to a number of decisions of the European Court of Human Rights. I have considered them with care. That said, by now, we surely fully appreciate that the principles to be found in Articles 6 and 10 of the European Convention are bred in the bone of the common law and indeed, in some instances at any rate, the folk understanding of the community as a whole.[47]

What, if any, is the Christian perspective on this history? Answering that question takes us back to where we started. Any one of us may play any part in the criminal justice process. When we do so, we do so as human beings, made in the image of God, though flawed through sin and in need of redemption. That redemption comes through the incarnation of Jesus Christ, by which Christians understand that God became one of us and came among us where he was not only rejected but was also accorded no dignity and was treated without even the due process that Jewish and Roman law should have accorded him. He was unjustly convicted and sentenced to what we now regard as a cruel and unusual punishment – death by crucifixion.

We can learn many things from these basic tenets of the Christian faith. We learn of human frailty and so should never be surprised that crimes are committed by all manner of people for all manner of reasons. We learn also that human frailty means that any justice system will be imperfect as it is operated by people who themselves are subject to the same frailties that afflict those who have committed the crimes. So judgment will be imperfect at best, at times mistaken and at times even malicious. That may be of some comfort not only to those who suffer injustice in places where there is no recognition of human dignity and due process, but also to all who recognise the imperfections of those regimes which do seek to uphold human dignity and due process.

Above all, it is those underpinning beliefs that will cause Christians whatever their particular role of the moment in the criminal justice system to aim to treat all the other persons they come across and deal with in the system with dignity and to respect them as people who equally with them were made in the image of their creator and who equally are people for whom Christ was incarnated and suffered death to bring about redemption.

46 Prior to his appointment as Lord Chief Justice. See Lord Judge's Preface to this volume.
47 *R (Bright) v Central Criminal Court* [2001] 1 WLR 662, at 679.

Further reading

Bingham, Tom. *The Rule of Law* (London: Penguin, 2011).

Griffith-Jones, Robin and Mark Hill. *Magna Carta, Religion and the Rule of Law* (Cambridge: Cambridge University Press, 2015).

McCrudden, Christopher. "Human Dignity and Judicial Interpretation of Human Rights", (2008) 19.4 *European Journal of International Law* 655–724.

Nurser, John S. *For All Peoples and All Nations* (Washington, DC: Georgetown University Press, 2005).

Pennington, Kenneth. *The Prince and the Law* (Berkeley: University of California Press, 1993).

Rosen, Michael. *Dignity: Its History and Meaning* (Cambridge, MA: Harvard University Press, 2012).

Waldron, Jeremy. *Dignity, Rank, and Rights* (New York: Oxford University Press, 2012).

Part III

Christianity and criminal offences

10 Christianity and crimes against the State

Nathan S. Chapman

10.1 Introduction

Christianity can inspire a dizzying array of responses to public policy. Take immigration: in June 2018, the United States began separating children and parents who arrived together at the southern border, ostensibly to discourage unlawful entry. Against public outcry, Attorney General Jeff Sessions cited Romans 13, which he described as the Apostle Paul's "clear and wise command" "to obey the laws of the government because God has ordained the government for his purposes". The news media lost no time pegging Sessions to other political groups who had relied on the same passage of Scripture: British loyalists and Southern slaveholders.[1] At the same time, hundreds of churches followed biblical injunctions to care for the poor and the alien by offering sanctuary to undocumented immigrants, placing themselves at risk of federal prosecution for "harbouring" them. Presumably, Sessions would apply his view of Romans 13 not only to unlawful immigrants, but also to these Christian dissenters. How could these opposite responses to the government's immigration policy emerge from the same religious tradition?

This chapter explores Christianity's contributions to the scope of the government's authority to punish crimes against the State. From its origins, Western Christianity has maintained two perspectives on earthly authority: God has authorised it for the purpose of restraining evil and promoting temporal peace, but Christians should resist its attempts to claim the loyalty and obedience due to God alone. Depending on the political and social context, Christian groups have emphasised one or the other of these teachings, or both at once. The result has been to alternately support and resist the government's authority, especially its authority to punish threats to its own political stability and operation.

By "crimes against the State", this chapter means offences that fall into three overlapping categories: those of political disloyalty; those that threaten constitutional order; and those that interfere with law enforcement. This would include

1 Julie Zauzmer and Keith McMillan, "Sessions Cites Bible Passage", *Washington Post*, 15 June 2018.

not only "political" crimes such as treason, espionage and terrorism, but also more pedestrian offences such as tax evasion, perjury, obstruction of justice and harbouring an undocumented immigrant. Most of these crimes do not directly harm persons and property. Rather, they resist the State's authority – either its right to exist altogether or its right to enforce a certain policy. These crimes sit at the nexus of the Christian belief that the government exercises authority from God and the belief that there are limits to that authority.

This chapter argues that Christianity's ambivalence towards the State's authority has inspired both expansions of and limitations to the State's legitimate exercise of power to punish crimes against the State. After sketching the historical, scriptural and institutional foundations of Christianity's perspectives on earthly government, the chapter examines three moments of constitutional crisis when Christianity affected the scope of crimes against the State. Section 10.3 focuses on the expansion during the reign of Henry VIII of the crimes of treason and *praemunire* as tools of religious and political uniformity. Section 10.4 considers the role of Christian Nonconformists in the development of the criminal jury's independence to implement religious tolerance in political trials. Section 10.5 brings the study up to date by showing how the Jehovah's Witnesses' refusal to swear allegiance to the State led the U.S. Supreme Court to articulate substantive constitutional limits on the government's authority to punish politically motivated conduct and speech.

Such a wide-angle history of the relationship between Christianity and crimes against the State must sacrifice some precision for perspective. Yet, I hope it will illuminate the enduring conceptual and political tendencies of Christianity.

10.2 Christianity's two views of the earthly city

From the beginning, Christianity has maintained two views of earthly political authority. The first is that God establishes and uses the earthly government for judgment; Christians should therefore honour and pray for earthly rulers. The second is that human government, in rebellion against God, claims the loyalty due to God alone. Christians have always struggled to know, and frequently disagreed about, the implications of these views for ethics. This section explores the scriptural and historical foundations for Christian thought about the proper relationship between Church and State. Since at least the fifth century, Christians have variously supported the State, including its authority to punish those who resist and, at times, resisted.

10.2.1 The Roman and Jewish antecedents

Christianity's origin within Second Temple Judaism under the Roman Empire shaped its views of the relationship between earthly and eternal politics. The Roman Empire, like most ancient polities, merged what moderns distinguish as religion and politics. Besides *Imperator* (general of the armies), the Roman emperor held the titles of *Augustus*, "signifying at once both [the emperor's] moral supremacy and the pleasure the gods took in his rule", and *Pontifex maximus*, the head of Roman state religion. Pagan polytheism was diffused throughout governmental and cultural practices. Holidays and festivals were religious, courts administered justice in the name of the gods and meat markets sold meat sacrificed to the gods. Christians likely earned a reputation for having "anti-social tendencies", as the historian Tacitus put it, for declining to participate in these customs.[2]

Although Rome let vassal states retain many of their political and cultural institutions, the emperor brooked no threat to Rome's hegemony. By the early first century, the Empire punished *perduellio* (treason) and an increasing number of acts as *maiesta minuta populi Romani*, literally, "the diminution of the majesty of the Roman people".[3] Additionally, local imperial officials maintained discretion to enforce loyalty on an ad hoc basis. Pliny the Younger, a Roman official in Bithynia in Asia Minor, investigated Christians, apparently upon private complaint, without knowing their alleged crime or the appropriate punishment. He executed those who refused to disavow the faith on the ground that their "stubbornness and unbending obstinacy" justified death.[4]

Christians inherited two perspectives on empire from Judaism. The first was one of potential conflict. Perhaps the most distinctive aspect of Jewish political theology was the belief that *Yhwh* demanded exclusive worship. *Yhwh* had delivered Israel from slavery in Egypt, given them land in Judaea and entered into a covenant with them. Foreign empires that merged polytheism and imperial cults were at odds with *Yhwh*'s call to holiness. The Hebrew Scriptures are thus critical of empire from the start: Cain, the primordial murderer, founds the first city, with its accoutrements of civilisation; the story of Babel portrays *Yhwh*'s opposition to worldwide political unity; Egypt, with its quasi-deity ruler, is throughout the Scriptures the avowed enemy of *Yhwh* and archetype of oppressive foreign rule; and the apocalyptic visions of Daniel portray empires as successively more powerful, degraded and destructive.[5]

Other passages in the Hebrew Scriptures emphasise that *Yhwh* uses even the vagaries of empire for the good of the Jewish people. Jeremiah 29 describes Nebuchadnezzar, who sacked Jerusalem and forced its leading families into exile in Babylon, as God's servant for the Jews' restoration. The prophet exhorts the exiles to "seek the welfare of the city where I have sent you into exile, and pray to

2 H.A. Drake, *Constantine and the Bishops* (Baltimore: Johns Hopkins University Press, 2000), 37, 91–2. John Jackson, trans., *Tacitus. Annals* (Cambridge, MA: Harvard University Press, 1980), 15.45.

3 See F.S. Lear, *Treason in Roman and Germanic Law* (Austin: University of Texas Press, 1965), 11–12.

4 B. Radice, ed. and trans., *Pliny the Younger. Letters and Panegyricus* (Cambridge, MA: Harvard University Press, 1975), 203–4, 10.96.

5 Oliver O'Donovan, *The Desire of the Nations* (Cambridge: Cambridge University Press, 1999), 88.

the LORD on its behalf, for in its welfare you will find your welfare" (v. 7).[6] The author of Isaiah 44–45 likewise represents Cyrus of Persia as *Yhwh*'s "shepherd" and "anointed" "to subdue nations" (45:1) and to rebuild Jerusalem (44:28). From this perspective, empire "offer[ed] constructive assistance on the one hand and secur[ed] protection on the other".[7]

10.2.2 The New Testament and early Church

Jesus Christ and his early followers, as recorded in the New Testament and other early writings, inherited and re-ordered the Jewish ambivalence about the relationship of God's kingdom to the Roman Empire.[8] Christ declared the Kingdom of God, a kingdom of service rather than power, of self-denial rather than violence. Although Christ's kingdom was "not from this world" (John 18:36), it was nonetheless fully embodied: his politics was not merely theoretical, intellectual or spiritual. The Son of God's incarnation, miraculous acts of healing and dispossession, teaching of the crowds, execution by those he came to save and resurrection by God were, altogether, the realisation of an alternative political order built on God's self-giving love, forgiveness and new life (Mark 10:32–52). That kingdom is not over. As Christians continue to confess in the Apostle's Creed, Christ "will come again to judge the living and the dead", assigning them to an eternal, embodied existence. The world, with its governments, is passing away. In the meantime, there is a transitory period in which "[t]he coming era of God's rule [holds] the passing era in suspension".[9] Christians live "as aliens and exiles" in the world (1 Peter 2:11). A "characteristic of Christian political theology down the centuries" has been a belief in the "qualitative difference between present and future" that rejects "the sufficiency of all present political arrangements".[10]

The Book of Acts illustrates this ambiguity. When the Jewish leaders threatened the apostles for preaching in the name of Jesus, they responded, "We must obey God rather than men" (Acts 5:29). At the same time, Acts repeatedly portrays the apostles relying on the legal and institutional protections of Rome. In Ephesus, for instance, the local silversmith guild was threatened by the conversion of Christians away from human-made gods, and initiated an assembly in the theatre bent on punishing Paul and his companions (19:23–30). The town clerk, however, quieted the crowd and told them that the silversmiths could "bring charges" in court against anyone who had wronged them, and that any other matter "must be settled in the regular assembly" (vv. 35–39). The Christian persecutors were the ones "in danger of being charged with rioting", itself a

6 All citations from Scripture are to the New Revised Standard Version.
7 O'Donovan, *Desire of the Nations*, 86.
8 Wayne A. Meeks, *The Origins of Christian Morality: The First Two Centuries* (New Haven: Yale University Press, 1993), 167–8.
9 O'Donovan, *Desire of the Nations*, 93.
10 Christopher Rowland, "Scripture: New Testament", in Peter Scott and William T. Cavanaugh, eds., *Blackwell Companion to Political Theology* (Malden: Blackwell, 2004), 22.

crime against the State (v. 40). While Acts portrays the Roman Empire, with its law and international institutions of peacekeeping, as an unwitting partner of the Church's expansion, the narrative simultaneously conveys Christianity as "an alternative total way of life". The "culturally destabilizing character of the Christian mission entail[ed] the potential for outsiders to construe Christianity as sedition or treason (as indeed it was so construed)".[11]

Perhaps the most influential New Testament passage on earthly government is Romans 13. The Apostle Paul instructs the church at Rome that God has given power to earthly authorities, "the servant[s] of God to execute wrath on the wrongdoer" (vv. 1–4), so Christians should pay them the taxes and honour they are due (vv. 4–5). Many scholars insist that the thirteenth chapter of the Apostle Paul's letter to the Roman Christians makes sense only in light of the twelfth. Read together, the chapters present a dual view of the believer's relationship to "wrath", or judgment. On the one hand, Paul expressly tells his readers to "never avenge yourselves, but leave room for the wrath" (12:19). On the other hand, he declares that "the authority", which is "from God", "is the servant of God to execute wrath on the wrongdoer" (13:1, 4). And he commands Christians to give "taxes", "revenue", "respect" and "honour" to whom they are due (v. 7; see also Mark 12:13–17). It is likely that Paul was writing to people who were not part of both groups – they were Christians, but they had no official role among the "governing authorities". Paul's view of earthly government echoes the view of empire presented by Jeremiah and Isaiah: God institutes and uses the earthly authorities to punish wrongdoers, protect the innocent and shape conscience (see 1 Peter 12:11–17; Titus 3:1).

Revelation 13 "represent[s] a radically different assessment of the relation of the Christian community to the Roman Empire".[12] Whether interpreted as predictive, historical or merely theologically evocative, the thirteenth chapter of Revelation paints a bleak picture of earthly government. Using the symbolic norms of apocalyptic literature, the passage depicts a world government founded by "the dragon" who has been cast out of heaven and now makes war on "those who keep the commandments of God and hold the testimony of Jesus" (12:17). The dragon gives authority to a blasphemous, seemingly immortal "beast" "to make war on the saints and to conquer them", and "over every tribe and people and language and nation" (13:1–8). This beast gives authority to another to "make the earth and its inhabitants worship the first" (v. 11–12). Christians are to see these governmental powers for what they are – false Christs who rail against the kingdom of God – and endure their persecution as a testimony to the true and coming kingdom, a kingdom ruled by a

11 C. Kavin Rowe, *World Upside Down: Reading Acts in the Graeco-Roman Age* (Oxford: Oxford University Press, 2009), 4–5.

12 Richard B. Hays, *The Moral Vision of the New Testament: Community, Cross, New Creation* (San Francisco: Harper, 1996), 190.

martyred and avenging Lamb.[13] On Revelation's vision of government, confessing Christ is itself a crime against the State.

The New Testament's perspectives on government reflect not only the early Christian communities' views, but also their experiences. Before the Edict of 250, Roman persecution of Christianity was local and sporadic. Imperial officials could execute Christians for little more than refusing to denounce Christ. Others were reportedly executed as political scapegoats or for refusing to participate in ceremonial gestures that were tantamount to worshipping Caesar. Martyrologies depicted Christians unjustly executed as witnesses for Christ and exhorted believers to courageously follow their path.[14]

Other early Christian thinkers sought to answer the difficult ethical question raised by Christ's declaration of the new kingdom and seeming acceptance of an ongoing legitimate role for earthly government: can someone follow Christ and serve as a magistrate, soldier or other law enforcement officer? In the early centuries, before many imperial office holders were Christians, the answers ranged from "no, of course not", to a more qualified "no".[15] Christians should pray for the government and faithfully hope that God would use the powers-that-be to serve the common good by punishing wrongdoers.[16] But a Christian's freedom to participate fully in the Empire's methods was dramatically limited by loyalty to a Lord who eschewed violence to suffer the shame of death on a Roman cross.[17] Given the New Testament's apparent ambivalence about "the State", it is perhaps unsurprising that Western Christian political thought has at once supported secular government and urged its limits.

10.2.3 Augustine, the two cities and the Middle Ages

By far the single most influential Christian account of politics has been Augustine of Hippo's *City of God*. In a synthesis of neo-Platonic philosophy and biblical narrative, Augustine retells the history of the world as a struggle between two allegorical cities – the earthly and the heavenly.[18] The cities are distinguished by their desires: the heavenly, in humility, loves God; the earthly, in pride, lusts for

13 Ibid., 176–81. David L. Barr, "The Apocalypse as a Symbolic Transformation of the World: A Literary Analysis", (1984) 38 *Interpretation* 39–50.

14 See, e.g. Meeks, *Origins of Christian Morality*, 168; Herbert Musurillo, ed. and trans., *The Acts of the Christian Martyrs* (Oxford: Oxford University Press, 1972).

15 See "The Patristic Age", in Oliver O'Donovan and Joan Lockwood O'Donovan, eds., *From Irenaeus to Grotius: A Sourcebook in Christian Political Thought* (Grand Rapids: William B. Eerdmans, 1999), 2–3.

16 See Theophilus of Antioch, "To Autolycus", in O'Donovan and O'Donovan, *From Irenaeus to Grotius*, 14.

17 See Tertullian, "The Military Chaplet", in O'Donovan and O'Donovan, *From Irenaeus to Grotius*, 27.

18 Augustine, *The City of God Against the Pagans*, ed. and trans. R.W. Dyson (Cambridge: Cambridge University Press, 1998), 2, 11–18.

"dominion".[19] For Augustine, the cities are intermixed until the final judgment. Citizens of the heavenly city will reign eternally with God, citizens of the earthly city will be punished eternally with the devil. Until then, citizens of the heavenly city are sojourners in the world, partaking of the goods of the earthly city, and, at the same time, citizens of the earthly city, participating in the human institution of the Church.

Augustine's account maintains the New Testament's ambiguity about the "earthly city". The earthly city desires "earthly peace", "without doubt [a gift] of God",[20] but temporal peace cannot compare to the eternal peace of the city of God. Citizens of the city of God are pilgrims in this life and therefore "make use of earthly and temporal things like pilgrims: they are not captivated by them, nor are they deflected by them from their progress towards God". While on earth, the heavenly city "does not hesitate to obey the laws of the earthly city, whereby the things necessary for the support of this mortal life are administered".[21]

To this duty of obedience, however, Augustine posits an important proviso. The earthly city worships a variety of gods. "But the Heavenly City knows only one God Who is to be worshipped, and it decrees, with faithful piety, that to Him alone is to be given that service which … is due only to God". For this reason,

> it has not been possible for the Heavenly City to have laws of religion in common with the earthly city. It has been necessary for her to dissent from the earthly city in this regard … thus she has had to bear the brunt of the anger and hatred and persecutions of her adversaries.[22]

What, for Augustine, is a "law of religion" that Christians must not follow? Presumably any law that requires something contrary to the worship of God. This suggests a potentially wide range of conflicts between the laws of the earthly city and obedience to God. And, for Augustine, this formula left room for the institutional church to enforce true worship, even with physical coercion, a view with an unfortunate legacy in mediaeval and early modern Christendom. Augustine thus explored the tension latent in the Christian Scriptures between the earthly government's proper sphere of power and the Christian's ultimate loyalty to God. His recognition that even the earthly city's pursuit of peace may result in the persecution of the citizens of the heavenly city points to how this tension may manifest itself through the punishment of crimes against the State.

The ensuing centuries of Christian thought on earthly government continued the scriptural ambivalence and built (not always self-consciously) on Augustine's theory of the two cities, but in a new way. Rulers were Christians. With Constantine as a model, those rulers often took responsibility for sorting

19 Ibid., 12.9.
20 Ibid., 15.4.
21 Ibid., 19.17.
22 Ibid.

out theological disputes among Christian bishops. Church leaders took it for granted that earthly rulers had authority from God to wield the sword; the question was the extent to which kings and emperors had authority over not only earthly matters, but spiritual matters too. Gelasius I's view, asserted in a letter to Emperor Anastasius, remained influential through the Middle Ages: "Two there are, august Emperor, by which this world is ruled: the consecrated authority of priests and the royal power". Kings must be "subordinate in religious matters", while "even the masters of religion, conscious that providence has conferred the empire upon you, obey your laws as public discipline requires".[23]

While the Byzantine Empire practiced what Westerners called "Caesaropapism", with the emperor as the head of the Church, the relationship between Western rulers and bishops, including the Pope, was more complicated throughout the early Middle Ages. The relative authority of secular and Church officials to appoint leaders, call doctrinal councils and decide religious matters waxed and waned with time, place and personality. One scholar has referred to the institutional arrangement as one of interpenetration – despite Gelasius's assertion in the fifth century, many Germanic kings took leading roles in "religious" questions and some clergy played roles in what we would now call secular judgment.

This period was followed by a revolution that upended many of the settled institutional and theological arrangements. The first was the "Investiture Crisis" or Gregorian revolution of the late eleventh and early twelfth centuries. Partly in an attempt to stem ecclesiastical corruption attending simony and clerical marriage, Gregory VII took two decisive steps with dramatic consequences for political history and theory. First, drawing on Scripture and traditional (but disputed) arguments, Gregory asserted the Pope's primacy over the Church.[24] Not merely the first among equals, the Bishop of Rome was the highest official in the Catholic Church, with authority to depose, reinstate and transfer bishops, to ordain clerics and to decide all matters of faith.[25] This would unify Western Christendom and result in the first complex international corporation. Second, Gregory asserted the Church's authority and jurisdiction over matters of religion, even over the person of the emperor and king. The Pope, he asserted, "alone may use the imperial insignia", "is the only one whose feet are to be kissed by all princes", "may be judged by no one", has "the power to depose Emperors" and "may absolve all subjects of unjust men from their fealty".[26] During the high Middle Ages and through the Renaissance, the Roman Church operated as a limit on the authority

23 Gelasius I, "*From* Letter to Emperor Anastasius", in O'Donovan and O'Donovan, *From Irenaeus to Grotius*, 179.

24 Gregory, "Letter 8.21", in O'Donovan and O'Donovan, *From Irenaeus to Grotius*, 243 (quoting Matthew 16:18).

25 See "Dictatus Papae", in O'Donovan and O'Donovan, *From Irenaeus to Grotius*, 242–3.

26 See Gregory, "Letter 8.21", 243.

of earthly kings by effectively operating as an international State itself.[27] In some sense, then, crimes against the Church were crimes against a State.

10.3 Christian dissent as treason against a Christian State

The legal relationship between the Church and State in late mediaeval England was complex. In broad strokes, the Pope was the head of the Church, the king the head of the secular realm. But the legal, political and social connections between the spheres were intricate. The Pope appointed bishops, but usually took the king's recommendation. For their part, the bishops swore overlapping, and therefore potentially conflicting, oaths to the Pope and to the Crown.[28] While clergy enjoyed a measure of immunity from punishment for serious common law crimes (though not for treason), several statutes provided for the criminal punishment for *praemunire*, essentially for using the process of the ecclesiastical courts to interfere with the Crown's affairs.[29]

In the early sixteenth century, Martin Luther's bold scriptural and theological arguments against the Pope's authority over the Church added fuel to a Europe-wide movement for ecclesiastical reform. The new teaching gained popular support and a number of sponsors among the northern nobility.[30]

Henry VIII of England resisted at first, but eventually broke with Rome over matters of state – and bedroom. Henry wanted a divorce. He believed that his marriage was cursed because he had married his brother's widow. In partial fulfilment of Leviticus 20, the marriage had produced only one surviving child, a daughter, and Henry worried about the stability of the throne, and thus the nation, without a male heir. He also, incidentally, fell in love with Anne Boleyn, who had the good sense to refuse his bed before marriage.

The Pope declined the annulment, so Henry decided to replace the Pope with himself as the head of the English Church. Parliament cooperated. The Appeals Act of 1533 declared the king "supreme head" of England, with "plenary, whole and entire power" "over all sorts and degrees of people, divided in terms, and by names of spiritualty and temporalty".[31] Archbishop Thomas Cranmer promptly declared sentence against Henry's marriage to Catherine and affirmed the validity of his marriage to Anne. The Succession Act of 1534 vested succession in Anne's daughter, Elizabeth, and made it high treason to slander the marriage in print

27 On the context and effects of the Gregorian Revolution, see generally Harold J. Berman, *Law and Revolution: The Formation of the Western Legal Tradition* (Cambridge, MA: Harvard University Press, 1983).

28 Peter Marshall, *Heretics and Believers: A History of the English Reformation* (New Haven: Yale University Press, 2017), 197.

29 Ibid., 96–7.

30 Diarmaid MacCulloch, *The Reformation: A History* (New York: Viking, 2005).

31 Marshall, *Heretics and Believers*, 205.

and misprision of treason to question it by speech. The Act also required all adults to take an oath to its terms.[32]

As the State's authority grew, so did its appetite to punish those who were disloyal. And as its authority grew at the expense of the Church, political disloyalty increasingly came in the form of religious dissent, and religious dissent was increasingly a threat to the body politic. The crimes took three principal forms. First, *praemunire*. Cardinal Thomas Wolsey was Henry's right-hand man. He was the Lord Chancellor and, at Henry's request, the Pope's legate. When it became apparent, however, that he would be unable to secure the Pope's consent to the divorce, Henry had him prosecuted for *praemunire*, "for obtaining from Rome the papal bulls making him a legate" – the very bulls Henry had requested.[33]

Second, throughout the English Reformation, "the spirit of inventing new and strange treasons was revived".[34] Parliament passed a number of bills of attainder and enacted statutes to punish those whose faith posed a unique threat to the Crown's newly asserted authority. The Pope, Reformers believed, was a foreign prince. Asserting his authority within the realm of England was tantamount to adhering to the king's enemies. Those who believed in the traditional division of temporal and spiritual authority between Crown and Church were executed as traitors. Probably the most well-known of these was Thomas More, who had succeeded Wolsey as Lord Chancellor. For refusing to take the succession oath, More spent a year in the Tower of London; he was executed for treason upon the further (probably unsubstantiated) charge that he had spoken against the marriage.[35] More's famous last words – he died "the king's good servant but God's first" – capture the crux of the dilemma latent in Christian political thought from the beginning: what, precisely, belongs to Caesar?[36] Under Protestant, Catholic and Presbyterian sovereigns, England would execute many more as traitors over the ensuing centuries for their disagreement about the limits that Christ's kingdom placed upon the State.

Third, with the king as head of the Church, the State claimed exclusive responsibility for defining, prosecuting and punishing heresy. Traditionalists and moderate evangelicals saw radical evangelicals, especially Anabaptists, as a threat not only to theological purity, but also to political stability. Wolsey, More and Thomas Cromwell, who served as Henry's vicegerent in the early days after the

32 Ibid., 209. For the text of the act, see Louis W. Karlin, Henry Ansgar Kelly and Gerard B. Wegemer, eds., *Thomas More's Trial by Jury: A Procedural and Legal Review with a Collection of Documents* (Woodbridge: Boydell, 2011), 137, Appendix 1.

33 Marshall, *Heretics and Believers*, 173.

34 William Blackstone, *Commentaries on the Laws of England* (Oxford: Clarendon Press, 1765–9), Bk IV, ch. 6.

35 See Peter Marshall, "The Last Years", in George Logan, ed., *The Cambridge Companion to Thomas More* (Cambridge: Cambridge University Press, 2011), 121–3.

36 Marshall, *Heretics and Believers*, 224. See also R.H. Helmholz, "Natural Law and the Trial of Thomas More", in Karlin, Kelly and Wegemer, *Thomas More's Trial by Jury*, 64–5.

Act of Succession, all burned evangelicals, even as they were each, in turn, executed for crimes against the State.[37]

England endured intermittent religious wars, and threats of wars, through the seventeenth century. Under Mary, Parliament repealed the Henrician treason laws, but for centuries after her reign it remained treason to support the Roman Catholic Church's authority within the realm. Adults, lawyers and judicial officers were liable for ***praemunire*** for failing to swear to the Crown's supremacy over the Church.[38] After the Glorious Revolution (1688) settled the Protestant Hanoverian line on the throne, several statutes made it treason to interfere in the Protestant succession.[39] While these were far from the only crimes against the State (the principal treason statute remained 25 Edw. III. c. 2), they are notable as offences inspired by Christian belief on both sides, the State and the offender. They were the legal manifestation of Christianity's ambivalence about the respective authority of Church and State in a society dominated by rival Christian theologies.

10.4 Christianity, religious toleration and political limits on the State

Christian religious toleration began to emerge in the late seventeenth century. Limits on the State's authority to punish politico-religious conduct were concrete manifestations of that toleration. Those limits were indirect at first. Today, such limits are "rights" that trump lower laws. In the early modern period, limits on the State's authority were usually structural – they involved dividing responsibility for decision-making among those with conflicting interests; in today's parlance, checks and balances. An important example was the jury's increased independence in political trials signalled by Chief Justice Vaughan's decision in *Bushell's Case* (1670).[40]

During the Restoration (1666–88), the Church of England was established by law. Non-Anglicans – Catholics and Nonconformists alike – were under various civil and political disabilities. The Quaker Act of 1662 and the Conventicle Act of 1664 outlawed meeting in groups of more than five persons for the purposes of non-Anglican worship. Quaker defendants and pamphleteers often turned to the jury for relief.

Traditionally, the judge decided questions of law; the jury decided facts based on the evidence. When a jury returned a specific verdict, it simply decided the facts and the judge applied the law to those facts. In a criminal trial, however, a jury ordinarily returned a general verdict, in which its duty was to take the law from the judge, apply it to the facts and then return a verdict of guilty or not guilty.

37 Marshall, *Heretics and Believers*, 186, 191, 222.
38 1 W. & M. st. 1. c. 8; 7 & 8 W III. c. 24.
39 13 & 14 W. III. c. 3; 17 Geo. II c. 39; 1 Ann. St. 2. C. 17; 6 Ann. c. 7.
40 124 ER 1006, Vaughan 135.

In this context, the government prosecuted a number of Quakers for violating the Conventicle Act. Since Quaker services are usually silent, judges instructed juries that the defendants had violated the Act if they had gathered for religious purposes without saying Anglican prayers. Some defendants and pamphleteers, though, argued that a conviction under the Act ought to require a showing that the meeting was seditious and not merely "under color of religion".[41]

On 14 August 1670, Quakers William Penn (future founder of Pennsylvania) and William Meade spoke to a large crowd in Gracechurch Street. The mayor of London arrested and indicted them for the common law crimes of unlawful assembly and disturbing the peace. At the trial, Penn admitted that he had gone to Gracechurch Street to preach and pray, but argued that he had not broken the law charged in the indictment.[42] He insisted that the prosecutor provide a copy of the indictment to the jury and urged the jury to find that he had not in fact violated that law. The jury first returned a special verdict, finding Penn "guilty of speaking in Gracechurch Street", but when the judge pushed them for a general verdict, they returned one of not guilty. The judge fined the four jurors who objected to a guilty verdict for returning a verdict contrary to fact and law.[43]

According to one historian, it is likely that the jurors

> both doubted the tumult and believed that the Crown had, in any event, to prove an unlawful intent, especially where the law of criminal trespass was being applied to a man of God preaching His Word to those gathered to hear him.[44]

As with the Conventicle Act prosecutions, the dispute between judge and jurors was likely about whether the law required the prosecution to show that the defendants had engaged in Christian worship with seditious intent. This was certainly Penn's interpretation of the verdict.[45]

Bushell, one of the four, refused to pay the fine, so the court detained him. He filed a petition for a writ of habeas corpus with the Court of Common Pleas, arguing that the mayor's court was detaining him against the law. The mayor's court justified the detention with a general argument that Bushell had violated the law, and pointed to *Wagstaffe's Case*, only five years old, where the King's Bench had upheld a judge's power to fine jurors.[46]

41 Thomas Andrew Green, *Verdict According to Conscience: Perspectives on the English Criminal Trial Jury 1200–1800* (Chicago: University of Chicago Press, 1985), 202–8.
42 The Trial of William Penn and William Meade (1670), 6 Cobbett's State Trials 955, 957–9 (1661–78: Charles II).
43 *State Trials*, 6:961–5.
44 Green, *Verdict According to Conscience*, 225.
45 William Penn, "An Appendix by Way of Defense", in *State Trials*, 6:970–1000.
46 See Green, *Verdict According to Conscience*, 236–9. See also *R. v. Wagstaffe*, 1 Keble 934, 83 Eng. Rep. 1328 (1665).

Chief Justice Vaughan, writing on behalf of all but one of the king's judges, overturned *Wagstaffe* and held that a court could not fine a juror for returning a sincere verdict, or one according to his conscience. He did not go so far as to say that the jury could decide the law as well as fact. Instead, he took it for granted that the jury was restricted to applying the law as stated by the judge to the facts of the case (as the jury saw them). But he emphasised that two people could look at the same facts and reasonably and sincerely come to different conclusions. "A man cannot see by another's eye, nor hear by another's ear, no more can a man conclude or infer the thing to be resolv'd by anothers understanding or reasoning".[47] Vaughan also noted that the jurors were traditionally expected to bring their own knowledge of the witnesses and circumstances of the case to bear on the verdict. If the judge were to simply substitute his judgment of the facts for the jury's, the jury would serve no purpose. Vaughan left open the possibility that a judge could sanction a juror for giving an insincere verdict, though in most cases it would be difficult to show that a juror had voted against his true knowledge of the case, or his "conscience".[48]

Bushell's Case by no means established a principle that a judge could not influence a jury verdict or fine jurors who acted in bad faith. Yet, it did stand as a hallmark of the jury's independence to render a verdict according to conscience without fear of reprisal. "Acquittals in such cases (as in later prosecutions for seditious libel) were clearly based on rejections of the bench's view of the law".[49] This shifted authority for deciding facts, and, tacitly, for defining the boundaries of crimes, from Crown appointees to laymen. In time, this would lead to an expanded role for the criminal jury, especially in trials for seditious libel. In 1680, a jury would acquit seven bishops of seditious libel who had merely petitioned the king to challenge their prosecution for declining to read the king's *Declaration of Indulgence*.[50] The *Seven Bishops' Case* and accompanying pamphlets would influence the jury's authority in political trials through the eighteenth century, especially in America. The late seventeenth- and eighteenth-century jury's independence in political trials (and others) did not give defendants a legal *right* under today's notion of constitutional law, but it was an important political and structural check on the government's authority to punish political dissenters, spurred by popular sympathy for Christian Nonconformists.

47 Bushell's Case (1670), 124 E.R. 1006, Vaughan 148.

48 See Kevin Crosby, "*Bushell's Case* and the Juror's Soul", (2012) 33.3 *Journal of Legal History* (2012), 258.

49 Green, *Verdict According to Conscience*, 243.

50 Seven Bishops' Case, in *State Trials* 12:183–434 (1688). See also Green, *Verdict According to Conscience*, 262.

10.5 Christianity and the rights of political dissent

Christianity has also played an important role in the modern development of contemporary constitutional rights against punishment for certain crimes against the State. In many respects, the disestablishment of religion in the United States reduced the scope of conflict between the government and religious minorities. The most important change was eliminating religious tests for political office – in theory, at least, this would ensure that the laws would reflect the religious diversity of the people. Moreover, religious crimes such as adhering to the Pope, *praemunire* and engaging in Nonconforming Christian worship simply disappeared. (In the nineteenth century the United Kingdom also abolished religious tests and religious crimes.)

Religious disestablishment did not eliminate the tension among Christian groups between support for the State and resistance to its spiritual pretensions. Through the middle of the twentieth century, most Americans identified with Protestantism, and federal and state governments sponsored a variety of religious practices that Protestants took for granted: national days of prayer, legislative and military chaplains, Protestant education in public schools and others. At the same time, the rise of symbols and rituals of nationalism, especially during and after the Civil War (1861–5) contributed to what sociologists call "civic religion". For many, by the Second World War, Christianity and civic religion had come together in a number of public displays of nationalism. This soft establishment of diluted Christianity united many Americans of various religious backgrounds against foreign threats of totalitarianism.

At this time, constitutional rights of political and religious dissent were much different than they are now. Contemporary lawyers are used to thinking of constitutional rights as "trumps" – they operate as higher law that overrides contrary statutes and executive action. In the early twentieth century, most of those rights were enforced, if at all, through the political process, not by courts. The U.S. Supreme Court had invalidated a host of state laws for interfering with private rights of contract, but it had rarely struck down laws for suppressing political dissent.[51] This changed in the 1940s, in large part because of the political dissent of the Jehovah's Witnesses.

The Jehovah's Witnesses were (and are) an Adventist group that "prophesied an imminent apocalypse" and "condemned political institutions as demonic and organized religion as spiritually bankrupt".[52] They drew these emphases from the apocalyptic tradition in Christian thought. For them, the Roman Catholic Church was the beast of Revelation, the whore of Babylon. All nations, including the United States, were idolatrous empires. The Witnesses' proselytisation strat-

51 The court did not invalidate a law under the First Amendment until 1939, when it held that a local ordinance banning certain labour demonstrations violated the Assembly Clause. See *Hague v. Committee for Industrial Organization* 307 U.S. 496 (1939).

52 Sarah Barringer Gordon, *The Spirit of the Law* (Cambridge, MA: Belknap Press of Harvard University Press, 2010), 16.

egy was aggressive because their gospel was unique. Only 144,000 souls would be saved and salvation depended on sharing the gospel. No-one was safe – not Protestants, not Jews and certainly not Catholics. So they descended on towns by the thousands to distribute handbills from door to door and drive through main streets with loudspeakers declaring the end of time.

To put it mildly, this message "disturbed many listeners".[53] Many, especially Catholics, viewed the Witnesses' gospel as sacrilege. The Witnesses' tactics spurred official condemnation, arrests and sometimes violence. Because of their beliefs about the State, many accused the Witnesses of being a "fifth column" of Nazis (though the Nazis persecuted the Witnesses alongside other Nonconformists). The Witnesses, emulating the Apostle Paul, embraced criminal prosecution as persecution for the gospel even as they turned to the courts for protection.[54]

In a series of landmark cases involving prosecutions of Jehovah's Witnesses, the Supreme Court inaugurated modern First Amendment rights. A number of the cases invalidated laws placing restrictions on unauthorised solicitation. The Witnesses' motivation for solicitation was to share the gospel, but these cases have had an important legacy in American constitutional law well beyond religiously motivated speech.

Perhaps the most well-known cases brought the Witnesses into direct conflict with American civil religion. The Witnesses believed that pledging allegiance to a nation was idolatry. This included saluting the American flag. Refusing to salute the flag played into the national narrative that Jehovah's Witnesses were dangerous and un-American.[55] In *Minersville School District v. Gobitis* (1940), the Supreme Court held that the Free Exercise Clause of the First Amendment did not forbid a local school board from expelling children for refusing to salute the flag. For many, the decision confirmed the Witnesses' political treachery. Some took it as a licence for rough justice against those who did not conform to the soft establishment of a quasi-Christian civic religion. The American Civil Liberties Union reported physical attacks against nearly 1,500 Witnesses in over 300 towns.[56] Only three years after *Gobitis*, the Supreme Court reversed course in a landmark decision that forbade the government from coercing people to engage in political speech.[57]

In *West Virginia Board of Education v. Barnette* (1943), Justice Jackson wrote some of the most enduring rhetoric of the modern era about the limits of the State's authority to punish religious and political dissent. Jackson first acknowledged the symbolic power of saluting a flag, comparing it to a religious ritual:

53 Ibid., 24.

54 See Shawn Francis Peters, *Judging Jehovah's Witnesses: Religious Persecution and the Dawn of Rights Revolution* (Lawrence, KS: University Press of Kansas, 2000).

55 Gordon, *Spirit of the Law*, 15.

56 Peters, *Judging Jehovah's Witnesses*, 84.

57 The reversal was the product of changed personnel as well as changed minds. Justice Jackson, who wrote the opinion in *Barnette*, joined the Court after *Gobitis*. Justices Murphy, Black and Douglas changed their vote.

"the compulsory flag salute and pledge requires affirmation of a belief and an attitude of mind".[58] Such "attempts to compel coherence" have a direct forebear in "the Roman drive to stamp out Christianity as a disturber of pagan unity".[59] The Court had already held that the First Amendment protects political speech that does not present a clear and present danger of conflict.

> To sustain the compulsory flag salute we are required to say that a Bill of Rights which guards the individual's right to speak his own mind, left it open to public authorities to compel him to utter what is not in his mind.[60]

The Court concluded that:

> If there is any fixed star in our constitutional constellation, it is that no official, high or petty, can prescribe what shall be orthodox in politics, nationalism, religion or other matters of opinion or force citizens to confess by word or act their faith therein.[61]

Few cases have had as important a legacy as *Barnette*. It stands for the proposition that the government may not coerce a person into saying something against his conscience. Such an individual "right" is different from the structural limits of an independent jury. A defendant can invoke it to halt a prosecution or preempt a punishment for any coerced political or religious speech. No need to appeal to the conscience of a legislature, executive officer or jury. The Jehovah's Witnesses' radical Christianity led to an important constitutional right of political dissent and, conversely, an important limit on the government's authority to punish political nonconformance.

10.6 Conclusion

This chapter has argued that Christianity has played an important role in the government's authority to punish a unique set of crimes: those that involve political disloyalty, threats to governmental stability or interferences with the government's law enforcement. From its origin, Christianity's ambivalence about the role of the earthly government has given Christians good reason to support the government's authority, and good reason to resist it. The former has tended to expand the government's authority to punish crimes against the State, including crimes of religious dissent. The latter has tended to mitigate that power, structurally and substantively.

58 *West Virginia Board of Education v. Barnette*, 319 U.S. 624, 633 (1943).
59 Ibid. at 641.
60 Ibid. at 657.
61 Ibid. at 642.

Further reading

Augustine. *The City of God Against the Pagans*, ed. and trans. R.W. Dyson (Cambridge: Cambridge University Press, 1998), books 19 and 20.
Gordon, Sarah Barringer. *The Spirit of the Law* (Cambridge, MA: Belknap Press of Harvard University Press, 2010).
Hays, Richard B. *The Moral Vision of the New Testament: Community, Cross, New Creation* (San Francisco: Harper, 1996).
Marshall, Peter. *Heretics and Believers: A History of the English Reformation* (New Haven: Yale University Press, 2017).
O'Donovan, Oliver. *The Desire of the Nations* (Cambridge: Cambridge University Press, 1999).
O'Donovan, Oliver and Joan Lockwood O'Donovan, eds. *From Irenaeus to Grotius: A Sourcebook in Christian Political Thought 100–1625* (Grand Rapids: Wm. B. Eerdmans, 1999).
Rowe, C. Kavin. *World Upside Down: Reading Acts in the Graeco-Roman Age* (Oxford: Oxford University Press, 2009).

11 Christianity and offences against the person

David Etherington QC

Violence to others and sometimes ourselves is part of the human condition, seated deep within our nature, and is perhaps an inevitable ingredient, necessary for our evolution as a species. Two themes recur in offences against the person: the ability to exercise control and the notion of justification, not primarily in its theological sense but in its more general sense of providing a good reason or explanation for violence, particularly in the sense of vindication.

11.1 An uncomfortable relationship

Christianity has had to confront, explain, control, mitigate and, on occasion, justify violence since its inception. In the Old Testament, God appears to have been thought to have been involved on occasion with invoking, encouraging, causing, punishing, forgiving and explaining acts of violence. Running alongside narrative incidents, particularly in the Old Testament, are the covenants between God and humankind whereby in exchange for certain canons of behaviour, God will act protectively towards humanity. Humans will be responsible for human misdeeds: "Who so sheddeth man's blood, by man shall his blood be shed" (Gen. 9:6). The good news of Jesus Christ marked a highly significant step-change in this evolution: preaching a gospel stressing the value of a peaceful response to physical force. Jesus himself died as a result of State violence: a judicial execution.

In the name of Christianity, its adherents have fought wars against other religions and persecuted perceived heresies in their own. They have themselves used the civil power to punish those perceived to be a threat to their religion. Sometimes, the complexity of this relationship has been so great that it has been difficult to disentangle the religious element from the political or secular: the religious trial and secular execution of Jeanne d'Arc is such an example. Her punishment needed to be carried out by the civil power, in this case the English, as only the secular power could *punish* the heretic as opposed to "rehabilitating" her with "measures". This distinction was at the heart of the power struggle in England between Church and King over "benefit of clergy" – one which the State won only by attrition over centuries, with its complete departure from English criminal law only occurring in 1827.

11.2 The law and violence

The criminal law prohibits certain conduct and imposes punishment for the commission of crime. It places some control on behaviour and discourages certain conduct. It is concerned with behaviour that is injurious not necessarily to individual citizens, but to society as a whole. Its reach may be narrow, concentrating on the minimum prohibition needed to keep the peace or more far-reaching, trying to change the way society behaves in (as the State sees it) the interests of the population as a whole. Central among the concerns of most communities since earliest times is a fear of the infliction of unlawful violence upon them, from murder at one extreme to simple (or "common") assault at the other. Sometimes, it is a fear for the safety of another as opposed to oneself. There is also concern about violence and injustice in other States and communities around the world – the news of which can be brought to public attention by the media in an instant.

11.2.1 A central element: loss of control

Violence often involves some loss of self-control, in the general sense of the phrase. Loss of self-control is not a defence to any crime with the exception of murder, where it acts as a special and partial defence, not relieving a defendant of liability, but reducing the culpability of the offender from murder to manslaughter.[1] A jury will only consider it if it has otherwise convicted the defendant of murder. Here, it does not bear its general meaning but a specific legal one, confining and constraining the extent to which the special defence will be available.

Loss of control in its general sense can, of course, occur following a premeditated decision (good or bad), but more often it arises spontaneously as a result of actual or perceived provocation, frustration, jealousy or, in the case of the inebriated, for no discernible reason at all or, at any rate, none that can be explained subsequently by the perpetrator. Sometimes, the circumstances of violence may involve permission to inflict it within certain limits which are not always easy to define. An example is war, where the use of violence is controlled to a degree by military orders or, as another example, in the apprehension or prevention of crime. In these kinds of situations, the need for self-control is still there and the potential for crossing it is sometimes very great.

Even when the violence is pre-planned, a reduced ability to control one's actions may arise as a result of a recognised mental disorder such as schizophrenia, a personality disorder or some other mechanism.[2] As with the special and partial defence of loss of self-control, impairment of responsibility can

1 Coroners and Justice Act 2009, s. 54.

2 The partial defence of "diminished responsibility" is available only to reduce murder to manslaughter under s. 2 of the Homicide Act 1957, as substituted by s. 52 of the Coroners and Justice Act 2009.

be reduced to a point where, although a defendant would otherwise be convicted of murder, his or her liability will again be reduced to manslaughter, this time by the operation of the special and partial defence of diminished responsibility.

Insanity is a defence that removes criminal culpability in all situations except those of strict liability, because the insane person cannot have the necessary mental functioning, the *mens rea*, to appreciate his or her actions, form an intent, realise the consequences of so acting or understanding the result of inaction. So, concepts such as intention, recklessness and negligence have no application. The M'Naghten Rules established that the test of insanity was to be extremely tightly drawn.[3] Essentially, it amounts to a defence of cognitive insanity: an inability on the part of the defendant, through such a defect of reason from disease of the mind, to know the nature and quality of the act in question, or, alternatively, to know that the act was wrong. It therefore encompasses only two possibilities: someone who is, in informal language, raving mad or someone who cannot distinguish between right and wrong.

However, in the case of offences against the person, short of murder, situations involving unlawful violence come in all shapes and sizes. It may be a drunken fight between young men and some young women, bullying – which can extend to intolerance of someone's race, culture, ethnicity, skin colour, gender or sexual preferences[4] – as well as online abuse,[5] sexual violence, violence in perceived retaliation for a wrong suffered by the perpetrator, violence in the course of stealing, over-enthusiastic self-defence right through to mass violence to inflict terror or even genocide itself.[6]

3 Daniel M'Naghten meant to assassinate Robert Peel, then prime minister, on 20 January 1843, but shot and killed by mistake his private secretary, Edward Drummond. While it was agreed that he was insane in general terms, the question at his trial was whether he had a valid *legal* defence of insanity. He pleaded not guilty by reason of insanity and, after a trial where both sides interpreted the law of insanity in a way more favourable to the defendant than the subsequent definition provided afterwards when the House of Lords sought the opinion of the judges, the jury agreed with M'Naghten's plea. There is little doubt that he would have been convicted of murder had the M'Naghten Rules been in force before his trial rather than afterwards. Tried today, he would have been likely to have run the defence of diminished responsibility, with what success can only be imagined. The M'Naghten Rules apply today, despite considerable and sustained criticism of them.

4 Aggravated offences under the Crime and Disorder Act 1998, s. 29 et seq. provide offences for racial and religious hatred involving violence. There are enhanced sentencing powers for the judge under ss. 145 and 146 of the Criminal Justice Act 2003 in relation to all crimes for the five characteristics – race, religion, sexual orientation, transgender and disability.

5 The government has now classified online offences of abuse as violent crimes.

6 See the International Criminal Court Act 2001; and K. Grady, "International Crimes in the Courts of England and Wales", (2014) 10 *Criminal Law Review* 693–722.

11.3 Biblical attitudes to violence

Biblical injunctions against the infliction of violence by one or more persons on another can be found both in the Old and New Testament. Biblically, the writers (or editors) can, on occasion, place this violence in a neutral or even positive light.

See, for instance, Genesis 34: it is a nasty tale concerning the rape of Dinah while on a visit to the Shechemites. However, the prince of the Shechemites repented as he had fallen in love with her. An agreement was reached whereby they would marry and the two groups amalgamate provided the male Shechemites were circumcised. While they were still suffering the after-effects, Jacob's sons, who had only pretended to agree to the marriage, killed the males and made off with the women, children and chattels. When Jacob chided his sons, the defence and the justification were given in the memorable final verse at Gen. 34:31 – "And they said, should he deal with our sister as with an harlot?" There is no further comment.

The story in Genesis illustrates the extent to which a wrong, such as the infliction of unjustified violence by one person or group upon another or others, is a private wrong to be rectified by those affected or a public wrong. Even today, in some societies, a murder (and, indeed, any unnatural death) might be seen primarily as a matter between the perpetrator and the family of the deceased. Although the State will facilitate punishment if the family wish it, the matter may be capable of being settled by the payment of compensation. In some Middle Eastern countries, the word *diya* represents that payment: a word meaning both "blood money" and "ransom". This was also known historically to English custom as well. Where this is not acceptable, it is replaced by equal retaliation, which also has a long history. It has both biblical recognition and was known to other legal systems – the *lex talionis* in Roman law for instance. It is part of the Mosaic law,[7] although rejected in Jesus' teaching.[8]

11.4 Christianity, the State and the law

The relationship between Christianity and secular law (including criminal law) against non-consensual violence can be analysed and narrated without necessarily raising any tension between the two. Christianity has a complex and historically variable connection with civil power. The practice of religion cannot but engage the attention of government. It provides, teaches and is reliant on a higher authority. Indeed, for a significant part of Western history, monarchs have relied upon their power being derived from God, expressed in its purest form by the concept of divine right espoused by most monarchs.[9] Religions can suggest a future imposition

7 Exod. 21:24–25; Deut. 19:21; Lev. 24:20.
8 Matt. 5:38–39; Luke 6:29.
9 James I, *Defense of the Right of Kings* (London, 1615); and see Rom. 13:1–7.

of a higher penalty for disobedience than merely imprisonment or even execution. Its tenets will be accepted by its adherents as objectively true. It can, and often will, appeal to part of the human psyche beyond that of reason. It will have a fabric and a network that can make it exceptionally difficult to suppress. Religion can, therefore, be a dangerous force to the State, particularly an autocratic one.

Equally, it can also be a force capable of supporting the civil State. It can act to restrain anti-social human behaviour (including riotous, unlawful and uncontrolled violence) and give a collective focus to national aspiration. The apparatus of religion can be helpful to the State. Christianity has run the gamut of the reactions of States to religion. Christ did not make opposition to Roman rule a feature of his teaching. Indeed, the Synoptic Gospels suggest the contrary – "Render unto Caesar what is Caesar's".

Christianity shaped and was shaped by the character of the States in which it had taken root and sooner or later it became the "State" religion in western Europe. Simon of Sudbury was Bishop of London for 14 years before becoming Archbishop of Canterbury in 1375 until his murder in 1381, having also become Lord Chancellor in 1380. He had crowned Richard II in 1377. Unfortunately, like others before and after him, he also made the mistake of involving himself with a poll tax and was a prime target of the Peasants' Revolt. When those who had released the priest John Ball, from incarceration in Maidstone arrived at the Tower of London, they found that Ball's servants had left all the doors open and so they dragged him out and beheaded him on Tower Hill in a mock-judicial murder. He had paid the price for the connection between Church and State, not for opposition to it – a striking example of the dangers of proximity between the spiritual and the secular.

Putting offences of violence into this frame seems relatively simple at first blush. The need for any society to protect itself against unlawful violence by one citizen or group of citizens against another or others is clear and obvious. In his 2019 history of the life of Louis XIV – *King of the World* – Philip Mansel relates how one reported argument for conversion made to King Phra Narai of Siam was that Catholicism was the best religion to permit princes who espoused it to reign supreme, because Christianity by its laws obliged Christians to be both loyal and obedient to their princes or face damnation.

11.5 The English common law

The development of the common law in England and Wales also marks an understanding that violence is not just a private matter between citizens, but it affects society as a whole. Recent legal reforms have tried to place victims and their families nearer the centre of the court's consideration than they had been for some time.[10] Treating the unlawful killing or maiming of a human being as simply a

10 See the chapter by John Saunders at pp. 301–313 of this volume with its discussion of victim involvement in criminal sentencing and the work of the Parole Board.

matter between the perpetrator and the victim's family and friends with the community acting as an arbiter was insufficient to assuage a feeling of public wrong that accompanied a crime as well as preventing the community from assessing, however crudely, the degree of risk posed by the offender. By the late twentieth century, the victim and/or the family had become spectators in the trial with limited access to the process other than giving evidence if required. The humanising effect of allowing the victim of crime to be the subject of the case rather than the object was plainly correct and long overdue. While these changes were not caused by any overtly religious sentiment, they are consistent with a belief, found in Christianity and other religions, of the importance of the individual irrespective of his or her circumstances, background or beliefs.

11.5.1 Murder

Murder has always attracted particular opprobrium. Not only is it considered the gravest crime of violence, but also the peculiarities of causation have engendered the partial defences of diminished responsibility and loss of self-control. The Bible deals with murder for the first time in Gen. 4:1–24. It is a particularly repellent type of murder, namely that of a sibling. Genesis gives a nuanced account of how Cain came to slay Abel. Abel kept sheep; but Cain tilled the ground. Cain's offerings to the Lord were not acceptable perhaps for reasons rooted in Cain's character. Cain murdered Abel, presumably out of jealousy, in that, while of sound mind, he killed him, neither by accident nor in reasonable self-defence, intending to kill him or cause him grievous bodily harm. He would be convicted today. The only possible defence would be loss of self-control, and it is almost certain that this would fail. The minimum sentence today would be life imprisonment with a starting point of 15 years, which would be increased to reflect the killing of a brother. If he had used a bladed article or other weapon, then that starting point would increase to 25 years upwards. Cain was cast from God's presence into the wilderness. This brief and painfully evocative story, probably in fact from a later period, has many features present in the history of murder as a crime: the overreaction to personal factors by a particular type of personality, a premeditated killing, the wound to the community, the elements of taboo both within the act of killing and of fratricide, the hue and cry and the removal of the offender from society. In the Ten Commandments, we read "Thou shalt not kill" (Exod. 20:13), widely regarded as meaning "murder". In Proverbs 6:17, seven things abominable to the Lord include "hands that shed innocent blood". The shedding of the blood of enemies was treated differently: Genesis 34 is but one example.

11.5.2 "Justified" homicide

It is no part of the definition of murder to require the unlawful killing to be unjustified in the general sense of the word. So, for instance, the deliberate killing of a killer (other than by lawful execution) is just as much murder as the slaying of a child. It would mitigate the sentence, of course. All kinds of "justified" homicide have abounded throughout history; those justified by religion itself, by war, blood revenge and even the inferiority of the person murdered. Some forms of life destruction, such as abortion and suicide, have caused immense difficulties for societies and continue to do so.[11] Those holding Christian beliefs may find these types of cases very hard to resolve. Suicide remains illegal in more than 25 countries, including a large number of African and Middle Eastern countries,[12] and assisting suicide is illegal today in all but a handful of countries. Those who object to legalising suicide, attempted suicide or euthanasia vary in their reasons: sometimes it is a view that the act is sinful and wicked, is forbidden by a religion or is a violation of our bodies. However, objections to it are not confined to those holding a religious belief. Many societies have come to view it as pointless and cruel to make suicide itself a crime; adding yet another layer of anxiety and fear for someone whose mental state may already be disturbed. When considering the possibility of euthanasia for the terminally ill, some doctrinal objections may fall away, but even these people can be peculiarly vulnerable and open to abuse by those who might benefit from the death. Nevertheless, some people have to die slow and painful deaths. Belgium, Switzerland, Luxembourg, Germany (with some exceptions), Finland and (as of 19 June 2019) the State of Victoria in Australia do permit euthanasia.

Christian sensibilities are evident in respect of the funeral and burial of a suicide in consecrated ground. In the Church of England, the prohibition on so doing was widely flouted. Until the nineteenth century, if the deceased had not been of sound mind or had not been baptised, then burial was officially refused. By the 1880s, burial was possible but with an alternative service. This caused immense pain to families and friends. The decision of the General Synod of the Church of England to end the ban in 2017 (with some exceptions) was generally welcomed. Likewise, the Catholic Church has also relaxed its similar stance on suicide – not by retracting its theological position but because knowledge of the complexity of mental health has increased.

11.6 The partial defences

Murder is alone in having so-called partial defences, whereby even if the offence of murder is proven, legal culpability is reduced. These partial defences arose initially out of a desire not to execute someone where his or her moral liability had been reduced either by the effects of a recognised mental illness or by a justifiable loss of control. This accords with general Christian principles of mercy and individual responsibility.

11 By way of recent example, see the various judgments of the United Kingdom Supreme Court regarding Northern Irish abortion law in *In the matter of an application by the Northern Ireland Human Rights Commission for Judicial Review (Northern Ireland)* [2018] UKSC 27.

12 In England and Wales, suicide ceased to be a criminal offence in 1961.

11.6.1 Diminished responsibility

While the concept of diminished responsibility had a long history in Scottish law, it was introduced in England and Wales only in 1957. It was reformulated in the Coroners and Justice Act of 2009, but its operation was considerably reduced by the Supreme Court in *R. v. Golds* [2016] UKSC 61. The defence was available to a defendant with an abnormality of mental functioning which arose from a recognised medical condition that provided an explanation for the defendant's acts (and omissions) in either killing someone or being a party to the killing.

The problem area, somewhat skirted by the 1957 legislation which preceded the 2009 Act, related to the final requirement, namely that the defendant's mental condition substantially impaired his or her ability to (a) understand the nature of the act committed; (b) form a rational judgment; and (c) exercise self-control where that mental abnormality provided an explanation for the defendant's conduct or was a significant contributory factor in causing the defendant to do what had been done. The approach up until *Golds* was to leave the matter of substantial impairment to the jury. However, two lines of approach considered by the courts had identified two plausible possibilities: first, that "substantial" as in "substantially impaired" meant "of substance" as opposed to "fanciful" or second, that "substantial" meant "important" or "weighty". The Supreme Court decided that in many cases it may not be necessary to define "substantial" but that if the jury had been introduced to the question of whether any impairment beyond the merely trivial would suffice, the judge should explain that the impairment needed to pass the trivial before it could be considered and that it is not the case that any impairment beyond the trivial would suffice. The Supreme Court doubted whether the issue of definition would necessarily arise very often. However, the experience of practitioners is that juries frequently dislike "mental" defences and the best chance for a defendant in this situation is to persuade the Crown to accept a plea to manslaughter by reason of diminished responsibility. The decision in *Golds* makes this more difficult. The Crown Prosecution Service may feel it would be much more difficult to accept pleas to manslaughter based on diminished responsibility, particularly as the burden lies on the defendant to prove this defence on the balance of probabilities.

For the Christian, the dilemma lies in distinguishing a justifiable finding of murder as against an unjustifiable conviction of a person whose ability to understand the nature of what they did is impaired, who could not form a rational judgment at the time or was unable to exercise self-control by reason of a recognised mental abnormality. As to the degree of impairment that might give rise to reduced liability, that is a matter of judgment over which Christians will differ as with any other citizens.[13]

13 For further consideration of this subject, see David McIlroy's chapter in this volume: "Christianity, *Mens Rea* and the Boundaries of Criminal Liability" at pp. 116–132.

11.6.2 Loss of self-control

The Coroners and Justice Act 2009 created the defence of loss of control, replacing the former partial defence of provocation. Three elements have to be present: first, whether it is reasonably possible that the killing resulted from the defendant's loss of control; second, whether the loss of control had a "qualifying trigger"; and third, whether a person of the defendant's age with a normal degree of tolerance and self-restraint and, in the circumstances of the defendant, might have lost self-control to the degree that the defendant did, provided that the defendant did not act with a considered desire for revenge. The qualifying triggers are either that the defendant's loss of control was attributable to the defendant's fear of serious violence from the deceased or was attributable to things done or said which constituted circumstances of an extremely grave character and caused the defendant to have a justifiable sense of being seriously wronged (or a combination of both) provided the defendant did not incite the behaviour complained of with the purpose of using it as an excuse to justify violence.

Loss of self-control is freighted with complex concepts for a jury to consider: "loss of control", "normal degree of tolerance and self-restraint", "considered desire for revenge", "justifiable sense of being seriously wronged" and more. Christians will sympathise with the desire to hold someone accountable for murder while reflecting reduced responsibility for justifiable loss of self-control. But lawyers, whether Christian or not, might wonder whether this highly conceptualised approach is the best way to achieve this end, particularly when the ultimate decision lies with a jury of lay men and women. Some would argue that, as done in many countries, the better approach is to have different categories of murder. The United States, for example, has first degree and second degree murder, followed by voluntary and involuntary manslaughter and ending with justifiable homicide, which is not a crime.

11.7 The Offences Against the Person Act (OAPA) 1861

This mid-Victorian Act is still the most used vehicle for prosecuting offences of violence falling short of murder or manslaughter. Sexual offences were removed from it and are now grouped together under the Sexual Offences Act 2003. The reform had begun in the reign of George IV, and the 1861 Act was, in fact, a revision and further consolidation of an earlier statute of the same name.[14] It paints an evocative picture of Victorian England, containing the full package of violent crime short of murder. It is expressed in concise and direct language,[15] and was exported to British territories overseas. Echoes of its provisions occur in much Commonwealth legislation in this area to this day. One thing not clear to the Parliament of 1861 was how, in fact, most acts of violence could be met by sections 18, 20, 47 and 34 of the Act, with the particular method of infliction

14 Offences Against the Person Act 1828.

15 OAPA 1861, ss. 1–2.

being treated as a feature of the charge rather than a defining element of a discrete crime.

Some of the original crimes created by the Act were very specific: see for instance section 17, Impeding a person endeavouring to save himself from shipwreck; section 21, Attempting to choke, suffocate, or strangle any other person with intent to enable himself or any other person to commit any indictable offence; section 22, Using chloroform to commit any indictable offence; section 28, Causing bodily injury by gunpowder; section 31, Setting spring guns etc. with intent to inflict grievous bodily harm; section 33, Casting stone etc. upon a railway carriage with intent to endanger the safety of any person therein; section 37, Assaulting a magistrate on account of his preserving wreck. All of them, and others, are still in force except for their sentencing provision. Today, when drafting an indictment dealing with deliberately inflicted violence falling short of murder, the lawyer in England will go up (or down) the spectrum of causing grievous bodily harm (or wounding) with intent (section 18), causing grievous bodily harm or unlawful wounding (section 20) and assault occasioning actual bodily harm (section 47). Common assault (that is assault without necessarily any battery or injury) is dealt with by section 39 of the Criminal Justice Act 1988.

The OAPA was passed in 1861 by British Members of Parliament who doubtless were observant Christians, in a society that epitomised as its public face moral rectitude and technological advance while in truth having a much darker underbelly exposed by writers such as Charles Dickens. The Act evidences a confidence and certainty of right and wrong. Its language is both simple and complete, untroubled by the uncertainty of future ages. Perhaps the reason for the durability of the Act has been the use of case law rather than the statute itself to provide a more flexible method of interpretation than the unyielding rigidity of legislation. However, there is a body of opinion critical of the Act for being outdated and in need of reform. The late and highly respected Professor J.C. Smith considered it a rag-bag of offences collected from a variety of sources. While it is desirable not to have obsolete or little-used offences littering our statute book, the need to repeal some of the more colourful sections has perhaps not been sufficiently urgent to command parliamentary time. It is also a fair criticism that the language is old-fashioned as was observed by the Law Commission in 2014,[16] although arcane terminology does not impede the practical use of the legislation.

There is, however, one serious criticism of the OAPA, namely the sentencing structure. Section 18 carries a maximum sentence of life imprisonment. Section 20 has a maximum sentence of five years. This is the same maximum as section 47 (assault occasioning actual bodily harm). To the Victorian mind this would not have been illogical as it is primarily concerned with what the defendant intended, but that view carried more weight in criminal sentencing

16 Law Commission, *Reform of the Offences Against the Person: A Scoping Paper*, Law Commission Consultation Paper No. 217, 2014, http://www.lawcom.gov.uk/app/uploads/2015/06/cp217_offences_against_the_person.pdf.

than it does now. In terms of punishment, there was a discernible change in the 1990s and 2000s to concentrate upon and reflect the *effect* of the offender's act. Nowhere has this been more noticeable than in causing death by dangerous driving. Features such as the number of people who are in a car that has been struck by a defendant can affect the sentence, although it was unbeknown to the perpetrator. Previously, it was assumed that the sentence reflected these variables and possibilities in its overall structure. Movement up and down the sentencing scale of severity was far more likely to result from the defendant's knowledge and intention, or the fact that the risk should have been appreciated by the defendant in the particular circumstances, as opposed to purely retributive considerations. There clearly was a major shift in this approach which has also been reflected in sentencing guidelines issued by the Sentencing Council.

How should Christian belief best consider what appears to be a move towards a more retributive approach? Is there a Christian view? Superficially, retribution may be viewed as a specific justification for a wrongful act – "an eye for an eye". However, retribution also has a positive value in protecting society as a whole from a breakdown of order or a loss of confidence in the law. If the victims of violent crime do not feel the law is reflecting, even assuaging, their hurt, then sooner or later they will seek their own redress or simply revile the legal system under which they live. It will affect their ability to overcome the suffering they have endured as a result of the crime. In that sense, retribution is not exclusively a retrograde concept but has both beneficial and necessary effects. Law often develops as a result of a political reaction to a particular situation. The politician is reacting to a perception about public opinion often arising from a particular case or crime and a perceived inadequacy of the State's response to it. This is magnified by attention coming from the media, and the likely scrutiny through print media, radio and television, and the ubiquitous social media will be intense and of unpredictable duration.

It is also far from clear that the apparently retributive stance taken at points in the Bible was simply evoking the principle of retribution for its own sake. An eye for an eye is one thing that may evoke concepts of reciprocity and proportionality, but taken to extremes can inspire blood feuds or worse. Mahatma Gandhi reputedly observed that an eye for an eye would render the whole world blind. Is Jesus telling us we should always respond to violence by turning the other cheek or presenting a startling concept to force us to think about whether violence for violence is the only, or best, response to an inflicted injury?

11.8 Consensual violence[17]

Thus far, this chapter has considered violence inflicted on another person without that person's consent. Except in situations where such violence on another

17 For a comprehensive review, see Law Commission, *Criminal Law: Consent in the Criminal Law*, Law Commission Consultation Paper No. 139 (London: HMSO, 1995); more gen-

is specifically allowed (medical intervention, competitive sport[18] and so on), the law does not generally permit anything more than the most minor violence on another[19] even if that other specifically wishes it either for its own sake or as an accepted consequence of something else that the other person desires. Such activity may be a by-product of religious fervour, sporting injury such as the punching game where consenting adults seek to withstand the punches of each other and prize fighting,[20] through to extreme violence inflicted for mutual sexual pleasure.[21] The message of Christianity and that of the criminal law may be coterminous in certain of these situations, but in some areas it is possible for Christianity not to condemn violence against another which is unlawful, or for Christians, and civil society more generally, to tolerate certain conduct that the law chooses not to criminalise. Some Christians may view mortification of the flesh for a godly purpose as entirely justified, some Christians may ally with the State's current view that one human being should not assist another to kill himself or herself and individual Christians may frown upon conduct in the field of sexual pleasure that is considered by the State not to be its business.

Our civilisation has reached a point where we are exploring, or possibly reverting to, bodily alterations involving pain, such as piercing, tattooing and tongue-splitting. Are these properly treated in the same category as medical interventions, particularly in the field of cosmetic surgery, or are they no more than permitting an individual to disfigure, maim or incapacitate himself or herself?[22] In the well-known prosecution arising from *Operation Spanner*, which had investigated and prosecuted instances of gay sadomasochism in England and Wales in the late 1980s, 16 men were charged with offences under the Offences Against the Person Act 1861. The trial began at the Central Criminal Court in October 1990, with defence submissions that all the behaviour described and, in many instances, filmed was consensual and thus lawful. The well-known prize-fighting case of *Coney*[23] had found bare-knuckle fighting to be illegal and the activities in

erally, see Alan Reed and Michael Bohlander (with Nicola Wake and Emma Smith), eds., *Consent: Domestic and Comparative Perspectives* (Abingdon: Routledge, 2017).

18 The House of Lords in *Brown* [1994] AC 212 explicitly exempted consensual violence perpetrated in the course of lawful sports and games. See Mark James, "Consent: Revisiting the Exemption for Contact Sports", in Reed et al., *Consent: Domestic and Comparative Perspectives*, 177–90.

19 It is usually overlooked or tolerated, rather than expressly permitted.

20 On the lawfulness of boxing, see Michael Gunn and David Ormerod, "The Legality of Boxing", (1995) 15 *Legal Studies* 181–203; and John Joseph Anderson, *The Legality of Boxing: A Punch Drunk Love?* (London: Birkbeck Law Press, 2007). On prize-fighting and similar, see *Coney* (1882) 8 QBD 534 and *Brown* [1994] AC 212.

21 See in particular *Donovan* [1934] 25 Cr App R 1 CCA, 2 KB 498. See also L.H. Leigh, "Sado-Masochism, Consent and the Reform of the Criminal Law", (1976) 39 *Modern Law Review* 130–46.

22 See *R. v BM* [2018] EWCA Crim 560, on which see also Tracey Elliott, "Body Dysmorphic Disorder, Radical Surgery and the Limits of Consent", (2009) 17 *Medical Law Review* 149–82.

23 *R. v. Coney* (1882) 8 QBD 534.

Spanner (irrespective of motive or consent) made *Coney* look very mild by comparison. A conviction in the 1930s for beating a woman with a cane was found by the judge to fall the wrong side of the line, notwithstanding that she was a willing participant.[24] The House of Lords in the *Spanner* appeal reviewed these and other authorities and concluded that the consent of the receiving party was not a valid legal defence to a charge of actual bodily harm inflicted by another.[25]

The difference between being maimed in the name of fashion and being injured for sexual pleasure may seem to involve a line that is easy to draw. In the first case, the piercing and inking of the body are because of the wish of the person to enhance his or her own appearance. In the second case, it is for the sheer pleasure of the infliction of the pain itself. But the change in appearance may often be with the aim of making the individual more attractive sexually. Some piercings today bear an uncomfortable resemblance to activities investigated in *Operation Spanner*, though in that case, the recipient derived pleasure from the violence and pain. The case itself drew protest marches, a support group and a newspaper, but the Law Commission's recommendation for decriminalisation was not taken up by the legislature. Various biblical injunctions condemn mutilation for appearance enhancement (vanity) and for sexual pleasure (perverting the true purpose of sexual union), but why should the criminal law forbid it? Christian denominations vary in their attitude to sexual acts committed other than for the procreation of children. Some stress the particular and sacred union of husband and wife and disapprove of sexual activity outside marriage. Others, explicitly or in practice, are more tolerant and liberal. There are people of faith, as well as others of none, who deplore what they see as a breakdown of civilised norms.

In the 1970s and 1980s, the debate on sexual mores was more ferocious than today. The National Viewers and Listeners Association, founded by Mary Whitehouse, was heavily influenced by Christian values and the perceived dangers of permissiveness. The Association promoted the National Festival of Light, a primarily Christian evangelical movement. Mrs Whitehouse herself provoked widely different reactions: support on the one hand and remorseless parodying on the other. She could be disarming, with a keen sense of humour. Trained as a teacher, she could use teaching skills, fierce determination and a certain dignity that appealed to people worried by the loosening of sexual morals. She also deployed the law in support of what she considered immutable Christian values. Malcolm Muggeridge (who supported the Festival of Light) proclaimed that without her there would have been a total destruction of Christian moral

24 *Donovan* [1934] 25 Cr App R 1 CCA, 2 KB 498.

25 *R. v. Brown* [1993] UKHL 19, 1 AC 212, 11 March 1993, HL. See also three of the defendants' appeals to the European Court of Human Rights: *Laskey and Ors v. The United Kingdom* 21627/9, 21826/93, 21974/93 Chamber Judgment [1997] ECHR 4. The ECHR upheld the House of Lords decision ruling that the laws were necessary in a democratic society for the protection of health, a similar view to that expressed by the trial judge.

values. Notably, she brought a successful private prosecution against *Gay News* for its publication of a controversial poem concerning a sadomasochistic fantasy by a fictional centurion present at the crucifixion. Neither Cardinal Hume nor the Archbishop of Canterbury consented to be witnesses for the prosecution. Whatever its artistic merits (not particularly trumpeted by anyone including the author), a storm of criticism arose following the verdict of guilty, which was subsequently overturned.[26] Mary Whitehouse was to say that her specific reason for bringing the prosecution was to protect Christ.[27] Sexual mores change – not only in one direction. Mary Whitehouse's *Gay News* campaign might have even more force today, with heightened religious sensitivities, although some of her other concerns about banning pornography have been overtaken by the internet, and her campaign against "sex toys" seems trapped in its own time. Her position on possessing child pornography and paedophilia would be, and has now become, obvious and unchallenged.

The police and the courts avoid the problematic issue of mortification of the flesh[28] in a religious context, as it seems did Mrs Whitehouse, particularly where those concerned are members of established religions and adults. For Christians, there are traditions of such mortification, sometimes severe. Sir Thomas More's hair shirt comes to mind. The Bible reminds us: "if by the spirit you put to death the deeds of the body, you will live" (Rom. 8:13). Matthew tells us that "if thine eye offend thee, pluck it out and cast it from thee" (Matt. 5:29–30). This may, of course, be deliberate exaggeration to drive home how great sacrifice is required to follow Jesus – and is worth the earthly cost.

While suicide was a mortal sin historically, perhaps St Paul's answer to whether any particular kind of behaviour can permanently destroy any possibility of redemption increasingly governs modern thinking. In Rom. 8:35, he asks rhetorically: who shall separate us from the love of Christ? Paul answers:

> I am persuaded, that neither death, nor life, nor angels, nor principalities, nor powers, nor things present, nor things to come, Nor height, nor depth, nor any other creature, shall be able to separate us from the love of God, which is in Christ Jesus our Lord.
>
> (Rom. 8:38–9)

Christian principles unsurprisingly coincide in part with secular views concerning acts of violence. Where violence is consensually inflicted, Christians are again likely to reflect the same divergence of opinion as secular society. Not

26 *R. v. Lemon* [1979] AC 617.

27 See Jeroen Temperman's chapter: "Crimes against God and the Church" at pp. 204–219 of this volume.

28 Mortification of the flesh is an act by which an individual or group seeks to mortify, or put to death, their sinful nature, as a part of a process of sanctification. In Christianity, common forms of mortification that are practised include fasting, abstinence, as well as pious kneeling.

everyone supports competitive boxing, for instance, whether Christian or not, and probably for similar reasons. Where violence is consensual but crosses a line judged by the law as unacceptable and not in a person's interest, a Christian perspective may support the law or may be indifferent to that law while having a view about the morality of the conduct. A Christian, like any citizen, may disapprove of the law being applied, believing the decision to be one for individual conscience. This is not easy. The age or mental state of the person, whether the individual has been corrupted or whether a financial motive is present, may all affect how it is viewed. The law sets out the conditions that make certain conduct criminal. However, the moral or religious aspect will involve a far more complex analysis.

Jesus is a remarkable teacher. He uses powerful and memorable imagery to introduce startling and unexpected events, encouraging the listener to think about the matter in a fresh way. It is not so much that he reminds us of a law that might have been forgotten, but that he makes one think differently about it. Jesus is critical of law and lawyers: for the Pharisees in particular, the law became an end in itself, and they did not practise what they preached. It is doubtful that Jesus, an observant Jew, disrespected the law. He disliked the way it was being used and how there was one law for some and another for everyone else. In his famous ordering of the law, Jesus prioritises two great commandments: first, to love God with all one's might; and, second, to love one's neighbour as oneself – on these hang all the law and the prophets. Religious law evolves, but Jesus does not disrespect it. The law on offences against the person evolves too with courts interpreting the words of the 1861 Act as new situations arise.

11.9 When the writing is on the wall

People may seek to justify the commission of crime by reference to their particular circumstances. However, it is extremely rare for defendants to attempt to justify, say, stealing, although the individual circumstances may well be relied upon in mitigation. In nearly all criminal cases involving dishonesty, the defendant will either deny the wrong-doing or accept occurrence of the dishonest act and attempt to mitigate it. However, in offences against the person, the position is different. It is common for defendants to justify the violence: "I was provoked", "I was defending myself", "I feared for my own safety", "I was trying to protect someone else". This is not usually a cynical ploy but represents the defendant's state of mind at the time. The problem multiplies with those who believe in a cause sufficiently to justify acts of extreme violence in promoting it. It can be hard to understand the mentality of someone killing or maiming another unless the violence is perpetrated in support of something in which we ourselves believe. Take the example of British agents operating in occupied France in the Second World War. Acts of violence might be justified in that situation, which we would deplore in the case of a terrorist operating in our own country in peacetime.

Justification is a potent force and a belief that one is carrying out God's will, or that of any other deity, can be an exceptionally potent justification. This is illustrated by the case of the Reverend Clive Blake.[29] He committed no act of violence but damaged property to draw attention to what he considered to be unlawful violence against innocent people being perpetrated by the Western alliance in Iraq, believing himself wholly justified in what he did and also innocent as a matter of law. In 1991, using a permanent felt-tip marker, Mr Blake reproduced the words written on the wall at Belshazzar's Feast (*mene, mene, mene, teckel u-pharsin* – interpreted as God has numbered the days of your kingdom and brought it to an end) on a concrete pillar at the corner of Bridge Street and Parliament Square. Conviction was perhaps inevitable, and Blake was conditionally discharged. He appealed to the Crown Court. The conviction was affirmed. Both courts found him both sincere and exceptionally courteous. He appealed again to the Divisional Court, Queen's Bench Division. He appeared in person. He had written the words. They constituted criminal damage to the pillar. He was sane. There was no duress. The governing statute was the Criminal Damage Act 1971. He would have had a defence under section 5 of the Act if he honestly believed the person(s) entitled to give consent had done so or would have done so had they known of the circumstances. Blake argued that he had acted as directed by God. He had thought and prayed and sought divine guidance. He firmly, genuinely and sincerely believed he was God's agent, as much as the finger that wrote the words at Belshazzar's Feast. The Court found, with regret, that a belief that God had authorised someone to commit what would otherwise be a crime did not afford a defence to the charge. For Stephen J had argued in an earlier case: "if a special divine order were given to a man to commit murder, I should certainly hang him for it unless I got a special divine order *not* to hang him".[30] But if Blake's belief had been genuinely and honestly held, the statutory defence would have been available and it is arguable that he was wrongly convicted.

11.10 Concluding thoughts

Law, particularly criminal law, is never simply a matter of people deciding what sort of conduct is worthy of prohibition and punishment and what is not. It is inextricably linked to our beliefs which, in most societies, will have been formed with reference to the divine. The precept "render unto Caesar" reminds us that citizens who profess any faith, owe duties both to the divine and to the State. Although in many respects, particularly concerning offences of violence, these duties will coincide, sometimes they do not. However, when it comes

29 An edited transcript of the judgment of Otton J in the Divisional Court may be found in: Mark Hill, *Ecclesiastical Law* 1st ed. (London: Butterworths, 1995), 13–17.

30 James F. Stephen. *A History of the Criminal Law of England*, 3 vols. (repr. Cambridge: Cambridge University Press, 2014), 160.

to consensual violence, or violence the State considers lawful, how does the Christian's duty stand as against his or her Christian beliefs? Should the Christian follow faith or secular law where the two conflict? The furore that occurred with *Operation Spanner* and consensual sadomasochism has largely subsided. If it still happens, no-one appears to be taking much interest. Christians have as much right as any other citizen to express their views on matters, including moral ones, and to take the steps allowed in a democracy to influence public opinion and register their approval or disapproval within the law. They have just as much of a duty and responsibility as any other citizen to obey the law as it stands at any one time. Ultimately, the rule of law is a protection without which the implied contract between governed and governors would cease to exist. Christians have to consider whether undermining or disobeying the law is justified if it weakens or destroys the rule of law itself. The twin features that run through offences against the person, loss of self-control and justification, have differing impacts on the acceptance of law. Loss of self-control is part of the human condition, and the law must balance justice to the victims with reflecting the culpability of the offender. Fairness looks in both directions, and at different times, the balance will shift to reflect political reality.

Justification provides an equal if different challenge. With the unhappy rise of religious and cultural intolerance in modern times, there is a risk of individuals or groups seeking to justify unlawful violence. As has been the case throughout our history, religious conflict can be a particularly pernicious catalyst for this kind of self-justification. Those who become convinced that breaking the law is justifiable can present a great danger to civil society as a whole. Those who commit outrages in the name of religion may do so in part to provoke hostility. Conflict within and between religious faiths is a sure way to increase human misery without useful purpose, just as does the persecution of any individual or group in the name of a religion. We should have *more* understanding as both Christians and non-Christians of what makes people lose self-control and inflict violence on others, and work together on how to help people manage those feelings or cope with mental illnesses and have less time for spurious justifications of violence, particularly violence inflicted in the name of any religion.

Further reading

Collins, John J., ed. *Does the Bible Justify Violence?* (Minneapolis: Augsburg Fortress, 2004).

Hobbes, Thomas. *Leviathan* (London: A. Crooke, 1651).

King, Peter J., ed. *Christianity and Violence* (Scotts Valley, CA: CreateSpace Independent Publishing Platform, 2016).

Ormerod, David and K. Laird, eds. *Smith, Hogan, and Ormerod's Criminal Law* (Oxford: Oxford University Press, 2018).

Reed, Alan and M. Bolander. *Loss of Control and Diminished Responsibility – Domestic, Comparative and International Perspectives* (Farnham: Ashgate, 2011).

Smith, John C. *Justification and Excuse in the Criminal Law*, Hamlyn Lectures (London: Stevens & Sons, 1989).

Steffen, Lloyd. "Religion and Violence in Christian Traditions", in M. Jerryson, M. Juergensmeyer, and M. Kitts, eds., *The Oxford Handbook of Religion and Violence* (Oxford: Oxford University Press, 2013).

12 Law like love like language

The Christian uses of property crime

John F. Stinneford[1]

12.1 A property crime caused the fall of man

As the Book of Genesis tells us, God created the heavens and the earth, the birds of the sky, the fish of the sea, the animals of the earth. He also created humans "in the image of himself, in the image of God he created him, male and female he created them" (Gen. 1:27). God commanded Adam and Eve, the first human beings, to "Be fruitful, multiply, fill the earth and subdue it", made them "masters of the fish of the sea, the birds of heaven and all the living creatures that move on earth" and gave them "all the seed-bearing plants everywhere on the surface of the earth, and all the trees with seed-bearing fruit" for their food (Gen. 1:28–29). He also "planted a garden in Eden" containing "every kind of tree, enticing to look at and good to eat, with the tree of life in the middle of the garden, and the tree of the knowledge of good and evil" (Gen. 2:8–9). God "took the man and settled him in the garden of Eden to cultivate and take care of it", and commanded him: "You are free to eat of all the trees in the garden. But of the tree of the knowledge of good and evil you are not to eat; for, the day you eat of that, you are doomed to die" (Gen. 2:15–17).

At first, Adam and Eve followed God's command. But one day a snake approached Eve and convinced her that if she ate the fruit of the tree of the knowledge of good and evil, she would not die. Rather, "the day you eat it your eyes will be opened and you will be like gods, knowing good from evil" (Gen. 3:5). Eve saw that the fruit was

> good to eat and pleasing to the eye, and that it was enticing for the wisdom that it could give. So she took some of its fruit and ate it. She also gave some to her husband who was with her, and he ate it.
>
> (Gen. 3:6)

1 The title of this chapter derives from some lines of Auden: "Like love we don't know where or why, / Like love we can't compel or fly, / Like love we often weep, / Like love we seldom keep". W H Auden, "Law, like love" in *Collected Shorter Poems 1927–1957* (London: Faber and Faber, 1969), 154.

The consequences of this act are familiar to us all: Adam and Eve became aware of their nakedness and so shame entered the world. When God asked what they had done, each found someone else to blame and so alienation entered the world. Adam and Eve were exiled from Eden and denied access to the tree of life. Death entered the world right on the heels of disobedience, shame and alienation (Gen. 3:7–24).

Adam and Eve's act of disobedience may be thought of not only as a sin but also as a crime. An authoritative lawgiver (and property owner) gave them a command backed by a sanction: "Do not eat the fruit from this tree. If you do, the penalty is death". If an English or American court had jurisdiction over this act, Adam and Eve could properly be charged with larceny – the trespassory taking and carrying away of the property of another with the intent to permanently deprive him thereof.[2] Or they could be charged with malicious mischief, for they intentionally destroyed or damaged the property of another.[3] Or perhaps (although it is a bit of a stretch) they could be charged with attempted identity theft, for they consumed God's property in the hope that this would enable them to assume God's identity.[4] If they had committed this act in England, they could be accused of "scrumping".[5]

Why is any of this important? Crime is not the same thing as sin, although the two often overlap. Blackstone defines crime as "a breach and violation of the public rights and duties due to the whole community, considered as a community, in its social aggregate capacity".[6] Sin, on the other hand, has been defined as "a transgression of the divine law and an offence against God".[7] When we commit a crime, we violate a duty to the community; when we commit a sin, we violate a duty to God. We can commit crimes without sinning and we can commit sins without violating the criminal law.

Nonetheless, crime and sin cannot be entirely disentangled. Both ordinarily require that the offender possess a culpable state of mind. Most criminal acts are also prohibited by divine law (although the reverse is not true in modern secular states). Even where the positive law prohibits an act that is not sinful in itself for example, a regulatory crime – Christians are normally bound in conscience to obey the law, so that a knowing violation of it might be considered a sin.[8]

2 See, e.g. Bryan A. Garner and Henry Campbell Black, eds., *Black's Law Dictionary*, 10th ed. (St. Paul: Thompson Reuters, 2014), entry for "larceny".

3 See, e.g. ibid., entry for "malicious mischief".

4 See, e.g. ibid., entry for "identity theft".

5 See, e.g. "scrump, v.", *OED Online*, Oxford University Press, December 2018, www.oed.com/view/Entry/173731 (accessed 20 January 2019), defining "scrump" as "To steal fruit, esp. apples, from an orchard or garden".

6 William Blackstone, *Commentaries on the Laws of England*, 4 vols. (Philadelphia, 1771–2), 4:5.

7 "sin, n.", *OED Online*, Oxford University Press, June 2018, http://www.oed.com/view/Entry/180030 (accessed 2 September 2018).

8 See, e.g. Romans 13:1: "Let everyone be subject to the governing authorities, for there is no authority except that which God has established".

The relationship between sin and property crime is even more complicated. Property can be an occasion of sin not only for the person who commits a property crime but also for the person who lawfully owns property or even wishes to own it. A person who commits a property crime such as theft, robbery, burglary or arson violates the command to love his neighbour as himself; but so, too, does a person who acts upon an inordinate love of his own property or a selfish desire for the property of others. Punishment for a property crime may awaken repentance in the heart of the offender and rekindle his love of God and neighbour. Similarly, victims of property crime may learn from their loss that they have vainly focused their love on something transitory rather than something eternal. Finally, when we take care of the victims of crime, or when others care for us after we have been victimised, this may help us recognise each other as neighbours who are proper objects of our love. In this sense, property crime has a redemptive use. The fact that property crimes occur and are punished may lead us from the love of perishable things to the love of God and neighbour.

In this chapter, I will explore the Christian uses of property crime. I will not attempt to show the influence of Christianity on the development of property crime doctrines or sentencing practices. Although Christianity doubtless had some influence on these doctrines and practices, such influence appears to be relatively limited. Property crimes under pagan Roman law seem pretty similar to property crimes under England's explicitly Christian common law.[9] Nor will I attempt to use Christianity to critique modern property crime doctrine or to argue for sentencing reform. Rather, I will explore the ways in which Christianity – particularly in the Gospels – uses property crime as an occasion to redirect our love away from transitory things and towards God and neighbour.

My primary analytical tool for this project is St Augustine's *On Christian Doctrine.*[10] Augustine wrote this work as an instruction manual for interpreting and expounding sacred Scripture. But in the course of providing such instructions, Augustine engaged in a profound meditation on the nature of language, sin, law and love. In this chapter, I will first discuss the treatment of these themes in *On Christian Doctrine* and then use this discussion as a framework for analysing the uses of property crime in the Gospels.

12.2 *On Christian Doctrine*

Two distinctions lie at the heart of *On Christian Doctrine*: the distinction between things that are signs and things that are not, and the parallel distinction between things that are to be used and things that are to be enjoyed. The first distinction tells us how to interpret Scripture and the second tells us how to live.

9 See James Fitzjames Stephen, *A History of the Criminal Law of England*, 3 vols. (London: Macmillan, 1883), 1:24–65.

10 Augustine, *On Christian Doctrine*, http://www.ntslibrary.com/PDF%20Books/Augustine%20doctrine.pdf (accessed 22 January 2019).

Augustine defines a sign as a thing that makes us think of something else. We might think of it as a kind of pointer. When we see a sign, our minds do not rest in the thing itself but instead move to the thing it signifies. Footprints on the ground make us think of the animal that made the footprints; smoke makes us think of a fire; the sound of a person's voice makes us think of the thoughts he or she is trying to communicate, as do that person's words on a page.

Augustine notes that some signs are natural and some are conventional. A natural sign is not created with an intention to communicate. For example, an animal's footprints signify the existence of the animal even though the animal did not intend such signification. Conventional signs, on the other hand, are signs that rational beings use to communicate the thoughts or feelings in their minds. Interpreters of conventional signs "seek nothing more than to find out the thought and will" of the speaker or writer.[11]

Christians believe that the writers of Holy Scripture intended to communicate the will of God and that they did so in an accurate and reliable way. The purpose of interpreting Scripture is to learn the will of God by understanding the ideas communicated by its writers. In other words, Scripture is meant to help bridge the nearly infinite gap between God and humanity. It is a sign that points from the finite to the infinite.

In order to help the Christian understand how to approach the interpretation of Scripture, Augustine provides several examples of what *not* to do – that is, examples of failed interpretation. The three primary examples he employs are the pagan reading of nature, the Jewish reading of the law and contemporary confusion between custom and moral truth.

Augustine argues that the fundamental error of pagan religion was to confuse signs with the things they signify. He takes as his example a statue of Neptune, the Roman god of the sea. Some pagans would worship the statue as though it were a god. This was a failure of interpretation, for the statue is manifestly a sign of Neptune – a thing that is meant to point the mind towards the idea of the god – not Neptune himself. But the problem goes even deeper, for Neptune himself was a mere sign, not the true object of signification. The pagans saw the beauty and sublimity of the ocean and thought that the ocean itself was a god. Similarly, they saw the glory of the sun and thought the sun was a god. They worshipped the sun, the ocean and other created things rather than recognising that the beauty, sublimity and glory of such things was meant to point their minds towards the beauty, sublimity and glory of the one who made them. From the perspective of truth, it is no better to worship the ocean than it is to worship a statue: "he is in bondage to a sign who uses, or pays homage to, any significant object without knowing what it signifies".[12] The pagans were in bondage to useless signs.

11 Ibid., 2.6.
12 Ibid., 2.9.13.

If the pagans were in bondage to useless signs, Augustine argued that the Jewish people prior to the time of Christ were in bondage to a "useful" sign – namely, the law. Unlike the pagans, the Jewish people knew that the purpose of the law was to lead them to God. Thus, St Paul wrote that the law was like a tutor for schoolchildren.[13] But the law could not itself bridge the gap between humanity and God, and so Augustine argued that many Jews were led to worship the law rather than using it as a sign. This was why Jewish leaders took offence when Jesus chose to heal on the Sabbath – they were in bondage to the law and so they could not recognise the one it signified, even when he walked among them.

Augustine's third example of failed interpretation is the tendency he noted in his own time to equate custom with the will of God. People tend to accept without question practices that are common to their culture, even where such practices are forbidden by Scripture, and to condemn practices that are countercultural, even where such practices are required by Scripture. If the people are Christian, they deal with the cognitive dissonance by claiming that the scriptural injunctions are "figurative", and that they do not really mean what they seem to mean. Augustine acknowledges that some scriptural passages really are figurative but asserts that the test for determining whether they are to be taken literally or figuratively is not whether a literal reading comports with custom. Rather, the question is whether the literal reading encourages love of God and neighbour. If so, the passage should be read literally. On the other hand, if a given reading of Scripture encourages "lust", which Augustine defines as "that affection of the mind which aims at enjoying one's self and one's neighbour, and other corporeal things, without reference to God",[14] it is to be rejected – even if it comports with the custom of the time.

In a sense, according to Augustine, these failures of interpretation were inevitable prior to the Incarnation. God is infinitely beyond human reason. Even to call God ineffable involves one in a contradiction, for the term describes something that is indescribable. In thinking of God, people imagine the highest form of excellence they can bring to mind. For some, imagination fastens on created things like the ocean or the sun, for others it fastens on the law, and for still others the focus is custom. Human reason cannot pass beyond these bounds because the finite cannot grasp the infinite.

Because humanity could not cross the gulf between them and God, God did so instead by becoming incarnate. By taking on flesh, Jesus became both sign and signified. He said, "I am the Way, the Truth, and the Life". He is the Way – the link between worldly creation and God, sign and signified; he is the Truth – he is God himself; and he is the Life – the place where we will rest and live when we are united with God in eternity. Viewed in this way, all of creation is a system of signification. All created things point to God, and Jesus is the link that connects them to him.

13 See Galatians 3:24.

14 Augustine, *On Christian Doctrine*, 3.10.16.

This brings us to Augustine's second major distinction in *On Christian Doctrine*: the distinction between things we are to use and things we are to enjoy. This distinction helps us understand not only how to interpret Scripture but also how to live. According to Augustine, we are to enjoy things that make us happy and we are to use things that "support us in our efforts after happiness, so that we can attain the things that make us happy and rest in them".[15] In other words, "to enjoy a thing is to rest with satisfaction in it for its own sake. To use, on the other hand, is to employ whatever means are at one's disposal to obtain what one desires."[16]

It is crucially important to understand what will make us happy and what will not. If we allow ourselves to be distracted by things that are proper objects of use rather than enjoyment, we may never obtain happiness. Augustine draws the analogy of a wanderer in a strange land, trying to find his way home. Such a traveller may become so charmed by the beauty of the lands through which he passes, and the pleasure of the motion, that he never finishes his journey. So it is with us: "We have wandered far from God; and if we wish to return to our Father's home, this world must be used, not enjoyed, that so the invisible things of God may be clearly seen".[17]

According to Augustine, the only thing that can truly make us happy is God. As he wrote in *The Confessions*, "You have made us for yourself, and our hearts are restless until they rest in you". But this raises a question. If God is the proper object of our enjoyment, how are we to relate to the world around us? Jesus said that all of the law and prophets are contained in these commandments: "Love God with all your heart, and with all your soul, and with all your mind" and "Love your neighbour as yourself" (Matt. 22:37–40). If God is the only proper object of our enjoyment and if all other things (including ourselves and our neighbours) are objects of use rather than enjoyment, in what sense are we to "love" them? And what should our attitude be to the things in this world that are neither self nor neighbour?

Augustine phrases this question as "Should man be loved for his own sake, or for the sake of something else?" His answer is that humans should not be loved for their own sake but for the sake of God. We should not even love ourselves for our own sake, for this cannot lead to happiness. Augustine supports this point with a surprising psychological insight: we are happiest when we are not thinking of ourselves but are focused on a good outside of ourselves. For a person is "never in so good a state as when his whole life is a journey towards the unchangeable life, and his affections are entirely fixed upon that".[18] Similarly, we are often most unhappy when we focus on ourselves for our own sake. A person whose love turns inward "does not enjoy himself at his best". A selfish kind of self-love is morally

15 Ibid., 1.3.
16 Ibid., 1.4.
17 Ibid.
18 Ibid., 1.22.

wrong because it is an attempt "to claim as due to itself that which is properly due to God only".[19] This kind of self-love is destructive and self-defeating, and is thus "more correctly called hate".[20] We should regard even ourselves as something to be used rather than enjoyed. To the extent we have built up habits of selfish self-love, we must be willing to die to ourselves so that we can be reborn to new life.

Since we are supposed to love our neighbours as ourselves, we must also regard our neighbours as objects of use rather than enjoyment. We must love them, but in such a way as to bring both ourselves and them closer to God:

> For in this way, loving his neighbour as himself, a man turns the whole current of his love both for himself and his neighbour into the channel of the love of God, which suffers no stream to be drawn off from itself by whose diversion its own volume would be diminished.[21]

Such love extends even to our enemies. If our love is properly ordered we have no need to fear our enemies, for they cannot take away the object of our love and enjoyment. We should pity them instead, because they are separated from God to the extent they hate us, and we should seek to draw them back into communion with God and with ourselves: "Now this is our highest reward, that we should fully enjoy Him, and that all who enjoy Him should enjoy one another in Him".[22]

Augustine regards love of our own bodies as flowing from our love of ourselves. Much of his discussion of this question centres around the psychological fact that we do love our own bodies and seek to take care of them. This is appropriate because our bodies are the primary instrumentality through which we express love of God and love of neighbour. But our love for our bodies must be subordinated to our love of higher things. We must love God in and for himself; we must love ourselves and our neighbours as beings capable of communing with God in love; and we must love our bodies as tools for effectuating our love of God and neighbour. But if we must choose between protecting our body and loving our neighbour, we should choose loving our neighbour.

On Christian Doctrine does not focus specifically on whether it is permissible to love any worldly thing other than oneself, one's body and one's neighbour. At times, Augustine implies that our love should focus exclusively on God and on beings capable of communing with God. At other times, however, he acknowledges the delights we can experience on our journey through this world to God. He does not condemn such delights as evil, but he warns us that they can be dangerous distractions that may prevent us from completing our journey. We should experience our love of worldly things "not with such love and delight as if it were

19 Ibid., 1.23.
20 Ibid.
21 Ibid.
22 Ibid., 1.32.

a good to rest in, but with a transient feeling rather, such as we have towards the road, or carriages, or other things that are merely means".[23]

In sum, *On Christian Doctrine* portrays all of creation as a system of intellectual and moral signification. When we gaze upon the beauty, the sublimity or the glory of created things, our minds should turn to the beauty, sublimity and glory of the one who created them. When we love ourselves, our neighbours or any created thing, this love should point us towards the love of God, for only God can be loved in and for himself. We sin when we treat the sign as the thing it signifies, loving or worshipping it for its own sake. In this light, the significance of the property crime committed by Adam and Eve becomes clearer. Before the Fall, God and humans communicated directly with each other. God walked in the garden and spoke to the man and the woman. Adam and Eve knew that all things were created by God and derived their goodness from God. There was no breakdown between sign and signified. But Adam and Eve's understanding of the relationship between the world and God was also a source of temptation. They saw that the tree of the knowledge of good and evil reflected an attribute of God, and they wanted to take this attribute for themselves. They chose to love themselves for their own sake, and this self-love led them to steal something that properly belonged to God. At the core of this property crime was their decision to turn their hearts inward upon themselves. This decision led to alienation from God, from each other (notice how quickly each of them tried to find someone else to blame for their actions) and even from themselves. And so shame, suffering and death entered the world.

12.3 Property crimes in the Gospels

Under Augustine's reading of Scripture, creation is a system of intellectual and moral signification that has been broken by sin and restored by the Incarnation and Resurrection. We can see this pattern of breaking and restoration in the Gospels' treatment of property and property crime. Property is a particularly useful example of breakdown and restoration because it is at the centre of many people's desire for security, sustenance and happiness. The good things property provides can lead us to recognition of the good things God provides and help us effectuate our love of God and neighbour – but too often it becomes a rival for our love and an obstacle to our relationship with God and each other. The remainder of this chapter will start by describing the Gospels' treatment of property as a failed sign that can undermine our ability to love God and neighbour. It will then illustrate the various ways in which the Gospels use property crime to restore the signifying function of property. The Gospels use property crime (1) to contrast the fleeting nature of worldly goods with the eternal goods offered by God; (2) to show how love of worldly goods can lead to rebellion against God; (3) to show how God breaks through our selfish

23 Ibid., 1.35.

self-love, sometimes violently, to warn or judge; (4) to show how caring for victims of property crime can restore our capacity to love our neighbours; and finally, (5) to show how forgiveness and reconciliation are always open to those who seek it.

12.3.1 Property as a failed sign

At several points in the Gospels, Jesus warns that love of property can be an obstacle to salvation. For example, the Gospel of Matthew recounts the story of a young man who approached Jesus and asked how to attain eternal life (Matt. 19:16–30). Jesus told him to obey the following commandments: do not murder, do not commit adultery, do not steal, do not bear false witness, honour your father and mother and love your neighbour as yourself. The man replied that he already did those things and asked what more he should do. Jesus responded: "If you want to be perfect, go, sell what you have and give to the poor, and you will have treasure in heaven; and come, follow me". Hearing this, the man walked away sad, "for he had great possessions". This encounter led Jesus to exclaim that "it is easier for a camel to go through the eye of a needle than for a rich man to enter the kingdom of God". When the apostles, in alarm, asked, "Who then can be saved?" Jesus responded: "With men this is impossible, but with God all things are possible".

This story shows how love of property can undermine love of God and neighbour. Jesus did not demand that the young man give up all his property to obtain eternal life. The only property-related command he gave was "Do not steal". But when the young man asked how to deepen his relationship with God, Jesus instructed him to use his property as an instrument to effectuate love of God and love of neighbour. By giving away his property and following Jesus, he could commit himself to total trust and dependence on God for the security, sustenance and comfort he currently derived from property. By giving the property to the poor, he could exercise his love of neighbour, helping those in need on their journey through life. But the young man just could not do it. His treasure on earth was more real to him than treasure in heaven. His property did not serve its proper signifying function, connecting him to love of God and neighbour. Instead, it caused him to focus his love inward, on the property and on himself. He ended by separating himself from Jesus – walking away – and Jesus remarked how difficult it will be for people like the rich young man to enter the kingdom of God.

Similarly, the Gospel of Luke recounts the story of the rich man and Lazarus (Luke 16:19–31). Jesus tells of a rich man dressed in fine linens who enjoyed all the good things of life while ignoring Lazarus, a poor beggar lying at his gate covered in sores. He did not give Lazarus even the scraps from his table. The dogs – Lazarus' competitors for those scraps – were kinder than the rich man, for at least they licked Lazarus' sores. When both men died, Lazarus went to heaven and the rich man went to hell. The rich man begged Abraham for relief, but Abraham told him:

> Son, remember that in your lifetime you received your good things, while Lazarus received bad things, but now he is comforted here and you are in agony. And besides all this, between us and you a great chasm has been set in place, so that those who want to go from here to you cannot, nor can anyone cross over from there to us.

Abraham also refused to send Lazarus to warn the rich man's brothers because they already had Moses and the prophets to warn them and, if they would not believe Moses and the prophets, they would not believe "even if someone rises from the dead".

This story carries the problem of property to its logical extreme. The rich man has given himself over to enjoyment of property to such an extent that he completely ignores the sore-covered beggar lying at his gate. Property has become his god, the thing he enjoys in and for itself. His love of property leads him to fail completely in his love of his neighbour. This love also separates him from God. Abraham's statement that an uncrossable chasm lies between the rich man and heaven demonstrates a total breakdown in signification. Whereas the story of the rich young man showed how the proper disposition towards property could lead to trust in God and love of neighbour, the story of the rich man and Lazarus shows how love that centres upon oneself will cut one off from God and neighbour. Abraham implies that even the Incarnation and the Resurrection – the ultimate restoration of the relationship between sign and signified – cannot reach those consumed by a selfish love of property. They would not change their ways "even if one should rise from the dead".

12.3.2 Property crime as a corrective sign

If property often acts as a failed sign, focusing our love on the thing itself rather than the thing it signifies, property crime sometimes appears in the Gospels as a means of correcting this failure. For example, in the Gospel of Matthew, Jesus says:

> Do not store up treasures for yourselves on earth, where moth and woodworm destroy them and thieves can break in and steal. But store up treasures for yourselves in heaven, where neither moth nor woodworm destroys them and thieves cannot break in and steal. For wherever your treasure is, there will your heart be too.
>
> (Matt. 6:19–21)

This statement echoes not only what Jesus told the rich young man about giving up treasure on earth in exchange for treasure in heaven, but also provides a practical reason for doing so: all earthly treasure is vulnerable and fleeting. Moths and woodworm will destroy it and thieves will take it. Jesus repeats this message about the transitory nature of worldly goods throughout the Gospels. For example, in the Gospel of John, Jesus tells the Samaritan woman at the well that earthly water will only satisfy her temporarily but that he can give her "living water" that will become in her "a spring of water welling up to eternal life" (John 4:10–14). Similarly, after Jesus performs the miracle of the loaves and the fishes, he tells the crowd: "Do not work for food that perishes but for the food that endures for eternal life, which the Son of Man will give you" (John 6:27).

The vulnerability of all worldly goods to thievery and other forms of corruption signals that it is a mistake to centre one's love upon them. Property should be used rather than enjoyed. It cannot provide lasting happiness because it cannot last.

12.3.3 Property crime as rebellion

Property crime also appears in the Gospels to illustrate how love of property can lead to rebellion against God. The core of property crime is the taking or destroying for one's own purposes something that belongs to someone else. Since all things belong to God, we rebel against him when we appropriate any created thing and turn it towards our own selfish purposes. We have already seen two examples of this rebellion in the discussion above. Adam and Eve rebelled against God's command by eating forbidden fruit in the hope of taking for themselves an attribute of God. The rich man in the Lazarus story rebelled against God by hoarding his property for himself and shutting himself off from the needs of his neighbour.

This rebellion appears most clearly *as* rebellion in the parable of the tenants. As recounted in the Gospel of Matthew, Jesus tells of a landowner who planted a vineyard and leased it to tenants (Matt. 21:33–41). At harvest time, he sent servants to collect his proceeds but the tenants repeatedly beat and killed them. Finally, he sent his own son to them, but they killed him in the hope of stealing his inheritance. Jesus then asks his listeners what the landowner will do when he returns, and they respond: "He will put those wretched men to a wretched death and lease his vineyard to other tenants who will give him the produce at the proper times".

The parable of the tenants uses property crime as a metaphor for rebellion against God. In a sense, the tenants are just like Adam and Eve. They are given a fruitful plot of land to tend, as well as instructions about what to do with this property. Like Adam and Eve, the tenants ignore the command of the landowner and try to take for themselves what properly belongs to him. But they go further, committing violence and murder, even against the landowner's son, to further their goal of wrongfully taking the landowner's property for themselves. Selfish self-love leads from property crime to murder to deicide.

The pattern of rebellion in the parable of the tenants repeats itself, of course, in the crucifixion of Jesus. As discussed above, Augustine argued that both the Jews and the pagan Romans were in bondage to failed signs – the Jews to the law and the Romans to created things that they worshipped as gods. Each group sought to kill Jesus in the name of its own failed sign: the Jews wanted him killed for claimed violations of the law, and the Romans actually killed him in the name of the false god Caesar. That this was a rebellion against the true God in the name of false gods is made clear in the mockery the Roman soldiers directed at

Jesus while prepared to crucify him: they scourged him, they gave him a purple robe and a crown of thorns and they pretended to worship him, slapping him in the face while exclaiming "Hail, King of the Jews!" (John 19:1–3). This mockery was explicitly framed as a denial of his authority as King and the Son of God. The final coda to this mockery was a property crime: they took his clothes and divided them up among themselves.

From a positivist viewpoint, the soldiers' appropriation of Jesus' clothes was not technically a crime, for the executioner had the right under Roman law to appropriate the clothes of the condemned person. But the Gospels present the entire crucifixion as unlawful – as the ultimate example of humans taking for themselves something that properly belongs to God. For this reason, John immediately follows his description of the soldiers taking Jesus' clothes with this lament from Psalm 22: "they divide my garments among them; for my clothing they cast lots" (John 19:24). In the Psalm, those who take the psalmist's clothes are described as "dogs" and "evildoers" who mock and torment the psalmist and seek his death. The wrongful taking of Jesus' clothes was of a piece with the wrongful taking of his life: an act of rebellion, taking for oneself that which properly belongs to God.

12.3.4 Property crime as warning and judgment

The Gospels use property crime not only as a metaphor for rebellion against God but also as a metaphor for God's capacity to break through our selfish self-love, either to warn us or to judge us. In Matthew 24, Jesus describes at some length what the end times will be like. Towards the end of this description, he says:

> In the days before the flood, they were eating and drinking, marrying and giving in marriage, up to the day that Noah entered the ark. They did not know until the flood came and carried them all away. So will it be at the coming of the Son of Man.
>
> (Matt. 24:38–39)

He then pivots to a series of metaphors and parables elaborating on the theme "get ready". The first metaphor is of a property crime, with God presented as the perpetrator:

> Be sure of this: if the master of the house had known the hour of night when the thief was coming, he would have stayed awake and not let his house be broken into. So too, you also must be prepared, for at an hour you do not expect, the Son of Man will come.
>
> (24:43–44)

This metaphor is followed by the parable of the faithful servant, the parable of the 10 bridesmaids, the parable of the talents and, finally, the story of the sheep and goats.

These parables give us a sense of what it means to be ready for God. The parable of the bridesmaids gives a general warning: the wise bridesmaids bring extra lamp oil while they wait for the bridegroom, the foolish ones do not. The remaining parables give us more detail: the faithful servant keeps his master's house prepared for his return; the unfaithful servant beats his fellow servants and gets drunk because he does not think the master will return any time soon. The good servants go out and increase the talents their master has given them; the bad one, acting out of fear, buries his talent in the ground. The sheep practised love of neighbour: "For I was hungry and you gave me food, I was thirsty and you gave me drink, a stranger and you welcomed me, naked and you clothed me, ill and you cared for me, in prison and you visited me" (Matt. 25:35–36). The goats did not.

Taken alone, the metaphor of God as a burglar seeking to break into one's house seems to imply that if one is ready for God, one can keep him out: "if the master of the house had known the hour of night when the thief was coming, he would have stayed awake and not let his house be broken into". But this cannot be what the metaphor means, because all the parables that follow tell us how to be ready to *welcome* God into our lives. They tell us to exercise love of God and love of neighbour: ready your lamp oil for the bridegroom so that he will invite you into the wedding, do not abuse each other, do not give yourself up to drunkenness, do something with the gifts God has given you and above all take care of those in need. In Augustinian terms, these parables tell us to prepare to enjoy God in and for himself and to use ourselves and our neighbours to get closer to God. Whether we experience God as a burglar or a bridegroom will depend on whether we are trying to keep him out or are prepared to let him in.

The metaphor of God committing a property crime to break through our selfish self-love becomes literal in Jesus' cleansing of the Temple. The Gospel of Mark describes the event this way:

> They came to Jerusalem, and on entering the temple area he began to drive out those selling and buying there. He overturned the tables of the money changers and the seats of those who were selling doves. He did not permit anyone to carry anything through the temple area. Then he taught them saying, "Is it not written: 'My house shall be called a house of prayer for all peoples'? But you have made it a den of thieves." The chief priests and the scribes came to hear of it and were seeking a way to put him to death, yet they feared him because the whole crowd was astonished at his teaching.
>
> (Mark 11:15–18)

This story (which should strike terror in the heart of church gift shop proprietors everywhere) demonstrates how the love of property can interfere with the love of God and neighbour, and also how God can break through that selfish love as both warning and judgment. The money-changers and dove-sellers in the Temple interfered with the love of God in at least two ways. First, they sold access to the act of worship, presumably at exorbitant rates (thus "den of thieves"), making it more difficult for their neighbours to worship God in the Temple. Second, they changed the focus of the Temple itself from worship to commerce. This change in focus cut the relationship between sign and signified, turning people's minds and hearts from God to money. By committing a property crime – overturning the tables and chairs and interfering with commerce – Jesus sought to deliver a warning: preserve the Temple as a "house of prayer for all peoples". Turn your thoughts and hearts from property to God.

12.3.5 Property crime and love of neighbour

Property crime can also be an occasion for expressing love of one's neighbour. When a person has been subjected to robbery, burglary or arson, he or she often needs help to recover. In the Gospel of Luke, Jesus uses property crime to demonstrate what it means to love one's neighbour. A lawyer tries to test Jesus by asking what he must do to inherit eternal life. Jesus turns the question back on the lawyer by asking what the law says. The lawyer responds: "You must love the Lord your God with all your heart, with all your soul, with all your strength, and with all your mind, and your neighbour as yourself" (Luke 10:27). The lawyer then asks "Who is my neighbour?" and Jesus responds with the parable of the Good Samaritan: a traveller is attacked by robbers who beat him, steal his clothes and leave him half-dead by the side of the road. A priest and a Levite both ignore this crime victim but a Samaritan takes him to an inn, tends his wounds and gives money to the innkeeper to care for the man until the Samaritan returns. Jesus then once again turns the question back on the lawyer and asks who proved to be a neighbour to the crime victim. The lawyer responded: "The one who showed pity towards him". Jesus then replied: "Go and do the same yourself" (10:37).

The parable of the Good Samaritan transforms our understanding of the command "love your neighbour". The lawyer thinks of a neighbour as "one who must be loved". Jesus changes the concept of neighbour to "one who loves". The Samaritan was a neighbour to the robbery victim because he chose to love and care for the robbery victim. Jesus then universalises the command by telling the lawyer to "go and do the same yourself". In other words, we are no longer supposed to make legalistic distinctions about whom we must love and whom we can ignore or hate. Instead, we must seek to *be* a neighbour to every person we meet, regardless of race, religion, nationality or social standing.

The act of helping those who have had what was theirs taken from them can bring both helper and victim closer to God. The helper comes closer to God by fulfilling God's command to love his neighbour. The victim may also be brought closer to God by experiencing an act of love that restores some of what was taken from him and serves as an example for him to follow in the future. In this way, the Gospel presents property crime as an occasion for further love of neighbour.

12.3.5 Property crime and reconciliation

Finally, the Gospels present punishment of property crime as an occasion for repentance and reconciliation with God. The Gospel accounts of the crucifixion describe two criminals who were crucified next to Jesus. In Matthew and Mark, they are specifically described as robbers – perpetrators of a violent property crime (Matt. 27:38; Mark 15:27). The Gospel of Luke recounts the following interaction between Jesus and the other condemned men, just as the crowd and the rulers were mocking Jesus:

> Now one of the criminals hanging there reviled Jesus, saying, "Are you not the Messiah? Save yourself and us." The other, however, rebuking him, said in reply, "Have you no fear of God, for you are subject to the same condemnation? And indeed, we have been condemned justly, for the sentence we received corresponds to our crimes, but this man has done nothing criminal." Then he said, "Jesus, remember me when you come into your kingdom." He replied to him, "Amen, I say to you, today you will be with me in Paradise."
>
> (Luke 23:39–43)

The interaction between Jesus and the robbers serves as a model for all criminal offenders, and indeed for all sinners (which is to say, all of us). Their decision to commit a serious property crime has led to a serious consequence: death. In this sense, the robbers are just like Adam and Eve. As with Adam and Eve, God comes to the robbers in the aftermath of their crime and offers them the choice of repentance or denial. The "bad thief", like Adam and Eve, directs his focus outward, mocking Jesus instead of coming to terms with his own actions. The "good thief", on the other hand, rejects the pattern of alienation and outward-directed blame that has been characteristic of humankind since the Fall. Instead, he takes responsibility for his crime ("We have been condemned justly") and asks Jesus for forgiveness and reconciliation ("Jesus, remember me when you come into your kingdom"). Jesus responds with immediate and total forgiveness: "today you will be with me in Paradise". Just as Adam and Eve's refusal to take responsibility for their property crime led to exile from God, the good thief's acceptance of responsibility and request for forgiveness brings reconciliation. Property crime expelled us from the Garden, and property crime shows us the way back home.

12.4 Conclusion

The Gospels use property and property crime as examples of humankind's misdirected love, as warnings about the consequences of such misdirected love and as examples of how to find our way back home. If the Incarnation restored the link between creation and God, sign and signified, it did so partially through the example of property crime.

Further reading

Augustine. *Confessions*, ed. and trans. William Watts, 2 vols (Cambridge, MA: Harvard University Press, 1960).
Augustine. *On Christian Doctrine*, http://www.ntslibrary.com/PDF%20Books/Augustine%20doctrine.pdf (accessed 22 January 2019).
Brown, Peter. *Augustine of Hippo: A Biography* (Berkeley: University of California Press, 2000; first published 1967).
Clement of Alexandria. *The Rich Man's Salvation*, ed. and trans. G.W. Butterworth (Cambridge, MA: Harvard University Press, 2003).
Gregory, Eric. *Politics and the Order of Love: An Augustinian Ethic of Democratic Citizenship* (Chicago: University of Chicago Press, 2010).
Hays, Christopher M. *Luke's Wealth Ethics: A Study in Their Coherence and Character* (Tübingen: Mohr Siebeck, 2010).
Jackson, Timothy P. *The Priority of Love: Christian Charity and Social Justice* (Princeton: Princeton University Press, 2000).
O'Donovan, Oliver. *The Problem of Self-Love in St. Augustine* (Eugene: Wipf & Stock, 2006).
Stephen, James Fitzjames. *A History of the Criminal Law of England*, 3 vols (London: Macmillan, 1883).
Wilken, Robert Louis. *The Spirit of Early Christian Thought: Seeking the Face of God* (New Haven: Yale University Press, 2003).
Witte, John Jr. and Frank S. Alexander, eds. *Christianity and Law: An Introduction* (Cambridge: Cambridge University Press, 2008).

13 Crimes against God and the Church

Jeroen Temperman

13.1 Introduction

Christianity did not invent crimes against God. In Judaism, not only blaspheming the name of the Lord but also such offences as breaking the Sabbath or breaking kashrut rules already constituted sins against God. Nor did Christianity invent crimes against religion: the Romans prohibited and punished different forms of sacrilege, such as non-compliance with divine laws or denying religious cults endorsed by the Roman state.[1]

Seventeen centuries of close entanglement between the State and Christianity served to secularise certain religious offences, effectively turning them into public offences – crimes against the people as much as crimes against religion. A combination of the disentanglement of the government and religion, a new human rights climate promoting freedom of speech and increased religious diversity, reversing the former homogeneity or dominance, have all contributed to the removal of the majority of the historic crimes against the Christian God and the Christian Church, although some vestiges remain. Whether such traces should be cherished as cultural remnants or vehemently opposed from a contemporary human rights perspective is the subject of intense academic, political, judicial and societal debate.

13.2 Secular criminalisation of offences against God and the Church

In past millennia, crimes against god(s) and religion have been both religious and secular offences – at times simultaneously religious *and* secular, at other times more one than the other. Generally speaking, and within what is now referred to as the "Christian world",[2] over the last 2,000 years or so one can discern the following: crimes against religion as a secular offence in ancient pre-Christian times;

1 Yulia Pershina, "Punishments for Crimes Against Religion and Christian Church in the Roman Criminal Law", (2015), 7 *Modern European Researches* 86.

2 By which is meant the sum of those nations and regions with predominantly Christian demographics, history and culture.

crimes against God and religion as a religious (and later a secular) offence in the Christian empire; continued secular entrenchment of religious offences throughout the modern era; and, finally, secular decriminalisation of religious offences and their replacement by offences in secular law against individuals or religious groups in the modern human rights era.

In Roman, pre-Christian times, sacrilegious crimes were not so much religious or specifically blasphemy offences as public order offences.[3] In fact, sacrilege was treated as a category of theft. It gradually acquired the figurative denotations that it still has: initially, the crime of stealing (literally: gathering) from a holy place – *sacrum* (holy), *legere* (to take) – was discussed as precisely that. Cicero, for instance, argued that stealing sacred items from a sacred place, such as a temple, amounted to sacrilege, while stealing sacred items from a location that was not sacred fell into a different category of crime (*furtum*).[4] A plausible rationale behind this approach is provided by Robinson:

> This more nationalistic and secular view of sacrilege, affected by the increasing dominance of the emperors, produced a range of crimes that were more easy to detect and punish, although the offence lay in the spirit world rather than in the world of men.[5]

At the same time, there were many attempts in the Senate to read elements of religious offence (qua religion) into sacrilege, usually triggered by major sacrilegious scandals.[6] Furthermore, religious authorities often had jurisdiction over the offence and, in any event, "vengeance of the gods" served "as a menace in reserve".[7] In addition to theft, there was a nexus between sacrilege and treason. Hence, in the pre-Constantine empire, Christians offended both religion and State, making them traitors both to the pagan gods and, more significantly, to the emperor.[8]

Nicene Christianity, as established by Theodosius as the religion of the empire, brought about a fresh impetus as to which crimes against religion should be prohibited and how such prohibition was to be enforced. Offences included such crimes as non-compliance with religious duties, various types of heresy or sacrilege and offences against the Church, including crimes against Church order and against Church property itself.[9] The later *Codex Theodosianus* (compiled under Theodosius II) was ground-breaking in that it contained a separate book (Book XVI) entitled "About the Universal or Catholic Church",[10] and included –

3 Olivia Robinson, "Blasphemy and Sacrilege in Roman Law", (1973) 8 *Irish Jurist* 356–71.
4 Ibid., citing Cicero, *De legibus* 2.16.41 and *Auct. ad Herenn.* 1.12.22.
5 Ibid., 360.
6 Ibid., 356–60.
7 Ibid., 360.
8 Ibid., 361–2.
9 Pershina, "Punishments for Crimes Against Religion", 87.
10 Ibid.

among more than 200 clauses – in addition to sacrilege, both sorcery and magic as crimes against religion.[11] It was the first time that a secular legal treatise had expressly differentiated religious matters from secular ones and devoted specific legal protection to the former.[12]

Those committing such crimes against Christianity and against the Catholic Church were deemed heretics and/or offenders against the Catholic Church and the punishments included dire ones. Notably, the property of heretics was confiscated; however, the law allowed for appropriation by the sons of heretics if they were devout Christians.[13] Heretical books were burned by judicial order; hiding them could incur the death penalty. Prescribed forms of worship and rituals, especially sacrificial rituals at pagan temples, were strictly forbidden. Persecution not only of pagans, but also of deviant Christian sects, was fierce and the typical punishments included exile (as in the case of the Arians), fines and various forms of capital punishment, in addition to land and property confiscation.[14] Roman emperors, however, differed as to how strictly they enforced these. For instance, Constantine stipulated that temples outside the city ought to remain intact for cultural reasons.[15] In 435, the total destruction of pagan temples was finally ordered under Theodosius and Honorius, alongside a law that ordered the erection of a cross on all such sites.[16] Jewish temples, on the other hand, were subject to some legal protection, although Jewish worship by Christians was deemed sacrilegious and certain Jewish rituals were banned.[17]

Specific attention was given to standards and burdens of proof. For instance, siblings could not bring charges of heresy against each other, but a father could against his children.[18] Incentives to prevent heresy were also legislated for: legal persecution sometimes ceased after conversion, although certainly not in all places, as the persecution of the Spanish *conversos* illustrates. Another example is that testamentary provision by non-Christians, such as Jews, which stipulated that children who had converted to Christianity would be disinherited was declared null and void.[19]

Before the Christian era, there was no precise equivalent to blasphemy. For one thing, there were too many gods who could take offence. But more importantly, "Romans believed that gods could protect themselves".[20] Nevertheless, one must distinguish between the introduction of blasphemy as a Christian religious offence and the introduction of blasphemy as an offence prosecuted by

11 Robinson, "Blasphemy and Sacrilege in Roman Law", 370.
12 Pershina, "Punishments for Crimes Against Religion", 87.
13 Ibid.
14 Ibid., 87–8.
15 Robinson, "Blasphemy and Sacrilege in Roman Law", 366.
16 Ibid., 367.
17 Ibid., 368
18 Pershina, "Punishments for Crimes Against Religion", p. 90.
19 Ibid., 89.
20 Ibid., 86.

the public authorities of the Christian empire. As a *religious* offence, the crime of blasphemy was acknowledged as such in the Hebrew bible which ordered the death penalty:

> The Lord said to Moses, saying: Take the blasphemer outside the camp; and let all who were within hearing lay their hands on his head, and let the whole congregation stone him. And speak to the people of Israel, saying: Anyone who curses God shall bear the sin. One who blasphemes the name of the Lord shall be put to death; the whole congregation shall stone the blasphemer. Aliens as well as citizens, when they blaspheme the Name, shall be put to death.
>
> (Lev. 24:13–16; NRSV)

Here we see the focus being on blasphemy against God, but in the New Testament this shifted to blasphemy against the Holy Spirit – in Jesus' words: "'Truly, I say to you, all sins will be forgiven the children of man, and whatever blasphemies they utter, but whoever blasphemes against the Holy Spirit never has forgiveness, but is guilty of an eternal sin' – for they were saying, 'He has an unclean spirit'" (Mark 3:28–29; ESV). According to Matthew, blasphemy against the Holy Spirit is the worst type of blasphemy and, unlike minor blasphemies, not to be pardoned:

> Whoever is not with me is against me, and whoever does not gather with me scatters. Therefore I tell you, every sin and blasphemy will be forgiven people, but the blasphemy against the Spirit will not be forgiven. And whoever speaks a word against the Son of Man will be forgiven, but whoever speaks against the Holy Spirit will not be forgiven, either in this age or in the age to come.
>
> (Matt. 12:30–32; ESV)

The introduction of blasphemy as a separate codified offence did not coincide with the establishment of Christianity as the religion of the empire. Blasphemy as a statutory crime emerged considerably later. It was Justinian (*c*. 482–565) who first devoted an entire treatise on the subject of *maledicere* (literally "speaking ill" or "cursing"; "blasphemy" does not exist in classical Latin).[21] Robinson points out that Justinian "condemned those who used blasphemous words and swore by the sacraments, provoking God to wrath, and also those who swore by … Christ's hair or head".[22] The superstitions that surrounded the offence made banning *maledicere* somewhat self-serving: it was thought that blaspheming could cause such ill-fated events as famines, earthquakes or defeat in wars.[23] Not surprisingly,

21 Robinson, "Blasphemy and Sacrilege in Roman Law", 371.
22 Ibid.
23 Ibid.

penalties were harsh, including capital punishment; in fact, those prefects who failed to punish blasphemers were themselves liable to "God's judgment and also to the imperial displeasure".[24]

From these moments of inception, crimes against God and religion gradually became ever more entrenched within canon law, common law and civil law. In the English context, while ecclesiastical authorities and judges enjoyed important competences (and extreme levels of discretion: Blackstone speaks of "a most arbitrary latitude"[25]) in the area of monitoring compliance, the gradual secularisation and hence appropriation of these crimes as public order offences by the State implied that secular authorities became vested with an enforcement mandate as well (or, sometimes, instead).

Thus far, the chief focus has been on heresy, sacrilege and blasphemy – the profound and, if you will, most direct transgressions against God and religion. Of course, "crimes against God and religion" is a much larger category of historical (and contemporary) crimes if one deems this notion to denote any offence against Christian teachings, or against "the revealed law of God" (to borrow Blackstone's phrasing).[26] In that light, many crimes in secular penal codes could be comfortably related to a Christian justice perspective, if not inferred from it. (Conversely, under that reading there would also be a vast number of offences that would be Christian wrongs that are no longer considered "in a criminal light", such as having bastard children.[27]) But even if, following Blackstone's endeavours, one were to concentrate exclusively on those offences "which are more immediately injurious to God and his holy religion", the list is vaster than those crimes alluded to thus far.

Engaging with English common law, statutory law and ecclesiastical law, Blackstone identified no fewer than 11 (sub-categories of) offences against God and religion:[28]

1. *Apostasy*: currently generally obsolete as a codified crime within the Christian world, with the exception of contemporary canon law (see below). Needless to say, under various Christian emperors (whereas Constantine punished conversion from Christianity to paganism, Judaism or other "false religions" with confiscation of goods, Theodosius stepped up the religious persecution by introducing capital crimes in this area), and throughout the Middle Ages and modern era, with the institution of the Inquisition as its repressive pinnacle, abandonment of the true faith and/or embracing false ones could trigger dire punishments.

24 Ibid.
25 William Blackstone, *Commentaries on the Laws of England*, 4 vols. (Oxford: Clarendon Press, 1765–9), vol. 4, ch. 4, II.
26 Ibid., Introduction.
27 Ibid., vol. 4, ch. 4, XI.
28 Ibid., vol. 4, ch. 4, I–XI.

2. *Heresy*: the main difference with apostasy is that it is not the entirety of Christianity that is denied, but certain essential doctrines are "publicly and obstinately" disavowed.
3. *Offences against religion affecting the established Church*: here, Blackstone distinguished between positive and negative sub-categories. The positive alternative is the worse offence: it amounts to "reviling the ordinances of the church", implying

    > the utmost indecency, arrogance, and ingratitude: indecency, by setting up private judgment in opposition to public; arrogance, by treating with contempt and rudeness what has at least a better chance to be right, than the singular notions of any particular man; and ingratitude, by denying that indulgence and liberty of conscience to the members of the national church, which the retainers to every petty conventicle enjoy.[29]

    The negative version is "Nonconformity to the worship of the church". Blackstone argued that the law should indulge a fair degree of nonconformity, which is after all "a matter of private conscience".[30] His argument resonates – in a modest way – with contemporary notions of religious freedom: "For undoubtedly all persecution and oppression of weak consciences, on the score of religious persuasions, are highly unjustifiable upon every principle of natural reason, civil liberty, or sound religion". Christian indulgence has its limits: in relation to that which "may endanger the national church: there is always a difference to be made between toleration and establishment".[31] Nonconformists include not only those who absent themselves from Church rituals but also those who, conversely, show a "mistaken or perverse zeal".[32] For a long time, this category included "papists" and Protestant dissenters, until the Acts of Toleration removed such legal penalties.[33]
4. *Blasphemy*: this crime against God arguably appeals most fiercely to the imagination. Of all the offences Blackstone lists, it is among the more significant and "live" crimes within the contemporary Christian world (if occasionally barely so, or in a legally "dormant" capacity). We will resume our discussion of blasphemy in the next section.
5. *Profane or common swearing and cursing*: related to, though different from, blasphemy, this can be listed as a crime against God and the Church, partly because, when it was on the law books, the fines levied typically benefited the parish. Using God's name in vain resulted in the highest fines, but these

29 Ibid., III(1).
30 Ibid., III(2).
31 Ibid.
32 Ibid.
33 Ibid.

were not forfeited in favour of (the poor of) the parish, ending up instead in the king's coffers.[34]

6. *Witchcraft or sorcery*: this is quite different from the previous categories. It was not so much the belief in witchcraft that was criminal, but the practices of conjuration or enchantment themselves, as well as, on the consumers' side, the act of consulting sorcerers and the like.
7. *Religious imposters*: in a way related to the previous category, these form a separate type of offender against the Church. By making false promises of rewards, by wrongly instilling fears and so on, such people abuse religion for their own benefit, but in so doing also subvert and ridicule religion, thus making this a profound crime against religion.[35]
8. *Simony*: (inducing) payment with a view towards securing an influential position within the Church[36] is quite clearly an offence against the Church and its internal order and procedures. The crime is named after Simon Magus (or Simon the Sorcerer), who committed the crime as recorded in the Bible:

   > And when Simon saw that through laying on of the apostles' hands the Holy Ghost was given, he offered them money, saying, Give me also this power, that on whomsoever I lay hands, he may receive the Holy Ghost. But Peter said unto him, Thy money perish with thee, because thou hast thought that the gift of God may be purchased with money. Thou hast neither part nor lot in this matter: for thy heart is not right in the sight of God. Repent therefore of this thy wickedness, and pray God, if perhaps the thought of thine heart may be forgiven thee. For I perceive that thou art in the gall of bitterness, and in the bond of iniquity. Then answered Simon, and said, Pray ye to the Lord for me, that none of these things which ye have spoken come upon me.
   >
   > (Acts 8:18–24; KJV)

   The crime is now generally dealt with ecclesiastically rather than under criminal law. Roman Catholic canon law devotes a specific canon to simony, punishing a "person who celebrates or receives a sacrament through simony" with suspension (Canon 1380). Moreover, there is an entire separate section dealing with numerous related crimes of "usurpation of ecclesiastical functions".[37] Office appointments made subject to simony are, naturally, declared void.
9. *Sabbath desecration*: "profanation of the Lord's day"[38] is a clear offence against God, though, as we shall see, it is rapidly losing sway within secular law.

34 Ibid., V.
35 Ibid., VII.
36 Ibid., VIII.
37 Code of Canon Law, Book VI, part II, s. III (Canons 1378–89).
38 Blackstone, *Commentaries*, vol. 4, ch. 4, IX.

10. *Drunkenness*: interestingly, this was deemed an offence against God/religion in former days. The offender was lucky if he or she got off with a fine, since the alternative penalty was a corporal – and humiliating – one: five hours in the stocks in order to sober up.[39]
11. *Lewdness*: a broad and shifting category – subject to the reigning morality at the time – this could include anything from "frequenting houses of ill fame" to committing public indecency, adultery and fornication.[40]

Few of these offences survive as indictable crimes within the Christian world today but, as we shall see, some still do.

13.3 Contemporary positive law examples of crimes against God and the Church

In sharp contrast with parts of the Muslim world,[41] apostasy and heresy – the religious offences par excellence – have no secular legal significance in virtually the entire Christian world. Contemporary Roman Catholic canon law, however, does touch on these crimes. Apostates from the faith, heretics and "schismatics" (i.e. those who create or incite schism and hence challenge the universal Church) are threatened with automatic excommunication from the Catholic Church (*latae sententiae* excommunication), while clerics may receive higher punishments (Canon 1364). A separate canon focuses on the role of parents and their duty to make sure that their children remain within the Catholic Church. Baptising or educating one's children in another religion may incur censure or another "just penalty" (Canon 1366). This same section on "Delicts Against Religion and the Unity of the Church" also lists two more subtle sacrileges: persons guilty of prohibited participation in sacred rites (*communicatio in sacris*) are to be punished with a just penalty (Canon 1365); and a

> person who throws away the consecrated species or takes or retains them for a sacrilegious purpose incurs a *latae sententiae* excommunication reserved to the Apostolic See; moreover, a cleric can be punished with another penalty, not excluding dismissal from the clerical state.
>
> (Canon 1367)

Out of the traditional offences against God and religion identified in the previous section, it is probably blasphemy[42] and the somewhat open-ended category of crimes against (the established) religion (especially when defined as offence

39 Ibid., X.
40 Ibid., XI.
41 Paul Marshall and Nina Shea, *Silenced: How Apostasy and Blasphemy Codes Are Choking Freedom Worldwide* (Oxford: Oxford University Press, 2011).
42 See e.g. Criminal Code of Austria, s. 115; Criminal Code of Cyprus, ss. 138, 141, 142; Criminal Code of Greece, Arts. 198–9; Blasphemy Act 2009 [Ireland], Bill No. 43/2006, Art. 36, which entered into force in July 2009.

against groups of believers)[43] that remain the most significant from the perspective of contemporary positive law. In a now somewhat outdated inventory, Pew Research Center lists eight predominantly Christian States (Denmark, Germany, Greece, Ireland, Italy, Malta, The Netherlands and Poland) that criminalise blasphemy; however, if one extends the variable somewhat so as to cover any "defamation of religion", well over 40 predominantly Christian countries would qualify.[44] From Pew's list of States with blasphemy laws, Denmark and The Netherlands ought to be deleted, as they have both annulled these laws in recent years.[45] Conversely, following the Pussy Riot incident and with vast support from the Orthodox Church, Russia has sharpened its blasphemy laws in recent times.[46] Hence, while the state of play within the Christian world is not completely static, the number of States upholding blasphemy laws has remained steady at around half a dozen.[47] Accordingly, such laws are clearly not as ubiquitous as in past ages or as in other parts of the world, notably the Middle East and North Africa. Moreover, penalties under enforceable blasphemy laws in the Christian world tend not to be as draconian as in other parts of the world, where the death penalty is not exceptional, at least as a potential punishment.

It may nevertheless be a surprise to find that blasphemy is still on the law books in some predominantly Christian States. Except for Russia, all those listed above are EU Member States. The fact that these States, through their EU membership and in particular the latter's external relations, ***lobby heavily*** for the abrogation

43 States that prohibit insults to religion, religious groups or religious believers include Germany, Iceland, Liechtenstein, Luxembourg, Monaco, Poland, Portugal, San Marino, Slovakia, Spain, Switzerland and Turkey. Crimes against houses of worship – i.e. in the physical sense of violence against churches, vandalising church property, etc. – are widely recognised as a criminal offence, but this category remains outside the scope of this chapter.

44 Pew Research Center, "Laws Penalizing Blasphemy, Apostasy and Defamation of Religion Are Widespread", 21 November 2012, http://www.pewforum.org/2012/11/21/laws-penalizing-blasphemy-apostasy-and-defamation-of-religion-are-widespread/ (accessed 22 January 2019). It should be noted, however, that Pew includes "hate speech laws" under this heading.

45 See Esther Janssen, "The Rise and Fall of the Offence of Blasphemy in The Netherlands", and Lars Binderup Grassmé and Eva Maria Lassen, "The Blasphemy Ban in Denmark", both in Jeroen Temperman and András Koltay, eds., *Blasphemy and Freedom of Expression: Comparative, Theoretical and Historical Reflections after the Charlie Hebdo Massacre* (Cambridge: Cambridge University Press, 2017), 619–42 and 431–55, respectively. Recent parliamentary initiatives to decriminalise blasphemy in Europe appear to have been fed by controversies surrounding blasphemy, such as the Danish cartoons row and the Charlie Hebdo massacre. See the Norway and Denmark chapters in ibid.

46 See, generally, Jeroen Temperman, "'Mother of God, Drive Putin Away': On Blasphemy and Activist Art in the Jurisprudence of the European Court of Human Rights", in Temperman and Koltay, *Blasphemy and Freedom of Expression*, 294–314. This same volume categorises Finland as being among the countries with a "live" blasphemy law.

47 This excludes those States where the crime is strictly formally speaking still on the books or part of common law yet wholly non-indictable on account of the reigning jurisprudence. For a comprehensive analysis of those dormant blasphemy clauses, see Temperman and Koltay, *Blasphemy and Freedom*, part VI.

of blasphemy laws worldwide is therefore indicative of a fair degree of double standards, if not outright hypocrisy. The *EU Guidelines on the Promotion and Protection of Freedom of Religion or Belief* provide that the European Union will "at all appropriate occasions" advocate the position and

> Recall at all appropriate occasions that laws that criminalize blasphemy restrict expression concerning religious or other beliefs; that they are often applied so as to persecute, mistreat, or intimidate persons belonging to religious or other minorities, and that they can have a serious inhibiting effect on freedom of expression and on freedom of religion or belief; and recommend the decriminalisation of such offences.[48]

So there are few blasphemy laws in the Christian world, but they do exist, and typically they are not extremely harsh, but they do criminalise speech and threaten speech acts with penalties. So what do these laws say? One thing that is striking is that, unlike the mediaeval heresy and sacrilege offences – and very much unlike Islamic blasphemy offences – the sheer denial of the existence of God is typically *not* part of the scope of the offence. There are exceptions, however, but these are found in blasphemy offences that are dormant or categorically unenforceable. Notable examples can be found within U.S. law at state level; for instance, the Criminal Code of Massachusetts provides:

> Whoever wilfully blasphemes the holy name of God by denying, cursing or contumeliously reproaching God, his creation, government or final judging of the world, or by cursing or contumeliously reproaching Jesus Christ or the Holy Ghost, or by cursing or contumeliously reproaching or exposing to contempt and ridicule, the holy word of God contained in the holy scriptures shall be punished by imprisonment in jail for not more than one year or by a fine of not more than three hundred dollars, and may also be bound to good behavior.[49]

What is typically prohibited under contemporary "Christian" blasphemy bans is deliberately defiling the dominant or established religion. This also commonly includes the notion that, for the act to be punishable, it must be *meant to offend, outrage, or shock the religious sensitivities* of members of the (established) religion – in fact, this question tends to be the chief legal yardstick.[50] As such, "blasphemy"

48 *EU Guidelines on the Promotion and Protection of Freedom of Religion or Belief*, adopted by the Foreign Affairs Council meeting, Luxembourg, 24 June 2013, para. 32(b), available at https://eeas.europa.eu/sites/eeas/files/137585.pdf (accessed 22 January 2019).

49 Criminal Code of Massachusetts, ch. 272, s. 36.

50 Eg, Irish Defamation Act 2009, Art. 36: "matter that is grossly abusive or insulting in relation to matters held sacred by any religion, thereby *causing outrage among a substantial number of the adherents of that religion*" (emphasis added). However, this provision was repealed on 17 January 2020 following a public referendum. The Russian Criminal Code,

has evolved from an offence against God to an offence against religion (as the sum of individual religious believers). While the law's focus of protection is groups defined by their belief, in practice it may be used occasionally to protect the reputation of religious leaders.

While blasphemy is probably what has survived longest from the extensive historical list of "offences against God and religion", there are some anomalies. Take Sabbath-breaking, for instance. In the Christian world, this is presently largely a municipal matter. Depending on the religiosity of the local religious or non-religious constituencies, opening hours of shops, working times and other activities may or may not be affected through municipal laws. While some parts of the Christian world are still more or less shielded from the 24/7 economy, it should be clear that Sabbath-breaking no longer carries the sense of taboo – and threat – of Exodus 31:15: "Six days shall work be done, but the seventh day is a Sabbath of solemn rest, holy to the LORD. Whoever does any work on the Sabbath day shall be put to death". Interestingly, Tonga is perhaps among the fiercest defenders of the sacredness of Sabbath. Article 6 of its Constitution provides:

> The Sabbath Day shall be kept holy in Tonga and no person shall practise his trade or profession or conduct any commercial undertaking on the Sabbath Day except according to law; and any agreement made or witnessed on that day shall be null and void and of no legal effect.

This clause is inserted in the opening chapter, which lists fundamental rights, and follows the freedom of religion clause, thus reading as a significant caveat. What serves as an explanation is that Methodism, and especially membership of the Free Wesleyan Church, is relatively widespread in Tonga and the royal family has traditionally had links to this denomination.

13.4 Blasphemy and human rights

The momentum within the Christian world to annul blasphemy laws has largely been fed by the contemporary human rights movement. Blasphemy laws, in that light, are seen not only as archaic and one-sided[51] – typically protecting exclu-

Art. 148 (inserted pursuant to the law of 11 June 2013, following the Pussy Riot church incident) criminalises "public actions clearly defying the society and committed ***with the express purpose of insulting religious beliefs***" (emphasis added), while the second paragraph of this provision adopts harsher punishments if the blasphemous act targets holy symbols or religious texts.

51 For the legal-political discussions in the UK, for instance, see House of Lords' Select Committee on Religious Offences in England and Wales, "Religious Offences in England and Wales: First Report, Session 2002–2003", Appendix 3: Blasphemy, para. 2, available at https://publications.parliament.uk/pa/ld200203/ldselect/ldrelof/95/9501.htm (accessed 22 January 2019), which holds, on the obsolete nature of the offence: "The legal notion of blasphemy dates back many centuries. Faith was seen to be the root of society's political

sively the dominant religions, or at least doing so more robustly than they do minority religions – but also and especially as contrary to important fundamental freedoms. The two freedoms mobilised in this debate are freedom of expression, naturally, and the right to freedom of religion or belief: after all, one person's blasphemy is another person's free manifestation of religion. Blasphemy has been abolished as a consequence of these legal, political and societal debates, but it would be more apt to say that it has been replaced: in many Western hemisphere States, the ancient crime of blasphemy has been replaced by one that accords better with the demands of contemporary international human rights law, namely standards against "hate speech" (or, more strictly speaking, hateful speech acts that incite violence or discrimination based on religion).[52]

Indeed, in recent years, international monitoring bodies and other international stakeholders have united in declaring blasphemy laws incompatible with the demands of modern human rights law. The UN Human Rights Committee, monitoring compliance with the UN International Covenant on Civil and Political Rights, provides: "Prohibitions of displays of lack of respect for a religion or other belief system, including blasphemy laws, are incompatible with the Covenant".[53] UN Special Rapporteurs have seconded this view.[54] The UN Special Rapporteur on freedom of religion or belief posits that "blasphemy laws typically

and moral behaviour. Therefore, to challenge that faith or to offend against it was to seriously threaten the very fabric of political and moral society and had to be punished severely. Clearly, that is no longer the case. Some might regret that, but it does not alter the fact that the law is now concerned with the preservation of the peace of the realm, and the concern is not so much with views of the deity as with the satisfactory state of society". For the Republic of Ireland, the Irish Law Reform Commission, *Consultation Paper on the Crime of Libel*, August 1991, para. 231, available at https://www.lawreform.ie/_fileupload/consultation%20papers/cpCrimeofLibel.htm (accessed 22 January 2019), similarly, and decades ago, developed a fierce position against maintaining the offence on the law books.

52 See the International Covenant on Civil and Political Rights, Art. 20(2). See also the International Convention on the Elimination of All Forms of Racial Discrimination, Art. 4, for a dissimilar anti-hate speech clause, not listing the ground of religion. It is not so in the United States, where such laws may be equally unconstitutional under the First Amendment of the Constitution (it should be noted that the United States has made an express reservation to Article 20 of the ICCPR upon ratification). That said, U.S. exceptionalism, as compared to other Western States, is both questioned in the literature (see e.g. Jeremy Waldron, *The Harm in Hate Speech* [Cambridge, MA: Harvard University Press, 2014]) and to some extent belied by legal reality (hate speech regulation is occasionally or perhaps even increasingly introduced "through the back door" not only through, for instance, university campus regulations, but also through criminal law by creating links – notably in the area of counterterrorism efforts – to notions of "complicity", "conspiracy" and so on).

53 Human Rights Committee, "General Comment 34: Article 19: Freedoms of Opinion and Expression" (CCPR/C/GC/34, adopted at its 102nd session, Geneva, 11–29 July 2011), para. 48. The Committee makes an exception for those speech acts that amount to incitement in the meaning of ICCPR, Art. 20(2).

54 Report of the Special Rapporteur on freedom of religion or belief, Asma Jahangir, and the Special Rapporteur on contemporary forms of racism, racial discrimination, xenophobia and related intolerance, Doudou Diène, further to Human Rights Council decision 1/107 on

have intimidating effects on members of religious minorities as well as on critics or dissenters".[55] The UN Special Rapporteur on freedom of expression similarly objects to blasphemy laws, deeming them to be "inherently vague and leave the entire concept open to abuse".[56] Recent freedom of speech benchmarks have picked up the baton and taken a position against blasphemy laws. Accordingly, the UN Office of the High Commission for Human Rights (OHCHR)-led initiative entitled the "Rabat Plan of Action", which seeks to define the line between protected speech on issues of religion and unprotected incitement, provides that

> many blasphemy laws afford different levels of protection to different religions and have often proved to be applied in a discriminatory manner. There are numerous examples of persecution of religious minorities or dissenters, but also of atheists and non-theists, as a result of legislation on religious offences or overzealous application of laws containing neutral language. Moreover, the right to freedom of religion or belief, as enshrined in relevant international legal standards, does not include the right to have a religion or a belief that is free from criticism or ridicule.[57]

The one notable exception to this trend is the European Court of Human Rights, which in a series of cases has sanctioned blasphemy restrictions on free speech.[58] Not only is this jurisprudence out of touch with the developments within wider (UN) international law noted above, but also the judgments concerned are also extremely badly reasoned. The biggest flaws in this body of jurisprudence are: First, in almost all such cases the Court stretches the right to freedom of religion or belief to unreasonable proportions. That is, the Court distils from the European Convention on Human Rights *a right not to be offended in one's religious feelings*, a right not specifically enshrined by the Convention and, more importantly, a right fundamentally at odds with that same right to have and manifest freely

incitement to racial and religious hatred and the promotion of tolerance, UN Doc. A/HRC/2/3, 20 September 2006, para. 42.

55 Special Rapporteur on freedom of religion or belief, "Tackling Manifestations of Collective Religious Hatred" (A/HRC/25/58, 26 December 2013), para. 59.

56 Special Rapporteur on the promotion and protection of the right to freedom of opinion and expression, "Report of the Special Rapporteur to the General Assembly on Hate Speech and Incitement to Hatred" (A/67/357, 7 September 2012), para. 53.

57 "Rabat Plan of Action on the prohibition of advocacy of national, racial or religious hatred that constitutes incitement to discrimination, hostility or violence", conclusions and recommendations emanating from the four regional expert workshops organised by the OHCHR in 2011, and adopted by experts in Rabat, Morocco on 5 October 2012, para. 19.

58 See e.g. *X. Ltd. and Y. v. United Kingdom* App. no. 8710/79 (European Commission on Human Rights, 7 May 1982); *Otto-Preminger-Institut v. Austria* App. no. 13470/87 (ECtHR, 20 September 1994); *Wingrove v. United Kingdom* App. no. 17419/90 (ECtHR, 25 November 1996); and *İ.A. v. Turkey* App. no. 42571/98 (ECtHR, 13 September 2005). See also, *mutatis mutandis*, *Murphy v. Ireland* App. no. 44179/98 (ECtHR, 10 July 2003) (not strictly a blasphemy case but sanctioning restrictions on speech about religion).

one's religion or belief, including religions and beliefs deeply offensive to others. Second, in such blasphemy cases the Court fails to apply the necessity test. At a very abstract level, freedom of expression may threaten freedom of religion or belief (notably in the context of incitement to violence or discrimination on religious grounds); yet, should that be the legitimacy behind restricting speech about religion, then that particular harm or the risk thereof must be firmly substantiated. In none of the blasphemy cases is this ever done, not by the respondent State and not, in its capacity as monitoring body, by the European Court of Human Rights itself.

There are indications, however, that the Strasbourg human rights court will revise its case law on blasphemy laws before long, or is already in the process of doing so. The Court's judges are deeply divided over this issue, as became very evident in some of the cases.[59] Moreover, the exact scope of permissible blasphemy laws is being eroded by the Court. For instance, profound criticism and even (offensive) satire aimed at religion and religious leaders may not be combated by States under the guise of blasphemy laws.[60] Importantly, the Court applied a more rigorous necessity test in these more recent cases, underscoring that not every form of satire or provocation, however insulting and offensive it may be, truly undermines core religious rights to have and manifest one's religion.[61] Finally, the Court came close to a full U-turn in the recent Pussy Riot case.[62] Members of this punk-rock group received custodial sentences over charges not of blasphemy but of "hooliganism for reasons of religious hatred and enmity and for reasons of hatred towards a particular social group", as a result of performing protest songs – aimed, *inter alia*, at the Putin regime and its collaboration with the Russian Orthodox Church – in, among other places, a Moscow church. It is the first time that the Strasbourg Court has explicitly posited that, for speech acts to be punishable by the State, the necessity test requires *an element of incitement to religious hatred.* Specifically, the Court

> accepts that as the conduct in question took place in a cathedral it could have been found offensive by a number of people, which might include churchgoers, however, having regard to its case-law and the above-mentioned

59 The case of *İ.A. v. Turkey* resulted in a split 4:3 decision and hence a very narrow decision in favour of sanctioning blasphemy laws. The three dissenting judges – Costa, Cabral Barreto and Jungwiert – argued that "the time has perhaps come to 'revisit' this case-law, which in our view seems to place too much emphasis on conformism or uniformity of thought and to reflect an overcautious and timid conception of freedom of the press". (Joint dissenting opinion of Mr Costa, Mr Cabral Barreto and Mr Jungwiert, para. 8.)

60 *Klein v. Slovakia* App. no. 72208/01 (ECtHR, 31 October 2006). Other decisions that may announce the Court's altering its course on this issue include *Albert-Engelmann-Gesellschaft mbH v. Austria* App. no. 46389/99 (ECtHR, 19 January 2006); and *Nur Radyo Ve Televizyon Yayinciligi A.S. v. Turkey* App. no. 6587/03 (ECtHR, 27 November 2007).

61 E.g. *Klein v. Slovakia*, paras 51–4; see also, *mutatis mutandis*, *Nur Radyo Ve Televizyon Yayinciligi A.S. v. Turkey*.

62 *Mariya Alekhina and Others v. Russia* App. no. 38004/12 (ECtHR, 17 July 2018).

> international standards for the protection of freedom of expression, it is unable to discern any element in the domestic courts' analysis which would allow a description of the applicants' conduct as incitement to religious hatred.[63]

This judgment may well be the final blow to European religious offence laws, including blasphemy laws, in predominantly Christian Member States of the Council of Europe, since these laws place the threshold for interference with free speech considerably lower than the criterion of "incitement".

13.5 Concluding remarks

Whether or not blasphemy laws, which in most parts of the Christian world are dormant,[64] have a chilling effect on free speech and on religious freedom, the main fault is that they seek to protect the amorphous concept of religion rather than believers (individually or collectively) or public order more generally. This focus leads to some perverse dynamics. The chief indicator as to whether the norm is breached is derived from the protected group itself. If that group takes offence, then a crime is constituted. One of the most recently enacted blasphemy laws within the Christian world, namely Ireland, serves as an excellent case in point:

> a person publishes or utters blasphemous matter if (a) he or she publishes or utters matter that is grossly abusive or insulting in relation to matters held sacred by any religion, thereby causing *outrage among a substantial number of the adherents of that religion*, and (b) he or she *intends, by the publication or utterance of the matter concerned, to cause such outrage*.[65]

What was up until recently the landmark European Court of Human Rights judgment on blasphemy, *Otto-Preminger-Institut*, further illustrates that – however the law is framed, blasphemy laws ultimately seek to foster respect for the religious sensitivities of the majority religion. Crucial in the Court's considerations were religious demographics:

63 Ibid., at para. 225.

64 Albeit with some fairly draconian exceptions. For example, in Greece and Russia, among other States, such legislation repeatedly leads to sentences, including custody. For Greece, see Effie Fokas, "God's Advocates: The Multiple Fronts of the War on Blasphemy in Greece", in Temperman and Koltay, *Blasphemy and Freedom of Expression*, 389–410; for Russia, see Temperman, "'Mother of God, Drive Putin Away'". For other fairly active blasphemy or religious defamation laws in predominantly Christian States, see the chapters on Finland (by Tuomas Äystö), Italy (by Cristiana Cianitto), Germany (by Matthias Cornils) and Poland (by Joanna Kulesza and Jan Kulesza) in the same volume.

65 Defamation Act 2009, Art. 36, emphasis added.

> The Court cannot disregard the fact that the Roman Catholic religion is the religion of the overwhelming majority of Tyroleans. In seizing the film, the Austrian authorities acted to ensure religious peace in that region and to prevent that some people should feel the object of attacks on their religious beliefs in an unwarranted and offensive manner.[66]

If one reverses the reasoning, the point is strengthened: since the overwhelming majority of locals adhered to the same dominant religion, no believer's capacity to perform his or her religious duties; no individual's right to have, hold, maintain and practise their religion; and no fundamental rights were ever going to be truly threatened, let alone affected, by the screening of a film which was, no doubt, blasphemous.

Further reading

Blackstone, William. *Commentaries on the Laws of England*, 4 vols (Oxford: Clarendon Press, 1765–9).

Marshall, Paul and Nina Shea. *Silenced: How Apostasy and Blasphemy Codes Are Choking Freedom Worldwide* (Oxford: Oxford University Press, 2011).

Robinson, Olivia. "Blasphemy and Sacrilege in Roman Law", (1973) 8 *Irish Jurist* 356–71.

Temperman, Jeroen. "Blasphemy, Defamation of Religions and Human Rights Law", (2008) 26.4 *Netherlands Quarterly of Human Rights* 517–45.

Temperman, Jeroen. *Religious Hatred and International Law: The Prohibition of Incitement to Violence or Discrimination* (Cambridge: Cambridge University Press, 2016).

Temperman, Jeroen and András Koltay, eds. *Blasphemy and Freedom of Expression: Comparative, Theoretical and Historical Reflections After the Charlie Hebdo Massacre* (Cambridge: Cambridge University Press, 2017).

66 *Otto-Preminger-Institut v. Austria*, para. 56.

14 Sex crimes and Christianity

John Witte

Sex has long excited an intimate union between theology and law in the Western legal tradition. For two millennia, both Churches and States issued detailed private laws and guidelines to define and facilitate licit sex within an enduring and exclusive marital bed. They also issued elaborate penal laws and procedures to prohibit and punish illicit sex. Church and State officials periodically fought over whose laws governed the sexual field. And they periodically shifted the line between sexual *sins*, which remained under church law alone, and sexual *crimes*, which were punished by the State (as well). Nonetheless, until the twentieth century, Churches and State alike played formidable roles in defining and regulating licit and illicit sex.

A typical early modern list of sex crimes – in civil law and common law lands alike – included abduction, abortion, adultery, bestiality, buggery, child abuse, concubinage, contraception, feticide, fornication, homosexual acts, illegitimacy, incest, infanticide, malicious desertion, masturbation, obscenity, polygamy, pornography, prostitution, rape, seduction and sodomy. Sometimes more exotic offences were added, such as castration, transvestism, mixed bathing, public nudity, sexual contact by or with clerics or monastics, and others. Sometimes defendants were charged with catch-all sex crimes such as "perversion", "indecency", "lewdness", "abomination" or "unnatural sex". Many of these sex crimes had shifting and sometimes eliding definitions over time and across legal systems and were variously classified as "offences against God", "religion", "morality", "nature", "public order" or "persons".[1] Until a century ago, sex offenders faced severe criminal punishment – execution in egregious cases.

Today, most of these traditional sex crimes have been eclipsed by the dramatic rise of new constitutional laws and cultural norms of sexual liberty. Traditional

1 See, e.g. J. Kohler and Willy Scheel, *Die peinliche gerichtsordnung kaiser Karls V. Constitutio criminalis Carolina* (Halle: Verlag der Buchhandlung des Waisenhauses, 1900), 62–4; Paul Johann Anselm von Feuerbach, *Lehrbuch des gemeinen in Deutschland geltenden peinlichen Rechts* (Giessen: G.F. Heyer, 1801), 484–508, §§ 413–36; G. Mueller, ed. *The French Penal Code* [1801] (New York: Fred B. Rothman & Co., 1976), Arts. 283–90, 316–17, 330–40; William Blackstone, *Commentaries on the Laws of England*, 4 vols. (Boston: Beacon Press, 1962; first published 1765–9), vol. 4, ch. 4.11, 15; James Fitzjames Stephen, *A History of the Criminal Law of England*, 3 vols. (Cambridge: Cambridge University Press, 2014; first published 1883), 3:10, 117–18.

crimes of contraception, abortion, fornication and sodomy have been struck down as antiquated and unconstitutional. Prohibitions on adultery, concubinage and non-marital sex and cohabitation have become dead letters, and modern law no longer visits "the sins of the fathers" or mothers upon non-marital children. Free speech laws protect all manner of sexual expression, short of obscenity, although the wildest unregulated frontiers of prurience are now only a mouse-click away. Privacy laws protect most forms of sexual conduct among consenting adults, including adult prostitution in some democracies. The classic sex crimes of incest and polygamy still remain on the books, but they are now the subjects of growing constitutional and cultural battles. Only one traditional sex crime has strengthened in recent decades: the crime of rape, now joined by strong new prohibitions against sexual assault, battery, stalking and harassment, as well as the sexual abuse and statutory rape of children. The sex crimes that remain, however, are now usually labelled as crimes against "persons", "dignity" or "sexual autonomy", rather than crimes against God, morality or nature.

This radical reduction of traditional sex crimes over the past century reflects not only the rise of modern constitutional liberty but also the shift of modern criminal law away from a "fault-based" to a "harm-based" system of liability. Traditional fault-based logic swept in many consensual and victimless sex acts that were considered to be just wrong (*malum in se*) – adultery, fornication, sodomy, bestiality, buggery, group sex, same-sex relations and other perceived sexual taboos. Modern harm-based logic ignores most such acts and instead focuses on crimes that inflict involuntary harm, particularly to vulnerable victims like young children or rape victims. To be sure, some traditional crimes remain hard to classify today: scholars debate whether pornography, prostitution and polygamy are *harm* crimes that should remain on the books or *fault* crimes that need to be removed. But many other traditional sex crimes based on moral fault have fallen aside.

Finally, the reduction of modern sex crimes reflects the transformation of modern family law. Historically, Western family law promoted the integration of marriage, sex and procreation within an enduring and exclusive marital household. Criminal law, in turn, prohibited sexual conduct that threatened or undermined this integrated domestic ideal. Today, family law countenances a far wider range of sexual activities and domestic relationships. And it accommodates several "striking new separations in the sexual field"[2] – separations between (1) marriage and sex; (2) marriage and childbirth; (3) marriage and child rearing; (4) childbirth and parenting; (5) sex and physical contact, given the advent of cybersex; and (6) childbirth, sexual intercourse and biological filiation, given the rise of artificial reproductive technology, sperm banks and surrogacy. This new family law regime has far less room and need for many traditional sex crimes.

2 Don S. Browning, "Family Law and Christian Jurisprudence", in John Witte, Jr. and Frank S. Alexander, eds., *Christianity and Law: An Introduction* (Cambridge: Cambridge University Press, 2008), 165.

Modern Christians living in Western liberal societies have variously celebrated or lamented all of these changes. Some Christians have been at the forefront of the sexual revolution and advocated and embraced at least some of these new sexual norms, while offering innovative theological arguments in support of them. Some churches have largely gone with the cultural flow on issues of sexuality and sexual liberty, with or without much change to their official teachings. Some churches have retained or re-emphasised strict standards of traditional sexual morality, with internal church laws holding their congregants to these standards as a condition for leadership, if not membership. Many churches have also been deeply challenged, and sometimes divided, over pressing new legal and moral issues about abortion, contraception, artificial reproductive technology, women's rights, children's rights, same-sex marriage, no-fault divorce, re-marriage and more. Finally, several churches have been roiled by massive scandals and criminal prosecution for clerical paedophilia and cover-ups by church leaders, as well as sexual and psychological abuses by pastors, counsellors, teachers, coaches and charity workers in religious organisations.

I touch lightly on these latter difficult topics at the end, knowing that they deserve much fuller treatment. I first review the main historical teachings on sex crimes in the Bible and the Western legal tradition. I then explore how traditional sexual morality may still be viable for modern liberal States and Christian Churches.

14.1 Sex crimes in the Bible

Many traditional Western sex crimes were rooted in the Bible. The Old Testament grounded its sexual prohibitions in religious narratives of personal purity and communal fidelity to God's covenant. The Mosaic law treated bestiality, buggery and most forms of incest as capital crimes. Adultery was a capital crime, too, although the sexual double-standard of the day restricted this offence to extramarital intercourse by the wife, not her husband. Similarly, it was a capital offence for a betrothed woman, but not her fiancé, to have consensual sex with another before the wedding. The Mosaic law prohibited castration, sex during menstruation, harm to a foetus and child sacrifice, joining pre-Mosaic customs that condemned men for "spilling [their] seed on the ground" (Gen. 38:9) after sexual contact. It further prohibited harlotry, interreligious marriage and sex between divorcees. It called for variant punishments for rape and seduction of a woman. If the victim was married, her innocent husband or the authorities could mete out (capital) punishment. If the victim was single, the rapist had to pay a dowry to her father; marry the victim if she and her father would have him; and waive his right to divorce. In most other cases, a husband could divorce his wife for her "indecency", leaving both parties free to re-marry another. A husband could also take multiple wives, and was obliged to do so in some cases of seduction, enslavement, famine, childless marriage or the premature death of his married brother.[3]

3 Exod. 20:14; 21:7–12, 22; 22:16–19; Lev. 18:6–23, 19:20–22, 29; 20:1–6, 10–22; Deut. 5:18; 7:3–4; 17:17; 21:15–16; 22:20–30; 23:17–18; 24:1–23; 27:21–23; Prov. 6:32–35,

The Mosaic law repeatedly called God's chosen covenant people of Israel to a higher plane of sexual morality than the Gentiles around them. "Do not defile yourselves by any of these things", reads Leviticus 18:24–29 after a lengthy recitation of "sins of the flesh".

> For whoever shall do any of these abominations, the persons that do them shall be cut off from among their people. So keep my charge never to practice any of these abominable customs which were practised before you, and never to defile yourselves by them [lest the holy land] vomit you out.

The New Testament not only echoed some of these Mosaic sexual prohibitions, but also called for greater equitable and egalitarian application of them. For example, the Gospel of Matthew reports that Joseph could have had Mary, his fiancée, stoned for her presumptive pre-marital adultery, but he endeavoured to break the engagement quietly without dishonouring her. Jesus rescued an adulterous woman sentenced to death. "[H]e who is without sin, cast the first stone", Jesus challenged her accusers, before ordering her to sin no more (John 8:7). Jesus called his followers to live by the letter and spirit of the laws on sexual purity. "You have heard that it was said, 'You shall not commit adultery'. But I say to you that everyone who looks at a woman lustfully has already committed adultery with her in his heart" (Matt. 5:27–28). He also ordered men to rein in divorce: "Everyone who divorces his wife, except on the ground of unchastity, makes her an adulteress; and whoever marries a divorced woman commits adultery" (Matt. 19:3–9).

St Paul offered similar teachings. While encouraging celibacy for the single and widowed, and repeating conventional norms about male headship, Paul also insisted that "the husband should give to the wife her conjugal rights" (1 Cor. 7:3) and told husbands "to love your wives, as Christ loved the church, and gave himself up for her" (Eph. 5:25). He also glossed Jesus' prohibitions on adultery and lust with denunciations of incest, sodomy, prostitution, polygamy, seduction, immoderate dress and grooming and other forms of sexual "immorality" and "perversion".[4] "Flee fornication!" (1 Cor. 6:18) was Paul's most famous admonition, which he directed to men and women alike. "Do you not know that he who joins himself to a prostitute becomes one body with her?" Paul challenged his male readers.

with discussion in Louis M. Epstein, *Sex Laws and Customs in Judaism* (New York: KTAV Publishing House, 1967); Ralph W. Scott, *A New Look at Biblical Crime* (Chicago: Nelson-Hall, 1979); Carolyn Pressler, "Sexual Legislation", in Brent A. Strawn, ed., *The Oxford Encyclopedia of the Bible and Law*, 2 vols. (Oxford: Oxford University Press, 2015), 2:290–302.

4 Rom. 1:24–27; 1 Cor. 5:1; 6:9, 15–20, 7:1–6; Eph. 5:3–4, 25; Col. 3:5–6; 1 Tim. 2:9–10; 3:2; 1 Thess. 4:3–8; Hebr. 13:4.

> For, as it is written, "The two shall become one flesh". Every other sin which a man commits is outside the body; but the immoral man sins against his own body. Do you not know that your body is a temple of the Holy Spirit within you?... Therefore, honour God with your bodies".
>
> (1 Cor. 6:16–20)

While repeating this general call for bodily purity and spiritual chastity, the early Church Fathers and Talmud Rabbis offered further biblical rationales for specific sex crimes.[5] Bestiality, they argued, defied the differences between species that God had separated at creation; after all, Adam could find no beast in Paradise like him, which had led God to create Eve whom Adam recognised as "bone of my bones, flesh of my flesh" (Gen. 2:23). Homosexual acts confused the genders that God had separated – "male and female he created them" (Gen. 1:27). Sex during menstruation, *coitus interruptus* and masturbation were lustful acts that defied the primal divine command to "be fruitful and multiply" (Gen. 1:28). Contraception, abortion, foeticide and infanticide also defied the primal command of procreation and raising up the next generation of God's people. Rape, fornication and adultery brought harm and shame to the innocent victim and her family, and could produce "bastards" who suffered significant legal disabilities, since "no bastard shall enter the assembly of the Lord" (Gen. 23:2). Incestuous marriages corrupted the blood, commingled the property, weakened the family tree and compromised the legacy and inheritance of the marital family and the strength of its alliances with other families and communities. These early interpretations of biblical sex crimes were incorporated into early Christian canon laws and penitential books, and into later Christianised Roman law as well.

14.2 Sex crimes in the Western legal tradition

14.2.1 Thomas Aquinas

At the height of the Middle Ages, the Dominican friar Thomas Aquinas (1225–74) integrated these biblical teachings into a natural law theory of sex crimes that became axiomatic in the Western legal tradition. Thomas knew the Roman law of sex crimes and the mediaeval civilian jurisprudence it had inspired. Emperor Justinian's sixth-century collection of laws, for example, outlawed as "contrary to nature itself" all forms of bestiality, sodomy, adultery, incest, rape, prostitution, seduction of virgins; sex with nuns, slaves and minors; and sex in groups or in public places, such as baths. These crimes Justinian variously branded as "abominable", "wicked", "execrable" and "insane" forms of "debauchery" that were

5 Sample texts in David G. Hunter, *Marriage in the Early Church* (Minneapolis: Fortress Press, 1992); Epstein, *Sex Laws and Customs.* The seventeenth-century English jurist John Selden offered a brilliant synthesis of these early teachings in his *On Jewish Marriage Law: The Uxor Hebraica*, trans. Jonathan R. Ziskind (Leiden: Brill, 1991).

"hateful to God" and God's laws. Any children born of such unions, he declared, were "bastards" who were "irredeemable" and "non-heritable".[6]

Thomas also knew the Church's canon laws on sex offences. By his day, the scholastics had arranged these offences in a hierarchy. Most began with the baseline of simple fornication and then added crimes of escalating gravity: prostitution, concubinage, seduction, bigamy, adultery, rape and incest. Graver still were "unnatural" sexual acts (gay and lesbian relations, bestiality, oral sex, anal sex and sex with children). Gravest of all were non- or anti-procreative sex acts (masturbation, contraception, sterilisation, abortion and infanticide). Each of these offences was worse, still, when committed by ordained clergy, avowed monastics or recidivists whether clerical or lay; or when aggravated by the commission of other crimes such as battery, theft, kidnapping or homicide.[7]

To sort out this legal inheritance and to devise his theory of sex crimes, Thomas began with several facts about the nature of human sexuality and reproduction. First, he observed, most humans crave sex all the time, especially when they are young and most fertile. Unlike other animals, humans do not have a short rutting or mating season, followed by a prolonged period of sexual inactivity. Second, human babies are born weak, fragile and utterly dependent for many years. Unlike most other animals, they cannot run, swim or fly away on their own upon birth or shortly thereafter. They need protection, food, shelter, clothing and education in order to survive, let alone thrive. Third, most human mothers have difficulty caring fully for their children on their own, especially if they already have other children. They need help, especially from fathers and their kin networks. Fourth, however, most human fathers will bond and help care for children only if they are certain of their paternity. Put a baby cradle in a public place and most women will stop out of natural empathy. Most men will walk by, unless they are unusually charitable or deputised to provide care. Once assured of their paternity, however, most men will bond deeply with their children, help with their care and support and defend them at great sacrifice. For they will see their children as a continuation and extension of themselves of their being, name, property and heritage.[8]

6 Bruce W. Frier, *et al.*, eds. and trans., *The Codex of Justinian: A New Annotated Translation, with Parallel Latin and Greek Text* (Cambridge: Cambridge University Press, 2016), 6.57.5.1, 5.27; Fred H. Blume, trans., *Justinian's Novels* (1952, unpublished), available at http://www.uwyo.edu/lawlib/blume-justinian/ajc-edition-1/novels/index.html (accessed 23 January 2019), 74, 77.1, 89.5, 141.

7 James A. Brundage, *Law, Sex, and Christian Society in Medieval Europe* (Chicago: University of Chicago Press, 1987) 207, 212–14, 225–6, 241–51; Vern L. Bullough and James A. Brundage, *Sexual Practices and the Medieval Church* (Buffalo: Prometheus Books, 1982), 89–101, 129–60, 176–87.

8 Thomas Aquinas, *Summa Theologica*, trans. Fathers of the English Dominican Province (London: Thomas Moore, 1948) (hereafter *ST*), I, q. 99, a. 1; V Supp., q. 41, a. 1–2; q. 49, a. 1–6; Thomas Aquinas, *Summa Contra Gentiles*, trans. Vernon J. Bourke (Notre Dame: University of Notre Dame Press 1975) (hereafter *SCG*), III.II.122–3.

Given these facts, Thomas concluded, rational humans have learned to develop enduring and exclusive marital unions as a good and advantageous form of sexual bonding and reproductive success. Such unions serve the ongoing sexual needs and desires of husband and wife. They ensure that both a father and mother are certain that a baby born to them is theirs. They ensure that both parents will care for, nurture and educate their children until they mature. And, these unions deter both spouses from dangerous sex outside the marital bed.[9]

But nature creates only a wobbly normative framework, given our perennial human sex drives and temptations, Thomas argued. Both Church and State thus need to enact firm and clear positive laws to guide and govern their members. The Church must offer comprehensive spiritual direction about sexual vices and virtues, drawing not only on natural law but also on sacramental, moral and biblical teachings. Accordingly, the Church's confessional books and canon laws contain far more detailed and expansive instructions about sex than what appears in the State's criminal law. The State has a more limited jurisdiction over sex based on natural law and natural justice alone, making its roll of sex crimes shorter and more focused. Thomas worked through these sex crimes, one by one, often leavening his arguments from nature with prudential and practical considerations.

"Simple fornication" between a single man and a single woman, he said, was criminal because it jeopardises the health and future of the woman and "tends to injure the life of the offspring to be born of this union". If a fornicating woman becomes pregnant, she may well be left alone to care for her child, which is risky for her and her children. Yes, a wedding could be hastily arranged before birth. This, however, risks a non-consensual marriage and the woman may be suspected of fornication with others, too, making it harder to determine the father of her child who will provide vital care when the infant child needs it most. Yes, an unmarried father or a stepfather might still provide child support and education to his illegitimate child, but doing so was not typical of most males. So, Thomas concluded, "human nature rebels against an indeterminate union of the sexes" in fornication, and the State must prohibit it clearly, though punish it quite lightly through fines or forms of public shaming or community service.[10]

Thomas was surprisingly tolerant of prostitution. He considered it a necessity of social order, given the realities that some men will always be unattached and will inevitably seek sex somewhere. Prostitution was rather like a "sewer" in a castle, Thomas said; without it, the castle would be filled with filth. Similarly, a society without prostitution would be filled with fornication, adultery, "sodomy" and other sex crimes, and sometimes with violence, too, born of rape or seduction of innocent women. It was better, on balance, to allow prostitution to continue discretely and allow prostitutes to keep their fees instead of banning the practice and imposing higher risks and costs on all others.[11]

9 *SCG* III.123; *ST* II-II, q. 26, a. 7–9; V, q. 49, a. 1–2.

10 *ST* II-II, q. 154, a. 2.

11 *ST* II-II, q. 10, a. 2; II-II, q. 60, a. 2, 5; II-II, q. 87, a. 2; II-II, q. 108, a. 8.

For Thomas, it was a graver offence when an unmarried man seduced a virgin or manipulated or tricked her into bed. Not only did this sexual encounter carry the same risk of harm to any child born of the union, but an additional "two-fold injustice attaches to it", Thomas wrote. The victim was now hindered from contracting a lawful marriage and likely put on the road to "a wanton life", since a non-virgin in that day had a much harder time finding a husband. The seduction was also unjust to the father, guardian or fiancé of the victim, whose investment in and relationship with her was damaged. The crime was even worse, other scholastics argued, when committed against a younger girl who could be more easily manipulated, or a "kept" woman such as a maid, ward, patient, tenant or passenger who had no real choice but to yield to a man's sexual predations. Seduction was a serious offence in Thomas' day, punishable by heavy fines and seizure of the criminal's property, sometimes banishment from the community, too.[12]

Rape was worse than fornication and seduction, Thomas argued, because it involved violence against the woman or against her family and was often accompanied by other violent crimes such as abduction or aggravated battery. Such violence exacerbated the harm and constituted an additional crime against the body of the victim and against the property and other interests of her family. Forcible rape was a major capital crime in the mediaeval world, on the same order of gravity as assassination and treason, and brazen or repeat offenders could face execution.[13]

"Adultery is more serious than seduction", Thomas continued, and even worse when "aggravated by the use of violence". When either the husband or the wife gained "access to another's marriage-bed", it breached marital fidelity and trust and caused harm to the entire family. It brought in sexual diseases that affected the innocent spouse and future offspring. It risked "bastard" children, who were either cast out of the home with slender chances of success or left in the home to become rivals to legitimate children and their mother. Adultery often led to separation of the married couple, yielding further dissipation of parental resources and care for children, and still greater temptation for both spouses to test the neighbour's bed. Even worse, it could lead to private revenge by the betrayed spouse, or murder of the betrayed spouse by the adulterous lovers. Adultery was thus a capital crime, Thomas argued.[14]

Polygamy constituted serial adultery, Thomas believed, and was a capital crime, too. Polyandry (one woman with multiple men), though rare, was unjust to children. A woman having sex with several husbands would undermine paternal certainty and investment in the children's care. The children would suffer from neglect and the wife would be overburdened trying to care for them and to tend to her multiple husbands and their sexual needs. Polygyny (one man with multiple women) was unjust to wives as well as children. Polygyny did not

12 *ST* II-II, q. 154, a. 6.
13 *ST* II-II, q. 154, a. 7; *SCG* III.122.
14 *ST* II-II, q. 154, a. 8, 12; II-II, q. 160; V q. 60, a. 1–2; V, q. 64, a. 1–4; V, q. 68.

necessarily erode paternal certainty, Aquinas allowed. As long as his multiple wives were faithful to him alone, a man could feel assured of being the father of any child born in his household. But this would require a man to pen up his wives like cattle, isolating them from other roving males, even when his own energies to tend to them were dissipated over the several women and children in his household. While locked up at home, the wives would be reduced to servants and set in perpetual competition with each other and with rival children for resources and access to their shared husband. This is not marriage but "a sort of slavery", said Aquinas.

> So, if it is not lawful for the wife to have several husbands, since this is contrary to the certainty as to offspring, it would not be lawful, on the other hand, for a man to have several wives, for the friendship of husband and wife would not be free, but somewhat servile. And this argument is corroborated by experience, for among husbands having plural wives the wives have a status like that of servants.

"Natural justice" thus calls for monogamy alone, and criminal law must punish polygamists.[15]

Incest was an "unnatural" sex crime, too, Thomas argued. "There is something essentially unbecoming and contrary to natural reason in sexual intercourse between persons related by blood". If allowed, it would obstruct the proper relationships of authority and obedience between parents and children, elders and youth. It would heighten the temptations to lust and produce an "excessive ardour of love" among relatives who lived together or near each other. It would also "hinder a man from having many friends" beyond his relatives, and in a peaceful society "it is most necessary that there be friendship among many peoples". Even animals, with only natural instincts to guide them, are "horrified" by sexual contact with their "close" blood relatives, Aquinas added. Rational human beings have built on this natural instinct to develop more refined impediments of consanguinity and affinity to avoid sex and marriage among even distant relatives.[16]

The gravest offences of all were what Thomas called "unnatural" acts of masturbation, sodomy, bestiality and "effeminacy". Thomas treated them only briefly as scandalous violations of the natural use of the sexual body and the natural procreative ends of sexual interaction. Even worse, these were offences against God himself and the natural order of creation. Thomas quoted favourably St Augustine's harsh instructions: "Those foul offences that are against nature should be everywhere at all times detested and punished", with the State emulating God's fiery wrath against "the people of Sodom".[17]

15 *SCG* III.123–4; *ST* V, q. 44, a. 1; V, q. 49, a. 2; V, q. 65, a. 1–2.
16 *ST* II-II, q. 154, a. 10; *SCG* III.125.6; *ST* V, q. 54–5.
17 *ST* II-II, q. 154, a. 12, reply obj. 1; *SCG* III.122, 126.

14.2.2 Later teachings

Thomas' wide-ranging arguments to encourage and enforce exclusive and enduring marriages while prohibiting and punishing extramarital sex remained a staple for the Western legal tradition until the twentieth century. Let me illustrate with a few statements by leading architects of the Anglo-American common law and political liberalism.

Many of these later writers started with the same facts about human nature, sexuality and pair-bonding. Leading Scottish philosopher David Hume (1711–76) put it concisely: "The long and helpless infancy requires the combination of parents for the subsistence of their young; and that combination requires the virtue of chastity or fidelity to the marriage bed".[18] "The God of nature has enforced conjugal society, not only by making it agreeable, but by the principle of *chastity* inherent in our nature" as rational humans, Scottish judge Henry Home (1696–1782) expounded.

> *Chastity and mutual fidelity* [are] essential to … the continuation of the human race. As the carnal appetite is always alive, the sexes would wallow in pleasure *and* be soon rendered unfit for procreation were it not for the restraint of *chastity*"

born of the natural law.[19] Both family law and criminal law underscore this natural reality, echoed leading common law jurist William Blackstone (1723–80): "The main end and design of marriage [is] to ascertain and fix upon some certain person, to whom the care, the protection, the maintenance, and the education of the children should belong". "The duty of parents to provide for the maintenance of their children is a principle of natural law". Family law facilitates that duty; criminal law enforces it.[20]

Indeed, criminal law must prohibit and punish all sex crimes that harm this natural configuration of sex, marriage and family life, others argued. English political philosopher John Locke (1632–1704) urged the State to punish all sex crimes that threaten the rights and interests of wives and children or erode a man's "natural obligation to continue in conjugal society with the same woman". Locke called for firm punishment of the "dishonesty and debauchery" of prostitution, concubinage, "simple fornication", incest, rape and "domestic abuse" in order to protect "the welfare and safety" of the victims and to spare a community the "greater inconveniences" of care for violated women and their children. Locke also castigated rape, adultery and polygamy as violations of the "natural rights" of

18 David Hume, *Enquiries Concerning the Human Understanding and Concerning the Principles of Morals*, ed. L.A. Selby-Bigge, 2d ed. (Oxford: Clarendon Press, 1902; first published 1748), 206–7.

19 Henry Home, *Sketches of the History of Man*, ed. James A. Harris (Indianapolis: Liberty Fund, 2007), 264–70.

20 Blackstone, *Commentaries*, vol. 1, ch. 15.1, ch. 16.1, 3.

women and children. Religious groups, he said pointedly, are not "exempt from the magistrate's power of punishing" such sex crimes just because they regard these activities as "articles of faith, or ways of worship". "[A] toleration of men in all that which they pretend out of conscience they cannot submit to, will wholly take away all the civil laws and all the magistrate's power".[21]

Other writers further developed the logic of individual sex crimes. English philosopher William Paley (1743–1805) defended the criminalisation of simple fornication in order to encourage marriage. "The male part of the species will not undertake the encumbrance, expense and restraint of married life, if they can gratify their [sexual] passions at a cheaper price; and they will undertake anything rather than not gratify them". Paley recognised that he was appealing to general utility, but he thought that decriminalisation of fornication would lead to forms of sexual libertinism that exploited and harmed women and children.

> The libertine may not be conscious that these irregularities hinder his own marriage, … much less does he perceive how *his* indulgences can hinder other men from marrying, but what will he say would be the consequence, if the same licentiousness were universal? or what should hinder it becoming universal, if it be innocent or allowable in him?[22]

Fornication can furthermore lead one or both parties to prostitution, Paley went on, with its accompanying degradation of women, erosion of morals, transmission of disease and production of unwanted and uncared-for children. Fornication is no better if it devolves into concubinage – the "kept mistress", who can be dismissed at the man's pleasure or retained "in a state of humiliation and dependence inconsistent with the rights which marriage would confer upon her" and her children. It is best to cut all this sexual pathos off at the root, Paley concluded, by prohibiting sex outside the marital bed and encouraging fit and capable couples to marry instead.[23]

Adultery is even worse than fornication, said Paley, because it causes harm to an existing family. To the betrayed spouse, adultery is "a wound in his [or her] sensibility and affections, the most painful and incurable that human nature knows". To the children of an adulterous parent, it brings shame and unhappiness as the vice is inevitably detected and discussed. To the adulterous party, it is a form of "perjury" that violates the marital vow and covenant. To all parties in the household, adultery will often provoke retaliation and imitation – another step in

21 John Locke, *A Letter Concerning Toleration and Other Writings*, ed. Mark Goldie (Indianapolis: Liberty Fund, 2010), 69, 84, 110–11; John Locke, *An Essay Concerning Human Understanding*, in *The Works of John Locke*, 10 vols. (London: Thomas Tegg, 1823), 2:96; John Locke, *Two Treatises of Government*, ed. Thomas Hollis (London, 1764), 264.

22 William Paley, *The Principles of Moral and Political Philosophy*, ed. D.L. Le Mahieu (Indianapolis: Liberty Fund, 2002), 169–72.

23 Ibid., 172–4.

the erosion of marriage and the endangerment of children and society. Adultery is thus a serious crime.[24]

This same concern for mutual fidelity and family stability informed the ongoing criminal prohibition on polygamy. Scottish philosopher Frances Hutcheson (1694–1746) argued that polygamy

> destroys all friendship in marriage; must be the cause of perpetual contentions; must tempt women so injuriously treated into adulteries; must corrupt the minds of men with wandering lust, destroying their natural affection to their children; and must occasion to some an offspring too numerous, which therefore will be neglected, and be void of all sense of duty to such dissolute parents.

Moreover, given the roughly equal numbers of men and women, polygamy would tend to exclude many men from the institution of marriage, "which chiefly civilize[s] and unite[s] men in society". Society will suffer gravely if too many men cannot marry because eligible women have been hoarded into the harems of men who may or may not be virtuous or capable of maintaining them and their children.[25]

The crime of incest has a more straightforward argument, wrote the leading utilitarian Jeremy Bentham (1748–1832). "Every people pretend to follow in this respect, what they call the law of nature, and they look with a sort of horror upon everything not conformed to the matrimonial laws of their own country" or with the laws of the Bible or the Church. But State prohibitions on incest are better rooted in four interrelated principles of utility, Bentham argued: (1) to reduce real or suspected rivalry among family members at the cost of household harmony; (2) to avoid seduction of young girls within the home which will prevent them from forming "permanent and advantageous" marriages when they grow up; (3) to avoid confusions in domestic relations "between those who ought to command and those who ought to obey"; and (4) to avoid physical injury from "premature indulgences" in sex. Utility was the best judge of incest laws, Bentham insisted. Worries about sexual taboos, "natural repugnance", "vulgar morality", weakened blood and fewer alliances are all just "pious frauds". It is worth noting, however, that almost all of Bentham's utilitarian arguments against incest echoed Thomas Aquinas' natural law arguments from five centuries earlier.[26]

While Western jurists and philosophers differed in their rationales for criminalising fornication, prostitution, concubinage, adultery, incest, rape and abuse of wives and children, few writers before the twentieth century argued for the

24 Ibid., 176–80.

25 Frances Hutcheson, *A Short Introduction to Moral Philosophy, in Three Books; Containing the Elements of Ethicks and the Law of Nature* (Glasgow: R. Foulis 1747), 248–60.

26 Jeremy Bentham, *Theory of Legislation*, trans. R. Hildreth (Boston: Weeks, Jordan, & Co., 1840), 248–61.

relaxation or expulsion of these crimes. Iconoclastic experimenters in "sexual communism" and "free love radicalism" were the exception, not the rule.[27] This is less true of the traditional "crimes of bestiality", sodomy, masturbation, contraception, polygamy, obscenity and other prohibited forms of "unnatural" "perversion", "indecency", "lewdness" and "abomination". These crimes remained on the books in common law and civil law lands until the twentieth century. However, a growing number of early modern detractors began to press for their removal, anticipating modern developments that struck many of these crimes for good.

14.3 Church, State and sexual morality today

In 1955, the American Law Institute declared that its new *Model Penal Code*

> does not attempt to use the power of the state to enforce purely moral or religious standards. We deem it inappropriate for the government to attempt to control behavior that has no substantial significance except as to the morality of the private actor. Such matters are best left to religious, educational, and other social influences.[28]

This striking statement about the limits of modern criminal law is now commonplace in modern pluralistic liberal societies. This statement seems especially apt for the sexual field, where a half-century of sexual liberty jurisprudence has strengthened the perceived separation of sin and crime, morality and liberty, tradition and modernity. Many modern liberal countries have also firmly committed to *laïcité* or the "disestablishment of religion", yielding a further separation of the roles of Church and State in dealing with sex.[29] Sexual morality is now commonly thought to be for private actors to work out for themselves, drawing as they wish "on religious, educational and other social influences". Even if one wanted to pursue a neo-Puritan sexual path today – I, for one, do not! – a new State criminalisation of a number of traditional sex offences could not pass constitutional or cultural muster in modern liberal societies.

But this does not mean that all the sex crimes listed in the Bible and articulated by the Christian tradition are now just relics of a bygone age. It is too simple to say that traditional moral standards have no place in modern criminal law. Some of the most serious crimes that liberal States actively prosecute today – murder, theft, rape, kidnapping, treason, conspiracy, perjury and others – are, in fact,

27 See, e.g. Faramerz Dabhoiwala, *The Origins of Sex: A History of the First Sexual Revolution* (Oxford: Oxford University Press, 2012).

28 American Law Institute, *Model Penal Code. Tentative Draft No. 4* (Philadelphia: ALI, 1955), 207.

29 See, e.g. Norman Doe, *Law and Religion in Europe: A Comparative Introduction* (Oxford: Oxford University Press, 2012).

deeply rooted in the moral teachings of the Bible and other religious texts, even if they now have other rationales. Moreover, many traditional sex crimes were not only inspired by the divine imperatives of sexual morality, bodily purity and godly chastity, but also infused with prudential and practical concerns that remain important for criminal law today. These included, as we have seen, concerns for the person, property and reputation of victims and other third parties; for the rights, liberties and interests of defendants, victims and their families; for the health, safety and welfare of the community; and more. Traditional sexual morality is part of modern criminal law on sex, whether we like it or not.

A more helpful distinction is between "the morality of duty" and "the morality of aspiration", as Lon Fuller once put it. The ***morality of duty*** guides and even coerces humans to avoid their worst inclinations. It "lays down the basic rules without which an ordered society is impossible, or without which an ordered society directed toward certain goals" of protecting life, liberty and property or pursuing justice, peace and the rule of law "must fail of its mark". By contrast, the ***morality of aspiration*** encourages humans to ascend to "the Good Life, of excellence, of the fullest realization of human powers".[30] It is directed to the Jekyll who sits alongside the Hyde within each of us – the saint who remains at perennial war with the sinner "within our members" (Rom. 7:23). It not only coerces persons against acts of violence and violation, but also cultivates in them virtues of charity and love. It not only punishes harmful acts of murder and theft, but also discourages evil thoughts of hatred and covetousness. The morality of duty is like the rules of grammar. Without them, there could be no coherent speech and literature. The morality of aspiration is like the quests for eloquence. With them, we get Shakespeare and Martin Luther King.

14.3.1 The role of the State

This simple framework gives us a different way to think through the distinctions between crime and sin, tradition and modernity, and the respective roles of State and Church in the sexual field. At the most elementary level, the State does and should use criminal law to enforce a baseline sexual morality of duty – laying down "the basic rules without which an ordered society is impossible" and without which the basic goods of life, liberty and property, justice, peace and the rule of law are imperilled. Included in most liberal penal codes today are prohibitions against the traditional sex crimes of abduction (now usually called kidnapping), castration (now punished along with involuntary sterilisation as aggravated battery), incest, infanticide (now usually a form of homicide), malicious desertion (now including failure to pay child support), obscenity, polygamy, prostitution, rape and sexual assault and battery. Each of these offences, if not prohibited and punished, would indeed harm the basic individual and collective goods of life, liberty and property, justice, peace and the rule of law. While some of these

30 Lon L. Fuller, *The Morality of Law*, 2d ed. (New Haven: Yale University Press,1964), 3–32.

traditional offences are now contested as violations of sexual liberty and autonomy, there are strong reasons, not least concern for the rights and liberties of vulnerable victims, for these crimes to remain on the books.[31]

The modern liberal State can, and in my view should, use other tools, besides criminal law, to "nudge" and "channel" its citizens towards a higher sexual morality of aspiration. "Nudging" is now a common legal strategy of promoting desirable public and private goods in many areas of life.[32] The liberal State facilitates, licenses, encourages, sometimes even pays for or rewards all kinds of desirable behaviour: think of voting in a State election, getting a free vaccine or going to college on a State scholarship. The State imposes taxes or fines or withholds State benefits or opportunities for those who indulge in undesirable behaviour: think of smoking, not wearing seat belts or dropping out of high school. The theory of "nudging" or "legal channelling" stipulates that, over time, the desirable behaviour encouraged by the State will become more customary, even natural or reflexive among citizens, and the undesirable behaviour will be viewed as aberrant and perhaps even stigmatised.

Without encroaching on sexual liberty, the modern liberal State can "nudge" citizens to integrate their sex, marriage and family lives as a public and private good to which they aspire.[33] The State can provide much stronger tax and social benefits for married couples, straight and same-sex alike. It can tighten its marital formation and dissolution rules to discourage an easy-in/easy-out marital culture. It can provide better comprehensive sex and family planning education as a matter of public and private health and safety. It can offer free contraceptives to vulnerable populations especially among the youth, gathered, say, at high school proms or in mixed college dormitories. It can provide more expansive pregnancy and maternal care and financial services, and more efficient and humane adoption options for women contemplating abortion. It can create a much more sophisticated system of biotechnology and information technology to find and hold fathers accountable for the children they produce. It can do much more to put all "children's interests first"[34] and to help protect and vindicate the fundamental rights of children. It can do much more to encourage better elder and intergenerational care. And State officials can and should model and promote responsible sex, marriage and family norms and habits in their own lives as a vital form of political and legal pedagogy.

31 See John Witte, Jr., *The Western Case for Monogamy over Polygamy* (Cambridge: Cambridge University Press, 2015).

32 Richard H. Thaler and Cass R. Sunstein, *Nudge: Improving Decisions about Health, Wealth, and Happiness* (New York: Penguin Books, 2008); Eric A. Posner, ed., *Social Norms, Nonlegal Sanctions and the Law* (Cheltenham: Edward Elgar, 2007).

33 Carl E. Schneider, "The Channeling Function in Family Law", (1992) 20 *Hofstra Law Review* 495–532.

34 Helen Alvare, *Putting Children's Interests First in U.S. Family Law and Policy* (Cambridge: Cambridge University Press, 2018).

But, in the end, the State and its laws can only do so much in the sexual field. Human families also need broader communities and narratives to stabilise, deepen and exemplify the natural inclinations and rational norms we have about responsible sex and procreation. Human families need models and exemplars of love and fidelity, trust and sacrifice, commitment and community, to give these natural teachings further content and coherence. They need the help of stable institutions beyond the State – churches, schools, charities, hospitals, neighbourhoods and others. They need the help of service professionals beyond judges, lawyers and State workers – preachers, teachers, doctors, mentors, counsellors, therapists, accountants, coaches and others. As Robert Bellah reminds us, while it takes a marriage to make a family, and a village to raise a child, it takes "a society to raise a family".[35]

14.3.2 The role of the Church

The modern Church plays a vital social role in "raising a family" and promoting healthy sexual morality in society. At minimum, the modern Christian Church must be as zealous as the modern liberal State in establishing a basic sexual morality of duty – making compliance with current State sex crimes a condition for Church leadership, if not membership. Some churches now do so in their canons of ordination and contracts of employment in sanctuaries, schools, charities, clubs and service organisations.[36] But all churches should have clear, detailed and enforceable "sexual morality" clauses with corresponding procedures for adjudicating complaints and cases.

This has become doubly imperative today given the grim reality of sexual abuse by some Catholic, Protestant and Evangelical clergy and cover-ups by some of their superiors. This fundamental "sacrilege" and betrayal of ordination vows has destroyed the lives of untold thousands of victims and has gravely harmed the moral standing and witness of the modern Church throughout the world.[37] Churches must root out and drive out all clergy and other religious leaders who abuse their wives, children, students, clients, patients or parishioners, as well as their accomplices after the fact who cover up these grave offences. These are serious sex crimes whose perpetrators can and should find no refuge behind constitutional walls or sacramental veils. Clerical pederasts, in particular, should remember that Jesus has reserved a special place in hell for those who

35 Robert Bellah, "Epilogue: It Takes a Society to Raise a Family", in Steven M. Tipton and John Witte, Jr., eds., *Family Transformed: Religion, Values, and Society in American Life* (Washington, D.C.: Georgetown University Press, 2005), 286–98.

36 See examples in Norman Doe, *Christian Law: Contemporary Principles* (Cambridge: Cambridge University Press, 2015); Mark Hill, *Ecclesiastical Law*, 4th ed. (Oxford: Oxford University Press, 2018).

37 Dominic Legge, O.P., "Cleansing the Church of Clerical Sacrilege", *First Things*, 16 August 2018, https://www.firstthings.com/web-exclusives/2018/08/cleansing-the-church-of-clerical-sacrilege (accessed 23 January 2019).

harm children (Mark 9:42; Luke 17:2). This biblical teaching merits regular repetition in churches and seminaries and ample elaboration in the Church's law books and disciplinary codes.

Rather than just following the secular status quo, however, or seeking to establish its spiritual norms by State positive law, modern churches in liberal societies should go further to teach a higher sexual morality of aspiration for its own voluntary community, setting out the norms and habits of sexual purity, bodily integrity and marital fidelity taught by Scripture and tradition. Among the most likely moral standards to consider are the repeated biblical injunctions against adultery, bestiality, buggery, fornication and sodomy. Some churches might also wish to add other long-standing sex prohibitions in the Christian tradition, such as abortion, contraception, prostitution and concubinage. Some modern churches support the continued enforcement of these sexual prohibitions within the Church – although same-sex actions and relationships have been under hot theological dispute.

A church may view this aspirational sexual morality – however specified – as essential or optional for church life and membership. It may have formal or informal methods of adjudication and enforcement of those rules. In a liberal society, no citizen may be compelled to be part of a church, nor barred from leaving it. But in a liberal society, every church has the right to maintain internal norms and procedures for its voluntary members without interference from the State, as long as there is no harm or threat to life and limb. Spiritual discipline in the form of fines, public confessions, mandatory charity, bans from the Eucharist, removals from church benefits or offices, shunning or ostracism from the community and the like can pass muster in a liberal society. But hard coercive power against life or limb is reserved to the State alone under strict due process constraints.

Churches need not, and in my view should not, banish from the pew, pulpit, lectern, keyboard or choir bench every person who falls short of their community's sexual standards. Nor should churches indiscriminately shun modern science and new insights about sex and sexuality. But churches do have a right and responsibility to teach, counsel and facilitate members to follow biblical teachings in their sex lives and to set realistic benchmarks for the spiritual growth of each member, with encouragement and appropriate consequences for those who fall short. This is doubly imperative for clergy and other religious leaders who are called to be faithful stewards of Scripture and tradition, and moral exemplars and teachers in their communities.

Sexual liberty is a hard-won prize of modern liberal life whose protection has allowed liberal citizens to escape some of the patriarchy, paternalism and plain prudishness of the past. But sexual violation and abuse remain a perennial reality of modern life, and sex crimes inflict some of the deepest scars on their victims. A liberal society must thus maintain minimum standards of sexual morality in its criminal law as a restraint on deviant and destructive "devices and desires" and as a bulwark against a society's slide into a sexual state of nature where life can be "brutal, nasty and short" for the most vulnerable. And a liberal society would do well to encourage its citizens and its communities of faith to pursue a higher morality of aspiration that views sex and the sexual body as a divine blessing to be enjoyed and exercised in the loving service of God, neighbour and self.

Further reading

Brundage, James A. *Law, Sex, and Christian Society in Medieval Europe* (Chicago: University of Chicago Press, 1987).
Bullough, Vern L. and James A. Brundage. *Sexual Practices and the Medieval Church* (Buffalo: Prometheus Books, 1982).
Epstein, Louis M. *Sex, Laws, and Customs in Judaism* (New York: KTAV Publishing House, 1948).
Feinberg, Joel A. *The Moral Limits of the Criminal Law*, 4 vols (Oxford: Oxford University Press, 1988).
Fuller, Lon L. *The Morality of Law*, 2d ed. (New Haven: Yale University Press, 1964).
Glendon, Mary Ann. *The Transformation of Family Law: State, Law, and Family in the United States and Western Europe* (Chicago: University of Chicago Press, 1996).
Griffith, R. Marie. *Moral Combat: How Sex Divided American Christians and Fractured American Politics* (New York: Basic Books, 2017).
Helmholz, R.H. *Marriage Litigation in Medieval England*, repr. ed. (Cambridge: Cambridge University Press, 2007).
Ingram, Martin. *Carnal Knowledge: Regulating Sex in England, 1470–1600* (Cambridge: Cambridge University Press, 2017).
Payer, Pierre J. *Sex and the Penitentials: The Development of a Sexual Code, 550–1150* (Toronto: University of Toronto Press, 1994).
Payer, Pierre J. *Sex and the New Medieval Literature of Confession, 1150–1350* (Toronto: University of Toronto Press, 2009).
Witte, John Jr. *The Sins of the Fathers: The Law and Theology of Illegitimacy Reconsidered* (Cambridge: Cambridge University Press, 2009).
Witte, John Jr. *Church, State, and Family: Reconciling Traditional Teachings and Modern Liberties* (Cambridge: Cambridge University Press, 2019).

15 Attempts, complicity, virtue and the limits of law

Richard W. Garnett

At first, criminal attempts and complicity might seem a strange, even poorly matched, pair of topics for a single chapter of a volume on Christianity and the criminal law. An "attempt", after all, is generally understood and treated as a free-standing – albeit inchoate, preparatory or incomplete – offence, while "complicity" or accomplice liability in the criminal law context is a theory or account of one actor's responsibility, and culpability, for the offence of another. In fact, both the basics and the details of these matters illustrate nicely and engagingly a long-standing and fundamental tenet of Anglo-American criminal law,[1] namely, that the blame and condemnation of the political community, which is directed at crimes and those who commit them and which gives criminal punishment its distinctive character,[2] attaches primarily to actors' states of mind – to their plans, purposes, awareness and recklessness – rather than (or at least more than) to the harms they cause or the results they bring about.[3]

It is well established that this focus, and insistence, on blameworthy states of mind not only replicates or reflects, but has also been shaped by, the similar emphasis in Christian Scripture, tradition and moral teaching.[4] It is, in the Christian tradition, appreciated that "evil things come from within", "out of the

1 This chapter considers criminal attempts and accomplice liability in the contemporary Anglo-American context only. For more on these matters in the contexts of other criminal law models and systems, see, e.g. Markus D. Dubber, "Criminalizing Complicity: A Comparative Analysis", (2007) 5 *Journal of International Criminal Justice* 977–1001; and Luis E. Chiesa, "Comparative Criminal Law", in Markus D. Dubber and Tatjana Hörnle, eds., *The Oxford Handbook of Criminal Law* (Oxford: Oxford University Press, 2014), 1104–13.

2 See generally, e.g. Henry M. Hart, Jr., "The Aims of the Criminal Law", (1958) 23 *Law and Contemporary Problems* 401–41.

3 See generally Larry Alexander and Kimberly Kessler Ferzan (with contributions by Stephen J. Morse), *Crime and Culpability: A Theory of Criminal Law* (Cambridge: Cambridge University Press, 2009).

4 For thorough examinations of this matter, see, for example, David McIlroy's and Brent Strawn's contributions to this volume, and also J.M.B. Crawford and J.F. Quinn, *The Christian Foundations of Criminal Responsibility: A Philosophical Study of Legal Reasoning* (Lewiston: Edwin Mellen, 1991). A helpful, standard overview of the role of *mens rea* in criminal law is provided in Francis Bowes Sayre, "Mens Rea", (1932) 45 *Harvard Law Review* 974–1026.

heart of men" (Mark 7:20–3).[5] Thus, an examination and discussion of criminal attempts and complicity can serve as an opportunity to illustrate Christianity's influence, past and present, on the theory, content and operation of the criminal law. In addition, though, running through the doctrines attached to and the debates regarding these matters is a concern – a caution, an unease – that might remind us of another central Christian concern, one that has been and is located, for the most part, outside the scope, or beyond the limits, of the criminal law: Christian moral teaching enjoins not only the avoidance of wrongful acts, but also the cultivation and practice of virtue, "an habitual and firm disposition to do the good".[6]

In Christian accounts or versions of virtue ethics, the aims of actors and policy-makers are not limited to deterring or responding to harms, to keeping the "benefits" side of the relevant ledger larger than the "costs" side, or to appropriately and accurately distributing blame and punishment. Yes, these are all important aims. Still, a Christian and "aretaic" account emphasises character, dispositions, projects, vocation, habits and habituation. It asks not only "what was done?" or "what came about and by whom?" but also "what sort of person did this?" It looks at the connections between who we are, on the one hand, and how we act, what we attempt and what we embrace, on the other. As one Christian moral theologian in the virtue ethics tradition has put it, a Christian "life of discipleship is not simply about performing certain types of actions. It is a vocation, a transformation of one's very self".[7] In Gilbert Meilaender's words:

> An ethic of virtue seeks to focus not only on … moments of great anxiety and uncertainty in life but also on the continuities, the habits of behavior which make us the persons we are … An ethic of virtue turns away not only from an overemphasis on borderline cases but also from the concept of duty as the central moral concept. *Being* not *doing* takes center stage; for what we ought to do may depend on the sort of person we are.[8]

However, this aretaic dimension of Christian morality and moral theology, unlike the nexus between culpability and choice, is difficult to find in the criminal law,[9] which is inclined more towards proscribing acts than prescribing character, more

5 Douay–Rheims translation.

6 *Catechism of the Catholic Church*, No. 1803.

7 William C. Mattison III, "Moral Virtue, The Grace of God, and Discipleship", *Church Life Journal*, 16 August 2016, https://churchlifejournal.nd.edu/articles/moral-virtue-the-grace-of-god-and-discipleship/.

8 Gilbert C. Meilaender, *The Theory and Practice of Virtue* (Notre Dame: University of Notre Dame Press, 1984), 5.

9 For some exceptions, see generally, e.g. Anthony Duff, "Virtue, Vice, and Criminal Liability", and Kyron Huigens, "On Aristotelian Criminal Law: A Reply to Duff", in Colin Farrelly and Lawrence B. Solum, *Virtue Jurisprudence* (Basingstoke: Palgrave Macmillan, 2008), 193–213 and 214–35, respectively.

towards forbidding bad conduct than facilitating good character, more towards deterring decisions than transforming selves. It is worth asking why.

Those who teach introductory criminal law courses would probably agree that attempts and complicity are engaging, and often entertaining, topics. The assigned cases and materials feature colourful characters and tricky conundrums: What to do with the drowsy lookout or the lost getaway driver, with a drug-buy involving oregano or an assassination scheme employing a voodoo doll, with "the superfluous accomplice"[10] and "Lady Eldon's Lace"[11] and so on? The subjects are often neighbours in tables of contents and syllabi, in part because the various rationales in the literature and in the cases for punishing attempts, on the one hand, and punishing accomplices, on the other, overlap, even if imperfectly.

What seems to stand out as justifying treating these two topics together in law courses and in this chapter is that, in each case, the relationship or connection between the actor being assigned criminal liability and the social harm element of the substantive offence in question – a relationship that is ordinarily required for criminal liability[12] – is complicated, attenuated or even non-existent. With respect to complicity, the general rule is that the assistance provided by the accomplice need not be a contributing or "but for" cause of the principal's conduct or of the harm caused by the principal's conduct.[13] And when it comes to attempts (whether classified as "complete", "incomplete", "impossible" or something else), it appears that the social harm with which the law is concerned does not occur at all (although it is sometimes argued that attempts do cause harms such as fear, apprehension, misallocation of police and insurance resources, etc.). In any event, these two topics are illustrations of the fact that the criminal law sometimes assigns liability – and, therefore, moral blame – to actors who are not even partially responsible for causing a social harm or for engaging in or contributing to conduct that is wrong in itself.[14] In both contexts, the law identifies an actor's intention, plan or project as blameworthy and deserving of punishment even though it is, or at least could be seen as, harmless. The law says that it is wrong, and blameworthy, to try to commit a criminal offence, even if – for

10 See Leo Katz, "The Story of *Tally*: Judge Tally and the Problem of the Superfluous Accomplice", in Donna Coker and Robert Weisberg, eds., *Criminal Law Stories* (New York: Foundation Press, 2013), 373–98.

11 The story of Lady Eldon's attempt at French-lace smuggling is discussed in Francis Wharton, *Criminal Law*, 12th ed., 3 vols (Rochester: Lawyers Co-operative Publishing Company, 1932), 1:304, §225.

12 Katz, "Story of *Tally*", 388: "Ordinarily, one is liable for a crime if one caused some harm—at least where the crime in question is a 'result crime'".

13 See generally, e.g. Sanford H. Kadish, "Complicity, Cause, and Blame: A Study in the Interpretation of Doctrine", (1985) 73 *California Law Review* 323–410.

14 See, e.g. John Austin, *Lectures on Jurisprudence*, 4th ed., 2 vols (1873), 1:523: "Generally, attempts are perfectly innocuous, and the party is punished … in respect of what he intended to do".

whatever reason – one fails;[15] the law says that it is wrong, and blameworthy, to assist or otherwise embrace another's criminal project, even if the other does not want or need help.[16] Each of these doctrines assigns blame to, and calibrates punishment or grades offences based on, the actor's state of mind with respect to a harm which that actor does not, or might not, bring about. Thus, as we will see, the doctrines and those applying them are concerned, as they should be, with the risks of this assignment and calibration, and so with safeguarding against the possibility of punishing bad thoughts[17] or bad character alone.[18]

Although the criminal law regimes of various jurisdictions have long found ways of responding to failed efforts to complete crimes, legal historians generally trace the Anglo-American approach to criminal attempts to a 1784 case called *Rex v. Scofield*.[19] Formulations and definitions vary from jurisdiction to jurisdiction and from time to time; however, for present purposes, an attempt is "an intent to do an act or to bring about certain consequences which would in law amount to a crime; and an act in furtherance of that intent which, as it is most commonly put, goes beyond mere preparation".[20] For purposes of analysis even if not for purposes of assigning liability and determining punishment, it is common to distinguish between "complete" and "incomplete" attempts; that is, between cases where an actor has done all that he or she intended to do, but for some reason (bad aim, for example) did not bring about the desired and planned result, and cases where, for some reason ("excellent work" by police, perhaps[21]) the would-be offender is interrupted before he or she finishes the job.

Several rationales for punishing attempts jostle for influence in the literature and the cases. Sometimes, the criminalisation of criminal attempts – that is, of

15 See generally Gideon Yoffe, "Criminal Attempts", (2014) 124 *Yale Law Journal* 92–156 (treating criminal attempts as "tryings").

16 See generally Joshua Dressler, "Reforming Complicity Law: Trivial Assistance as a Lesser Offense?", (2008) 5 *Ohio State Journal of Criminal Law* 427–48.

17 See, e.g. Alan Brudner, *Punishment and Freedom: A Liberal Theory of Penal Justice* (Oxford: Oxford University Press, 2012), 108: "If there is any one proposition that commands general agreement among theorists and practitioners of criminal law, it is that judicial punishment ought not to be inflicted for private thoughts, wishes, inclinations, or states of character where these have not manifested themselves in conduct".

18 See Jeffrie G. Murphy, *Punishment and the Moral Emotions: Essays in Law, Morality, and Religion* (Oxford: Oxford University Press, 2012), 75–6: "[I]f a sentencing judge, … adds on a little extra [punishment] because of the defendant's vicious character … is that not simply to punish him for an aspect of his character that has no victim?"

19 See generally, e.g. Eugene Meehan and John H. Currie, *The Law of Criminal Attempt* (Scarborough, Ontario: Carswell, 2000), 11–12.

20 Wayne R. LaFave, *Criminal Law*, 3rd ed. (St. Paul: West Group, 2000), §6.2. See also, e.g. Joshua Dressler, *Understanding Criminal Law*, 8th ed. (Durham, NC: Carolina Academic Press, 2018), 356: "[A] criminal attempt occurs when a person, with the intent to commit an offense, performs 'some act done towards carrying out that intent'".

21 See, e.g. *People v. Rizzo*, 246 N.Y. 344, 158 N.E. 188 (N.Y. Court of Appeals 1927): "The police of the city of New York did excellent work in this case by preventing the commission of a serious crime".

incomplete or failed criminal offences – is defended on quite practical, harm-prevention grounds, as a way of providing "a basis for law-enforcement officers to intervene before an individual can commit a completed offense".[22] Other consequentialist justifications might emphasise the common-sense concern that one who tries but fails to commit a crime has, notwithstanding his failure on the present occasion, "shown his willingness to try to bring about a proscribed consequence", his "dangerousness" and, therefore, his need for incapacitation and constraint.[23] These utilitarian explanations do not tell the whole story, though. Contemporary law and scholarship on criminal attempts fundamentally reflect the intuition – or, better, the conviction – that it is wrong to try to do what is wrong, that "moral luck" or the fortuity of failure or detection is not relevant to blameworthiness, and that, for purposes of assigning culpability, results matter less than intention and risk-creation.[24] As one commentator put it, a "person who casts off the burden of self-restraint deserves punishment", notwithstanding the fact that "[i]n criminal endeavours, as in other spheres of life, things do not always turn out as one expects".[25]

The treatment of three particular questions that arise in the law of criminal attempts seems to confirm the primacy of these latter, "subjectivist" accounts and also to illustrate the consonance of this law with deeply rooted Christian accounts of action, intention, responsibility and culpability. First, it is fair to say that it has proved much easier to report that a criminal attempt requires some "act in furtherance of [criminal] intent which ... goes beyond mere preparation" than to identify precisely and consistently the location of the going-beyond point:

> Both as fascinating and as fruitless as the alchemists' quest for the philosopher's stone has been the search, by judges and writers, for a valid, single statement of doctrine to express when, under the law of guilt, preparations to commit a crime become a criminal attempt thereat.[26]

Some "tests" or methods focus on how far the actor has moved towards completion while others look at how close or "dangerously proximate" to success he or she comes before being interrupted or thwarted;[27] some ask whether the actor's

22 Ira P. Robbins, "Double Inchoate Crimes", (1989) 26 *Harvard Journal on Legislation* 12.

23 Andrew Ashworth, "Criminal Attempts and the Role of Resulting Harm under the Code, and in the Common Law", (1988) 19 *Rutgers Law Journal* 738.

24 See, e.g. Alexander and Ferzan, *Crime and Culpability*, 195: "Results do not matter for blameworthiness or punishability".

25 Ashworth, "Criminal Attempts", 735.

26 John S. Strahorn, Jr., "Preparation for Crime as a Criminal Attempt", (1939) 1 *Washington and Lee Law Review* 1–30, cited in Joshua Dressler and Stephen P. Garvey, *Criminal Law: Cases and Materials*, 7th ed. (St. Paul: West Academic Publishing, 2016), 779. See also, e.g. *United States v. Mandujano*, 499 F.2d 370 (1974): "The courts in many jurisdictions have tried to elaborate on the distinction between mere preparation and attempt".

27 See *Commonwealth v. Peaslee*, 177 Mass. 267, 59 N.E. 55 (1901).

conduct unequivocally reveals a criminal plan, or provides sufficient confirmation or corroboration of the actor's blameworthy intent, while others are concerned with the point beyond which he or she is unlikely to be deterred or to undergo a change of heart; we see at work not only a worry about allowing an actor to come too close to causing harm before liability kicks in and police intervention is authorised, but also a concern with criminalising too early and marking as a punishable offence what is better regarded as a fleeting, and forgivable, unworthy thought.[28]

A second question worth highlighting here is whether it is or should be relevant to liability for criminal attempt – in other words, to the blameworthiness of failure – that success was "impossible".[29] Real-world and hypothetical cases involving impossible attempts have tangled the minds of more than a few law students, lawyers and judges. An actor shoots at a tree stump, believing it to be her enemy; a would-be child molester arranges a meeting online with a law-enforcement officer posing as an underage child; a man engages in sexual intercourse with the corpse of a woman who has died but who he believed had passed out from intoxication; and an aspiring thief reaches into his victim's pocket, which turns out to be empty. Even more colourfully, a prison inmate obtains a lock of hair taken from the judge who sentenced him to prison and sends it, along with the judge's picture, to a "voodoo priest" with instructions to cast a death curse on the judge.[30] Generally speaking, and in keeping with the long-standing tendency in Anglo-American criminal law to treat as culpable and punishable the intentions that failed, even doomed and impossible, projects reflect, the impossibility-of-success is not a defence to criminal attempt.[31]

A third illustrative matter is the significance of a would-be criminal's abandonment or "renunciation" of his or her plan or purpose.[32] The enterprise of finding, or constructing, a line between "mere preparation" and attempt has long reflected the realisation that, with "incomplete" attempts, there will almost always be, regardless of the "test" employed, a *locus poenitentiae* – a "chickening out zone", as one student called it[33] – during which an actor who has crossed the blurry line separating bad thoughts from criminal attempts still has the meaningful capacity to change his or her mind, to desist and perhaps even to repent. Should the law care – should we care – if he or she does?

28 See generally Dressler, *Understanding Criminal Law*, 371–6.

29 See generally, e.g. John Hasnas, "Once More unto the Breach: The Inherent Liberalism of the Criminal Law and Liability for Attempting the Impossible", (2002) 54 *Hastings Law Journal* 1–77 (2002); George P. Fletcher, "Constructing a Theory of Impossible Attempts", (1986) 5 *Criminal Justice Ethics* 53–69.

30 Mark Curriden, "Voodoo Attempt? Two Face Conspiracy Charges in Failed Death Hex of Judge", (1989) 75.9 *ABA Journal* 48.

31 See, e.g. American Law Institute, Model Penal Code, §5.01(1)(a).

32 See ibid., §5.01(4).

33 Robert Batey, "Minority Report and the Law of Attempt", (2004) 1 *Ohio State Journal of Criminal Law* 695.

Certainly, to the extent the law punishes completed offences more severely than attempted offences, it is relevant that an actor abandoned (or otherwise failed to complete) a criminal project; that actor will be punished, if at all, for the attempted, and not the completed, offence. The more interesting, and controversial, question is whether sincere repentance and voluntary abandonment of a criminal undertaking can wipe the slate clean, un-ring the bell or detach the already incurred liability, and culpability, for the attempt? A slayer's regret at having killed his or her enemy might be relevant for sentencing purposes, but the law has never thought such regret could, by itself, operate as a defence to liability. Given that a criminal attempt is, again, a free-standing, even if inchoate, offence, should things be any different here? The answer is unclear; that is, the question is answered in different ways. Generally, and again in keeping with the theme that actors are blameworthy and punishable for the projects they undertake as well as for the harms they cause, "abandonment" has not been treated as a defence to attempt.[34]

"Complicity", or accomplice liability, is, as was noted at the outset, not an offence in itself, but is instead a "means by which a substantive crime may be committed".[35] An "accomplice" is a "secondary" actor who has done (or, in some cases, omitted to do) something "that makes it appropriate to blame him for what [a] primary actor does".[36] We might say that an accomplice is one who, by his or her own voluntary act, decision or choice, fully embraces, endorses or adopts another's criminal project as his or her own. In the words of Judge Learned Hand, an accomplice is one who "associate[s] himself with the venture, … participate[s] in it as in something that he wishes to bring about, … [and] seek[s] by his action to make it succeed".[37] It is important to see that complicity is only superficially like vicarious liability; accomplice liability, after all, is derivative, but not assigned; it is chosen, not imposed.

Complicity is controversial in some of its particulars and applications, but it is still "deeply rooted" in the criminal law.[38] In the United States, during the last decade or so, the idea became more familiar by virtue of the role that arguments about complicity, and about religiously grounded obligations to avoid culpable cooperation with others' wrongful acts, played a central role in the legal challenges to the contraception coverage requirements imposed on many employers, including religious institutions, by the 2009 Patient Protection and Affordable

34 See *People v. Kimball*, 109 Mich. App. 273, 311 N.W. 2d 343 (1981): "[O]nce a defendant has gone so far as to have committed a punishable attempt, the crime is 'complete' and he or she cannot then abandon the crime and avoid liability anymore than a thief can abandon larceny by returning the stolen goods". The Model Penal Code, however, does allow a limited "renunciation" defence: American Law Institute, Model Penal Code, §5.01(4).

35 Robert Weisberg, "Reappraising Complicity", (2000), 4 *Buffalo Criminal Law Review* 225.

36 Kadish, "Complicity, Cause and Blame", 337.

37 *United States v. Peoni*, 100 F.2d 401 (2d Cir. 1938).

38 See generally, e.g. Francis Bowes Sayre, "Criminal Responsibility for the Acts of Another", (1930) 43 *Harvard Law Review* 702.

Care Act.[39] Contrary to the suggestions of some commentators, however,[40] there was and is nothing especially exotic or novel, in moral philosophy or in criminal law, about the idea that an actor may be culpable, and even punishable, for aiding, assisting or cooperating in another's wrongful or criminal acts. Roman Catholic moralists, in particular – perhaps most notably, in recent years, in the increasingly fraught arena of bioethics – have long engaged the challenge of evaluating cooperation, and have developed careful, fine-grained distinctions between formal and material, and remote and immediate, forms of cooperation with evil.[41]

In the criminal law context, of course, the paradigm case is not that of a secondary party who is concerned with avoiding blameworthy or scandalous cooperation with another's wrongdoing; it is that of an alleged accomplice who is said to have acted in such a way, and with such a state of mind, that he or she shares fully in the criminal liability for the conduct of or harm caused by another. In the Model Penal Code's formulation, a person is "guilty of an offense if it is committed by his own conduct or by the conduct of another person for which he is legally accountable" – and, one is legally accountable for another's conduct when one is an accomplice of that other person in the commission of a crime.[42]

As is the case in the law of attempts, the tight nexus between a person's criminal complicity and his or her state of mind is of principal importance. After all, a criminal's success (or, indeed, his or her criminal attempt) is, in any particular case, almost certainly facilitated by the activities, movements, perceptions, errors, locations and interpretations of many, many others. That a successful criminal might be said to owe his or her project's outcome to many others – a sleeping security guard, a slow-footed officer, a naïve and trusting doorman, an attentive trainer at the shooting range – does not mean these others do or should derive or share blame, responsibility or liability. Again, an accomplice is one who

39 A full description of the many lawsuits, administrative proceedings, scholarly explorations and public interventions having to do with the so-called "contraception coverage mandate" is beyond the scope of this chapter. See generally, e.g. Josh Blackman, *Unraveled: Obamacare, Religious Liberty, and Executive Power* (New York: Cambridge University Press, 2016); Brief of 50 Catholic Theologians and Ethicists as *Amici Curiae* in Support of Petitioners, *Zubik v. Burwell*, 578 U.S. ___ , 136 S. Ct. 1557 (2016); W. Cole Durham and Robert Smith, "The Affordable Care Act: *Burwell v. Hobby Lobby* and *Zubik v. Burwell*", *Religious Organizations and the Law* §6.22 (March 2017 update).

40 See, e.g. Amy J. Sepinwall, "Conscience and Complicity: Assessing Pleas for Religious Exemptions in *Hobby Lobby*'s Wake", (2015) 82 *University of Chicago Law Review* 1897–1980.

41 See generally, e.g. Germain Grisez, *The Way of the Lord Jesus. Volume 3: Difficult Moral Questions* (Chicago: Franciscan Press, 1997); Anthony Fisher, "Cooperation in Evil: Understanding the Issues", in Helen Watt, ed., *Cooperation, Complicity, and Conscience* (London: Linacre Centre, 2005), 27–64; Kevin L. Flannery, *Cooperation with Evil: Thomistic Tools of Analysis* (Washington, DC: Catholic University of America Press, 2019); Benedict M. Ashley, Jean K. deBlois and Kevin D. O'Rourke, *Health Care Ethics: A Catholic Theological Analysis*, 5th ed. (Washington, DC: Georgetown University Press, 2006).

42 American Law Institute, Model Penal Code, §2.06(1)–(3).

"associate[s] himself with the venture", as with "something that he wishes to bring about".[43]

So, what is it that distinguishes the unwitting bystander from the criminal and that creates a connection or link between the principal and another, enabling the latter to justly share in the blame, and the punishment, that attaches to the conduct of the former? Terms such as "aid", "abet", "assist", "promote", "encourage", "stimulate", "instigate", "incite" and "embolden" are common, but each of these terms raises, rather than answers, the "what counts?" question. One widely used criminal law textbook uses, as teaching examples, one case where it was enough to flip the complicity switch that a writer for a Jazz magazine "failed to get up and protest in the name of the musicians of England" when an American saxophone player performed in a London theatre without the required authorisation, and another in which a teenager was found to be complicit in her friend's convenience store burglary by virtue of having "expressed a desire for some bananas".[44]

Precisely what it is that opens the circuit through which derived culpability and criminal liability can flow is, like the location of the line separating bad thoughts and mere preparation from attempts, difficult to determine with confidence. And yet, as with attempts, a blameworthy intent to step outside the constraints to which one has, like one's fellow members of the political community, presumably agreed to submit is key. "Mere presence" at the scene of another's crime does not make one the other's accomplice, but such presence accompanied by a communicated intent to warn the other, if necessary, of an approaching police officer, does. Indeed, some approaches would impose liability via complicity on a person who attempts or intends to aid but does not, and even if the principal actor is entirely unaware of the "accomplice's" support.[45]

A controversial feature of accomplice liability in the criminal law context is that, at least in some jurisdictions, "one can be an accomplice even if [one's] assistance is not a 'but for' cause of the crime".[46] Some commentators insist that "trivial", ineffective or otherwise non-causal "assistance" should not give rise to derivative criminal liability or, at the very least, should result in liability for a lesser offence than the one committed by the principal actor.[47] To be sure, dispensing with a causation requirement in the accomplice liability context creates or contributes to the risk that liability, blame and punishment will be imposed on

43 See *United States v. Peoni*.

44 *Wilcox v. Jeffery*, 1 All England Law Reports 464 (King's Bench Division, 1951); and *State v. Helmenstein*, 163 N.W. 2d 85 (Supreme Court of North Dakota, 1968), cited in Dressler and Garvey, *Criminal Law*, 915–20.

45 See Dressler, *Understanding Criminal Law*, 467.

46 Dressler and Garvey, *Criminal Law*, 921 (citing and quoting *State ex rel. Martin v. Tally*, 102 Ala. 25, 15 So. 722 (1894)): "The assistance given … need not contribute to the criminal result in the sense that but for it the result would not have ensued". See generally Katz, "Story of *Tally*".

47 See, e.g. Dressler, "Reforming Complicity Law".

actors who, conceding their *mens rea*, are tenuously connected or located at a far distance from the actual offence. And, it could be argued, it opens the door to disproportionate punishments, at least if one believes that the severity of a punishment should reflect one's real-world, actual responsibility for wrongs, harms and costs.

And yet, we might say that even a remote, ineffective, redundant, non-causal "accomplice" is – like the one who attempts an impossible crime or who is apprehended well before he or she presents any meaningful danger – blameworthy and appropriately subject to condemnation and punishment, by virtue of the evil that he or she, however uselessly, embraced. The objections to complicity in cases of non-causal assistance would seem to have more to do with the risk of abuses of discretion or judicial and prosecutorial mistakes than with principle.

Clearly, much more could be said about the foundations, details and implications of criminal liability for criminal attempts and via complicity. The goal for the discussion so far is a modest one, i.e. to illustrate a harmony – the causes of which others have explored and elaborated in detail – between Christianity's insistence on a compromised but still meaningful capacity to deliberate, intend and choose well or badly, on the one hand, and Anglo-American criminal law's signature theme of assigning blame and condemnation to plans and purposes, on the other. Accompanying this harmony, though, is a cautious reluctance to go further, and to move beyond subjective accounts of desert and blame to enlisting the criminal law in efforts to transform and shape character and to inculcate virtue. Christian morality and ethics propose, among other things, that we are creatures beloved by God and that understanding human flourishing requires an understanding of what it means to be human and of what human persons are for.[48] The virtues, Christianity teaches, "enable a person 'to attain the furthest potentialities of his nature'", they "picture for us what a person would be if his or her nature were fully realized" and they "fit us to live a life characteristic of flourishing human beings".[49]

It has been more than 60 years since Elizabeth Anscombe famously declared that "it is not profitable for us at present to do moral philosophy", and at the heart of her diagnosis was the complaint that, "at present", those purporting to "do moral philosophy" lacked and showed little interest in developing an account of moral praise and blame that was connected to ideas of human flourishing and the virtues that facilitate it.[50] Since then, of course, there has been a significant "revitalization of virtue ethics" – not only among Christian moral theologians and theorists – and an increased appreciation for the fact that "the good for human persons" is not merely to avoid causing harms or violating prohibitions but instead "to flourish as persons, to realize our own nature, to develop in full-

48 See generally, e.g. Richard W. Garnett, "Sectarian Reflections on Lawyers' Ethics and Death-Row Volunteers", (2002) 77 *Notre Dame Law Review* 795–830.

49 Meilaender, *Theory and Practice of Virtue*, 19, 11.

50 G.E.M. Anscombe, "Modern Moral Philosophy", (1958) 33.124 *Philosophy* 1–19.

ness what we actually are".[51] Alasdair MacIntyre's landmark *After Virtue* is, of course, a prominent and widely engaged example in moral philosophy[52] and many specifically Christian, yet differing, treatments have also been proposed. What would seem to unite, or at least hold together, these accounts is an insistence that morality is about more than rule-following and obligation and a concern with ethical formation, habituation and character development, usually in community. The moral life is seen as a journey, the end of which is supplied by our nature as beloved creatures made for Beatitude. Virtue ethics, Christian Smith explains, "are concerned not centrally with rules and duty, but with the kind of persons we are and are becoming, with the formation and living out of good, moral personal character".[53] Human persons, precisely because we are persons, "can't not be headed somewhere", as one Christian theologian nicely put it. "We live leaning forward, bent on arriving at the place we long for".

And yet, with a few notable exceptions,[54] theorists and practitioners of criminal law seem to be leery about an Aristotelian or aretaic turn.[55] They are sceptical not only of suggestions that criminal liability and criminal punishment should attach to bad character or failures to flourish, but also of claims that this liability and punishment can play a substantial role in the development of practical wisdom or the habituation into virtue. Of course, there is a well-pedigreed tradition in Christian thinking about the law of humility and modesty when it comes to the role of law in "leading men to virtue". "[N]ot all the vices from which virtuous men abstain are prohibited by human law", Aquinas said, and "human law does not issue commands concerning all the acts of all the virtues".[56]

For all the emphasis in contemporary Anglo-American criminal law – including, as we have seen, in the doctrines relating to criminal attempts and complicity – there is a no less firm insistence that we do not punish "bad guys" for being "bad guys" but only for acting wrongly.[57] We saw in the discussion above that various aspects and specifics of accomplice and attempt liability display a

51 See Christian Smith, *What Is a Person? Rethinking Humanity, Social Life, and the Moral Good from the Person Up* (Chicago: University of Chicago Press, 2010), 385 and note 2 (collecting works and sources reflecting the virtue ethics revival).

52 Alasdair MacIntyre, *After Virtue: A Study in Moral Theory*, 3rd ed. (London: Duckworth, 2007).

53 Smith, *What Is a Person?*, 408.

54 Kyron Huigens' work is probably the leading example of an attempt to develop a thoroughly aretaic approach to criminal liability. See, e.g. Kyron Huigens, "Virtue and Criminal Negligence", (1998) 1 *Buffalo Criminal Law Review* 431–58; Kyron Huigens, "Virtue and Inculpation", (1995) 108 *Harvard Law Review* 1423–80.

55 See, e.g. Duff, "Virtue, Vice, and Criminal Liability", 209 (insisting that "criminal liability is, at least paradigmatically, not for choices, or character traits, or vices, but for actions").

56 Thomas Aquinas, *Treatise on Law: The Complete Text*, trans. Alfred J. Freddoso (South Bend: St. Augustine's Press, 2009), q. 96, aa. 2–3.

57 Ekow N. Yankah, "Good Guys and Bad Guys: Punishing Character, Equality, and the Irrelevance of Moral Character to Criminal Punishment", (2004) 25 *Cardozo Law Review* 1019–67.

tight nexus between culpability and states of mind, with harmful results caused by actors' conduct playing less of a role. Still, with attempts and other inchoate crimes, the actor is not punished for having a bad character, for defects in habituation or for being "the sort of person" who concocts criminal plans and projects. Similarly, one is not an accomplice simply for approving (or just not minding) another's wrongdoing; one must do something – not much, perhaps, but something – to embrace the other's offence, and make it one's own, in order to derive and share liability.

And so, this chapter's two criminal law topics not only confirm a moral teaching that is central to and informed by Christianity, but they also, through their reticence, point towards another fundamental Christian concern, while reminding us of the limits – this side of Heaven – of law.

Further reading

Anscombe, G.E.M. "Modern Moral Philosophy", (1958) 33.124 *Philosophy* 1–19.

Aquinas, Thomas. *Treatise on Law: The Complete Text*, trans. Alfred J. Freddoso (South Bend: St. Augustine's Press, 2009).

Besser-Jones, Lorraine and Michael Slote, eds. *The Routledge Companion to Virtue Ethics* (London: Routledge, 2015).

Cloutier, David and William C. Mattison III. "Review Essay: The Resurgence of Virtue in Recent Moral Theology", (2014) 3.1 *Journal of Moral Theology* 228–59.

Crawford, J.M.B. and J.F. Quinn. *The Christian Foundations of Criminal Responsibility: A Philosophical Study of Legal Reasoning* (Lewiston: Edwin Mellen, 1991).

Dressler, Joshua. *Understanding Criminal Law*, 8th ed. (Durham, NC: Carolina Academic Press, 2018).

Farrelly, Colin and Lawrence B. Solum, eds. *Virtue Jurisprudence* (Basingstoke: Palgrave Macmillan, 2008).

Flannery, Kevin L. *Cooperation with Evil: Thomistic Tools of Analysis* (Washington, DC: Catholic University of America Press, 2019).

MacIntyre, Alasdair. *After Virtue: A Study in Moral Theory*, 3rd ed. (London: Duckworth, 2007).

Mattison, William C. III. *Introducing Moral Theology: True Happiness and the Virtues* (Grand Rapids: Brazos Press, 2008).

Meilaender, Gilbert C. *The Theory and Practice of Virtue* (Notre Dame: University of Notre Dame Press, 1984).

Pieper, Josef. *The Four Cardinal Virtues*, trans. Richard Winston and Clara Winston (Notre Dame: University of Notre Dame Press, 1966).

Porter, Jean. *The Recovery of Virtue: The Relevance of Aquinas for Christian Ethics* (London: SPCK, 1994).

Solum, Lawrence B. "Virtue Jurisprudence: Towards an Aretaic Theory of Law", in Liesbeth Huppes-Cluysenaer and Nuno M.M.S. Coelho, eds., *Aristotle and the Philosophy of Law: Theory, Practice and Justice, Ius Gentium: Comparative Perspectives on Law and Justice 23* (Dordrecht: Springer, 2013), 1–31.

Yaffe, Gideon. *Attempts: In the Philosophy of Action and the Criminal Law* (Oxford: Oxford University Press, 2010).

Part IV

Christianity and the enforcement of criminal law

16 Defences: justification, excuse and provocation

Chloë Kennedy

16.1 Introduction

There are many ways of thinking through the relationships between Christianity and law. These might, to greater and lesser extents, be historically informed, concerned with explication or critique, and situate Christian approaches within global, multifaith contexts. In this chapter, I think through some of the relationships between Christianity and criminal law defences with two aims and, for reasons of space, without engaging in any interfaith comparison. The first aim is to discern how traditional Christian beliefs have shaped criminal law defences as a matter of doctrine and practice. The second aim is to consider whether alterations to these defences might be supported through relying on alternative strands of Christian thinking. This approach is informed by what I take to be the two main benefits of examining law in conjunction with religion: first, attaining a deeper and more critical understanding of the laws we have and, second, identifying different ways of addressing the challenges that arise within, or because of, these laws.

In the rest of this chapter, I consider the full and partial defences of self-defence, necessity, "insanity" (now more commonly termed mental disorder), provocation and consent. I discuss these defences in particular not only because their scope and operation are well explained by the influence of traditional Christian beliefs but also because they present pressing challenges for contemporary criminal law scholars. To foreground the nature of these challenges, the analysis in the following sections is structured around three themes: adult human capacities, sanctity of life, and heteronormativity and patriarchy.

Under "adult human capacities", I examine the tension between broader and narrower iterations of the insanity defence and the role that Christian conceptions of free will have played in keeping the ambit of this excuse small. Section 16.3 on "sanctity of life" explores the exclusion of intentional homicide from the defence of necessity and the difficulty of accommodating both "pro-life" and alternative views of euthanasia and assisted suicide in contemporary, pluralistic societies. In Section 16.4, I argue that the heteronormativity and patriarchy of traditional Christian marriage contribute to the continued existence of the marital rape exemption and the defence of provocation by infidelity in some jurisdictions, and have prevented consent from being recognised as a defence to "assault" in the context of bondage/discipline/dominance/submission/sadism/masochism (BDSM). Finally, I question whether these phenomena are necessary corollaries of a Christian contribution to criminal law.

16.2 Adult human capacities

The idea that adults who would otherwise be responsible agents should not be punished for their crimes if they lack mental capacity is ancient, with roots that extend into the Greek and Roman worlds.[1] In the hands of the canonists, this notion developed into the now widely held view that an offender may be excused from criminal liability if the relevant acts were committed while the offender was "out of his [*sic*] mind", so long as it could be proved that (i) as a result of his condition he could not know that he was doing wrong and (ii) he had not wrongfully brought about his condition.[2] Both of these requirements must be understood alongside the Christian belief that afflictions such as insanity are punishments for sin and the strong Christian faith in free will. The effect of these commitments was to keep the insanity defence within narrow bounds, confined to cognitive failings of the most serious kind that the offender had no (perceived) role in bringing about. In accordance with this, the legal definition of insanity that was accepted within early Anglo-American criminal law was total deprivation of understanding.

Over time and as inter-personal relations grew in number and complexity, legal actors were increasingly called on to adjudicate capacity claims. In the face of this, confidence in the law's prototypical agent – the largely unfettered individual – began to erode. This process gained pace over the course of the eighteenth and nineteenth centuries with the emergence of a body of expert knowledge which suggested that criminal misconduct might be caused by mental deficiencies, which could in turn be attributed to environmental or physical factors. Such suggestions not only undermined the voluntarism on which the law was based, but they also raised questions about how to distinguish causes that ought to preclude liability, i.e. disease, from those that should not, i.e. depravity. Layered over these difficulties was the prospect of *manie sans délire* – insanity without any reasoning defect, delusion or hallucination, which might afflict only the sufferer's volition or emotions. Such maladies posed even more pronounced epistemic anxieties than cognitive defects, and threatened to widen the scope of non-responsibility well beyond the narrow core suggested by the presumed existence of universal and largely uniform free will.

1 Daniel N. Robinson, "The Insanity Defence as a History of Mental Disorder", in K.W.M. Fulward *et al.*, eds., *The Oxford Handbook of Philosophy and Psychiatry* (Oxford: Oxford University Press, 2013), 18–36.

2 Harold J. Berman, *Law and Revolution: The Formation of the Western Legal Tradition* (Cambridge, MA: Harvard University Press, 1983), 189.

Faced with these seemingly intractable difficulties, judges have often fallen back on traditional, theologically informed beliefs about human agency, according to which all behavioural deficiencies, bar the clearest cases of cognitive impairment, are the responsibility of the delinquent and merely evidence of her choice to give in to vicious habits.[3] The same is true in respect of provocation which, though only formalised into a partial defence in the sixteenth and seventeenth centuries, has operated to mitigate punishment from at least mediaeval times. Importantly, this leniency has only been exercised when it is thought that the anger could have been resisted but was instead indulged. In essence, the notion that individuals can and should control their passions, and work to develop their consciences, has informed the way the exculpatory dimension of anger has functioned in criminal trials.[4]

Many of these challenges have not abated. Law is still considered by some to lag behind advances in understanding the human mind, especially where determinism, moral responsibility and criminal punishment are concerned. To hard-line determinists, developments in neuroscience undermine the case for retributive punishment altogether and suggest that a public health-quarantine model should be used to handle criminal offenders instead.[5] There also remains disagreement over whether to hold individuals with purportedly faulty moral reasoning, such as those with psychopathic personality disorder, fully responsible for crimes they commit. The Christian contribution to these debates continues to rely on the claim that humans are born in sin but retain the capacity to know good from evil and choose the good. Hence, the range of situations in which an excuse is thought appropriate is very limited. To advocates of this approach, "scientific materialism" has failed to deliver on its promises, revealing the "inherent shortcomings" of attempting to understand human nature in wholly scientific terms.[6]

Despite this continuity, within Christian communities there has been a move away from conceiving of mental illness as something for which the sufferer is responsible and which can be overcome through acts of will. This view has been replaced by a sense that human beings are better understood as existing at the

3 Susanna Blumenthal, *Law and the Modern Mind: Consciousness and Responsibility in American Legal Culture* (Cambridge, MA: Harvard University Press, 2016); Chloë Kennedy, "'Ungovernable Feelings and Passions': Common Sense Philosophy and Mental State Defences in Nineteenth Century Scotland", (2016) 20.3 *Edinburgh Law Review* 285–311.

4 Kennedy, "'Ungovernable Feelings and Passions'"; Elizabeth Papp Kamali, "The Devil's Daughter of Hell Fire: Anger's Role in Medieval English Felony Cases", (2017) 35 *Law & History Review* 155–200.

5 E.g. Gregg D. Caruso, "Justice Without Retribution: An Epistemic Argument Against Retributive Criminal Punishment" (2018) *Neuroethics*, https://doi.org/10.1007/s12152-018-9357-8; Gregg D. Caruso, "The Public Health-Quarantine Model", in Dana Nelkin and Derek Pereboom, eds., *Oxford Handbook of Moral Responsibility* (New York: Oxford University Press, forthcoming).

6 Philip E. Johnson, "Human Nature and Criminal Responsibility: The Biblical View Restored", in Michael W. McConnell *et al.*, eds., *Christian Perspectives on Legal Thought* (New Haven: Yale University Press, 2001), 426–34.

interstices of finitude and freedom and with an acknowledgement that mental illness can often be considered a response to a disordered world, replete with collective human failings.[7] It is debatable whether taking these insights seriously might lead to an expansion in mental disorder defences, though. The criminal law's individualistic blaming relations are notoriously hard to unsettle and the repercussions of doing so for the justice system are perhaps too radical for this to prove a realistic prospect.[8] At the very least, meaningful support should be provided to those suffering from mental illness and over-inclusive criminal laws should be amended so that mentally ill people are not punished for engaging in self-destructive behaviour patterns, such as substance abuse.

16.3 Sanctity of life

Where the insanity defence dictates who may be excused from criminal punishment, the question of what kinds of conduct may be excused is, of course, equally important. For the most part, so-called general defences (those that are not particular to specific crimes) are unrestricted in their application. An exception to this is the defence of necessity and, by extension, duress, which have been held to be unavailable to charges of intentional homicide on account of the inviolability of human life.[9] Since in homicide cases the defence of necessity demands an assessment of the relative worth of human lives, it is inconsistent with the idea that life has sacred, irreducible value – a difficulty that is most pronounced when the deceased has been selected from a multitude of potential victims, as in the (in) famous shipwreck case of *R v Dudley & Stephens*.[10]

As is well known, in this case two of the crew, who had been adrift for 18 days and without food for a week, killed and ate the flesh of the young cabin boy – Richard Parker – who was weaker than the others and, unlike them, had no children to support. It became clear when the surviving crew were convicted of murder that weighing the comparative value of human lives in this way is incompatible with the deontological, and implicitly Christian, ethic that appears, through closer examination of the judgment, to underpin this defence. Preserving

7 Marcia Webb, "Toward a Theology of Mental Illness", (2012) 16.1 *Journal of Religion, Disability & Health* 49–73.

8 Benjamin J. Berger, "Mental Disorder and the Instability of Blame in Criminal Law", in François Tanguay-Renaud and James Stribopoulos, eds., *New Canadian Perspectives on the Philosophy of Domestic, Transnational, and International Criminal Law* (Oxford: Hart, 2011), 117–39.

9 In contrast, the Model Penal Code suggests that intentional homicide should be justified under the defence of necessity when there is a "net saving" of innocent lives: see John Alan Cohan, "Homicide by Necessity", (2006) 10 *Chapman Law Review* 133–5.

10 (1884) 14 QBD 273. This case has been influential in the common law world and has shaped the law's trajectory in the United States and the United Kingdom. See Joshua Dressler, "Reflections on *Dudley and Stephens* and Killing the Innocent: Taking a Wrong Conceptual Path", in Dennis J. Baker and Jeremy Horder, eds., *The Sanctity of Life and the Criminal Law* (Cambridge: Cambridge University Press, 2013), 126–47.

one's own life at the expense of another innocent person's does not cohere with this moral framework either, so necessity is also unavailable in homicide cases where only one victim is involved.

Each of these points comes out clearly in the *Dudley & Stephens* judgment, in which Lord Coleridge asks, rhetorically, who could be the judge of this kind of necessity and on what basis individual lives might be compared. Quoting from Milton's *Paradise Lost* – "So spake the Fiend, and with necessity, / The tyrant's plea excused his devilish deeds"[11] – he acknowledges that the defendants faced extreme temptation but nevertheless rules that reprieve was the most they could expect. In addition to the impropriety of assessing the relative worth of human lives, the reasons given for this decision include concerns over the effect of formally sanctioning such conduct and the claim that, other than in cases of self-defence, one has a duty to sacrifice one's own life to save another's. I will return to the second issue below; for now, it is worth teasing out the final reason in a bit more detail because it reveals more about why necessity was considered unavailable to the defendants and the theological rationale behind this restriction.

The answer lies in the deep roots of self-defence, which are found in the just war theory created by St Augustine and extended by St Thomas Aquinas. In an effort to smooth the alliance between Christianity and the imperial Roman world, Augustine undertook to reconcile the highly pacifist teachings of the New Testament with Ciceronian views on the legitimacy of force. By fusing elements of the Judeo-Christian tradition with select Roman law concepts, Augustine conceived of just war as a punitive response to sin. He argued that if adversaries sin, through disturbing "right order" and peace, then their punishment, if delivered in the right spirit (i.e. without revenge or pleasure in the suffering of others) and with the authority of the sovereign, amounts to nothing more than an act of love that would prevent future sinning. This reconfiguration of Christian teachings did not condone defensive violence in a private capacity, though. When a Christian used lethal force against another outside the context of war, the act was simply presumed to be motivated by hatred or a lack of love, even if it had been undertaken in self-defence. When Aquinas eventually expanded self-defence to encompass dyadic encounters, this was facilitated by the doctrine of double effect. This doctrine teaches that although it is impermissible to intend to end another's life, a lethal act of self-defence against an aggressor is permissible so long as the intention is good (to preserve one's life), the bad outcome (death) is accidental and the intended good end is proportionate to the bad outcome.[12]

It is clear that Lord Coleridge's judgment contains elements of both these schools of thought, expressed in theological language, when he holds that the only defence available to the defendants was self-defence, which could not apply

11 (1884) 14 QBD 288.

12 Onder Bakircioglu, *Self-defence in International and Criminal Law: The Doctrine of Imminence* (Abingdon and New York: Routledge, 2011), ch. 2; John Langan, "The Elements of St Augustine's Just War Theory", (1984) 12.1 *Journal of Religious Ethics* 19–38.

on account of the innocence (indeed helplessness) of Richard Parker. Moreover, according to Lord Coleridge, this was exactly how things should be. "[I]t is enough in a Christian country", he wrote, "to remind ourselves of the Great Example whom we profess to follow". By this view, the fact that we may never be able to reach the standards set by this example is unproblematic because we are often compelled to lay down rules of law we cannot satisfy.[13] These remarks help make sense of the court's reluctance to countenance anything other than the possibility of post-conviction leniency. To allow the defence of necessity in cases of intentional homicide would be too formal an endorsement of the defendants' act, which would compromise the law's unqualified condemnation of taking the lives of innocent non-aggressors. As Lord Coleridge put it, it was not possible to "allow compassion for the criminal to change or weaken in any manner the legal definition of the crime".[14]

This desire to avoid diluting the legal opprobrium that has traditionally attached to intentionally taking innocent life has also arisen, in an increasingly fraught way, in the debate over legalising euthanasia and assisted suicide. In common with other theological traditions, the Christian position on these practices is that they are totally impermissible, with the exception of administering palliative care that incidentally shortens life or withdrawing futile treatment, which are considered acceptable by some Christians in accordance with the doctrine of double effect.[15] Many Western legal systems broadly cohere with this view such that euthanasia and assisted dying remain criminal offences. Furthermore, for the reasons already mentioned, necessity is generally not available as a defence. Although in *Re A*[16] the English Court of Appeal relied on the defence of necessity to hold that it would be permissible for doctors to separate conjoined twins in the knowledge that the operation would kill the more vulnerable of the two (an act that was deemed to satisfy the definition of murder), the court was keen to limit the effects of the judgment. It emphasised that its decision turned on the particular facts in question, and commentators have distinguished the case from *Dudley & Stephens* on the basis that there was no choice between innocent lives to be made.[17]

That said, public opinion on these matters is far from unified and challenges to laws criminalising assisted suicide and compassionate killings, as well as attempts to decriminalise these practices, continue to occur in various jurisdictions. Given the strongly held views on either side of the debate and the impossibility of

13 (1884) 14 QBD 287.

14 (1884) 14 QBD 288.

15 Damien Keown and John Keown, "Killing, Karma and Caring: Euthanasia in Buddhism and Christianity", (1995) 21.5 *Journal of Medical Ethics* 265–9.

16 [2001] WLR 480.

17 Penney Lewis, "The Failure of the Defence of Necessity as a Mechanism of Legal Change on Assisted Dying in the Common Law World", in Baker and Horder, *Sanctity of Life and the Criminal Law*, 280. This seems questionable: even if the poor condition of one twin meant that the choice was easy to make, a choice was made.

coherently accommodating both simultaneously, strategies have emerged that effectively attempt to appease both "pro-life" and "pro-euthanasia" cohorts. In England and Wales, for example, the doctrine of double effect has been used to ensure that doctors and other medical professionals who administer pain-relieving medication and, by doing so, hasten death will not be guilty of murder.[18] This was achieved – notably by Lord Devlin, who believed that British law ought to uphold Christian morality[19] – not by providing these doctors with a defence like necessity that would amount to an endorsement of the homicidal action, but through an unorthodox interpretation of the law of intention to take account of primary and secondary purposes. In cases of active killing that do not involve medical professionals, it is harder to claim there is any non-homicidal primary purpose, since relieving pain or suffering and hastening death are, in these cases, inextricable. Instead, juries have simply elected to acquit where their sympathies have been sufficiently aroused.[20]

In the case of assisted suicide, the public prosecution service has been compelled to make explicit and publicise the factors that will influence its decision to prosecute, following a successful human rights challenge to the pre-existing, less specific prosecution policy.[21] Although welcomed by many, this move has been criticised on the basis that it requires open and prospective determinations of the comparative value of human lives, which brings with it undesirable symbolic and practical consequences. High among these is the possibility that a permissive "can" might morph into an obligatory "ought" that would lead people, often those who are already vulnerable, to choose an early death. Importantly, it is the formalisation of these factors, which will determine the decision of whether to prosecute, that underlies these apprehensions; the implicit legitimisation of assisted suicide, and assisted dying more generally, is what matters here.[22]

As mentioned previously, this is precisely the concern that has partly fuelled judicial reluctance to allow necessity, and by extension duress, to be pled in response to a charge of intentional homicide. It may be, however, that this caution is unnecessary if a distinction is drawn between necessity as a justification and necessity as an excuse. Whereas justification defences apply when an offence has been committed but is not considered wrongful, excuse defences apply when an offence is considered wrongful but not culpable. Only the former can properly be interpreted as "undoing" the prohibition of an otherwise sanctioned act.

18 Withdrawal of medical treatment which results in death has also been held to be permissible (*Airedale NHS Trust v Bland* [1993] AC 789).

19 T.A. Roberts, "Law, Morality and Religion in a Christian Society", (1984) 21.1 *Religious Studies* 79–98.

20 Alan Norrie, "Legal Form and Moral Judgment: Euthanasia and Assisted Suicide", in R.A. Duff *et al.*, eds., *The Structures of the Criminal Law* (Oxford: Oxford University Press, 2011), 134–56.

21 *R.(Purdy) v. DPP* [2009] UKHL 45.

22 Kate Greasley, "*R (Purdy) v DPP* and the Case for Wilful Blindness", (2010) 30.2 *Oxford Journal of Legal Studies* 310–26.

Allowing the defence of necessity to excuse intentional homicide would therefore allow those who are motivated by compassion to be acquitted without going so far as to formally amend the condemnation of intentional killing that the law has traditionally upheld.

The difficulty with this possibility is that general verdicts, such as "not guilty", do not communicate whether an acquittal is based on the conduct being excused rather than justified, so the ameliorative effect of this solution, when it comes to the symbolism of the law, is minimal. For these reasons, it may be that the strategies of compromise set out above remain the optimal way of handling the sensitive disagreements that arise within this area of law. For strict adherents to the sanctity of life, such as Christians and many other peoples of religious faith, these compromises are likely to be unacceptable. They do not officially condone deliberate killings, but they allow them to go unpunished. In modern, pluralistic societies, however, this probably cannot be determinative. For many people, the law ought to concede to reasonable human frailties. In other words, *contra* Lord Coleridge, it should not condemn people for failing to meet standards they cannot realistically meet. To many, killing out of compassion is a wholly understandable, perhaps even laudable, response to witnessing extreme suffering, so inflicting censure and punishment is not a justifiable exercise of State power. Perhaps the main lesson to be derived from this discussion is that laws, including criminal laws, are always applied with a particular notion of what human beings are, and what they should be, in mind. Even when covert, this notion, with all the expectations and assumptions it carries with it, undergirds who will be afforded a defence to criminal liability and when.

16.4 Heteronormativity and patriarchy

The most striking and contentious illustrations of the law presuming what people are and ought to be like come from its regulation of sexual practices. Here, the heteronormative and patriarchal dimensions of traditional Christian marriage have shaped, and continue to shape, the extent to which "non-standard" sexual practices are deemed lawful and, conversely, the extent to which conduct that would ordinarily constitute a crime is permitted when it coheres with these conventional views. At least, this is what I aim to show in this penultimate section with reference to the role of consent in BDSM and marital rape, and the defence of provocation by infidelity.

The specific views that are relevant to this undertaking are represented across the Catholic, Lutheran, Calvinist and Anglican traditions, despite their different interpretations of the soteriological capacity and social function of marriage.[23] They include the ideas that marriage is a monogamous relationship between a

23 See John Witte, Jr., *From Sacrament to Contract: Marriage Religion, and Law in the Western Tradition*, 4th ed. (Louisville: Westminster John Knox Press, 2012). Cf. the different, more egalitarian, Quaker views of gender relations in and outside marriage: Petra L. Doan and Elizabeth P. Kamphausen, "Quakers and Sexuality", in Stephen W. Angell and Ben Pink

man and a woman; that the terms of marriage are not set by the parties; that the goods of marriage are fidelity, procreation and protection from sexual sin; and that the husband rules over his wife. As scholars have pointed out, even though the language of mutuality and reciprocal duties has been found within descriptions of marriage since the advent of the New Testament, this jars with the gendered hierarchy that has subsisted within traditional Christian notions of marriage and which has, moreover, been performed in a way that subjugates women.[24] The same is true of the injunctions against adultery that have appeared, with punishments of varying severity, over the years as a complement to these beliefs about marriage. Even when formally neutral, their application has affected women more harshly (to say nothing of the many explicit double standards). For example, Calvin famously abhorred all adultery, advocating its capital punishment, and thought that a man's otherwise natural superiority over his wife did not apply in matters of conjugal sex. Yet, even while chastising both adulterous men and women for breaking their promise to each other and to God, he condemned adulterous women for exposing their husbands to shame and despoiling the names of their families and unborn children.[25] For unfaithful women, then, breaching the marital vow brought greater stigma on themselves and, crucially, on their husbands. Regrettably, all of these gender differentials remain extant in law and cultural attitudes. A recent report by the UN Working Group on discrimination against women in law shows that ostensibly gender-neutral crimes of adultery are, in practice, directed overwhelmingly towards women and girls.[26] Furthermore, research shows that female adulterers are shamed more than their male counterparts and that the mistresses of male adulterers, and even their wronged partners, also face negative treatment.[27]

Together, these conventional Christian marriage tenets and their contemporary successors are heteronormative in the broad sense of the term, wherein it dovetails with patriarchy. Put simply, these tenets create a structure that privileges heterosexuality, and its related binary understanding of gender, and supports systemic male dominance.[28] With this in mind, it is not difficult to see that there is at least a *prima facie* case for assuming that the hetero-patriarchal facets of criminal

---

Dandelion, eds., *The Oxford Handbook of Quaker Studies* (Oxford: Oxford University Press, 2013), 445–57.

24 Yolanda Dreyer, "De-centre-ing Sexual Difference in Public and Ecclesial Discourses on Marriage", (2008) 64.2 *Theological Studies* 715–38.

25 Witte, *From Sacrament to Contract*, 195–6.

26 UN Working Group on Discrimination, "Adultery as a Criminal Offence Violates Women's Human Rights", https://www.ohchr.org/Documents/Issues/Women/WG/AdulteryasaCriminalOffenceViolatesWomenHR.pdf (accessed 23 January 2019).

27 Alyssa Miller, "Punishing Passion: A Comparative Analysis of Adultery Laws in the United States and Their Effects on Women", (2018) 41 *Fordham International Law Journal* 425–72.

28 Lilly Nortjé-Meyer, "Deconstructing the Heteronormative Image of the Early Christian Household: Reconsidering Gender as a Key Concept of Family Functioning", (2010) 21.2 *Acta Patristica et Byzantina* 141–51.

law analysed in this section can be traced to the privileging of a specific set of religiously informed norms about sex and gender relations. To substantiate this suggestion, however, it is necessary to consider each of the facets in more detail.

A useful starting point is the marital rape exemption which, of the three areas of law under discussion, is probably the most alien to contemporary sensibilities. Now eradicated from many, though not all, legal systems, the marital rape exemption operated – as the name suggests – to exclude married men from being held criminally liable for non-consensual sex with their wives. Put differently, it allowed men to rape their wives. The most commonly cited origin of this rule is Sir Mathew Hale's *Historia Placitorum Coronae*, which states that "[a] husband cannot be guilty of a rape committed by himself upon his lawful wife, for by their mutual matrimonial consent and contract the wife hath given up herself in this kind unto her husband, which she cannot retract".[29] Even though it is unlikely that Hale actually created the exemption, he seems to have provided its theoretical basis and, in doing so, seems to have been making a normative as well as a descriptive statement.[30]

Four aspects of Hale's explanation of the marital rape exemption are significant in unpacking the Christian conception of marriage that can be discerned within it. First and second are the facts that marriage is conceived as a contract and that the terms of this contract are not set by the parties (or at least one of them). Third is the fact that matrimonial consent, and by extension sexual access to one's spouse, is considered irrevocable. Fourth is the fact that although consent and contract to marriage are described as mutual, their operation is very clearly asymmetrical: it is the wife who has given herself unto her husband. All of these features cohere with the conception of marriage that Hale, a Puritan Anglican, is likely to have endorsed,[31] and a number of these features continue to be exalted within some contemporary Christian jurisprudential thinking.[32] It also maps onto the justifications that have continued to be offered for the marital rape exemption into the modern age.[33] According to this view of marriage, it is unimportant

29 Sir Matthew Hale, *Historia Placitorum Coronae*, vol. 1 (Philadelphia: Robert H Small; first published 1736), 628.

30 Jill Elaine Hasday, "Contest and Consent: A Legal History of Marital Rape", (2000) 88.5 *California Law Review* 1375–1506 at 1396–1400.

31 Alan Cromartie, "Hale, Sir Mathew (1609–1676)", *Oxford Dictionary of National Biography* (Oxford University Press, 2004), https://doi.org/10.1093/ref:odnb/11905 (accessed 23 January 2019).

32 E.g. Don S. Browning, "Family Law and Christian Jurisprudence", in John Witte, Jr. and Frank S. Alexander, eds., *Christianity and Law: An Introduction* (Cambridge: Cambridge University Press, 2008), 163–83. Browning laments the decline of covenantal marriage and suggests that different but "equal" roles for husbands and wives are desirable (a notion that is rejected by the majority of feminists on account of its proven tendency to lead to the subordination of women).

33 Keith Burgess, "Wife Rape", (1998) 12.1 *Public Affairs Quarterly* 1–22 (refuting the purported justifications but not mentioning their overlap with traditional Christian views of marriage).

whether a wife gives her consent to sexual intercourse at any time after she has consented to be married. Both parties have mutually and irreversibly consented to marriage and all that entails (sexual intercourse, procreation and fidelity) and, since the husband is the head of the household, he dictates the terms on which this "mutuality" will operate.

The association with procreation is not especially clear in Hale's account of the marital rape exemption, but it was crucial in the efforts of early women's rights groups to eradicate the defence. Although denunciations of the marital rape exemption only gained sufficient traction to effect legal change in the twentieth century, the exemption attracted criticism from the middle of the nineteenth century and the women who voiced these concerns were wholly cognisant of the links between marriage, procreation and denial of their bodily autonomy. In fact, they turned the oppressions generated by these associations (which prevented them access to the public sphere) to their advantage to argue that since women were expected to undertake the childcare that "successful" procreative sex necessarily gave rise to, women should have the right to determine how and when they would be expected to undertake this work.[34]

This strategy ultimately failed, which is not surprising given the prevailing views on the place of women in society at the time. It is instructive, however, because it highlights the importance of understanding how intersecting marital expectations have come together to help men escape criminal liability that they would otherwise face. It also demonstrates that loosening the grasp of these expectations has for a long time been recognised as a strategy for abolishing such defences in the name of gender equity. This is significant because there remain other areas of criminal law where these lessons could be put to use.

A good example is the defence of provocation which, when pled successfully, typically serves to mitigate murder to a lower category of homicide. In several jurisdictions, discovering that a spouse has been unfaithful can constitute a provoking act that is capable of grounding this defence. While plenty of scholarship has pointed out the unpleasant, and gendered, implications of this defence, few have considered its links with Christian conceptions of marriage beyond pointing out that these condemn adultery. The links appear stronger, though, upon examination of the circumstances under which this strand of the provocation defence emerged. As one of the last forms of provocation to be recognised by courts, provocation by infidelity first entered English criminal law as a formal defence in 1671 at a time when adultery was an offence that was justiciable in church courts and, briefly, as a secular crime too. At this time, however, the defence protected men who killed their wives' paramours; it was not a defence employed by men who killed their spouses, as is the case today.[35] The position was similar in Scotland where, according to the jurist Sir George Mackenzie, husbands might be spared death or even offered clemency when they killed their wives' lovers,

34 Hasday, "Contest and Consent".
35 Ibid.

and fathers might be treated the same if they killed their daughters, and their daughters' lovers, on discovering their infidelity. Mackenzie explains that these rules, which were derived from the civil law, reflected hatred of the act of adultery, rather than sympathy with the passionate response of those who discovered it. Since adultery was by Scots law a capital offence when "notorious", this would cohere with the legal position on spousal infidelity at the time.[36] Yet, the prejudicial effects on women of these doctrines did not go unnoticed by Mackenzie, who pointed out that women enjoyed neither the protection of this defence nor the general prerogative over their spouse that was afforded to men. He suggests that women may have been considered too passionate to be trusted with these privileges or that it might have been considered indecent to arm women. Whatever the cause, in his view "women may complain that men, being the only legislators, have taken too great a measure of favour to themselves in this law".[37]

What is noteworthy about these laws is that they reflect the two-fold asymmetry of traditional Christian views on marriage as related to gender: infidelity was worse when committed by a woman and it was therefore worthier of shame and condemnation when committed this way. As the defence developed through subsequent centuries, the same attitudes can be detected, although the defence increasingly came to be pled by men who killed their unfaithful (or, more accurately, suspected-to-be-unfaithful) wives. Even as judges tried to steer jurors away from accepting these pleas, which were out of step with circulating discourses about manly self-control and chivalry, sympathy for the cuckolded killer endured, no doubt exacerbated by the nineteenth-century premium on female chastity.[38]

It is particularly striking that these shifts coincided with the decline in official punishments for adultery and with the emancipation of women from a number of the legal strictures they had previously faced, and that all of these changes came about around the same time as the liberalisation of marriage.[39] In this context, it seems plausible to read both the homicidal actions of men who killed their allegedly adulterous wives and the sympathetic response they elicited as a misogynistic backlash against the blow to patriarchy that each of these changes represented.[40] In addition to the perceived need to restore the "rightful" balance of power, the

36 Brian P. Levack, "The Prosecution of Sexual Crimes in Early Eighteenth-century Scotland", (2010) 89 *Scottish Historical Review* 172–93.

37 Sir George Mackenzie, *Laws and Customs of Scotland in Matters Criminal* (Edinburgh: Stair Society, 2012; first published 1678), Title 11. Note that Mackenzie could not point to any case or statute that suggested that these civilian rules actually applied in Scotland.

38 Martin J. Wiener, *Men of Blood: Violence, Manliness, and Criminal Justice in Victorian England* (Cambridge: Cambridge University Press, 2004), ch. 6.

39 K.J. Kesserling, "No Greater Provocation? Adultery and the Mitigation of Murder in English Law", (2016) 34 *Law & History Review* 199–225; Levack, "Prosecution of Sexual Crimes"; Witte, *From Sacrament to Contract*, ch. 8.

40 I understand misogyny to be the policing, controlling and punishing of women who challenge male dominance. The sympathetic response might usefully be described as "himpathy", i.e. excessive sympathy extended to a male wrongdoer over his female victim. See Kate Manne, *Down Girl: The Logic of Misogyny* (Oxford: Oxford University Press, 2017).

fact that women agitated for these changes is likely to have been significant. Their rejection of the status quo granted these women a publicly visible sense of agency that had been lacking in earlier times, when women were treated more like chattels to be fought over. Allied to this capacity for agency is, of course, the capacity for blame, so it is perhaps unsurprising that uxorial punishment would become the norm at this time.

Even as the defence has been widened to accommodate same-sex and unmarried couples, it continues to be underpinned by the same hierarchical power dynamics that typify hetero-patriarchal marriages, irrespective of the gender identity or marital status of the parties to the relationship. This is a stark reminder of how ostensibly neutral laws and practices can embody the expectations and structural relationships that support religious norms. Before moving on to consider what it might take to overcome these damaging and highly gendered assumptions, I want to consider the final example of how the privileging of traditional Christian ideals has shaped the range of criminal defences available and how this has been to the detriment of marginalised groups.

Cohering with the notion that procreation and enrichment of "valuable" (i.e. monogamous, marital, man/woman) relationships are the ends that render sexual activity worthwhile, alternative forms of sexual expression have traditionally been deprecated and proscribed through law. Same-sex sexual activity is one obvious example which, though now legal throughout much of Europe and North and South America, is still criminalised in a number of other countries. The example that is more relevant for present purposes, because it involves the availability of an affirmative defence, is BDSM. BDSM refers to sexual practices that involve bondage, discipline, domination, submission, sadism and masochism, which can include acts that are considered to satisfy the definition of assault. Unlike other "assaults" that are consensual, such as tattooing,[41] surgery, engaging in contact sports and so on, in a number of jurisdictions BDSM cannot be rendered lawful through the consent of the "victim".

It has been robustly argued by others that there are few uncontentious distinctions between BDSM and those instances where consent is allowed to operate as a defence, other than worries over the potential for abuse (especially in the case of male "perpetrators" and female "victims") and the risk of compounding or belittling real oppressions through their re-enactment.[42] The decision to exclude BDSM from the range of activities in respect of which consent can lawfully be given instead appears to rest on the controversial determination that sexual or erotic pleasure, in and of itself, is not valuable.[43] This explanation is supported by

41 Although not, by analogy, body modification: see *R. v. BM* [2018] EWCA Crim 560.

42 Concerns which might be alleviated through requiring the "victim" to testify that he or she consented and prohibiting simulations of, for example, slave abuse and Nazi concentration camps. See Jonathan Herring, "*R v Brown* (1993)", in Philip Handler, Henry Mares and Ian Williams, eds., *Landmark Cases in Criminal Law* (Oxford: Hart, 2017), 333–55.

43 The tests of "public interest" and "good reason" have been used to decide when consent may operate as a defence to assault: see *R. v. Brown* [1994] 1 AC 212.

its conformity with other legal developments. Where the law has shifted to ratify non-traditional sexual acts, such as those involving same-sex participants, this has been accomplished by emphasising their potential to further traditional – notably, Christian – values, such as marriage, procreation and emotional intimacy, rather than through relying on the inherent merit of sexual pleasure.[44] Although BDSM may serve some of these purposes, it does not fit this mould easily; indeed, part of the appeal of BDSM to its practitioners is its transgressive decoupling of erotic pleasure from these more traditional goods, including, sometimes, by rejecting the label "sexual" (perhaps on account of its long-standing association with these traditional goods).[45] This seems to be one of the major reasons behind the reluctance to allow consent as a defence in this context or even to recognise BDSM acts as sufficiently valuable that their commission would only be an offence in the absence of consent (as with other "normal" sex acts).[46]

The inversion of traditional gender roles that BDSM sometimes involves is another reason why it is rejected by those who advocate adherence to traditional Christian marital norms. This comes out especially clearly when BDSM is contrasted with so-called Christian domestic discipline, a movement that relies on literalist biblical interpretation to champion patriarchal marriage and wifely submission (while incoherently trying to maintain that gender hierarchy does not entail inequality). The women who choose this model of relationship are quick to distance the spankings they receive as punishment from BDSM practices, denouncing "female dominance" and "alternative lifestyles", by which they mean BDSM and "homosexual relationships".[47] There is, of course, a world of difference between the two. While BDSM is motivated by desire and characterised by scrupulous attention to always-revocable consent, Christian domestic discipline is motivated by behaviour modification and shame and depends on the irrelevance of the wife's consent to the beatings.

From this overview, it is clear that hetero-patriarchal Christian marriage norms have shaped the ambit of defences available to those accused of crime and that this has been to the severe detriment of women and other non-dominant groups. But, it is equally clear that this is not inevitable. Queer and feminist theologians have worked to show that gendered articulations of Trinitarian personhood have warped both our inter-personal relations, such as marriage, and our understanding of God.[48] Others have suggested that Christianity can not only endorse BDSM practices, but may also have something valuable to learn from its commu-

44 Margo Kaplan, "Sex-positive Law", (2014) 89 *New York University Law Review* 89–164.

45 Jeremy Carrette, "Intense Exchange: Sadomasochism, Christianity and the Politics of Late Capitalism", (2005) 11 *Theology and Sexuality* 11–30.

46 Sharon Cowan, "Criminalizing SM: Disavowing the Erotic, Instantiating Violence", in Duff *et al.*, *Structures of the Criminal Law*, 59–84.

47 R. Claire Snyder-Hall, "The Ideology of Wifely Submission: A Challenge for Feminism?", (2008) 4 *Politics & Gender* 563–86.

48 Marie Linn Tonstad, *God and Difference: The Trinity, Sexuality, and the Transformation of Finitude* (London: Routledge, 2015).

nity of practitioners. Away from the productive pleasures of the traditional family unit, BDSM offers a vision of non-productive pleasure that intricately connects body, fantasy, heart and passion.[49]

16.5 Conclusion

Publicly upholding alternative ways of living as viable and valuable is essential to any genuine effort to ameliorate some of the negative consequences that have arisen as a result of the law's being imbued with traditional Christian norms. To do this, it is necessary to acknowledge, and to acknowledge through law, that these alternatives have the potential to be as full, transformative and rewarding as their more traditional counterparts. This may be difficult to imagine, even for members of those marginalised groups who have most to gain, because these norms are readily internalised in a culture where they still, to an extent, pass as neutral.

That the alternatives can come from *within* Christian discourse shows, however, that vindicating them is not the same as denigrating religion. It is not even the same as denigrating traditional Christian views, since these can co-exist alongside alternative views, as long as they are not allowed to remain hegemonic. It is simply a case of trying to ensure that people, especially oppressed groups, are presented with an opportunity to live in a way that affords them the dignity and protection from psychic and physical violence that they deserve. If others wish to live a life that coheres with patriarchal heteronormativity, they should not be lambasted or demeaned for doing so, but they have an obligation to understand what this means for their own personhood and, more importantly, for the society of which they are a part. This is only possible if different ways of being are presented as genuinely worthy alternatives. Given the tenacity of the Christian norms outlined in the previous section,[50] this is likely to require removing the various State privileges that still attach to marriage. As a result, marriage would remain an option for those who wish to partake in it, but it would lose its exalted status.

These suggestions apply equally to the other traces of Christian influence I have identified in this chapter. It is vitally important to understand their form and function within contemporary law, but they should not be afforded any determinative normative force merely on account of their longevity. For any scholars genuinely invested in exploring how Christian thought can make a meaningful contribution to contemporary legal debates, this should not be a cause for concern. There is plenty of scope for Christian contributions to have a place in these

49 Carrette, "Intense Exchange".

50 As evidenced by the slow death of the marital rape exemption and the fact that provocation by infidelity continues to shape sentencing patterns, even where it is no longer a formal defence. See Jeremy Horder and Kate Fitz-Gibbon, "When Sexual Infidelity Triggers Murder: Examining the Impact of Homicide Law Reform on Judicial Attitudes in Sentencing", (2015) 74.2 *Cambridge Law Journal* 307–28.

debates but only as one voice among others, and only, I would suggest, when advanced with an awareness of how these contributions have perpetuated, and continue to perpetuate, structural and inter-personal violence.

Further reading

Blumenthal, Susanna. *Law and the Modern Mind: Consciousness and Responsibility in American Legal Culture* (Cambridge, MA: Harvard University Press, 2016).

Chambers, Clare. *Against Marriage: An Egalitarian Defence of the Marriage-Free State* (Oxford: Oxford University Press, 2017).

Fletcher, George. *Rethinking Criminal Law* (Boston: Little, Brown, 1978).

Gruber, Aya. "A Provocative Defense", (2015) 103.2 *California Law Review* 273–334.

Horder, Jeremy. *Provocation and Responsibility* (Oxford: Oxford University Press, 1992).

Scrutton, Anastasia Philippa. "Is Depression a Sin or a Disease? A Critique of Moralizing and Medicalizing Models of Mental Illness", (2015) 19.4 *Journal of Disability and Religion* 285–311.

Spain, Eimear. *The Role of Emotions in Criminal Law Defences: Duress, Necessity and Lesser Evils* (Cambridge: Cambridge University Press, 2011).

Sumerau, Edward J. "'Little Girls Unwilling To Do What's Best for Them': Resurrecting Patriarchy in an LGBT Christian Church", (2015) 44.3 *Journal of Contemporary Ethnography* 306–34.

Tonstad, Linn Marie. *God and Difference: The Trinity, Sexuality, and the Transformation of Finitude* (London: Routledge, 2015).

Wiener, Martin J. *Reconstructing the Criminal: Culture, Law, and Policy in England, 1830–1914* (Cambridge: Cambridge University Press, 1994).

Wiener, Martin J. *Men of Blood: Violence, Manliness, and Criminal Justice in Victorian England* (Cambridge: Cambridge University Press, 2004).

Witte, John Jr. *From Sacrament to Contract: Marriage Religion, and Law in the Western Tradition*, 2d ed. (Louisville: Westminster John Knox Press, 2012).

17 Punishment, forgiveness and mercy

Jeffrie G. Murphy[1]

17.1 Introduction

Speaking in Cairo in 2017, Pope Francis stated that

> True faith is one that makes us more charitable, more merciful, more honest, and more humane ... It makes us see the other not as an enemy to be overcome but a brother or sister to be loved, served, and helped.[2]

If one accepts the accuracy of the Pope's expression of the nature of Christian love then one might understandably think that devout Christians must reject, and even regard as sinful, the whole practice of criminal punishment – a practice that inflicts hard treatment on criminals from a motivation that seems itself hard and not charitable – either seeing criminals as enemies who must be made to suffer to keep the law-abiding safe or to give criminals the suffering that is felt to be what they deserve because of their iniquity or both. In either case, we tend to brutalise them and thereby brutalise ourselves – an observation that prompted Nietzsche to remark (hardly from a Christian motivation, of course) that "We must mistrust the person in whom the desire to punish is strong and take care that, when we set out to do battle with monsters, we do not become monsters". Should we then abandon the whole corrupt and corrupting practice of punishment in a spirt of Christian love, forgiveness and mercy? Is this what Jesus would demand of us?

Presumably not. Even though Jesus and Paul speak eloquently of the virtues of love, forgiveness and mercy, they never condemn the practice of punishment

1 I want to thank all of those (I hope I remember them all) who were kind enough to read and give me comments on earlier drafts of this chapter: Terence Ball, Robert Cochran, Richard Dagger, Stephen Garvey, Zachary Gubler, Thomas Hill, Jr., Jonathan Jacobs, Herbert Morris, Mark Murphy, Ashraf Rushdy, Meghan Ryan, Mary Sigler, James Boyd White, Michael J. White and John Witte, Jr. A version of this chapter was published as Jeffrie G. Murphy, "Punishment, Forgiveness, and Mercy", *Journal of Law and Religion*, (2020) 35.1. This original version, as presented to the round table symposia, is published with permission.

2 Homily of His Holiness Pope Francis, Cairo, Egypt, 29 April 2017. https://w2.vatican.va/content/francesco/en/homilies/2017/documents/papa-francesco_20170429_omelia-viaggioapostolico-egitto.html (accessed 16 March 2020).

itself. What they do condemn is a certain *attitude* towards punishment – an attitude of dismissive contempt of those who have done wrong and thus a tendency to stop thinking of them as part of the human community and as sinners, like the rest of us, for whom redemption and salvation should still be hoped. Because of this hope the counsel is not the abolition of prisons but rather a stress on *visiting* those in prison in order to show them that, though they have done wrong, they have not been forgotten or forsaken but are still valued as members of the human community and that there is still hope for them (Matt. 25:36). This will seek to save them from the great sin of *despair*.

17.2 Some definitions and some problems

In many of my own writings on punishment, forgiveness and mercy, I have generally conceptualised these concepts (and their differences) in the following way. *Punishment* is a social practice to be defended mainly in terms of the values of crime control and deserved retribution for wrongdoing.[3] *Forgiveness* is *personal* – the overcoming, on moral grounds, of the negative passions (such as anger and resentment) that are generally present in victims against the persons who have wrongfully harmed them.[4] *Mercy* is the reduction, on moral grounds, of the punishment that might reasonably be thought to be required for crime control or retributive desert. I use the phrase "on moral grounds" to rule out motives for forgiveness or leniency that would keep them from counting as virtues. Purely selfish or evil motives, for example, would keep leniency from counting as a virtue. So if one wanted to give someone a good example of mercy as a virtue, one would not be tempted to use judge Angelo's promise (in Shakespeare's *Measure for Measure*) to spare Isabella's brother from execution if she will have sex with him and would not use it even if Angelo had intended to keep that promise.

3 It is important to emphasise that, in spite of a common confusion, retribution does *not* mean vengeance or harsh punishment and does not mean (indeed explicitly rejects) punishment based on hatred, anger or resentment. It simply means the punishment that is *deserved* – a value that will often incline the retributivist to argue for reduced punishment. Note also that, when punishment is described as imposing suffering, this is not to be taken as pain. It is rather the sense of suffering as *enduring* (think of "he does not suffer fools gladly"), where the criminal is simply being required to endure a period of confinement in which he or she no longer enjoys full voluntary control over his or her life. In short, and as the old saying goes (although many in our increasingly cruel society no longer seem to think in this way, alas), we send people to jail *as* punishment, not *for* punishment. I am personally drawn to a justification of punishment that combines both crime control and retributive elements. I defend such a view in some detail in my "Last Words on Retribution", in Jonathan Jacobs and Jonathan Jackson, eds., *Routledge Handbook of Criminal Justice Ethics* (London: Routledge, 2017), 219–35.

4 For an elaboration of my previously stated views on forgiveness and mercy, see Jeffrie G. Murphy, *Getting Even: Forgiveness and Its Limits* (Oxford: Oxford University Press, 2003). My views have been greatly influenced by the sermons "Upon Resentment" and "Upon Forgiveness of Injuries" by Bishop Joseph Butler.

Although these definitions may be serviceable as an initial framework in which a discussion can be started, they rather soon can be seen as problematic. For example, the virtue of mercy as defined above immediately seems in conflict with the virtue of justice – a point well made by St Anselm: "What justice is it that gives him who merits eternal death everlasting life? How then, gracious Lord, good to the wicked, can you save the wicked if this is not just, and you do nothing that is not just?" (*Proslogium* IX). Difficulties also arise if one thinks of forgiveness as defined above. If forgiving is simply the personal overcoming of victim resentment (out of love or some other moral reason), then it seems that forgiveness can only come *from victims* and is a duty only for them. If that is the case, however, there can be little tension between forgiveness and even severe punishment if we retain the common view that crimes (unlike torts) are not simply injuries to individuals but rather injuries to the community as a whole. This is why tort cases bear names such as Jones v. Smith whereas criminal cases generally bear such names as *State v. Smith*. Even if victims forgive the criminals who have harmed them, this will rarely have any relevance (other than evidential problems caused by uncooperative victim witnesses) to the State's decision to prosecute. Some States even compel victim witnesses to testify and will sanction them if they do not.

Finally, it may seem that punishment itself is not properly understood or justified if, as is common in contemporary philosophical writings on punishment, it is discussed only in terms of crime control and retribution. One might, for example, want to consider a justification for punishment that goes back as far as Socrates and Plato and can be found in at least some strands of Christianity. According to Plato, as his views are expressed by the character of Socrates (in *Gorgias*, for example), punishment must be justified in terms of the value of *goodness* as revealed in the attempt to improve the wrongdoer's character and make that wrongdoer a better or more virtuous person. This idea of caring about the character or soul of the wrongdoer first appeared in ancient Greece when Socrates (in *Apology* and *Crito*) argued that it is the one who acts unjustly who is really harmed rather than the one who is treated unjustly since the unjust actor has damaged the thing that is of greatest value and should matter the most – his character or soul. This is why Socrates is able to say, very paradoxically in his day and still in ours, that a good person cannot be harmed. Surely Christians would find some version of this view congenial. The crucified Jesus was being harmed as the world generally understands harm, but he was not being harmed in the Socratic sense.

17.3 A fresh start

I have written a great deal about punishment, forgiveness and mercy within the framework set by the analyses of those concepts as defined above, and I do not want simply to repeat here what I have said in those other writings. Rather, I want to pursue the following line of thought: instead of thinking of mercy and forgiveness as *acts* – as things we *do* or gifts we *bestow* – I want to think of them as aspects of *character* and focus not so much on what it is to perform acts of forgiveness or mercy as on *what it means to be a merciful or forgiving person.* I hope that this will allow us to see how such virtues of character might have some interesting and valuable impacts on our thinking about criminal punishment itself – in particular, on how we apply such values as crime control and retribution. My surprising (to many) inspiration for this hope has come from the Protestant Christianity (often quite unorthodox) of Immanuel Kant. (Kant's Christianity was of the liberal kind that was a product of the Enlightenment and will, of course, not be embraced by all Christians.) Most people who have been taught Kant's views on punishment have learned them in undergraduate or law college anthologies (even, alas, in my own anthology *Punishment and Rehabilitation*) from excerpts of his *Doctrine of Right.* In that book (the first part of his *Metaphysics of Morals*), he offers in just a couple of pages an extreme (even primitive) form of retributivism in which he claims, for example, that murderers must be punished with death (even if a society is to abandon itself and thus will not need to worry about crime control) in order to prevent the "bloodguilt" of the offence from falling upon the remaining citizens. (This sounds more like something to be expected in ancient Greek tragedies than in the thinking of the greatest philosopher of the Enlightenment.) He also claims that punishment must be exactly proportional to the "inner viciousness" (*inneren Bösartigkeit*) of the offender and that, in order to achieve this, the criminal should (where possible) be punished by having the exact thing done to him that he has done to his victim – a death for a death, for example. These passages are useful in allowing students to see a pure (even if extreme) form of retributivism. If they really represented Kant's full and considered views on punishment, however, he would have to be regarded as something of a monster or at the very least as inviting secular political authorities to presume to play God.

Fortunately (particularly for one who wants to retain admiration of Kant), these brief passages do not represent his full and considered views relevant to punishment, for in other works he offers some valuable correctives to the harshness expressed in the *Doctrine of Right* – correctives that should help to overcome the common view of Kant as a cold rationalist formalist in ethics with no sympathy at all for love or any other emotion. The correctives occur mainly in his *Doctrine of Virtue* (the second part of his *Metaphysics of Morals*) and *Religion Within the Limits of Reason Alone.* Here are some brief samples:

> It is … a duty of virtue not only to refrain from repaying another's enmity with hatred out of mere revenge but also never even to call upon the world-judge for vengeance – partly because a man has enough guilt of his own to be greatly in need of forgiveness and partly, and especially because no punishment, no matter from whom it comes, may be inflicted out of hatred. Hence [while still seeking to protect the public] men have a duty to cultivate a *conciliatory spirit.* (*Doctrine of Virtue*)[5]

5 Immanuel Kant, *The Metaphysics of Morals*, trans. Mary J. Gregor (Cambridge: Cambridge University Press, 1991), 253.

> [I]t is an indirect duty to cultivate the compassionate natural ... feelings ... in us. It is therefore a duty not to avoid places where the poor, who lack the most necessary things, are to be found; instead, it is a duty to seek them out. It is a duty not shun sickrooms or prisons and so on in order to avoid the pain of pity, which one may not be able to resist. For this feeling, though painful, nevertheless is one of the impulses placed in us by nature for effecting what the representation of duty might not accomplish by itself. (*Doctrine of Virtue*)[6]
>
> [People] may picture themselves as meritorious, feeling themselves guilty of no such offenses as they see others burdened with; nor do they ever inquire whether good luck should not have the credit, or whether by reason of the cast of mind which they could discover, if they only would, in their own in-most nature, they would not have practiced similar vices, had not inability, temperament, training, and circumstances of time and place which serve to tempt one (matters which are not imputable), kept them out of the way of these vices. This dishonesty, by which we humbug ourselves and which thwarts the establishing of a true moral disposition in us, extends itself outwardly also to falsehood and deception of others. If this is not to be termed wickedness, it at least deserves the name of worthlessness, and is an element in the radical evil of human nature. (*Religion Within the Limits of Reason Alone*)[7]

I have quoted these passages from Kant for two reasons. First, I want to correct the very common misunderstanding of Kant's thinking about punishment that is based on the few passages generally quoted from his *Doctrine of Right*. Second, and much more important for present purposes, is that these passages in my view contain insights that should moderate to a considerable degree the uncritical righteous enthusiasm with which the values of crime control and retribution are often applied in our own society – an enthusiasm (reaching for some the point of fanaticism of the sinful kind spoken of by Pope Francis) that often results in radically excessive punishments and unspeakably cruel prison conditions. This does not show that there is something wrong with these values, since society must for the common good control crime (a clear utilitarian value), if just must constrain its crime control measures in ways that respect the dignity and humanity of offenders and thereby treat them with due consideration of their actual moral culpability for the wrong that they have done and for which they deserve to suffer (core retributive values). In short, I will argue that if the criminal law is applied by those with certain Christian (but admittedly not uniquely Christian) virtues (love, humility and dispositions to forgive and show mercy), then the practice of criminal punishment will be made more just and thus there will be no inherent conflict

6 Ibid., 251.

7 Immanuel Kant, *Religion Within the Limits of Reason Alone*, trans. Theodore M. Greene and Hoyt H. Hudson (New York: Harper Torchbooks, 1960), 33–4.

between forgiveness and mercy and the values of crime control and retribution will be properly understood. This will reveal, for example, that there is considerable truth in the cliché that mercy is not in conflict with justice but rather *tempers* it, thereby making it stronger, and the insight in Shakespeare's famous observation (in *The Merchant of Venice*) that justice should be *seasoned* with mercy and thus made more morally palatable. If Christian purity of heart is to will one thing, then surely that one thing must be *love* as expressed in the great commandment (found originally in Jewish law) "Thou shalt love thy Lord thy God with all thy heart, and with all thy soul, and with all thy strength, and with all thy mind; and thy neighbour as thyself". If a Christian is to accept the institution of criminal punishment, a way must be found to incorporate such love into the institution. I will now suggest how one might make at least a start towards doing this.

17.4 Humility and love: loving your crooked neighbour with your crooked heart

The commandment that we are to love our neighbour (and to regard every human being as a neighbour) is a hard saying when we realise that many of the humans we are to regard as neighbours seem anything but lovable or even likeable. Kierkegaard refers to them as "our very unpoetic neighbours" and argues in his *Works of Love* that, absent a command of God, we would have no reason to love them.[8] It is perhaps hardest of all to love those – many criminals, for example – who have done us or our communities serious wrongful injury. The natural instinct is to resent them, become angry at them or even hate them and wish them ill. And yet, as a Christian, one is supposed to overcome those natural inclinations and love them, wish them well and approach them with what Kant called a "conciliatory spirit". Is this not to demand of us the impossible?

Difficult, yes; but impossible, no – and Kant has given us a variety of ways in which we can overcome or at least blunt our natural inclinations with respect to criminals. What Kant offers in the quoted passages is, in effect, a philosophical elaboration of the deeply insightful cliché: "There, but for the grace of God, go I". He advocates a posture of radical humility by arguing that we simply do not know enough and are not good enough to presume a right to make totally dismissive judgements of any fellow human being – to regard any member of our

8 The issue of whether or not the command to love one's neighbour as oneself can be accepted with independence from the metaphysical claims that are a part of orthodox Christianity (the promise of eternal life, for example) is not one that I am able to explore here. Perhaps those of us who are initially sceptical of many of these metaphysical claims can be drawn to them (on certain interpretations) because of the immediate appeal of the value of love. If so, then Kierkegaard may be mistaken in thinking that the belief in a divine command must precede belief in the fundamental value of love. I suspect that more people are drawn into Christianity because of the appeal of the love commandments than because of those metaphysical arguments about God's existence and nature that are generally made central in introductory philosophy courses.

species (every one of them a beloved child of God and created in his image) as so evil at the core as to be beyond any hope of redemption. Even Judas might have been redeemed had he not succumbed to despair and killed himself in the false belief that he had fallen outside the scope of God's love and forgiveness.

So what is the virtue of humility, how does one acquire it and how might it function to make our treatment of criminals more just? I have argued elsewhere that humility is what I call a "cluster virtue" – a virtue that consists of three other virtues: attention, recognition of one's own luck and empathy. I will briefly summarise here what I have explored at greater length elsewhere.[9]

As a start towards understanding the virtue of attention and the vice of its lack, consider one of the most moving passages in Shakespeare's *King Lear*. We find old Lear – suffering on the storm-tossed heath the torments of lost status, abandonment by family, hunger and bitter cold – having an epiphany of self-transformation when he notices (for the first time in his life) the suffering of others, sees an equality with them and seeks to assist them in the small ways still available to him. He says this to his Fool:

> In, boy, go first – You houseless poverty –
> Nay, get thee in. I'll pray, and then I'll sleep.
> Poor naked wretches, wherso'er you are,
> That bide the pelting of this pitiless storm,
> How shall your houseless heads and unfed sides,
> Your loop'd and window'd raggedness, defend you
> From seasons such as these? O, I have ta'en
> Too little care of this! Take physic, pomp;
> Expose thyself to feel what wretches feel,
> That thou mayst shake the superflux to them,
> And show the heavens more just. (Act III, Scene 4)

Being aware only of his status and power as king, Lear had previously never even noticed those around him as people of a moral worth and dignity equal to his own; and to see other human beings – even ones that were previously despised – as having human dignity is an important kind of humility – one that breaks down the sharp us–them distinction that the comfortable like to make when they despise the poor or the sick or those who have done wrong. When Chief Judge Richard Posner dissented in the prison conditions case of *Johnson v. Phelan*, he captured this aspect of humility very well and showed its clear application to criminal punishment:

9 Jeffrie G. Murphy, "Humility as a Moral Virtue", in Everett L. Worthington, Jr., Don E. Davis and Joshua N. Hook, eds., *Handbook of Humility: Theory, Research, and Applications* (New York and London: Routledge, 2017), 19–32.

> There are different ways to look upon the inmates of prisons and jails in the United States ... One way is to look upon them as members of a different species, indeed as a type of vermin, devoid of human dignity and entitled to no respect. I do not myself consider ... inmates of American prisons and jails in that light. We should have a realistic conception of the composition of the prison and jail population before deciding that they are scum entitled to nothing better than what a vengeful populace and a resource-starved penal system chooses to give them. We must not exaggerate the distance between "us", the lawful ones, the respectable ones, and the prison and jail population; for such exaggeration will make it too easy for us to deny that population the rudiments of humane consideration.[10]

Chief Judge Posner is not an enemy of criminal punishment and appreciates both its crime control and its retributive value. He also appreciates, however, how these values will be corrupted and will depart from justice (instead of realising justice) if approached with an attitude of arrogant dismissal of the very humanity of those being punished. This is certainly not to approach them as Jesus, Paul, Shakespeare or Kant would approach them. Indeed, in addition to advocating a "conciliatory spirit" in such matters, Kant insisted that punishment must be "freed from any mistreatment that could make the humanity of the person suffering it into something abominable".

In addition to paying attention to the dignity and humanity of those who do wrong, any initial contempt that those who are law-abiding and otherwise virtuous might feel for wrongdoers should be substantially diminished if one is properly humbled by bringing to consciousness the role that luck (many Christians would say grace) has played in one's own law-abiding life. Kant stresses in the final quoted passage above from his *Religion Within the Limits of Reason Alone* that what he calls the "radical evil in human nature" (his version of the doctrine of original sin) is dramatically and essentially revealed in our self-deceptive tendency to celebrate our own moral virtue (and thus feel superior to those who have done wrong) without an awareness of how much that virtue may have depended on pure good luck and that we might have "practiced similar vices, had not inability, temperament, training, and circumstances of time and place which serve to tempt one kept them out of the way of these vices". (It is not for nothing that the Lord's Prayer contains "lead us not into temptation" as an essential element.) Before one happily embraces the self-deception of "I could never be one of those evil and vile criminals who are just getting what they deserve if they are thrown into prisons that are run by gangs and rape is the order of the day or that subjects them to soul-destroying long-term solitary confinement", one should Google and learn about the Milgram Experiment and the Stanford Prison Experiment, read the books *Ordinary Germans* by Christopher R. Browning and

10 *Johnson v. Phelan*, U.S. Court of Appeals, 7th Circuit, 24 October 1995.

Hitler's Willing Executioners by Daniel Jonah Goldhagen, and read or see the powerful play (or film) *Death and the Maiden* by Ariel Dorfman.

In *Death and the Maiden*, we are given, collapsed from many actual cases, one fictional representative, Doctor Miranda, of the kind of monstrous evil that existed in Chile under Pinochet – a regime that, like Nazi Germany, successfully tempted many "good" people to cooperate in atrocities – in torture, rape and murder all in the name of keeping the country safe from a communist takeover. (This play might, of course, make many Americans think of "Gitmo".)

Doctor Miranda had for many years been a conscientious physician and family man – a generally kind person. He was then asked to serve as a physician for interrogation sessions of the dictatorial regime. His role was to make sure that the interrogation was not so severe that those being interrogated would be rendered incapable of cooperation or even killed. Since it was not really possible to refuse such a request under the regime in power, he agreed and thought that his task was consistent with his role as a physician. He was at first shocked by the torture and rape that took place in the sessions, but still believed that those being treated in this way were better off with his care than if he refused to play his physician role. Soon he began to be drawn into this web of evil, however, and became a torturer and rapist himself. He describes his descent into evil this way:

> The prisoners were dying on them, they told me, they needed someone to care for them, someone they could trust … [I agreed] for humanitarian reasons. We're at war, I thought, they want to kill me and my family, they want to install a [Communist] dictatorship, but even so, they still have a right to some sort of medical attention. It was slowly, almost without realizing how, that I became involved in more delicate operations, they let me sit in on sessions where my role was to determine if the prisoners could take that much torture, that much electric current. At first I told myself that it was a way of saving lives [and I ordered them to stop or the prisoner would die]. But afterwards I began to bit by bit, the virtue I was feeling turned into excitement … A kind of brutalization took over my life, I began to truly like what I was doing. It became a game. My curiosity was partly morbid, partly scientific. How much can this woman take? More than the other one? How's her sex? Does her sex dry up when you put the current through her? Can she have an orgasm under these circumstances? She is entirely in your power, you can carry out all your fantasies, you can do what you want to her – everything they have forbidden you since ever, your mother ever urgently whispered you were never to do … and finally I – but not one ever died on me, not one of the women.[11]

The moral of this for our purposes here is simple: before having utter dismissive contempt for the crooked heart of the criminal, reflect on the crookedness of

11 Ariel Dorfman, *Death and the Maiden* (New York: Penguin Group USA, 1991), 58–60.

your own heart either actual or potential. This should at least force you to consider a more modest and realistic conception of the punishment that the criminal actually deserves as a matter of justice. And before you let yourself believe that you are certain that, whatever your potential for evil, there is no actual evil that can be attributed to you, recall this insightful observation on self-deception from Nietzsche: "'I have done that' says my memory. 'I could not have done that' says my pride and remains inexorable. Eventually memory yields".

Simply accepting intellectually the claims that one's pride in one's own virtue can be misplaced because of insufficient attention to the humanity of others or a failure to recognise the role that luck has played in one's own life does not yet produce the full virtue of humility. Intellectual acceptance is not full and genuine acceptance unless it produces an emotional impact and is accepted in one's heart of hearts. (A good illustration of this point is in a story told by Peter Geach about an Anglican archdeacon who was asked by a member of the congregation what he expected after death. The archdeacon replied, "I expect to sit at the feet of my Lord and Saviour enjoying eternal bliss, but please let us stop talking about such depressing matters".) And what should the emotional payoff of these intellectual insights of attention and vulnerability to luck be in order to allow them to develop into the full virtue of humility? The answer, I think, is *empathy*.

What is empathy? I think that there are two different senses of empathy – empathy as love or compassion and empathy as seeing the world (to the degree possible) from another person's (in our case the wrongdoer's) way of conceptualising himself and his place in the world – to "walk a mile in his shoes" as the cliché goes. In his book *The Better Angels of Our Nature*, the cognitive scientist Steven Pinker sees the close relation between these two senses of empathy and even offers a suggestion for how one might develop empathy if one is lacking in it:

> "Empathy" in the sense of adopting another's viewpoint is not the same as "empathy" in the sense of feeling compassion toward the person, but the first can lead to the second by a natural route … Realistic fiction, for its part, may expand readers' circle of empathy by seducing them into thinking and feeling like people very different from themselves.[12]

We human beings have a strong preference for being around and thinking about people like ourselves, and thus it is easy to see "the other" as so mysterious as to be potentially dangerous or even as less than fully human. It is particularly easy to view criminals in this way. Contact with them by visiting them in prison, writing letters for them, teaching a class for them and other ways of showing them some concern and respect might not just benefit them but might also benefit the one who does the visiting in that it might allow that person to develop a more nuanced and sympathetic understanding of why the offender developed in the

12 Steven Pinker, *The Better Angels of Our Nature* (New York: Viking Press, 2011), 175.

way he did and acted in the way he did. Even if he did some terrible things, is truly dangerous and should be in prison, getting to know him might at least allow one to see human connections with him and to see that his time in prison should not be one of cruel abuse and neglect.

As Pinker points out, reading literature can also expand our empathy by allowing us to live vicariously for a bit inside the minds of characters who initially seem so different from us and in the minds of characters who have a human way of relating to characters whom many would despise and shun. Consider, for example, the characters of the murderer Raskolnikov and the policeman Porfiry in the very Christian novel *Crime and Punishment* by Dostoevsky. Most readers will develop some sympathy (limited) for Raskolnikov as they read the novel and see his youthful innocence, his hunger and poverty, his low self-esteem that allows him (like many present-day American terrorists recruited by ISIS perhaps) to be seduced by crackpot but influential moral, political and religious ideas that are current in his culture. They will also come to appreciate Porfiry's refusal to give up on Raskolnikov. Continuing to hope for Raskolnikov's redemption, he will not regard Raskolnikov as a "finished man" and will not let Raskolnikov see himself in that way. He counsels Raskolnikov to confess so that his prison sentence will not be so long that he will not still be a reasonably young man when it is finished, and he believes that Raskolnikov can lead a meaningful life when his sentence is over if he uses his time in prison to overcome the corruptions of character that led him to become a murderer.

Finally, at least for Christians, an important way to become more empathetic and expand one's humility is, of course, to *pray* for it. In saying this, I am thinking of Kierkegaard's important view of the best kind of prayer – namely, praying not to change God, but to change ourselves.

17.5 Criminal punishment constrained by humility

Let us imagine that one approaches criminal punishment with the "conciliatory spirit" advocated by Kant and with the kind of humility that I have suggested as a complex of attention (Iris Murdoch called this "loving attention"), recognition of luck and empathy. What will the consequences be?

They will not be the total rejection of punishment as a mechanism to control crime or the rejection of the retributive constraints of limiting, as a matter of justice and fairness, punishment to what is deserved given the criminal's actual culpability for the wrong done. (As a former Archbishop of Canterbury William Temple said, "It is axiomatic that love should be the predominant Christian impulse and that justice is the primary form of love in social organization".) A civilised society must seek the common good and protect itself from those who do their fellow citizens wrong or inflict grave harms upon them. In so doing, however, such a society will never impose punishments that are excessive or that treat the offender with less than the full respect and dignity that he deserves. As Dostoevsky wisely said, the degree that a society is truly civilised can be seen in the way it treats its prisoners. This is a test that our American system of "criminal justice", alas, fails dramatically in a variety of ways – for example, excessively long sentences, horrendous prison conditions (gang rape very common) and such soul-destroying punishments as long-term solitary confinement.

How will the virtue of humility be of help here? First, it will incline those who would punish to see this not as something to be celebrated but as something to be done with great regret and always with a sense of loss and disappointment, always open to the possibility that the offender has failed us because to some degree we have failed him. This, of course, is not always the case, but its possibility should be among the things that influence our judgements. We must be careful here, of course, not to carry the idea that social injustice often plays a role in criminality to such an extreme degree that we deprive disadvantaged people of their human dignity by claiming that they are just victims and in no sense responsible for the wrong that they do.

Second, those who punish in humility will try to keep vividly in mind their own shortcomings and limitations and, having forgiving and merciful characters, will always be seeking the least intrusive way to accomplish the legitimate aims of punishment – hoping to find ways to punish less rather than more. They will thus be at constant war against the American tendency to deal with crime simply by adding more years on to oppressive mandatory sentences and to throw convicted wrongdoers into prisons that are in effect Hobbes' state of nature wherein life is solitary, nasty, brutish and short – a world in which gangs control much of prison life and prison rape is tolerated or even joked about.[13]

Third, humility should incline one to seek in prisons an environment that will be truly rehabilitative and will provide opportunities for people to become better people and to develop habits of mind and conduct that will aid them in living lives as productive citizens when their term of imprisonment is over, instead of, as is now so often the case, making them worse people when they get out than they were when they went in. Certainly, spending a few years in a gang-controlled environment of rape and other forms of abuse is hardly character-improving, but there are positive things that could be done as well – more mental health care, for example, since so many people who are currently incarcerated in America have serious mental health problems. There are also many small things that could be done. I, for example, as a passionate lover and respecter of dogs, am particularly fond of the Prison Dog Project as a way of helping to build virtuous characters – characters that are built, if Aristotle was correct, by a process of habituation – learning by doing. In the Prison Dog Project, prisoners care for dogs and thereby at least some of them develop the virtues that come from giving and receiving love (dogs are marvellously uncritical in giving love). This healthy exchange of love was something missing in the earlier life of many prisoners and the programme seems, at least for some inmates, to help them in developing a sense of responsibility and empathetic kindness. The programme is only one small thing,

13 See Mary Sigler, "By the Light of Virtue: Prison Rape and the Corruption of Character", (2006) 91 *Iowa Law Review* 561–607.

of course, but great things often consist of many small things. Those whose characters are filled with love, humility and dispositions of character to forgive and show mercy will no doubt be motivated to think of many more small things and perhaps even some bigger things. A society that truly values freedom must be careful about forcing programmes of character cultivation on unwilling prisoners, but there is surely no such objection to offering such *opportunities* to inmates – or perhaps even providing positive incentives (possibility of early release, for example) to those who successfully complete such programmes.

Fourth and finally, those whose hearts are filled with the virtue of loving humility will always be on the lookout for viable *alternatives* to punishment and will tend to see punishment as a sometimes necessary last resort but never simply uncritically taken as the first resort. Here, I take up again the Socratic/Platonic idea that I mentioned earlier – the idea that what is most important in dealing with wrongdoers is to save them from the damage that they do to their characters or souls simply by being wrongdoers. If we can help them to mould better characters only through humane punishment, then humane punishment it will be. Alternatives to criminal punishment that are better at potential character improvement than even humane punishment, however, are clearly to be preferred – at least with respect to many non-violent offenders.

A good example here is to be found in America's so-called "war on drugs". The use of drugs is out of control in America – deaths from opioid addiction rising all the time – and our system of criminal punishment has shown itself to be radically mal-adapted to deal with the problem (and the related problems of prostitution and theft in support of drug habits) through its ham-handed mania for mass incarceration with longer and longer prison terms even for those guilty of fairly minor and non-violent crimes with respect to drugs.

Are there alternatives? Anyone who reads Susan Burton's new book *Becoming Ms. Burton: From Prison to Recovery to Leading the Fight for Incarcerated Women* (and Nicholas Kristof's essay about her in the *New York Times*) may come to see that there can be alternatives.[14] From a life of drug addiction and prostitution, her downward spiral ended when she chanced into a drug treatment programme, overcame her addiction, ended the cycle of frequent jail times and decided if, with the right kind of help, she could do it then others could as well. With the start-up help of billionaire philanthropist Theodore Forstmann, she founded the non-profit A New Way of Life Re-entry Project. This project (now with five homes) helps women who have been imprisoned for drug and related offences – some for so long that they have lost all ability to do such simple things in the outside world as shop or apply for a social security card. In addition to receiving some financial support, these women are provided with counselling, shelter, sobriety support and, where necessary, instruction and help in developing the basic survival skills

14 Susan Burton, *Becoming Ms. Burton: From Prison to Recovery to Leading the Fight for Incarcerated Women* (New York: The New Press, 2017); Nicholas Kristof, "From Prisoner to Modern-day Harriet Tubman", *New York Times*, 4 May 2017.

for living a viable life outside of prison. Kristof closes his essay on Burton with these words:

> I am celebrating Burton's new book and amazing second career – but with a bittersweet feeling that there are so many other Susan Burtons out there who never get the help or drug treatment they need, and are still incarcerated in ways that diminish them and all of America.

Surely those with Christian love, humility and forgiving and merciful characters will join Kristof's celebration but will also share his bittersweet sadness and may want to do their part to find viable alternatives to the heartless and cruel system of mass incarceration that dominates America's approach to crime and criminals.

In this chapter, I have suggested that approaching criminal punishment with love (what Kant called a "conciliatory spirit" or a disposition towards forgiveness and mercy) will, rather than undermining justice, make us better at doing justice. If I am right about this, the supposed conflict between justice and love (the conflict that worried Anselm) is, at least to some degree, resolved. *Legis plenitudo caritas.*[15]

Further reading

Adams, Marilyn McCord. "Forgiveness: A Christian Model", (1991) 8.3 *Faith and Philosophy* 277–304.

Bash, Anthony. *Forgiveness: A Theology* (Eugene: Cascade Books, 2015).

Butler, Joseph. "Sermons 8 ("Upon Resentment") and 9 ("Upon Forgiveness of Injuries")", in David McNaughton, ed., *Fifteen Sermons and Other Writings on Ethics* (Oxford: Oxford University Press, 2017), 68–74 and 75–83.

Hampton, Jean. "Forgiveness, Resentment and Hatred" and "The Retributive Idea", in Jeffrie G. Murphy and Jean Hampton, eds., *Forgiveness and Mercy* (Cambridge: Cambridge University Press, 1998), 35–87 and 111–61.

Holmgren, Margaret. *Forgiveness and Retribution* (Cambridge: Cambridge University Press, 2014).

Murphy, Jeffrie G. *Getting Even: Forgiveness and Its Limits* (Oxford: Oxford University Press, 2003).

Nussbaum, Martha. *Anger and Forgiveness: Resentment, Generosity, Justice* (Oxford: Oxford University Press, 2016).

Pettigrove, Glen. *Forgiveness and Love* (Oxford: Oxford University Press, 2012).

Rushdy, Ashraf. *After Injury: A Historical Anatomy of Forgiveness, Resentment, and Apology* (Oxford: Oxford University Press, 2018).

15 "The law will be fulfilled, but only by love".

18 Justice, mercy and equality in discretionary criminal justice decision-making

Albert W. Alschuler[1]

18.1 Introduction

Discretion not to punish runs from the start of the criminal justice system through to the end. A police officer who observes a crime may make an arrest or may let the offender go. A prosecutor may decline to file charges even when guilt is clear. A prosecutor may also allow a defendant to plead guilty to a less serious crime than the one he or she apparently committed and the prosecutor may agree to recommend a lenient sentence.

Whether a grand jury has the same authority as a prosecutor to free the guilty is unclear. A few states tell grand jurors they have this power; a larger number tell them they do not; and still more do not instruct them on the question.[2] Some early state constitutions, statutes and decisions expressly authorised trial juries to acquit defendants whose factual guilt was clear, but that power of juries, which was never recognised in England, vanished in America more than a century ago.[3] Judges now insist that authorising trial juries to "nullify" would be inconsistent with the rule of law.[4] (Oddly, judges do not say the same thing about prosecutors' decisions to free the guilty, which often occur.) Although jurors are told not to nullify, jurors who do acquit clearly guilty defendants are not sanctioned and their verdicts are not set aside.[5]

Like a jury, a judge deciding guilt or innocence has no authority to acquit a guilty defendant. Following conviction, however, a judge may be empowered to sentence the offender to prison for a long term or a short term or to place him or

1 I am grateful to Rachel Barkow, Paul Larkin, Jeffrie Murphy and Mark Osler for valuable comments. A version of this chapter was published as Albert W. Alschuler, "Justice, Mercy, and Equality in Discretionary Criminal Justice Decision-making", *Journal of Law and Religion* 35, no. 1 (2020). It is republished with modifications by permission of the *Journal of Law and Religion* and the Center for the Study of Law and Religion.

2 See *United States v. Navarro-Vargas*, 408 F.3d 1184, 1197–98 (9th Cir. 2005).

3 Albert W. Alschuler and Andrew G. Deiss, "A Brief History of the Criminal Jury in the United States", (1994) 61 *University of Chicago Law Review* 902–11.

4 E.g. *United States v. Kleinman*, 859 F.3d 825, 835–38 (9th Cir. 2017); *United States v. Thomas*, 116 F.3d 606, 614–16 (2d Cir. 1997).

5 *United States v. Thomas*; see also *Bushell's Case*, Vaughn 135, 124 Eng. Rep. 1006 (1671).

her on probation. A parole board may be authorised to release the offender long before he or she has completed the sentence set by the judge. Other correctional authorities may have discretion to determine the conditions of the offender's confinement. Finally, many state governors, like the U.S. president, have almost entirely unfettered authority to commute an offender's sentence or to pardon him or her altogether.

In exercising their discretion, criminal justice officials should do justice, but whether they should also be merciful is a more challenging issue. In some translations, the Bible tells them to do both. "[W]hat doth the Lord require of thee", the prophet asks, "but to do justly, and to love mercy, and to walk humbly with thy God?" (Micah 6:8; KJV).[6]

Can officials do both? Philosophers since Aristotle have doubted that they can.[7] Jeffrie Murphy explains the dilemma:

> [I]f we simply use the term "mercy" to refer to certain of the demands of justice (e.g., the demand for individuation), then mercy ceases to be an autonomous virtue and instead becomes a part of … justice. It thus becomes obligatory, and all the talk about gifts, acts of grace, supererogation, and compassion becomes quite beside the point. If, on the other hand, mercy is totally different from justice and actually requires (or permits) that justice sometimes be set aside, it then counsels injustice. In short, mercy is either a vice (injustice) or redundant (a part of justice).[8]

The word "mercy" is indeed slippery. Does it consist, as Alwynne Smart maintained, of "deciding not to inflict what is agreed to be the just penalty, all things considered"?[9] Smart's definition may seem under-inclusive because the baseline from which mercy reduces suffering need not always be "justice". When a kidnap victim begs a kidnapper to show mercy, he or she is not seeking the remission of just punishment. Is the relevant baseline, then, any painful or undesired condition that might exist in the absence of the merciful action? Can mercy include seeking less punitive ways of *doing* justice? Can the word sometimes refer not to an act or omission at all, but simply to a character trait – a merciful disposition?

6 Other translations speak of loving "goodness" or "kindness" rather than loving "mercy".

7 See Aristotle, *Nicomachean Ethics*, trans. W.D. Ross, ed. Lesley Brown (Oxford: Oxford University Press, 2009), 5.1137b: "it seems strange if the equitable, being something different from the just, is yet praiseworthy; for either the just or the equitable is not good, if they are different; or, if both are good, they are the same".

8 Jeffrie G. Murphy, "Mercy and Legal Justice", in Jeffrie G. Murphy and Jean Hampton, *Forgiveness and Mercy* (Cambridge: Cambridge University Press, 1988), 169.

9 Alwynne Smart, "Mercy", (1968) 43 *Philosophy* 349; see also in this volume, Chapter 17, Jeffrie G. Murphy, "Punishment, Forgiveness and Mercy", p. 269 at p. 270. This defines mercy as "the reduction, on moral grounds, of the punishment that might reasonably be thought to be required for crime control or retributive desert".

Smart's definition may also seem over-inclusive, for it speaks of foregoing just punishment without specifying an accompanying mental state or motive. A prosecutor who decides not to seek just punishment only because a trial would consume three days of his or her time does not appear to be merciful. Compassion for the person whose punishment is remitted seems essential, though perhaps this motivation need not be exclusive.

Echoing Ludwig Wittgenstein's analysis of the word "game", Alex Tuckness and John Parrish declare that mercy is "a 'family resemblance' concept: one where the concept can retain usefulness even though one cannot give a definitive account of its necessary and sufficient conditions".[10] Unlike pornography, however, one does not always know mercy when one sees it and use of the undefined term can muddy rather than clarify.

Without fully defining the term, this chapter accepts the conventional view that mercy must be supererogatory. It must be something given, not owed. This requirement does not extend to every use of the word. The kidnapper who spares a victim merely does his or her duty, and Immanuel Kant maintained that developing a merciful spirit is obligatory.[11] When one seeks to call some acts justice and others mercy, however, the line between obligation and supererogation seems crucial.

Focusing on this characteristic reveals that the question ultimately is one of ethics, not linguistics. In exercising their discretion, when, if ever, should criminal justice officials remit or forego punishment they consider just partly or entirely out of compassion for the person whose punishment is foregone? When, if ever, should they forego punishment simply to be merciful? In some situations, mitigating punishment is a moral duty; in others, it is improper. If these situations exhaust the field, justice is what matters and mercy is an impossible virtue.

In examining the duties of criminal justice officials, this chapter focuses particularly on the power of chief executives to grant commutations and pardons. This power is likely to seem the least problematic place for official acts of mercy. The chapter considers not only whether and when chief executives should be merciful but also the extent to which they should treat applicants for clemency equally. Of course, the chapter offers only the perspective of one Christian, not *the* Christian perspective. It begins by considering a case in which Jesus Christ pardoned a criminal.

18.2 The example of Jesus Christ

The woman's guilt was clear. "Teacher, this woman was caught in the very act of committing adultery". The prescribed punishment was clear as well. "Now in

10 Alex Tuckness and John M. Parrish, *The Decline of Mercy in Public Life* (Cambridge: Cambridge University Press, 2014), 250.

11 See Immanuel Kant, *The Doctrine of Virtue*, trans. Mary J. Gregor (New York: Harper Torchbooks, 1964; first German edition 1797), 459–60.

the law Moses commanded us to stone such women". But when Jesus challenged anyone without sin to throw the first stone, the accusers left the scene. Then Jesus said to the woman, "Go your way, and from now on do not sin again" (John 8:4–11).[12]

An inspiring story, you say? Suppose a U.S. president were to free someone guilty of a capital offence with no punishment at all, simply warning her not to do it again. Suppose that, when challenged to defend such action, the president declared that no-one is entitled to punish unless he or she is without sin him- or herself. Suppose the president granted clemency without mentioning any redeeming virtue of the offender or any extenuating circumstance of the crime. Suppose he or she said nothing to distinguish the pardoned offender's case from that of any other offender.

One might wonder whether this president opposed criminal punishment altogether. If only people without sin are entitled to punish, no-one is. And if the president did not mean to bring the punishment of criminals to an end, did he or she free this one at random? Did the president see clemency as sport or as an expression of tender sentiments on a lovely day? Is there an alternative? However you look at it, the president's pardon was outrageous. He or she should be impeached.

Was Jesus' view of clemency as radical as the case of the woman taken in adultery makes it seem? John Calvin said that "although Christ remits one's sins, He does not subvert the social order or abolish legal sentences and punishments". Calvin condemned as "Popish theology" the idea that "Christ has brought in the law of grace, by which adulterers may be freed from punishment".[13]

Someone seeking support for Calvin's tough, "non-popish" view can suppose that the Bible provides an incomplete account of the woman's case. They can, if they like, accept the imaginative reconstruction offered by J. Duncan M. Derrett.[14] Derrett noted that Jewish law allowed conviction only on the testimony of two witnesses[15] and that people committing a capital offence would have made every effort to conceal it. In all probability, Derrett said, witnesses did not simply stumble upon the woman in the act of adultery. Instead, the woman's husband learned of her disloyalty. Because the husband could not testify against his wife, he arranged to have two or more witnesses observe a later tryst. These witnesses might have warned the woman and prevented her crime, but they conspired with the husband to cause her death. When Jesus said, "Let anyone among you who is without sin be the first to throw a stone at her", he was not broadly condemning the hypocrisy of punishing others while leaving one's own sins unacknowledged.

12 This and all subsequent biblical quotations in this chapter are from the New Revised Standard Version.

13 John Calvin, *The Gospel According to St. John*, trans. T.H.L. Parker (Edinburgh: T. & T. Clark, 1959), 209.

14 J. Duncan M. Derrett, *Law in the New Testament* (Eugene: Wipf & Stock, 2005; first published 1970), 156–88.

15 See Deut. 19:15.

Rather, he was inviting any accuser who was not complicit in the woman's crime to begin an execution. Confronted with this challenge, the accusers slunk away one by one.

One can also, if one likes, attribute to Jesus a modern recognition of the injustice of the ancient law of adultery. This law required death for a married woman who had sex with someone other than her husband and it demanded death for her lover as well. But it did not punish either participant in sexual intercourse between a married man and a woman other than his wife.[16]

John's Gospel does not reveal the fate of the man caught in the act with the woman. Perhaps he was a fast runner or perhaps he had already been executed. Perhaps he was recruited by the husband to entrap the woman and then was allowed to go free. Perhaps he paid a bribe to escape prosecution (something a married woman, unable to own property independently, could not have done). Or perhaps the man was simply the beneficiary of discriminatory prosecution. (An aside: many scholars do not believe that the story of the woman taken in adultery was part of John's Gospel. In 383, however, St Jerome included this story in the Latin version of the Gospels he prepared on the basis of earlier Greek texts. The Church declared Jerome's version authoritative at the Council of Trent more than 1,100 years later.)

Could one reasonably applaud Jesus while booing the modern president by distinguishing between divine and earthly justice? In about 386, St Ambrose, the Bishop of Milan, replied to a judge who asked whether, as a Christian, he could properly sentence offenders to death. Ambrose said that the Church did not forbid capital punishment, because this punishment might repress crime and because "clemency should proceed from [the judges'] own free will and forbearance, rather than from any legal necessity".[17] After reciting the story of the woman taken in adultery, however, Ambrose said of Jesus:

> Being the Redemption, He refuses to condemn her, being the Life He restores her, being the Fountain He washes her … Jesus … stoops down … that He may raise the fallen … Here is an example for you to follow, for it may be that there is hope of amendment for this guilty person … See how many roads there are to redemption![18]

Pardons appear to be as old as punishment. As best I can tell, every legal system has provided for them. At a minimum, Jesus' teachings suggest a liberal use of this power.

16 Deut. 22:22; Lev. 20:10–12.
17 H. Walford, ed. and trans., *The Letters of S. Ambrose, Bishop of Milan, Translated with Notes and Indices* (Oxford: James Parker & Co., 1881), 1184. The Tertullian Project has placed the text of this edition of Ambrose's letters online, and the letter to Studius appears at http://www.tertullian.org/fathers/ambrose_letters_03_letters21_30.htm#letter25 (accessed 23 January 2019).
18 Ibid.; see also 1184–90 (Letter XXVI, to Irenaeus).

18.3 Equality

Someone who sought to identify the most troublesome presidential pardon in American history might consider Bill Clinton's pardon of Marc Rich. Clinton pardoned Rich, a billionaire fugitive from justice, on his last day in office, only hours before the inauguration of George W. Bush. Rich had fled the United States as he was about to be charged with tax evasion and conspiring to purchase more than six million barrels of oil from Iran while that country was holding 52 U.S. hostages.

Although Clinton's chief of staff and his White House counsel opposed clemency for Rich, Rich's ex-wife, Denise Rich, supported it. She had contributed more than $1 million to the Democratic Party and its candidates, $450,000 to Clinton's library fund, $100,000 to a fund supporting Hillary Clinton's Senate campaign, $10,000 to the president's legal defence fund and $7,375 worth of furniture to the Clintons. She had also presented a gold-plated saxophone to the president at a charity ball. Denise Rich not only wrote letters to the president but also pressed a White House social secretary for an invitation to a White House dinner. Seated at Clinton's table with such notables as Barbra Streisand and Maya Angelou, she sought a private moment with the president to emphasise that pardoning her former husband would mean a great deal to her.[19]

On the day Clinton pardoned Rich, he also granted clemency to his half-brother (Roger Clinton), two former members of his cabinet (John Deutch and Henry Cisneros), one cabinet member's son (Richard Riley, Jr.), a former cabinet member's chief of staff (Ron Blackley), a former Member of Congress (Mel Reynolds), a former governor who had been a college friend (J. Fife Symington III), a lawyer who had managed Clinton's Georgetown campaign for student body president (Paul Prosperi), one of the president's partners in the Whitewater real estate venture (Susan McDougal) and two applicants who, apparently without Clinton's knowledge, had paid a brother of Hillary Clinton more than $200,000 apiece to support their applications.[20]

Clinton's last-day pardons lent support to the argument of some notable opponents of pardons (at least in democratic societies) – Kant, Bentham, Montesquieu, Blackstone and Beccaria. These critics maintained that pardons inevitably render justice unequal.[21] President George W. Bush, who himself incurred criticism for remitting the sentence of his vice-president's chief of staff, wrote in his memoirs: "I came to see the massive injustice in the system. If you had connections to the

19 Albert W. Alschuler, "Bill Clinton's Parting Pardon Party", (2010) 100 *Journal of Criminal Law and Criminology* 1137–42.

20 Ibid., 1142–60.

21 See, e.g. Immanuel Kant, *Metaphysical Elements of Justice*, trans. John Ladd, 2d ed. (Indianapolis: Hackett Publishing Co., 1999; first German edition 1787), 144, describing clemency as "the most slippery of all the rights of the sovereign" and a means by which the sovereign can "wreak injustice to a high degree".

president, you could insert your case into the last-minute frenzy".[22] Reformers have proposed that a body of rules should replace "case-by-case pardons" to promote the equal treatment of similarly situated applicants.[23]

Jesus' championship of people at the bottom of the social pyramid – Samaritans, prostitutes, women, children, the poor, the hungry, the thirsty, the meek, the naked, the homeless, the lepers, the tax collectors and the prisoners – makes clear that he would have disapproved of partisanship towards the rich and powerful in granting clemency.[24] Yet, Jesus' miracles and his pardon of only one adulteress also raise issues of equality. Why did he restore the sight of some and not others? Jesus made little or no effort to treat like cases alike.

Perhaps equal treatment does not matter in working miracles – supernatural events to which no-one is entitled. And although equal treatment does matter in granting clemency, it may matter less in this phase of the criminal process than in most others. In granting clemency, can governors and presidents be seen as mini-miracle workers?

Consider this thought experiment: President P has known Member of Congress C for many years, and when C was indicted for mail fraud, convicted and sentenced, P followed her case closely. P believes that C was treated unjustly. If the merits of C's application were all that mattered, P would pardon her. Nevertheless, P hesitates. He thinks: "There may be other applicants who were treated as unfairly as C. Indeed, there probably are many of them. But because I do not know their cases as well as I know C's, I cannot be sure. To find out, I would need to investigate their cases in depth and it isn't my job to do over what the criminal justice process has already done. Unlike C, the other applicants haven't overcome my presumption that the criminal justice system got it right". P also thinks: "My friend C is a wealthy, white college graduate, and many of the others who are likely to have meritorious cases are none of those things. To favour applicants whom I know or whose friends have my ear is systematically to favour the already advantaged". Should P's concern about equal treatment lead him to reject C's application for a pardon? Or should he conclude that neither his inability to provide equal justice nor his predicable tilt in favour of wealthy white people should keep him from redressing the injustice he sees in C's case?

22 George W. Bush, *Decision Points* (New York: Crown, 2010), 104.
23 Daniel J. Freed and Steven L. Chanenson, "Pardon Power and Sentencing Policy", (2001) 13 *Federal Sentencing Reporter* 124.
24 See Luke 4:17–18: "He unrolled the scroll and found the place where it was written: 'The Spirit of the Lord is upon me, because he has anointed me to bring good news to the poor. He has sent me to proclaim release to the captives.'"; James 2:1–4: "My brothers and sisters, do you with your acts of favouritism really believe in our glorious Lord Jesus Christ? For if a person with gold rings and in fine clothes comes into your assembly, and if a poor person in dirty clothes also comes in, and if you notice of the one wearing the fine clothes and say, 'Have a seat here, please', while to the one who is poor you say, 'Stand there', or, 'Sit at my feet', have you not made distinctions among yourselves, and become one with evil thoughts?"

In granting clemency, presidents have an obligation not to treat like cases differently, but they may have no obligation to treat like cases alike. To put the point less cryptically, presidents have an ethical duty not to discriminate, but they may have no duty to act affirmatively or to expend resources to ensure equal treatment. Obviously, a policy of granting clemency to whites and not blacks would be outrageous, and so would a policy of granting clemency to political supporters simply because they are supporters. Perhaps, however, affirmative measures to ensure equal treatment should be regarded as supererogatory – admirable when they can be undertaken without unduly sacrificing other goals, but not imperative. In this respect, chief executives may differ from judges and other criminal justice officials. Although presidents do not promise to render justice in every case, judges do, and prosecutors seem more like judges than like presidents.

18.4 A place for mercy in criminal procedure

Asking whether chief executives render justice or grant mercy when they pardon poses a false dichotomy. They sometimes grant clemency without doing either one and they sometimes do both at the same time. President Kennedy's commutation of the sentence of the Soviet spy Rudolf Able to facilitate his exchange for the U-2 pilot Francis Gary Powers was clemency that did neither.[25] This commutation implied neither that the president considered the commuted sentence unjust nor that he felt merciful towards the spy. Other situations, however, show presidents both rendering justice and granting mercy. Even when pardons correct substantive injustice, granting them can be merciful.

When a president approves clemency because a prisoner's innocence has been shown or because the prisoner's punishment is excessive, the president does justice. Yet, if presidents need not treat like cases alike – if they have no obligation even to listen – affording any procedure at all is merciful. If presidents are entitled to treat the judgments of the "regular" criminal justice system as conclusive, granting relief from any of these judgments is supererogatory. Presidents commonly do render justice when they pardon, but because they have no obligation to render justice, they also grant mercy.

This view of clemency as a hybrid of justice and mercy (just in substance and merciful in procedure) becomes plausible only when clemency is seen as a dispensable safety valve at the far end of a just legal system. Chief Justice Marshall took this view when he wrote for the Supreme Court in 1833, "A pardon is an act of grace".[26] Justice Holmes, however, apparently took a different view when he wrote for the Court in 1927, "A pardon in our days is not a private act of grace

25 See *Bridge of Spies* (Touchstone Pictures, 2015); Tom Wicker, "Powers is Freed by Soviet in an Exchange for Abel; U-2 Pilot on Way to U.S.", *New York Times*, 18 February 1962, A1, available at https://archive.nytimes.com/www.nytimes.com/learning/general/onthisday/big/0210.html#article (accessed 23 January 2019).

26 *United States v. Wilson*, 32 U.S. 150, 160 (1833).

… It is part of the Constitutional scheme".[27] When clemency is seen as simply one more tier of review and presidents are thought responsible for doing justice, the distinction between clemency and other phases of the criminal justice system collapses.

For example, a new technology might enable authorities to identify a substantial number of wrongly convicted prisoners with a high degree of certainty, and a legal system that provided no mechanism for releasing these prisoners would be unjust. Without affording any judicial or administrative remedy, however, courts and legislatures might look to executive clemency to do the job. These authorities might say with the U.S. Supreme Court, "Clemency … is the historic remedy for preventing miscarriages of justice when judicial process has been exhausted".[28] In this situation, reviewing convictions produced by the "regular" criminal justice system would not seem supererogatory.

18.5 Should public officials be merciful in substance as well as procedure?

This chapter has used the word "mercy" in a different way from the definition propounded by Alwynne Smart (a decision "not to inflict what is agreed to be the just penalty, all things considered"). It has maintained that doing justice can be merciful when an official has no obligation to consider an applicant's case. But the chapter now turns to Smart's kind of mercy. Should officials be merciful in substance as well as procedure? When, if ever, should they remit punishment agreed to be just for reasons that include compassion for the person whose punishment is foregone? When, if ever, should they remit punishment agreed to be just *only* out of concern for the person whose punishment is foregone?

One cannot sensibly answer these questions without considering how broad the concept of justice should be. The more sophisticated one's understanding of justice becomes, the less room it allows for mercy. With a primitive concept of justice – an eye for an eye – mercy has much work to do. Acknowledging that justice depends as much upon circumstances and personal characteristics as upon physical action and harm, however, shrinks mercy's role. And recognising that developments after an offence (such as unprompted repentance) can bear on what punishment an offender deserves diminishes the role of mercy still further.

Should the concept of justice grow to the point that the space for mercy simply vanishes? A president may approve a pardon because a prisoner deserves it (say, because new evidence establishes his or her innocence) or he or she may approve a pardon for instrumental reasons (say, to facilitate an exchange of prisoners). If the applicant does not deserve a pardon and the pardon serves no instrumental purpose, however, it seems improper. Mercy alone looks like a bad reason for clemency. Perhaps the recognition of mercy as a virtue always reflects

27 *Biddle v. Perovich*, 274 U.S. 480, 486 (1927).

28 *Herrera v. Collins*, 506 U.S. 390, 412 (1993).

an impoverished concept of justice – one that does not truly render to each his or her due.[29]

For private individuals, a line between duty and supererogation seems useful (difficult though the line is to draw). Buying a stereo system with funds the purchaser could have donated to Doctors Without Borders is not wrongful even if making the donation would have been more virtuous. An aspiring musician has no duty to pattern his or her life on that of Mother Teresa rather than Elvis even if emulating Mother Teresa would be nobler. One's moral obligation stops short of making the most virtuous choice.

A public official, however, stands in a different place. He or she is a fiduciary, charged with advancing the public's interest rather than his or her own. Unlike a private individual drawing on his or her bank account, an official cannot properly draw on the public treasury to make a gift to Doctors Without Borders and, just as an official may not give public cash to people not entitled to it, he or she may not make personal gifts of non-cash benefits.[30]

When an official must decide whether to remit criminal punishment, supererogation seems impossible. In exercising his or her discretion, the official must advance the public interest as best he or she can. Serving any other goal is a violation of his or her duty and doing better than his or her best is impossible. No space is left for supererogation. In the absence of an instrumental public purpose or a clear indication that the public favours making unmerited gifts, an official should not grant undeserved clemency. This chapter will note, however, that an undeserved remission of punishment sometimes can reflect the willingness of society as a whole to forgive.

To test whether, as I have just argued, officials should never view mercy alone as a sufficient reason for remitting punishment, this section considers three cases. They are among the strongest I can think of for calling legitimate official action merciful.

First, consider compassionate release of the dying. Someone who has been imprisoned 20 years for a robbery has only weeks to live, and his wife and children ask the governor to allow him to die at home. Describing the governor's release of the prisoner as an act of mercy seems natural and conventional, but this characterisation implies that the governor has made a gift, that she would not have violated any moral duty by leaving the prisoner confined and that she had no obligation to base her decision on what the prisoner, his family and the public deserved. Might it be better for the governor to view her task as one of

29 See Cicero, *De Natura Deorum (On the Nature of the Gods)*, trans. Francis Brooks (London: Methuen & Co., 1896), Book XV, describing justice as "the virtue which assigns to each his due" (available at https://oll.libertyfund.org/titles/cicero-on-the-nature-of-the-gods [accessed 23 January 2019]).

30 A variation on a familiar Bible story illustrates how the moral and legal positions of principals and agents differ. Suppose that, when the prodigal son returned, his father was absent. If the father's property manager had taken it upon himself to kill the fatted calf and host a feast, he would have been liable to the father in damages.

doing justice – including justice to the prisoner who, despite his crime, remained entitled to humane treatment as his life approached its end?

Or consider a hypothetical case posed by Saul Touster.[31] The Civil War has ended and a recently emancipated slave has stolen a horse and wagon in order to search for members of his family who were sold to a plantation owner in another state. The former slave might be a plausible candidate for a defence of necessity, but recognising this defence would declare his action justified and would encourage others to engage in similar conduct. Recognising a formal defence would license the former slave to continue to steal wagons until he achieved his goal. The use of a low-visibility discretionary mechanism – refusal to prosecute, jury nullification or executive clemency – would be less problematic. A virtuous prosecutor might decline to prosecute and then take up a collection to buy the former slave a horse and wagon.

The prosecutor's private donation of a wagon could be seen as supererogatory. Should his refusal to prosecute be regarded as supererogatory as well? If the only measure of justice were what the law provides, the prosecutor's action would fit Alwynne Smart's definition; he would have chosen not to inflict the penalty deemed just. In this case, however, the law book badly missed the mark (or rather it would have if it had not authorised the prosecutor to make exceptions). The prosecutor did justice by declining to prosecute, and perhaps he would have violated his moral duty by doing anything else.

Finally, consider a case in which private mercy influenced public punishment. On 26 October 2018, the remains of Matthew Shepard were interred in the National Cathedral, a shrine where visitors can also view the tombs of Woodrow Wilson, Helen Keller and other notable Americans. It had been 20 years since Aaron McKinney and Russell Henderson lured Shepard from a Laramie bar, beat his skull with a .357 Magnum, burned him and strung him on a fence to die. McKinney and Henderson killed Shepard because he was gay. His interment was delayed for two decades because his parents feared desecration of his grave by people like those who demonstrated at his funeral with signs reading "Matt in Hell" and "God Hates Fags".

One of Shepard's killers, Russell Henderson, avoided capital punishment by agreeing to testify against the other, Aaron McKinney. Shepard's parents, Dennis and Judy Shepard, then persuaded a reluctant prosecutor not to seek the death penalty for McKinney. Here are excerpts from Dennis Shepard's courtroom remarks on the subject of mercy:

> My son was taught to look at all sides of an issue before making a decision or taking a stand ... When he did take a stand, it was based on his best judgment. Such a stand cost him his life when he quietly let it be known that he

31 Saul Touster, *The Treatment of Jewish Survivors of the Holocaust, 1945–1948: Dilemmas of Law, Care, and Bureaucracy* (Boston: Heller School for Advanced Studies in Social Welfare, Brandeis University, 2000), 12–13.

> was gay. He didn't advertise it, but he didn't back away from the issue either. For that I'll always be proud of him. He showed me that he was a lot more courageous than most people, including myself … Matt's beating, hospitalization, and funeral focused worldwide attention on hate. Good is coming out of evil … [Mr. McKinney, y]ou made this world realize that a person's lifestyle is not a reason for discrimination, intolerance, persecution, and violence … [M]y son has become a symbol, a symbol against hate and people like you … I would like nothing better than to see you die, Mr. McKinney. However, this is the time to begin the healing process. To show mercy to someone who refused to show any mercy. To use this as the first step in my own closure about losing Matt … I'm going to grant you life … because of Matthew … I give you life in memory of one who no longer lives. May you live a long life, and may you thank Matthew every day for it.[32]

Dennis and Judy Shepard supported the death penalty. They saw their choice to spare McKinney as merciful – a gift to an undeserving beneficiary. One could accept this characterisation without viewing the prosecutor's acquiescence in their choice the same way.

Whether survivors should have a voice in determining a murder's punishment is a challenging issue.[33] Delegating part of this choice to these private parties affords authority over offenders' lives to people whose interests would disqualify them from serving as jurors and it ensures the unequal administration of justice. Whether an offender lives or dies may turn, not on a judgment by a community's authorised representatives, but on whether the offender victimised someone whose family is charitable or vindictive or someone who had no family at all. The separation of criminal law from tort law in England roughly 1,000 years ago was a civilising step, and turning back from that step may diminish the sense that crime wrongs all of us.[34]

Many champions of the death penalty, however, see this form of punishment as a means of providing closure to victims' families – in Franklin Zimring's words, as State-sponsored psychotherapy.[35] One implication of viewing "closure" as a justification for the death penalty is that a survivor should be able to say with

32 Dennis Shepard's full statement appears at https://www.matthewshepard.org/statement-court-1999/ (accessed 13 March 2020).

33 Compare *Booth v. Maryland*, 482 U.S. 496 (1987) (holding that the Cruel and Unusual Punishment Clause prohibits a jury from considering a "victim impact statement" during the sentencing phase of a capital murder trial because this evidence has no bearing on an offender's personal responsibility and moral guilt), with *Payne v. Tennessee*, 501 U.S. 808 (1991) (overruling *Booth* and noting that sentencing authorities have long considered "the specific harm caused by the crime in question").

34 See generally in this volume, Chapter 8, David McIlroy, "Christianity, *Mens Rea* and the Boundaries of Criminal Liability", p. 116.

35 Franklin Zimring, *The Contradictions of American Capital Punishment* (Oxford: Oxford University Press, 2003), 60.

Dennis Shepard that mercy, not death, is his path towards closure. If taking account of survivors' wishes is appropriate and if these parties may approve an undeserved remission of punishment, there is a place for substantive mercy in the administration of criminal justice. Even on this questionable hypothesis, however, the prerogative of mercy ordinarily belongs to victims or their representatives, not public officials.

18.6 Did Shakespeare and Jesus get it right?

The finest speech ever given in the English language on the subject of mercy took a different view from the one this chapter has advanced. Although this chapter has maintained that public officials have less justification for being merciful (in the Alwynne Smart sense) than private individuals, Shakespeare declared mercy one of a ruler's noblest virtues:

> The quality of mercy is not strained;
> It droppeth as the gentle rain from heaven
> Upon the place beneath. It is twice blest;
> It blesseth him that gives and him that takes;
> Tis mightiest in the mightiest; it becomes
> The throned monarch better than his crown:
> His sceptre shows the force of temporal power,
> The attribute to awe and majesty,
> Wherein doth sit the dread and fear of kings;
> But mercy is above the sceptred sway;
> It is enthroned in the hearts of kings,
> It is an attribute to God himself;
> And earthly power does then show likest God's
> When mercy seasons justice. Therefore, Jew,
> Though justice be thy plea, consider this,
> That, in the course of justice, none of us
> Should see salvation: we do pray for mercy;
> And that same prayer doth teach us all to render
> The deeds of mercy. I have spoke thus much
> To mitigate the justice of thy plea;
> Which if thou follow, this strict court of Venice
> Must needs give sentence 'gainst the merchant there.[36]

Did Shakespeare err? Although the character who declaims these great lines purports to plead for mercy rather than justice, does she in fact plead for justice? In urging a nobleman to temper justice, does she mistakenly take the law as the

36 William Shakespeare, *The Most Excellent Historie of the Merchant of Venice* (London: printed by I.R. for Thomas Heyes, 1600), Act IV, Scene 1, 190–212 (spelling modernised).

measure of justice? Does she in fact favour tempering only an unjust law? Does she truly beg for an official gift to an undeserving wrongdoer or does she decry a cruel and brutal law, one that allowed a creditor to enforce a vicious penalty clause?

Opposing Alwynne Smart–style mercy implies no support for harsh punishment. On the contrary, it may make mandatory the generosity and lenient treatment that pleas for mercy treat as optional. This chapter has advocated narrowing the concept of mercy only as far as the concept of justice expands. An appropriate concept of justice sees humane treatment as a public official's obligation and an offender's right. And yet, however expansive the concept of justice becomes, occasions for undeserved mercy will remain. "Be merciful", Jesus Christ said, "just as your Father is merciful" (Luke 6:36). "Forgive, and you will be forgiven" (Luke 6:37). And at the end: "Father, forgive them; for they do not know what they are doing" (Luke 23:34).

Although Jesus accompanied his final plea for mercy with an appeal to justice ("they do not know what they are doing"), he repeatedly championed Alwynne Smart–style mercy – the remission of punishment as a gift to the undeserving. Consider, for example, this familiar passage of the Sermon on the Mount – one that links forgiving wrongdoers and foregoing punishment with giving to the poor:

> You have heard that it was said, "An eye for an eye and a tooth for a tooth." But I say to you, Do not resist an evildoer. But if anyone strikes you on the right cheek, turn the other also; and if anyone wants to sue you and take your coat, give your cloak as well; and if anyone forces you to go one mile, go also the second mile. Give to everyone who begs from you, and do not refuse anyone who wants to borrow from you.
>
> (Matt. 5:38–42)

The sacred texts of Jesus' own religion endorsed the principle he repudiated – an eye for an eye.[37] In place of this principle, he urged, not a broader concept of justice, but radical forgiveness. Inviting a burglar who steals your cash to take your jewels as well is supererogatory, if indeed it is virtuous at all. (Your offer might shame some burglars and lead to their reform, but many others would be likely to say, "Thanks, Sucker". Allowing them to take your jewels with your blessing probably would not be good for them, for you or for society.[38])

Jesus commended a father who, rejecting his prodigal son's proposal for justice ("Father, I have sinned against heaven and before you; I am no longer worthy to

37 Exod. 21:23–25; Lev. 24:19–20; Deut. 19:21.

38 See Jeffrie G. Murphy, *Punishment and the Moral Emotions: Essays in Law, Morality and Religion* (Oxford: Oxford University Press, 2012), 154: "If one forgives the unrepentant wrongdoer, then one risks sacrificing one's own self-respect through complicity in or tacit endorsement of the insulting and degrading message contained in the wrongdoing".

be called your son; treat me like one of your hired hands"), pardoned the son and celebrated his return (Luke 15:11–32). And although Jesus directed his prescription for mercy and forgiveness primarily to private individuals ("forgive us our debts, as we also have forgiven our debtors" [Matthew 6:12]), the case discussed at the beginning of this chapter suggests that he also favoured Alwynne Smart–style mercy in the administration of the criminal law. It bears repetition that, in freeing the woman taken in adultery, Jesus mentioned neither any mitigating circumstance of her crime nor any redeeming virtue of her character.

A central tenet of Christianity is that Jesus' crucifixion and death were themselves an act of Smart-style mercy: "while we still were sinners, Christ died for us" (Rom. 5:8); "Here is the Lamb of God who takes away the sin of the world" (John 1:29); "For this is my blood of the covenant, which is poured out for many for the forgiveness of sins" (Matt. 26:18); "we have been sanctified by the offering of the body of Jesus Christ once for all" (Hebr. 10:10). Some Christians have seen in Jesus' atonement only his sacrifice of his life for undeserving others. In their view, Jesus saved sinners simply by offering a moral example. Others, however, have recognised a dark side of the story – a God who demanded blood for the remission of sins and accepted the blood of the innocent (at least for a time). This vision cannot be reconciled with most modern understandings of either justice or mercy.

The forgiveness offered by some of Jesus' followers continues to astonish – for example, that voiced by survivors and family members within hours of a white supremacist's murder of nine congregants at the Emanuel African Methodist Episcopal Church in Charleston. A jury, however, may have taken an appropriate stand for justice when it rejected the wishes of many of these survivors and family members and sentenced the killer to death.[39]

This chapter has contended that public officials should be less willing than private individuals to approve Alwynne Smart–style mercy. Sometimes, however, deciding not to inflict the just penalty can reflect the willingness of an entire society to forgive. Consider the amnesties that public authorities have approved following wars, rebellions and the fall of oppressive governments.

The U.S. Constitution established a government of checks and balances, but the Framers seemed to overlook this principle in Article II, section 2, clause 1. This provision gave the president an unchecked power to pardon[40] – a power even broader than the king's.[41] When Alexander Hamilton explained the Framers'

39 See Jelani Cobb, "Inside the Trial of Dylann Roof: The Complicated Moral Calculations that Followed a Horrific Crime", *New Yorker*, 6 February 2017, https://www.newyorker.com/magazine/2017/02/06/inside-the-trial-of-dylann-roof (accessed 23 January 2019).

40 U.S. Constitution, Art II, s. 2, cl. 1: the president "shall have Power to Grant Reprieves and Pardons for Offenses against the United States, except in Cases of Impeachment".

41 See John Somers, *The Security of Englishmen's Lives* (London: Effingham Wilson, 1821; first published 1681), 38–9; James N. Jorgensen, "Federal Executive Clemency Power: The President's Prerogative to Escape Accountability", (1993) 27 *University of Richmond Law Review* 349–52.

choice in Federalist 74, he argued first that leaving "the prerogative of pardoning … as little as possible fettered or embarrassed" would serve justice: "The criminal code of every country partakes so much of necessary severity, that without an easy access to exceptions in favor of unfortunate guilt, justice would wear a countenance too sanguinary and cruel". Hamilton added, however, that remitting even deserved punishment could serve public goals: "in seasons of insurrection or rebellion, there are often critical moments, when a well-timed offer of pardon to the insurgents or rebels may restore the tranquillity of the commonwealth".[42]

Hamilton focused on restoring public peace, but amnesties typically reflect compassion for amnesty recipients as well. After George Washington granted amnesty to participants in the Whiskey Rebellion and remitted the death sentences of two of its leaders, he told Congress that it was "consistent with the public good … to mingle in the operations of Government every degree of moderation and tenderness which the national justice, dignity, and safety permit".[43] Similar sentiments influenced John Adams' pardon of participants in Fries' Rebellion, James Buchanan's pardon of Brigham Young and other participants in the Utah War of 1857–8, Abraham Lincoln and Andrew Johnson's amnesties for Confederate rebels, Theodore Roosevelt's pardon of participants in the Philippine insurrection, Warren Harding's pardon of Eugene V. Debs and others convicted of subverting military recruitment during the First World War, Calvin Coolidge's pardon of First World War deserters, Harry Truman's amnesty for many Second World War draft violators and deserters, Gerald Ford's amnesty for some Vietnam-era draft violators and deserters and Jimmy Carter's amnesty for nearly all the rest who refused to serve in Vietnam.[44]

Truth and reconciliation commissions have been described as a third way between general amnesties and Nuremberg-style war crimes trials.[45] Notably, the South African commission granted 1,500 amnesties (from more than 7,000 applications) for crimes committed by government officers and political activists during the apartheid era. Applicants were eligible only if they disclosed their actions fully and established they acted for political reasons.[46] Although the commission is widely credited with promoting social reconstruction and facilitating

42 *The Federalist No. 74* (Hamilton), available at http://avalon.law.yale.edu/18th_century/fed74.asp (accessed 23 January 2019).

43 James D. Richardson, comp. *Messages and Papers of the Presidents*, vol. 1 (Washington, D.C.: Government Printing Office, 1896), 184.

44 See generally Charles Shanor and Marc L. Miller, "Pardon Us: Systematic Presidential Pardons", (2001) 13 *Federal Sentencing Reporter* 139–46.

45 See generally in this volume, Chapter 20, Daniel Philpott, "Judicial Punishment in Transitional Justice", p. 314 at p. 324.

46 See Desmond Tutu, "Truth and Reconciliation Commission, South Africa", *Encyclopedia Britannica*, https://www.britannica.com/topic/Truth-and-Reconciliation-Commission-South-Africa (accessed 23 January 2019); Therese Abrahamsen and Hugo van der Merwe, "Reconciliation Through Amnesty? Amnesty Applicants' Views of the South African Truth and Reconciliation Commission", http://www.csvr.org.za/docs/trc/reconciliationthroughamnesty.pdf (accessed 23 January 2019).

South Africa's transition to constitutional democracy,[47] some South Africans bitterly protested the exemption of murderers and other violent offenders from the punishment they deserved.[48]

When truth and reconciliation commissions exempt offenders from punishment, they do so primarily for forward-looking public reasons, and compassion for offenders seems subordinate. Yet, the goals they advance are those commonly associated with private forgiveness and mercy – healing, reconciliation and moving on. A commission can accomplish these purposes only when most of a society is willing to forgive, and a society that has authorised a truth and reconciliation commission through democratic processes evidently is. Such a commission is likely to be the faithful agent of a public ready to put aside past wrongs and start over. Amnesty that public officials approve because it advances public purposes, however, is not supererogatory.

Mercy unmixed with instrumental and self-serving goals may be rare. Jesus repeatedly emphasised that mercy would be rewarded.[49] Jesus himself, however, exemplified pure mercy – selfless mercy, mercy unaccompanied by any instrumental objective, the remission of punishment simply as an undeserved gift. May a public body properly approve this kind of mercy? This chapter has argued that, in the absence of clear authorisation, it may not.

18.7 Conclusion

In opposing grants of mercy by public agencies unless they serve forward-looking public purposes, this chapter may seem – or even be – heretical. The case of the woman taken in adultery makes it likely that Jesus took a different view. Few Christians through the centuries, however, have approved non-instrumental gifts of unmerited leniency by public officials. Officials could make these gifts only by distributing them as miraculous lightning bolts (as Jesus did during his ministry) or by granting them to all offenders (as Jesus did in the atonement), bringing criminal punishment to an end. The clearest strategy for avoiding, denying or concealing the heretical position of this chapter is to say that criminal punishment is so clearly essential that Jesus could not have wanted to remit all of it, and many Christians have taken this tack. These Christians have offered little support

47 See Desmond Tutu and Mpho Tutu, *The Book of Forgiving: The Fourfold Path to Healing Ourselves and Our World* (New York: HarperCollins, 2014), 3: "I have often said that in South Africa there would have been no future without forgiving".

48 See Ashraf H.A. Rushdy, *After Injury: A Historical Anatomy of Forgiveness, Resentment, and Apology* (Oxford: Oxford University Press, 2018), 3–4.

49 See, e.g. Matt. 6:14–15: "For if you forgive others their trespasses, your heavenly Father will also forgive you; but if you do not forgive others, neither will your Father forgive your trespasses"; Rushdy, *After Injury*, 32: "Jesus' point, then, is that interpersonal forgiveness must be unconditional, recurrent, and pervasive, while divine forgiveness is conditional – precisely, on the exhibition of interpersonal forgiveness".

for their position, however,[50] and perhaps Jesus was willing to approve mercy in every case. It would have been out of character for him to say no and no-one has pointed to a case in which he did. Jesus instructed followers to “judge not”, “condemn not” and “forgive” (Luke 6:37). He may have opposed criminal punishment altogether.

Further reading

Crouch, Jeffrey. *The Presidential Pardon Power* (Lawrence, KS: University of Kansas Press, 2009).

Griswold, Charles. *Forgiveness: A Philosophical Exploration* (Cambridge: Cambridge University Press, 2007).

Moore, Kathleen Dean. *Pardons: Justice, Mercy and the Public Interest* (Oxford: Oxford University Press, 1989).

Murphy, Jeffrie G. *Getting Even: Forgiveness and Its Limits* (Oxford: Oxford University Press, 2003).

Osler, Mark. “A Biblical Value in the Constitution: Mercy, Clemency, Faith, and History”, (2012) 9 *University of St. Thomas Law Journal* 769–81.

Rothchild, Jonathan, Matthew Myer Bolton and Kevin Jung, eds. *Doing Justice to Mercy: Religion, Law, and Criminal Justice* (Charlottesville, VA: University of Virginia Press, 2007).

Rushdy, Ashraf H.A. *After Injury: A Historical Anatomy of Forgiveness, Resentment, and Apology* (Oxford: Oxford University Press, 2018).

Tuckness, Alex and John M. Parrish. *The Decline of Mercy in Public Life* (Cambridge: Cambridge University Press, 2014).

50 The nearest they have come seems to be Matt. 18:15–17 (approving the shunning of persistent, unrepentant sinners) and Matt. 12:30–32 (declaring blasphemy against the Holy Spirit unforgivable).

19 Parole, risk assessment of offenders and Christianity

Sir John Saunders

From the government's point of view, one of the main, if not the principal, reasons for having a parole system is to eliminate or reduce overcrowding, which exacerbates the appalling conditions in our prisons; however, that is not the only reason. In the House of Lords decision in *R. (Smith & West) v. Parole Board*, which concerned prisoners serving determinate sentences, Lord Bingham said:

> While ... it is true that early release provisions have the practical effect of relieving overcrowding in prisons, that is not their penal justification. But such justification exists. All, or almost all, determinate sentence prisoners are expected to return to the community on release from prison after serving their sentences. It is in the interests of society that they should, after release, live law-abiding, orderly and useful lives. For a host of practical, psychological and social reasons, the process of transition from custody to freedom is often very difficult for the prisoner. It is accordingly very desirable that the process of transition should be professionally supervised, to maximise the chances of the ex-prisoner's successful reintegration into the community and minimise the chances of his relapse into criminal activity.[1]

19.1 Background

The role of the Parole Board has changed considerably over its 50 years of existence. It started life as a body which advised the home secretary and had no power to order release. European human rights jurisprudence made this an untenable position and the power to direct release was transferred in the cases set out below to the Board. In the early days, there were very few members of the Board and all were judges. There were no oral hearings; all decisions were made on paper. Now there are over 8,000 oral hearings per year. This number increased substantially following a decision of our Supreme Court in 2013 which meant in practice that the majority of parole decisions are now made following an oral

1 [2005] 1 WLR 350 at para. 25.

hearing.[2] Of those prisoners who request an oral hearing, two-thirds get one. The remaining cases are decided on paper. A far greater number of members of the Board were required to conduct this number of oral hearings. There are currently 238 members of the Board. A relatively small percentage of them are serving or retired judges. In addition to judges and independent members, there are specialist members, psychologists and psychiatrists, who are increasingly in demand to sit on cases of prisoners with mental health problems.

19.2 Automatic release of prisoners serving determinate sentences

The Parole Board plays no part in the initial release of prisoners serving determinate sentences. They are automatically released at the end of one half of their sentence and remain on parole licence until the end of their sentence. Whether spending that percentage of the sentence on licence in the community is necessary to maximise the chances of successful reintegration into society may be doubtful but it is certainly necessary for the purposes of reducing overcrowding in prisons. Conditions are attached to any period of licence including a condition to be of good behaviour. If a prisoner breaches the terms of his or her licence, he or she is liable to be recalled to prison by the secretary of state. A breach of the terms of a prisoner's licence will not necessarily involve committing a criminal offence but the overall re-conviction rate for prisoners who have been released from prison runs at about 40 per cent.

If prisoners who have been released on parole are recalled to prison and are not re-released by the secretary of state for justice, the Parole Board will have to consider whether their recall was justified and, whether or not it was justified, whether they are safe to be re-released.[3] If the Board concludes that a prisoner is safe to be released, it directs that the prisoner shall be released and, subject to any appeal to the High Court, the secretary of state has to comply with that direction. Prisoners recalled for breaching their parole licence make up a significant number of cases which are considered by the Board.

19.3 Release of prisoners serving life sentences or extended sentences

There are another group of prisoners who are not automatically released at the halfway point in their sentence and can only be released on licence by the Parole Board. They are prisoners who are serving mandatory life sentences for murder, prisoners serving discretionary life sentences and prisoners serving extended sentences. In the case of prisoners serving a life sentence, the judge will have prescribed a minimum period that the prisoner has to serve before he or she is

2 *Osborn v. the Parole Board, Booth v. the Parole Board* [2013] UKSC 61.
3 *R. (Calder) v. Secretary of State for Justice* [2015] EWCA Civ 1050.

eligible for parole. In cases of murder, that minimum period is assessed having taken account of starting points for different categories of murder set out by the legislature.[4] For those prisoners sentenced to a discretionary life sentence, the judge will fix the minimum period by determining what would have been the appropriate determinative sentence for the offence, had he or she not imposed a life sentence and then dividing it by two.[5]

The minimum term represents the retributive part of the sentence and, once it has been completed and the matter has been referred by the secretary of state for justice, the Parole Board considers whether the prisoner is safe to be released. If the Board concludes that the prisoner is safe to be released, then the Board has to direct his or her release. If the prisoner is not safe to be released, the Board may, as an alternative to release, recommend to the secretary of state for justice that the prisoner should be transferred to an open prison in order to prepare for release into the community on licence. This recommendation does not have to be accepted by the secretary of state, who retains the ultimate decision whether to transfer a prisoner to open conditions. In making his or her decision, the secretary of state is bound by any findings of fact made by the Board.

19.4 The public protection test

The test to be applied is that the Parole Board will only release a prisoner if satisfied that it is no longer necessary for the safety of the public that the prisoner remains confined (the public protection test). If the Board is satisfied on the evidence that the release test is met, it has no discretion and has to direct release. This is frequently misunderstood by the public and politicians who comment that the Parole Board should not have released a particular prisoner after so few years when he or she has committed such an awful crime or crimes. The Parole Board is not responsible for fixing the minimum period reflecting the appropriate retribution or just desserts for the crime. That is for the judge to do. The Parole Board cannot review whether the judge got it right or was too lenient; only the Court of Appeal can do that.

The test for recommending open conditions is whether the prisoner can be safely contained in open conditions taking into account any risk of escape and whether, in the particular prisoner's case, a period in open conditions will help progress the prisoner towards release.

19.5 Assessment of risk

Risk assessment, which is what the Parole Board is primarily required to do, is fraught with difficulty. There are tools which are based on statistical data and

4 Schedule 21 of the Criminal Justice Act 2003.

5 It is divided by two because prisoners serving determinate sentences are automatically released halfway through their sentences.

other static factors. There are dynamic assessments where there is normally input from a psychologist who has met and examined the prisoner. Both of these different types of tools can only be trusted as a guide. The Supreme Court in *Osborn* placed heavy emphasis on having oral hearings in a large proportion of cases. They reached that decision having concluded that procedural fairness demanded an oral hearing in many cases. That included, according to Lord Reed, who gave the leading judgment, cases where the prisoner could contribute little which was relevant to the decision but was entitled to be involved. He said:

> justice is intuitively understood to require a procedure which pays due respect to persons whose rights are significantly affected by decisions taken in the exercise of administrative or judicial functions. Respect entails that such persons ought to be able to participate in the procedure by which the decision is made provided they have something to say which is relevant to the decision to be taken.[6]

It may be that experience suggests that oral hearings do not necessarily result in more reliable outcomes. Some prisoners can be manipulative, have learned what they should say to improve their chances of getting parole and give a very convincing performance. To support his view in favour of normally giving the prisoner a say, Lord Reed cited Fortescue J in Dr Bentley's case (*R. v. Chancellor of Cambridge ex parte Bentley*):

> The laws of God and man both give the party an opportunity to make his defence, if he has any. I remember to have heard it observed by a very learned man, upon such an occasion, that even God himself did not pass sentence upon Adam before he was called upon to make his defence.[7]

The point of the *dictum* was that Adam was allowed a hearing notwithstanding that God, being omniscient, did not require to hear from him in order to improve the quality of his decision-making. Although God can be expected to see through any dissembling or deception, the Parole Board, not being omniscient, cannot always do so.

If the Board gets it wrong, and releases someone who goes on to commit a further serious offence, the media are quick to criticise and politicians quick to react. Even when it cannot be demonstrated that the Board got it wrong, the grant of parole to someone whom the public and politicians think should not be released, leads to heavy criticism, and the reaction from politicians and the press is sometimes extreme. Those who criticise will not have seen the large amount of material on which the Board will have made its decision.

6 Ibid. at para. 68.
7 (1748) 2 Ld Raym 1334.

19.6 Pressure to release

Sometimes, but unusually, the pressure from politicians and the public is not to keep prisoners in custody but to release them. From April 2005 when the dangerousness provisions introduced by the Criminal Justice Act 2003 came into force up until the Legal Aid, Sentencing and Punishment of Offenders Act 2012 was passed, there was an additional sentence that the courts could impose on dangerous offenders and that was imprisonment for public protection (IPP). It was similar in the way it operated to a life sentence. The prisoner could only be released by the Parole Board applying the public protection test (see above). The judge was required to pass a minimum term which the prisoner had to serve before he or she could be released on parole. IPP could be passed for a variety of violent and sexual offences set out in schedules to the Criminal Justice Act 2003. When the Act was first brought into force, the judge had to pass a sentence of IPP if the prisoner had committed an offence contained in the schedules and the judge found the prisoner to be dangerous. The potential unfairness in this was that the offences set out in the schedules could be quite minor and merit nothing more than a short determinate sentence. That consideration was not relevant to the task of the Parole Board, who could only release the prisoner at the end of the minimum period if satisfied that it was safe to do so. The consequence of this was that offenders, particularly young offenders, were remaining in custody for long periods, well in excess of the minimum period which represented the prisoner's just desserts for the crime or crimes he or she had committed. The most extreme example of this was a sentence of IPP that was passed with a minimum period to be served of 28 days. The appropriate determinate sentence to reflect the seriousness of the offence was two months. That prisoner served far longer than two months. The provisions surrounding IPPs were amended in 2008 but that did not solve all the problems and in 2012 the sentence was abolished.[8]

The decision whether or not to give parole to a prisoner sentenced to an IPP for a relatively minor offence who has been in custody for many years past his or her minimum period, can be extremely difficult. On the one hand, there is a clear injustice in keeping a prisoner in custody long after the time that he or she has paid the appropriate penalty based on the seriousness of the offence he or she has committed. On the other hand, the test the Board has to apply is clear: it must be "satisfied that it is no longer necessary for the protection of the public that the prisoner remains confined". It is a very difficult test for a prisoner to satisfy. Prison may make a prisoner more difficult to rehabilitate rather than less. The only guidance which the Supreme Court has been able to give in this complex situation is that the Board should consider whether to release ever more anxiously the longer the prisoner has been in prison beyond his or her tariff. That suggests

8 That abolition did not affect those serving IPPs. So some prisoners serving sentences of IPP for relatively minor offences remain in custody because the Board is not satisfied that it is not necessary for the protection of the public that they remain in prison. There are IPP prisoners still in custody despite being many years over tariff.

that the Board does not anxiously consider release in all the cases it considers. It does. The only possible justification for considering that the length of time past the tariff is a factor in the release decision is that it is to be hoped that the longer a person spends in prison, the more chance there is that he or she will have been rehabilitated. That is a hope which may not always be realised.

19.7 Christian principles in parole decisions

So where, if anywhere, do the principles of Christianity impinge on issues of parole? Forgiveness is a Christian virtue – but it is not the Board's function to forgive. It does not even take into account, when deciding whether to release, any overt expression of forgiveness by the victim. The same principle applies in the criminal courts where the forgiveness of the victim is not normally to be treated as a mitigating factor in arriving at the appropriate sentence. More often and understandably, the reaction of the victim is not to forgive the prisoner but to urge the Board not to release the prisoner because of the effect that the crimes had on his or her life. This cannot usually affect the Parole Board's decision as the Board is only concerned with assessing future risks.

Christians believe that it is a pre-condition of divine forgiveness that the sinner truly repents of his or her sins. Many prisoners will express regret to the Board for the crimes they have committed as part of their commitment to live a law-abiding life in the future. The difficulty for the Board is to assess whether that repentance is genuine or feigned as part of a process of manipulation. Even if the repentance and remorse are genuine, it does not mean that a prisoner, if released, will necessarily refrain from committing further crimes. It is probably fair to say, however, that repentance, which is assessed as genuine, is likely to assist a prisoner in the grant of parole.

While repentance may assist a prisoner get parole, lack of repentance does not mean that a prisoner will not get it. It may make it more difficult, but it does not make it impossible. It may mean the prisoner is not eligible to go on courses available in prison which are designed to lessen the risk of re-offending. For example, convicted sex offenders cannot go on courses designed to reduce their risk of re-offending if they deny committing the offences of which they have been convicted. That does not mean that sex offenders serving an indeterminate sentence who deny that they committed the offences can never be released, but it is more difficult for the Board, who have to assume that they did commit the offences, to conclude that it is safe to do so.

Victims are encouraged to take part in the parole process. Not infrequently, the Board receives statements from victims setting out the enduring effects that the crime has had on them and urging the Board not to release the prisoner. As that does not impinge on future risk, should it be ignored? Does it help victims to be encouraged to submit a statement saying how they have been affected if it cannot influence the Board's decision? There are areas where their input is relevant. For example, if they have received threats directly or indirectly from the prisoner of what he or she will do upon release. That would obviously be taken into account as it is relevant to future risk. Further, victims play an important part in decisions as to any conditions on the licence and, in particular, exclusion zones so that they do not have to meet their attacker unexpectedly after he or she is released. Victims should be treated with compassion, but is it compassionate to pretend that they can influence the parole process when, in most circumstances, they cannot? Compassion is a Christian virtue but should be meaningful, not superficial.

The decision of the Administrative Court in the Worboys case[9] will have encouraged more victims to contest a release decision made by the Parole Board. Most often, the victims' motivation will be that the prisoner should not be released because of the appalling nature of the crime committed which is still causing them intense suffering. They will also say that they fear coming face to face with their attacker. That risk can be reduced by requiring the offender to wear an electronic tag and/or imposing exclusion zones that he or she is not allowed to enter. The extent of the ongoing suffering of a victim or victims is irrelevant to any issue the Parole Board has to consider in deciding whether to release. So, for victims who want to prevent release, it is left to prison lawyers to trawl through the available material to try to find something in the way the Board reached its decision that might provide possible grounds for legal challenge.

19.8 Comparisons with judicial sentencing

Where Christianity can have a practical effect on the grant of parole is the issue of rehabilitation. This corresponds to the Christian belief in the possibility of redemption. If we believe that humans are created in the image of God, then redemption and therefore rehabilitation must always be possible. Maintaining this belief is not always easy. Members of the Board have to shut their ears to press and public reaction to the possibility of the release of a prisoner who has committed terrible crimes. This is different from sentencing by a judge. The judge will always have half an eye on the likely reaction of the public to any sentence which, at the least, will be reflected in their sentencing remarks. It is important that the public should have trust in the sentencing process and that depends to some extent on whether the public consider that the criminal has received his or her just desserts for the crime. Many feel that, for the sentencing process to take much account of the public's reaction, is wrong. The public often do not see the full picture. They get their information from the media which may not fully or accurately report the sentencing hearing or the judge's sentencing remarks. Frequently the public do not read the full report but rely on headlines which are designed more to catch attention than to accurately reflect the substance of the article. Despite the limits on the public's understanding of why a sentence has

9 *R. (DSD and NBV) v. the Parole Board and the Secretary of State for Justice* [2018] EWHC 694 (Admin).

been imposed, public opinion does play a part in the sentencing process. Whether it should or not is a more difficult issue.

The Criminal Justice Act 2003 was a major reforming statute. Among many other things, it sets out the purposes of sentencing to which every judge must have regard.[10] Included as one of those purposes is the reform and rehabilitation of offenders. While it is to be hoped that the judges believe in the reform and rehabilitation of offenders, it is not certain that the public do, nor that it should play any part in sentencing. The government periodically produces Green Papers proposing that a greater focus be placed on the rehabilitation of offenders. It seems that little gets done, perhaps because most politicians fear being regarded as soft on crime if they were to promote rehabilitation.

19.9 Public opinion and parole

Whatever influence public opinion may have on sentences, there seems no reason why it should influence the parole process. While it is important that the public have confidence in the parole system, their consideration as to whether a prisoner should be released on parole will inevitably be ill-informed. The public will normally be opposed to parole for a prisoner either because they believe that the nature of the crime he or she has committed was so awful that he or she should not be released or because they cannot believe that there will not be a significant risk to the public if the prisoner is released. As to the first, the prisoner has already served his or her tariff sentence before becoming eligible for parole. That reflects what the judge considered to be the appropriate punishment for the crime. It is not the Parole Board's job to revisit that decision. The Parole Board cannot be influenced by considerations simply based on the seriousness of the crime or crimes which were committed. As to the second, the public will have no idea whether or not a prisoner has been rehabilitated; they will not know how he or she has reacted to courses which are designed to improve his or her behaviour; and they will not have seen any of the reports on which the Board is likely to base its decision. It is to be hoped that the recent innovation of providing summaries of the Board's decisions will assist in public understanding of the process and will result in a greater acceptance of what the Board does, but I doubt it.

19.10 The functioning of the Parole Board panels

At present, panels who make decisions about release on behalf of the Parole Board make them, I believe, on the evidence that is presented to them and not with an eye to public opinion. They do release, even if the prisoner has committed a horrible crime or crimes, if they are satisfied that he or she is safe to be released. Whether a panel can remain focused on the issues it properly has to consider, and disregard misinformed public opinion, may become more difficult

10 Criminal Justice Act 2003 s. 142(1).

as Parole Board proceedings become more open. Open justice is an important principle. The Board should not be immune from critical assessment, but I am not convinced that more openness in its proceedings will lead to better understanding of what the Board does. The public find out what the Parole Board does by reading about it in the newspaper and newspapers sometimes have an agenda which they wish to promote.

Assessment of risk is, of course, difficult. There is no crystal ball, but that does not mean that it is a waste of time and should not be undertaken. Even where the assessment of risk was correct at the time it was made, there are imponderables which may affect the accuracy of any assessment. Family support, which may be a critical protective factor, might unpredictably disappear. Drug addicts who seem to have made good progress in coping with their addiction may relapse under some intense personal pressure. No panel can make allowances for every unpredictable event. If it did, no-one would ever be released on parole.

Experience tells us that rehabilitation can work provided there is the right support for the prisoner when released. It is not always easy to get the right support when cutbacks have affected all public services. In the case of assistance for prisoners in the community, that may be a false economy as keeping prisoners in custody is more expensive than giving them adequate support in the community. People leaving prison on parole can find it very difficult to adjust to freedom, particularly when they have been incarcerated for a long time. It may be easy for prisoners to say and believe while in custody that it will be possible to resist the blandishments of anti-social peers or the attractions of hard drugs, but, faced with the reality, it can be much more difficult. Nevertheless, the number of prisoners who commit a serious further offence within three years of release by the Parole Board are few. The current figure is less than 1 per cent, suggesting that the risk assessments that are made are more reliable than people think.

19.11 Public reaction and pressure

Public reaction to the release by the Parole Board of a criminal who has committed a particularly horrible crime or crimes can be extreme, as we have recently seen in the United Kingdom.[11] What starts as criticism of the decision, which may or may not be justified, rapidly extends to the vilification of those who have made the decision or have supported release at the hearing in a professional capacity. One of the psychologists who gave evidence in support of Worboys' release had to change all her phone numbers to escape the attentions of the press. While those on the Parole Board who have to make decisions whether or not to release say, and no doubt believe, that they are immune to these pressures, it is difficult to be sure that the fear of widespread condemnation in the press does not affect decisions and lead to prisoners who are safe to be released staying in custody

11 John Worboys and Stephen Mitchell. See *R. (DSD and NBV) v. the Parole Board and the Secretary of State for Justice* [2018] EWHC 694 (Admin).

longer than they need to. It is vitally important that the courts, when they review decisions of the Parole Board are not swayed by public opinion.

Rehabilitation of prisoners in the community can be made much more difficult if not impossible by the actions of the public. Some prisoners convicted of notorious crimes have changed their names by deed poll in order to escape retribution in prison and to increase their chances of avoiding public attention on release. Some members of the press consider that if a notorious prisoner is released into the community, the public should know where they are so that they can avoid any danger that they may present. The result, however, may be that the released prisoner becomes the victim of vigilante attacks or his or her life becomes so difficult that he or she cannot remain outside prison and is returned. That happened to a notorious prisoner on two occasions when he was sent to open prisons as a preparation for release. On each occasion, he did well at open prison and behaved himself when he was allowed out to work in the community and when allowed out overnight in a hostel. Other prisoners released his name to the press and as a result of the details they published it was deemed unsafe for the prisoner to remain at an open prison. He was returned to a closed prison where he has had to remain for many years. In 2000, the *Sun* newspaper ran a campaign to name all convicted paedophiles living in the community. This followed the murder of a girl by a convicted paedophile who, unknown to anyone, lived in her area. The result of this was, in some cases, vigilante activity against those who were named in the newspaper.

19.12 Christian support for release of offenders on parole

The support, and more importantly the vocal support, of Christians in the community who believe in the possibility of redemption would help to create more of a balance in the reaction of the public to unpopular decisions that the Parole Board make. Importantly it would make it easier to rehabilitate prisoners after they have paid their debt to society.

Most mainstream churches believe in the concept of giving prisoners who have served their time in prison the opportunity to rehabilitate themselves in the community. They urge that an ex-prisoner should be treated as an individual and not defined by his or her offending. They provide support to released prisoners and urge their congregations to assist with this in practical ways. There are difficulties in practice. How far is it right for a church to welcome into their congregation an ex-offender without informing the congregation of the offence or offences which were committed? This is a particular concern where the released prisoner was convicted of a sexual offence.

Not all the churches resolve this difficulty in the same way. Cardinal Vincent Nichols, head of the Catholic Church in England and Wales, has proposed that an ex-offender should not be required to reveal his or her criminal convictions when applying for a job. Whether such a proposal would receive general acceptance may be doubtful. It ought to be possible for a prisoner to be given a chance to rehabilitate himself or herself even if his or her crimes are made known to members of the community in which he or she lives.

It is a Christian virtue, as well as a legal requirement, for parole hearings to be fair.[12] While objectively fair in terms of legal requirements, trials, and particularly criminal trials, are not always fair to defendants. The court surroundings, the formality, what the lawyers wear in court and the presence of an often hostile public can make a court an intimidating place in which to give evidence. Most criminal lawyers can give accounts of their clients giving a fluent and credible account when seen in a client meeting who go to pieces in the witness box. Of course, that may be because they are giving an untruthful account which is later exposed; sometimes, the intimidating atmosphere of a court serves to stifle honest evidence.

Panels conducting parole hearings do their best to provide an atmosphere which is conducive to all witnesses, including the prisoner, giving of their best and not feeling intimidated. It is not always easy to do that. Prisoners can become frustrated that panels seem to concentrate on the downsides of his or her case: the details of the index offence, which may have occurred 20 years ago, and any bad behaviour which may have occurred in custody, however long ago and whatever the circumstances. Equally, many prisoners have mental health problems or are of very limited intelligence which can make a parole hearing very difficult.

The consequence of creating an atmosphere where everyone can give of their best may be that the questioning at parole hearings can be less probing than in a criminal court. While the secretary of state for justice is a party to every parole hearing and is entitled to be represented, he or she seldom is. This is no doubt for reasons of cost but it does mean that demanding questions, if they are needed, have to be asked by the panel.[13] While no doubt it is possible to be fair and ask probing questions, it may be difficult to always appear fair to the prisoner, who may get the impression that the panel has taken against him or her.

Parole Board hearings are relatively informal, and the prisoner has the central role so that the way in which the proceedings are held is adapted to the needs and abilities of the prisoner. This seems both humane and fair, but would no doubt give rise to criticism if the public were admitted to the hearings. As other authors have written in this volume, what is necessary to be fair is to have empathy for the prisoner: only then is the correct decision likely to be made.

Is parole a waste of time? Some commentators believe that most criminals will stop offending when they reach a certain level of maturity and that courses in prison are of marginal if any use. We simply need to wait until they have grown out of crime. While it would be possible to dispense with the parole licence for prisoners serving determinate sentences, it would be impossible, while we pass indeterminate sentences on "dangerous" offenders, to do without parole in their cases. As Lord Judge said in the decision of the Supreme Court in *R. (Walker) v. Justice Secretary*:

12 Article 5(4) of the European Convention on Human Rights.

13 *R. (on the application of DSD and NBV) v. the Parole Board and Radford, formerly Worboys* [2018] EWHC 694 (Admin).

> The statutory regime for dealing with indeterminate sentences is predicated on the possibility that, save for those for whom the punitive element of the sentence requires that life imprisonment should indeed mean imprisonment for the rest of the offender's natural life, prisoners maybe or will reform themselves. A fair opportunity for the rehabilitation and the opportunity to demonstrate that the risk they presented at the date of sentence has diminished to levels consistent with release into the community should be available to them.[14]

Someone will have to make the decision whether or not the risk has "diminished to levels consistent with release into the community" and there seems no reason why that should not be the Parole Board which has long experience and expertise in risk assessment.

Lord Judge made clear that what he said did not apply to those serving "life means life" sentences. These are prisoners who, because of the nature of their crimes, will never be released. There are currently in excess of 40 prisoners serving such a sentence. While the European Court of Human Rights has ruled that the arrangements in England and Wales for possible release of prisoners serving whole life sentences mean there is no breach of Article 3 of the Convention, it is to be hoped that the number will not increase significantly. To sentence a human being to a life in prison without hope of release would seem to most people to be inhumane (and unchristian) unless the circumstances are truly exceptional.

19.13 Conclusion

What is required by panels conducting parole hearings is an ability to decide whether to release a prisoner on the evidence presented to it, and not to be influenced by public opinion or the consequences to the panel of making an unpopular decision. Panels have to believe in the possibility of rehabilitation whatever the prisoner has done. Of course, the result of a hearing may be that the panel remain unconvinced that the time when release into the community is possible has arrived, but it must not close its mind to the possibility whatever the crime the prisoner has committed.

If the Board does all those things then parole hearings will be fair and the Board will conduct itself in a manner which is in line with Christian teaching and, it is to be hoped, will get the understanding and support of all who aspire to follow and spread that teaching. The Board needs support. The Parole Board's decisions to release are being challenged more frequently. The basis of the challenge is generally that the prisoner should not be released because of the awful crime he or she has committed. Christian teaching is that, once a prisoner has served his or her debt to society, he or she should be given support to rehabilitate himself or herself into society and encouraged to live a law-abiding life. If Christians live this teaching out in their lives, then Christianity can make a very practical contribution to the parole process.

14 [2010] 1 AC 553 at para. 134.

Further reading

Caplan, Joel M. "Parole Release Decisions: Impact of Positive and Negative Victim and Nonvictim Input on a Representative Sample of Parole-Eligible Inmates", (2010) 25.2 *Violence and Victims* 224–42.

Evans, Donald G. "Community-Focused Parole", (December 2006) 68.7 *Corrections Today* 216–18.

McBride, Elizabeth C. "Note: Policing Parole: The Constitutional Limits of Back-End Sentencing", (2009) 20.2 *Stanford Law and Policy Review* 597–621.

Ogletree, Charles J. Jr. and Austin Sarat. *Life Without Parole: America's New Death Penalty?* (New York: New York University Press, 2012).

Petersilia, Joan. *When Prisoners Come Home: Parole and Prisoner Reentry* (New York: Oxford University Press, 2003).

Phillips, Dan. *Probation and Parole: Current Issues* (New York: Routledge, 2009).

Stevens, Duncan N. "Off the Mapp: Parole Revocation Hearings and the Fourth Amendment", (1999) 89.3 *Journal of Criminal Law and Criminology* 1047–60.

Tewksbury, Richard and David Patrick Connor. "Predicting the Outcome of Parole Hearings", (June–July 2012) 74.3 *Corrections Today* 54–6.

Thompson, Anthony C., *Releasing Prisoners, Redeeming Communities: Reentry, Race, and Politics* (New York: New York University Press, 2008).

20 Judicial punishment in transitional justice

A Christian restorative approach

Daniel Philpott

One of the trends that has defined global politics over the past generation is a wave of transitions from dictatorship, war and genocide to democracy and nascent peace. These transitions have caused an accompanying wave of efforts to confront the injustices of the past: truth commissions, trials, reparations, apologies, peace enforcement operations, new constitutions and forgiveness. Among what is known as the international community – a global network of officials, diplomats, international lawyers and human rights activists espousing the norms of international law – pride of place among these efforts belongs to judicial punishment. The international community's most fervent dream has been to bring to justice Yugoslavia's Slobodan Milosevic, Liberia's Charles Taylor and Uganda's Joseph Kony, just as the Nuremberg Trials once tried and punished Rudolf Hess, Ernst Kaltenbrunner and Hermann Goering.

Amid these same efforts, an unexpected set of voices, espousing an unexpected set of claims, has been those of Christians – bishops, pastors and laypeople speaking directly from the Christian tradition. Their role is unexpected, at least in the West, where religion and politics are far less enmeshed than they are in countries where these Christians have exercised what has been at times a remarkable influence. The Nuremberg Dream has been much less central in their approach to past injustices than it has been for members of the international community. Associated indelibly with political transitions is the image of Archbishop Desmond Tutu chairing South Africa's Truth and Reconciliation Commission in his purple episcopal robes in the late 1990s, urging reconciliation and forgiveness as an explicit alternative to Nuremberg. Bishop Juan Gerardi of Guatemala was assassinated in 1998 after he released the report of the truth commission that he helped to form and conduct in the aftermath of that country's civil war, a report stressing the central importance of the revelation of truth. Bishop Carlos Belo in Timor-Leste spoke of reconciliation while calling for the trials of Indonesian generals who had committed atrocities in Timor-Leste's long civil war and independence referendum of 1999. Archbishop John Baptist Odama of Uganda called for forgiveness amid peace talks in the 2000s while opposing the intervention of the International Criminal Court (ICC), which he viewed as a barrier to peace.

This chapter emanates from these voices and confronts the question: How ought a Christian to view the question of judicial punishment in the setting of countries facing past human rights violations on a large scale while trying to establish new or renewed political orders based on constitutional liberal democracy, a peace settlement or a combination of both? This context of society-wide crimes makes this chapter distinct from others in this volume. Here, unique questions arise such as: How is it possible to perform fair trials when the alleged perpetrators number in the thousands? Or, may judicial punishment be justly foregone if it stands in the way of a peace agreement? That is, are amnesties ever justified? What about alternatives to trials such as vetting or "lustration" arrangements or else community forums based on tribal traditions such as Rwanda's *gacaca* courts?

The approach for which I will argue, restorative punishment, entails a Christian approach to judicial punishment in general, but also, I contend, is uniquely and appositely suited to the predicament of entire societies undergoing political transitions.[1] The chapter begins with a summary of the past generation's explosion of judicial punishment. It then offers a critique of the two leading Western views of punishment in the past 250 years: utilitarianism and retributivism. Next, it presents restorative punishment as an alternative. It subsequently explains how restorative justice contributes to the restoration of political orders that are facing past injustices in the context of a transition to democracy and peace. The chapter concludes with some short reflections on institutions for restorative punishment.

20.1 Judicial punishment in political transitions

Towards the end of the twentieth century, a global explosion of judicial punishment for individual perpetrators of large-scale human rights violations took place. The Nuremberg Dream – that individual perpetrators of human rights violations could be tried and punished – was revived after having been on ice during the decades of the Cold War. Political scientists Kathryn Sikkink and Carrie Booth Walling show that from the mid 1980s to 2004, a marked acceleration in trials undertaken by countries around the world took place. Another political scientist, Leslie Vinjamuri, reports that of all the tribunals that took place from 1945 to 2007, 61% took place following the end of the Cold War in 1989. Along with these strong claims comes the caution of other scholars who point out that when trials are counted as a percentage of countries in transition, they decreased from the mid 1980s onwards.[2] Perspective also comes from the observation that trials

1 The argument of this chapter is based on the arguments in Daniel Philpott, *Just and Unjust Peace: An Ethic of Political Reconciliation* (Oxford: Oxford University Press, 2012).

2 Kathryn Sikkink and Carrie Booth Walling, "Argentina's Contribution to Global Trends in Transitional Justice", in Naomi Roht-Arriaza and Javier Mariezcurrena, eds., *Transitional Justice in the Twenty-First Century: Beyond Truth Versus Justice* (Cambridge: Cambridge University Press, 2006), 312; Leslie Vinjamuri, "Judicial Interventions, Amnesties and Ongoing Conflict", paper presented at the Annual Meeting of the American Political Science Association, Boston, MA, 2008; Andrew Reiter, Tricia D. Olsen and Leigh Payne, "Behind the Justice Cascade: Sequencing Transitional Justice in New Democracies", unpublished paper,

and convictions are dwarfed by the scale of human rights violations and violence. Still, the dramatic increase in the absolute number of trials following the end of the Cold War makes judicial punishment in society-wide conflicts worthy of ethical consideration.

Some of the most dramatic human rights trials have taken place in national-level courts. These were rare prior to the 1980s, exceptions being Germany's trials of Nazi criminals following Nuremberg and Greece's trials of leaders of its military junta, which reigned from 1967 to 1974. The contemporary wave of judicial punishment began in the mid 1980s in Argentina, where courts tried nine and convicted five generals from the Dirty Wars of 1976 to 1983, though the convictions were voided by an amnesty in 1990. Over the next couple of decades, domestic trials also took place in Chile, Germany (concerning Communist East Germany), Ethiopia and Rwanda.

Reviving Nuremberg even more robustly were three international courts created in the 1990s. The UN Security Council created two ad hoc courts, the International Criminal Tribunal for the former Yugoslavia (ICTY) and the International Criminal Tribunal for Rwanda (ICTR), after which a standing permanent body, the ICC, was established through the Rome Treaty of 1998 and went into operation in 2002. Important also are a set of hybrid courts that combine international and national authority, including ones in Timor-Leste, Sierra Leone, Kosovo and Cambodia.

Other innovations in accountability include practices of vetting, sometimes called lustration, in which wrongdoers of a previous regime or armed conflict are prohibited from holding office in a post-transition government, either temporarily or permanently, and sometimes in private sector or civil society organisations. The most well-known of these arrangements took place in post-unification Germany, post-communist eastern Europe and Iraq under U.S. administration following the fall of Saddam Hussein.

Community justice forums are also innovative approaches to accountability and, as we will see, promising settings for restorative punishment. The most significant of these were the *gacaca* courts in Rwanda and the community reconciliation panels of Timor-Leste, both of which took place mostly during the 2000s. Such forums tried perpetrators through community gatherings that also involved the public testimony of victims and witnesses, confession and apologies on the part of perpetrators, forgiveness on the part of victims and punishment of a kind that would reintegrate perpetrators back into their community (for instance, building houses for displaced victims).

Finally, the role of amnesties – where judicial punishment is foregone – cannot be overlooked. These are frequent in global politics and a critical part of debates over judicial punishment and their outcomes. Louise Mallinder, an international

---

2007, cited in Oskar N.T. Thoms, James Ron and Roland Paris, *The Effects of Transitional Justice Mechanisms: A Summary of Empirical Research Findings and Implications for Analysts and Practitioners* (Ottawa: Centre for International Policy Studies, 2008), 16.

legal scholar, has documented over 420 amnesty processes since the Second World War and a dramatic upsurge in them since the mid 1970s, roughly the period in which trials also burgeoned.[3] Amnesties vary in their terms and can be quite elaborate, some of them blanket and some of them conditional, some covering all perpetrators and others only some.

In the advocacy and argument surrounding all of these new forms of punishment, a frequently voiced term is "transitional justice". I adopt the term in its broadest sense to mean the subject of how political orders deal with past injustices committed in the context of political struggle. It is in the setting of transitional justice, broadly construed, then, that we may pose the question: How ought a Christian view judicial punishment as it has come to be practised in the past generation?

20.2 The leading alternative views

I argue that a Christian ought to judge judicial punishment in the context of transitional justice through the same theological, philosophical and jurisprudential commitments that a Christian ought to bring to bear upon punishment in general. These commitments entail an approach that I will call restorative punishment. What differs in the transitional setting is the institutional forms of punishment that best address these special circumstances. Restorative punishment, I will also argue, is well-suited to these circumstances.

The rationale for and virtues of restorative punishment can be seen best through a comparison with the two leading views of punishment in the West over the past two-and-a-half centuries or so: consequentialism and retributivism. These views may be characterised as secular not only because they have been prominent in modern Western philosophy and criminology but also because they emerged at a point in European history when classical Christianity was being challenged.

In the past generation's explosion of judicial punishment, it is striking that the international community's arguments regarding this punishment have been predominantly consequentialist. That is, they focus on the effects of trials rather than on the intrinsic justice of punishing arch war criminals. What do these effects include?

In what stands as a classic article on the case for judicial punishment, legal scholar Diane Orentlicher argues that "The fulcrum of the case for criminal punishment is that it is the most effective insurance against future repression".[4] This insurance is achieved by deterring future crimes, she explains. Likewise, the preamble to the Rome Statute, which established the ICC, states that the court seeks

3 Louise Mallinder, *Amnesty, Human Rights, and Political Transitions* (Portland: Hart Publishing, 2008).

4 Diane F. Orentlicher, "Settling Accounts: The Duty to Prosecute Human Rights Violations of a Prior Regime", (1991) 100.8 *Yale Law Journal* 25–42.

to "put an end to impunity for perpetrators of these crimes and thus to contribute to the prevention of crimes".

Second to deterrence is the promotion of the rule of law. When a new democracy places yesterday's dictators in the dock, it is argued, its citizens will have more confidence that their government secures the rule of law and will view it as more legitimate.

Trials are also touted for channelling revenge out of the hands of citizens into the hands of the judicial authority, contributing to peace between warring communities by convincing each side that the other's arch murderers are receiving justice, and placing in prison the most potent instigators of belligerence. Confidence in all of these effects motivates the international community to advocate passionately for new innovations in global judicial justice and to decry "impunity".

Judicial trials for egregious war crimes and human rights violations also have sceptics, who also typically argue in consequentialist terms. They question all of the alleged fruits of trials, doubting that they will deter heinous crime, especially across borders, or promote the rule of law. International tribunals are rarely even-handed in their prosecution and are prone to try the criminals of only one side of a conflict, thus undermining peace. Even if trials are balanced, they may have little effect on the ground and often cost enormous sums of money, it is argued.[5]

On the terms of this argument, the case for judicial punishment is ultimately empirical. We must assess and weigh effects. Echoed here is the utilitarian school of punishment, the most prominent version of consequentialist approaches, whose founders, Cesare Beccaria and Jeremy Bentham, sought to supplant what they viewed as a harsh retributivism that cared little for the welfare of the criminal with an approach that focused solely on the effects of punishment, including rehabilitation and deterrence.

Utilitarian rationales for punishment, though, encountered withering criticisms and eventually fell out of favour. Rehabilitation programmes were often unsuccessful, returning criminals to the street to commit more crimes. The theory came under scrutiny as well. If the effects of punishment are all that matter (as must be the case for utilitarianism), then guilt, innocence and procedural fairness must also be placed on the balancing scales and can potentially be overridden. What barriers prevent, for instance, giving extra punishment to a famous person who is popularly considered guilty, or even punishing such a person who is innocent, in order to achieve deterrence? Or, why not seize and give therapeutic treatment to people who are judged likely to be criminals but have committed no crime yet? Or apply heavy-handed "reprogramming" treatments to criminals without respect for their free will – a scenario from Stanley Kubrick's film *A Clockwork Orange*? While, to be fair, most utilitarians have favoured leniency, not such frightening scenarios, the deeper problem is their failure to identify

5 For an example of consequentialist scepticism, see Adam Smith, *After Genocide: Bringing the Devil to Justice* (Amherst, NY: Prometheus Books, 2009).

the intrinsic connection between guilt, desert and punishment. Deterrence and rehabilitation may be legitimate aims of punishment, but alone these rationales are vulnerable to Hegel's criticism that they treat criminals like dogs to be trained rather than citizens to be respected for their free choices. The same criticisms find resonance in the Christian tradition, where punishment, both divine and temporal, is always associated with sin, a free act for which an agent is deemed responsible.[6]

The other modern paradigm, retributivism, revolves around the principle that utilitarianism lacks, namely that a person who commits a criminal act incurs guilt and deserves punishment. This connection, agent–act–guilt–desert–punishment, is retributivism's core. Central to retributivism is also the principle that guilt ought to be determined through a fair set of legal procedures. The guilty ought to be punished only for the crime that they commit and proportionately to the scale of this crime and to their level of culpability. Proponents often maintain that retribution is not revenge, which does not respect proportionality, principle or fair procedure and involves personal payback.[7] Retributivists also do not necessarily reject other ends of punishment such as rehabilitation, deterrence or the protection of society, but they insist on guilt and desert.

Rationales and defences of retributivism vary greatly. One scholar identified nine varieties.[8] In one version, deserved punishment is self-evident, a principle that people grasp through an act of the intellect without proof or demonstration. Immanuel Kant, history's most famous retributivist, was keen to stress that legitimate punishment is a principle known through reason, and is not tied to its consequences for persons or societies. To seek to advance well-being through punishment would be to treat persons as means and not as ends. To treat them as ends is to respect them and their choices by responding commensurately to their violation of the law. Thus, in *The Metaphysics of Morals*, Kant argued that punishment

> can never be inflicted merely as a means to promote some other good for the criminal himself or for civil society. It must always be inflicted upon him only *because he has committed a crime*. For a human being can never be treated merely as a means to the purposes of another or be put among the objects of rights to things: His innate personality protects him from this, even though he can be condemned to lose his civil personality.[9]

6 For a good account of problems with utilitarian justifications, see Jean Hampton, "The Moral Education Theory of Punishment", (1984) 13.3 *Philosophy and Public Affairs* 208–38.

7 On the difference between retribution and revenge, see Robert Nozick, "Retributive Punishment", in *Philosophical Explanations* (Cambridge, MA: Harvard University Press, 1981), 366–8.

8 John Cottingham, "Varieties of Retribution", (1979) 29.116 *Philosophical Quarterly* 238–46.

9 Immanuel Kant, *The Metaphysics of Morals*, trans. Mary Gregor (Cambridge: Cambridge University Press, 1991), 140, emphasis in original.

As Alex Tuckness and John M. Parrish point out in their book *The Decline of Mercy in Public Life*, Kant's views are closely related to his more general critique of eudaimonism, the view that morality promotes happiness.[10] Kant argues elsewhere in the same work that the principle of retaliation "is by its form always the principle for the right to punish since it alone is the principle determining this idea *a priori* (not derived from experience of which measures would be most effective for eradicating crime)".[11] It is "pure and strict justice", and not consideration of the consequences, that ought to govern punishment, Kant thought.[12]

Other forms of retributivism revolve around the notion of balance, vivified by the blind Greek goddess of justice, who holds scales in her hands. In these versions, punishment balances out the gain that a perpetrator has wrought from his crime with a corresponding hardship. Evil is thus repaid with evil and the balance is restored. Balancing satisfies justice apart from any actual restoration of the well-being of the perpetrator, victim or society. Justice is simply done.

Still other versions of retributivism exist, but the above varieties, recounted briefly here, vividly capture retributivism's central commitments. It is remarkable how rare retributivist arguments are today among advocates of courts that would render judicial punishment for the greatest of crimes.[13] Is it not exactly these cases where payment for misdeeds would seem most plausible? In any case, it is not hard to imagine retributivist arguments for today's tribunals. Indeed, courtroom procedures alone, with their concern for the careful determination of guilt, culpability, magnitude and proportional punishment, already embody retributivism's core commitments.

Is retributivism a satisfying way to think about criminal justice? It is difficult to answer this question thoroughly in the space here. I am sympathetic to the claim that the intellect can grasp the idea that a person incurs guilt for a crime that she has committed, that she deserves a countering response and that culpability and proportionality are relevant in determining this response. I doubt, though, that the most abstract form of this principle, that a person ought to be punished "only because he has committed a crime", as Kant put it, can be grasped reliably in this way. If a sceptic were to reply that it is equally intuitive that this person ought to apologise, be rehabilitated or be forgiven without punishment, it is not clear what Kant's answer would be. What does punishment do? Perform? Bring about? Rectify? Defeat? Accomplish? Apart from answers to these questions, the pure principle of retribution is hard to sustain.

10 Alex Tuckness and John M. Parrish, *The Decline of Mercy in Public Life* (Cambridge: Cambridge University Press, 2014), 226.

11 Kant, *Metaphysics of Morals*, 168.

12 Ibid., 141.

13 There are a few exceptions. See, for instance, the arguments of Amy Gutmann and Dennis Thompson, "The Moral Foundations of Truth Commissions", in Robert I. Rotberg and Dennis Thompson, eds., *Truth v. Justice: The Morality of Truth Commissions* (Princeton: Princeton University Press, 2000), 22–44.

Excessively abstract is also the balancing justification for punishment, which calls for harms to balance out the perpetrator's gains. While the metaphor of scales is intuitively clear, deeper probing raises questions about the notion of gain. In what sense does a criminal gain from his crime? If gain means a true moral good, then there is no gain. Even if gain means some kind of benefit, it remains dubious whether this is derived from crime. Does the rapist benefit from his sordid act in any meaningful way? Along with alleged benefits, crime also brings perpetrators injury, anxious guilt, danger and a disintegrated soul. Do not these losses considerably complicate the calculation of gain?

The common problem with these standard versions of retributivism is that they are too formal and abstract. While they rightly tie punishment to the misdeed of a freely acting person, they do not describe well the moral rupture that crime causes.

There are also reasons to doubt whether retributivism is Christian. Portions of Scripture do point this way, for instance: Genesis 9:6, "Whoever sheds human blood, by humans shall their blood be shed"; passages referring to God's "recompense"; episodes of God punishing harshly; and passages referring to the death penalty. There is also much in Scripture, however, that runs against retributivism. Just a few chapters prior to the Genesis 9 passage, God places a mark on Cain, a murderer, to prevent him from being killed for his crime – thus acting contrary to precisely what Cain deserves on retributivism's proportionality argument. God's harshest punishments, by contrast, often seem disproportionate to wrongs and thus also a violation of retributivism. Then, though, there are the many episodes where God makes clear that he is not requiting sinners as they deserve. Some passages describe God as "slow to anger and abounding in mercy" or something similarly worded, while at least four passages describe God as vowing to punish and then refraining from it.[14] Neither pure desert nor balance seem to describe God's principle. A better candidate would be God's willingness to continually restore his covenant with the people of Israel, which God does variously through punishment, mercy, forgiveness, exile and return from exile.

The laws of the community of Israel as described by the Torah do not square neatly with retributivism, either. The three *lex talionis* passages seem to be based on retributive metaphors – eye for an eye, tooth for a tooth – but the point of these principles was to place limits on retribution and keep it proportionate in a milieu in which blood revenge was common.[15] Judicial punishment in the community sought to restore the integrity of God's covenant among Jews, which took place most often through restitution.[16] Admittedly, it is difficult to square the death penalty, which the Torah prescribes for more than 20 crimes, with restorative punishment, but even its purpose was to cleanse the community

14 Hosea 11; Amos 5, Jer. 30:11, 18; Jonah.

15 See Christopher D. Marshall, *Beyond Retribution: A New Testament Vision for Justice, Crime, and Punishment* (Grand Rapids: Eerdmans, 2001), 78–89.

16 Ibid., 125–7.

and to restore covenantal relations among the people, not to satisfy an abstract principle of balance or desert.[17]

Jesus' teaching regarding the *lex talionis* – "You have heard it was said 'eye for eye and tooth for tooth', but I tell you, do not resist an evil person" – has been widely regarded in the tradition as deepening the proportionality principle and forbidding retributive paybacks altogether.[18] Jesus is not calling for the abolition of law courts, but if they were to be based on his counsel, they would have to find a basis for punishment other than retributivism.

Jesus' death and resurrection, regarded by the dominant Christian tradition as atoning for the sins of humanity, is also difficult to square with retributivism. A wide consensus in the tradition holds that Jesus' suffering was a gift to humanity and not something it deserved, a gift that Jesus offered "while we were still sinners" (Rom. 5:8) rather than demanding that humanity pay up first. While some views of the atonement see Jesus as rendering satisfaction for the debt of sin (Anselm) or even receiving humanity's punishment from the Father (Calvin, or at least later Calvinists) – seemingly a retributivist logic – even these more legalistic theologies hold that Jesus mercifully suffered in place of humanity, a vicariousness that cannot be squared with retributivism's demand that the perpetrator and only the perpetrator be punished.

Finally, as Tuckness and Parrish point out, major formators of the Western tradition such as Augustine and Thomas Aquinas did not justify punishment in the temporal realm along retributive lines. They argue that this was in part because Augustine and Aquinas saw God enacting retribution at the final judgment, a motivation to deploy temporal punishment to lead criminals to repentance and conversion.[19] Even today, the *Catechism of the Catholic Church* teaches that "The primary effect of *punishment* is to redress the disorder caused by the offense … it has a medicinal value: as far as possible, it should contribute to the correction of the offender".[20] Generally, the Eastern Church is far less retributivist than the West and prides itself on having avoided what it regards as an unfortunate turn towards legalism in the West.

The classical Christian tradition is not utilitarian, though. Punishment, both God's and that inflicted in the temporal order, was always directed at the sinner for his sin – thus preserving the agent–act–guilt–desert–punishment connection on which retributivism insists. But the rationale for punishment is neither pure desert nor balance but rather the restoration of the sinner and of right relationship. This synthesis was lost when philosophers who rejected classical Christian

17 Ibid., 204–8.

18 Ibid., 84–9; Augustine, "From *Against Faustus*, Book 19", in Oliver O'Donovan and Joan Lockwood O'Donovan, eds., *From Irenaeus to Grotius: A Sourcebook in Christian Political Thought 100–1625* (Grand Rapids: Eerdmans, 1999), 115–16.

19 Tuckness and Parrish, *The Decline of Mercy*, 110, 122.

20 *Catechism of the Catholic Church* (San Francisco: Ignatius Press, 1994), s. 2266.

theology gave us modern retributivism and utilitarianism, but is retained in the view that I call restorative punishment.

20.3 The justice of restorative punishment

Restorative punishment, on a Christian view, reflects justice as set forth by the Bible. Here, justice means – and is translated interchangeably with – righteousness, which, in turn, means right relationship as manifested by God's covenants.[21] Biblical justice, like all justice, has two valences: a state or condition of right relationship; and a process of restoring right relationship with respect to past wrongs. Justice in the Bible virtually converges with another concept of prime theological importance, reconciliation, which also means a restoration of right relationship to a state of right relationship.

Justice in the Bible, I argue, both contrasts and converges with the classic notion of justice rendered as the constant will to render another what is his due. This conception, revolving around the notion of due, entails respect for subjective claim rights as well as deserved punishment (i.e. wrongdoers receiving their due). I hold that whereas justice rightly enfolds these senses of due, biblical justice is wider than these senses. For instance, it involves "wide duties" – such as the duty to assist the poor – whose discharge is open-ended and does not correspond neatly with rights. The Bible even uses the language of justice to describe God's saving act of atonement in Christ, which, again, is not humanity's due.

These features of biblical justice resonate strongly with what has become known as restorative justice. Having arisen in the past generation and been enacted, especially at the community level, in New Zealand, Australia, Great Britain, the United States and elsewhere,[22] restorative justice offers a critique of Western criminal law's emphasis on abstract law, an impersonal State and an inordinate stress on imprisonment, which do little to help offenders, victims or members of a community who have been harmed by crime.[23]

Restorative justice purports to promote human flourishing more widely and fully than do concepts of justice based on desert, due and rights. It can be summarised through three claims. The first is that crime is not only a violation of the law but also a rupture in right relationship among victim, offender and members of the community, and that this rupture can be described through harms, or wounds, to persons and relationships. Second, a community's response to crime ought to aim to repair these relationships with respect to the range of harms that

21 For a good summary of this claim about justice and righteousness, and references to the scholarship behind it, see Marshall, *Beyond Retribution*, 35–7.

22 Here I refer to explicit restorative justice programmes. John Braithwaite argues that restorative justice is the most widespread way of conceiving of justice across history and geography. See John Braithwaite, "Restorative Justice: Assessing Optimistic and Pessimistic Accounts", (1999) 25 *Crime and Justice* 1–127.

23 A classic statement of restorative justice can be found in Howard Zehr, *Changing Lenses: A New Focus for Crime and Justice* (Scottdale, PA: Herald Press, 1990).

the crime has inflicted on its members. Third, this justice involves the active participation of stakeholders – victims, offenders and members of the community – in this work of repair.

Restorative justice is well-suited to the predicament of political orders facing pasts of large-scale injustice, a setting in which wounds are widespread and varied and in which their repair is critical for the prospects of just government and peace. In my book, *Just and Unjust Peace: An Ethic of Political Reconciliation*, I present restorative punishment as bundled with several other practices that also address various and particular wounds: reparation, apology, acknowledgement, forgiveness and the building of just institutions. These practices together make up restorative justice, which is synonymous with reconciliation.

Restorative punishment offers a third way between consequentialist and retributivist approaches, one that aims to combine the best features and avoid the major flaws of both. It draws upon a set of theorists who have also sought to forge such a third way in recent decades, ones whose views of punishment go under names like expressivist, communicative and moral education.[24] Like consequentialism, restorative punishment addresses actual human flourishing, its harm and its repair. Unlike utilitarianism and like retributivism, it preserves the linkage of agent–act–guilt–desert–punishment, and affirms that the principle stating this link is intelligible as a basic one. Restorative punishment recasts the principle, though, so as to be less formal and more substantive. It is no longer exactly "crime deserves punishment" but rather "crimes that wound human flourishing warrant practices that restore this flourishing, ones that take account of the responsibility of the wrongdoer for the damage to right relationship that she has inflicted". Restorative punishment affirms proportionality and the principle "treat likes as likes", but understands these principles as broad and soft, not strict and exacting, and calls for flexibility towards the wide range of ways in which crimes rupture relationship – a range that is especially wide in the context of political transitions.

The Christian basis for restorative punishment lies first in the Old Testament's norms of the Jewish community and Jesus' teachings about how his followers ought to respond to injustice. Broadly, restorative justice can be seen in the broad arc of salvation history, involving God repeatedly restoring his covenant with the people of Israel, the climax of this restoration in the death and resurrection of Jesus Christ, and the ultimate consummation of this restoration in the final judgment and general resurrection, where creation is renewed and restored. This restorative justice is multivalent, involving a judgment upon evil, the vindication of truth, solidarity with victims and the poor, forgiveness, an actual restoration of right relationship and, at every stage, punishment. God disciplines the people

24 Marshall, *Beyond Retribution*; Hampton, "The Moral Education Theory"; Herbert Morris, "A Paternalistic Theory of Punishment", (1981) 18.4 *American Philosophical Quarterly* 263–71; R.A. Duff, *Punishment, Communication, and Community* (New York: Oxford University Press, 2001); Joel Feinberg, *Doing and Deserving: Essays in the Theory of Responsibility* (Princeton: Princeton University Press, 1994).

of Israel through punishment of their sin; Jesus satisfies the demands of punishment on the cross (though through a vicariousness that does not square with retributivism); and God renders ultimate judgment on sinners on the last day. Punishment furthers comprehensive restoration.

20.4 How punishment contributes to the restoration of political orders

Restorative justice, the justice of reconciliation, is enacted in political orders through practices that bring repair to wounds in persons and relationships. These wounds are real diminishments of human flourishing, not abstractions. As one of these practices, restorative punishment aims at repair with respect to several forms of woundedness. The most important of these is what I call the standing victory of injustice.

In committing a political injustice – that is, an unjust act performed towards a political end – a perpetrator violates right relationship with the victim, who holds rights, and with the political community, which properly recognises and upholds these rights. What remains in the aftermath of this injustice are various harms that the act caused, but in every case the ongoing triumph of the perpetrator's deed, which persists unchallenged. This standing victory of injustice is a "moral fact" whose existence is clear to everyone involved. To take an example of a moral fact, if Dave insults Jennifer, he has created a new reality in their relationship, one that now cannot be avoided. Jennifer must now decide how to respond, whether through returning the insult, forgiving it, refusing to talk to Dave or ignoring it – itself a form of response. For his part, Dave may decide to apologise for the insult, try to explain it away, make an excuse for it or stand by it – acts that each presupposes the moral fact that his insult has established.

Examples of victims of human rights violations decrying the standing victory of injustice within political transitions are not hard to find. Such victories are what human rights activists have in mind when they decry "impunity". Hear the words of a Rwandan whose family was killed in the genocide of 1994:

> The problem is that they ask us for reconciliation. It is true that it is necessary, because we can't continue with cyclical massacres. But you feel bad when you see those who killed your family strolling around with impunity. I say this because it is the case for me. I lost all my family in the genocide. My home was destroyed, and I live badly. But I feel bad when I know that the author of all this lives in Kigali. I know that [when he visits] he arrives at night and leaves early the next day [to avoid] arrest. How can I be reconciled with him when he doesn't come to ask my forgiveness or at least to reimburse my goods that he destroyed?[25]

25 Timothy Longman and Théonèste Rutagengwa, "Memory, Identity, and Community in Rwanda", in Eric Stover and Harvey Weinstein, eds., *My Neighbor, My Enemy: Justice and*

What this survivor rues is precisely the "impunity" with which the killer of her family strolls around. She holds out the possibility that a request for forgiveness (i.e. an apology) or reparations could allow her to be reconciled, both actions that would involve the killer addressing the persistent moral fact to which she draws attention. The standing victory of injustice may also be the best way to think about what Chilean human rights activists were seeking to redress when they demanded the prosecution of General Augusto Pinochet long after he had left power and become an infirm elderly man, yet continued to enjoy high honours within Chile. It was these high honours for which they demanded an authoritative counter communication.

This is what judicial punishment does – delivers a communication of censure that purports to bring down, or defeat, the standing victory of injustice. It is critical that this communication be voiced by the State or by a legally established international authority who has the legitimacy to speak and make judgments on behalf of, and to restore, the community's laws. This authoritative censure is directed above all to the perpetrator. The hardship, or deprivation, involved in the punishment is part and parcel of its message, for only an imposed hardship can communicate the gravity of the crime (taking into account soft proportionality). Should the perpetrator accept the punishment willingly, recognising its message, he will effectively participate in the defeat of her injustice – something much like penance in the Christian tradition. Together, the communication of censure and the accompanying hardship are a good and not an evil or harm that is delivered in return for the harm that the injustice caused. The communication is also directed to the victims and to the members of the community, all of whom have a valid interest in the defeat of injustice and the vindication of justice.

Judicial punishment defeats the standing victory of injustice most effectively when it bears two qualities: strong legal authority and popular participation. Strong legal authority is gained through principles that fall under the heading "rule of law" and provides for a fair determination of guilt and punishment. Generally, the human rights tribunals of the past generation have met these standards. More informal forms of punishment such as Rwanda's *gacaca* courts did not, having been hobbled by ill-trained and sometimes illiterate judges and counsel, trials of victims in groups, unreliable witnesses and frequently false testimony. An important achievement of trials is individuation of guilt, culpability and punishment: individuals are not held responsible for the misdeeds of their group. An unbiased distribution of punishment among factions is important, too. When members of only one faction in a civil war are punished, the conflict only deepens.

Popular participation, the other criterion, can add depth to the punishment's message and helps to link punishment with other practices of reconciliation such as apology, truth-telling and forgiveness. Victims, perpetrators and community members alike have an opportunity for their story and their suffering to be heard,

---

Community in the Aftermath of Mass Atrocity (Cambridge: Cambridge University Press, 2004), 162–82.

and often they collaborate in forging and agreeing upon a punishment. Here is enacted the kind of interactive processes that restorative justice often recommends. On this measure, local justice forums such as Rwanda's *gacaca* courts and Timor-Leste's community reconciliation panels perform strongly, and traditional law courts more poorly due to the constraints that their procedures pose.

Legal authority and popular participation, then, stand in some tension. One imperfect solution to this dilemma is to try the most serious and socially devasting crimes – murder, rape and the ordering of atrocities from above – in traditional courts of law, where potentially long prison sentences place a strong premium on rule of law standards. By contrast, "less serious" crimes that are committed in the course of conflict – arson, theft and assault – might be tried in community forums. It is also worth bearing in mind that Rwanda's *gacaca* courts, which did try murder among other crimes, were adopted because of the sheer impracticability of bringing to trial over 100,000 perpetrators of genocide through a prison and court system limited in its capacities. Community forums, then, might be adopted for practical reasons as well as for their benefits for popular participation.

Apart from the standing victory of injustice, there are five other wounds that judicial punishment addresses and that merit brief mention. One wound that secular views of punishment usually overlook but that a Christian perspective takes quite seriously (along with most other religions and Plato) is the wounded soul of the perpetrator. Indeed, a Christian might argue that it is the perpetrator who is damaged most by her crime, without diminishing what the victim has suffered. Philosopher Herbert Morris wrote, "His soul is in jeopardy as his victim's is not".[26] Apart from its intrinsic value, the damaged soul of the perpetrator is important because if neglected, it might lead her to commit future crimes and refuel conflict. Judicial punishment, the community's communication to the perpetrator, invites her to repent and to accept her punishment as a sincere expression of her repentance. The record of judicial punishment in political transitions shows that repentance is most common in community forums where the perpetrator is exposed to the stories of victims and her punishment is oriented towards the repair of the community.

Judicial punishment can also serve to confer recognition on victims, whose public vindication accompanies the defeat of the standing victory of injustice. Next, judicial punishment can elicit the truth about the source and circumstances of injustice, ignorance of which is one of the wounds of injustice. Further, judicial punishment can contribute to the payment of reparations, which can help to alleviate material harm to victims. Finally, the very practice of judicial punishment can give expression to the legitimacy of human rights and the rule of law, which is denied by regimes and conflicts in which human rights are regularly violated.

In all of these respects, judicial punishment enacts the logic of restorative justice, bringing repair to the actual wounds to human flourishing that injustices and violence inflict. Importantly, with respect to these wounds, judicial punishment

26 Morris, "A Paternalistic Theory", 268.

instantiates this repair, performing it through its very enactment, as opposed to bringing it about as a further consequence of punishment. However, it is also possible that judicial punishment can bring about further positive consequences for transitional societies in addition to the repair that it enacts intrinsically. There is no reason why a theory of punishment that is not generally consequentialist may not also welcome the potential positive consequences of social punishment.[27]

These prospective consequences take three forms, which can be assessed empirically. The first is deterrence, which, as we have seen, is a common argument for international tribunals. If Radovan Karadzic is tried and imprisoned in the Hague, it is argued, a potential war criminal in Congo or Burma will think twice before massacring civilians. Empirically, there is almost no evidence for deterrence, and its possibility depends on international enforcement processes that are nowhere in the offing.[28]

Second, it is claimed that punishment advances the rule of law through giving legitimacy to a new regime or peace settlement, through teaching citizens the meaning of law and human rights or through strengthening democratic discourse by stimulating civil public debate. Three empirical studies of trials in the recent global wave of judicial punishment together offer significant but not overwhelming evidence that trials strengthen the rule of law.[29]

A hotly debated question is whether judicial punishment promotes peace in settings of armed conflict. Proponents argue that trials can lend legitimacy to a peace settlement by infusing it with justice, especially when they prosecute criminals from all sides of the conflict. Sceptics argue that trials can undermine peace, especially when they are held before an agreement is concluded, in which case the fear of prosecution creates a disincentive for combatants to sign. While trials following a peace agreement might in theory yield legitimacy, sceptics doubt the possibility of even-handed prosecution. If one faction in the conflict retains power following the peace, its leaders are quite unlikely to allow its own members to be prosecuted. Empirically, the evidence is mixed. In any given case, it is very difficult to tell whether peace would have fared better in the absence of a trial or worse had trials been present where they were in fact absent. This conclusion

27 The point here is parallel to the sense in which a retributivist can welcome purposes of punishment other than retribution – rehabilitation, deterrence, protection, enhancing respect for the rule of law – even while affirming retribution as the central purpose of punishment. In *Just and Unjust Peace*, I distinguish between "primary restorations", which are forms of repair that a practice (e.g. punishment) enacts through its very performance, and "secondary restorations", which are further, additional, consequences that the practice brings in its train. What I am about to explore as "consequences" are what I call "secondary restorations".

28 Hun Joon Kim and Kathryn Sikkink, "Explaining the Deterrence Effect of Human Rights Trials", (2010) 54.4 *International Studies Quarterly* 939–63.

29 Ibid.; Tricia Olsen, Leigh Payne and Andrew Reiter, *Transitional Justice in Balance: Comparing Processes, Weighing Efficacy* (Washington, D.C.: United States Institute of Peace, 2010); Jane Stromseth, David Wippman and Rosa Brooks, eds., *Can Might Make Rights? Building the Rule of Law after Military Interventions* (Cambridge: Cambridge University Press, 2006).

supports neither side of the debate and thus neither adds nor detracts from the moral achievement of judicial punishment.

Closely related to the debate about peace is the most hotly contested issue surrounding judicial punishment, amnesties. The international community detests them. Witness the reaction of Richard Goldstone, the lead prosecutor of the International Criminal Tribunal in Yugoslavia, upon being told that leading Serbian war criminals might be given amnesty: "What politicians have the moral, legal, or political right to forgive people charged with genocide and crimes against humanity – for the deaths of tens of thousands of people – without consulting the victims? I find it abhorrent".[30]

Yet, others argue that amnesties are sometimes critical for bringing a colossally bloody conflict to an end or for effecting a transition to democracy. Amnesty becomes even more appealing when it is conditional upon other practices that contribute to peace such as truth-telling, reparations or apologies – what Mallinder has called a "restorative amnesty".[31] In South Africa's transition from apartheid to multiracial democracy, amnesty was a key component of the agreement by which the apartheid government agreed to leave power and was conditional upon alleged perpetrators' full disclosure of truth as well as reparations – the deal that made possible the renowned Truth and Reconciliation Commission. Political scientists Leslie Vinjamuri and Aaron P. Boesenecker report that out of 77 peace agreements between 1980 and 2006, 30 included amnesty mechanisms and maintain that amnesty facilitated peace in Namibia, Mozambique, El Salvador, Macedonia, Cambodia and Afghanistan.[32] A more recent case, Colombia, can be plausibly added.

How shall a Christian approach of restorative punishment regard amnesty? The importance of judicial punishment to restorative justice delivers a presumption against amnesty. In situations where the prospect appears strong that trials will stand in the way of a peace agreement or a transition to democracy, this presumption may be overridden, though even here, a conditional amnesty ought to be pursued that will facilitate other restorative practices. Amnesty also ought to be as restricted as much as possible, for instance, by allowing for prosecution at a later date. Amnesty must be evaluated case by case, but always carrying the burden of proof.

30 Gary R. Bass, *Stay the Hand of Vengeance: The Politics of War Crimes Tribunals* (Princeton: Princeton University Press, 2000), 243.

31 Louise Mallinder, "Amnesties in the Pursuit of Reconciliation, Peacebuilding, and Restorative Justice", in Jennifer J. Llewellyn and Daniel Philpott, eds., *Restorative Justice, Reconciliation, and Peacebuilding* (Oxford: Oxford University Press, 2014), 138–73.

32 Leslie Vinjamuri and Aaron P. Boesenecker, "Accountability and Peace Agreements: Mapping Trends from 1980–2006", report for the Centre for Humanitarian Dialogue, https://www.hdcentre.org/publications/accountability-and-peace-agreements-mapping-trends-from-1980-2006 (accessed 10 December 2018), 5, 9–11.

20.5 Conclusion: the importance of institutions

Section 20.4 showed how restorative punishment addresses a range of wounds of injustice, most prominently, the standing victory of injustice. This repair of wounds is the hallmark of restorative justice, reflecting its Christian foundations. From Section 20.4 also emerges the insight that the possibilities for restorative punishment are dependent on the fraught realities on the ground in political transitions. As I have argued, restorative punishment (and, more widely, restorative justice) not only finds warrant in Christianity, but also is well-suited to the variegated moral demands of political transitions, in which entire societies are addressing wounds on a large scale and in which punishment ought to accompany the just restorative tasks of making peace, building just institutions, reparation, apology, acknowledgement, the revelation of truth and forgiveness. Persistent social tensions and weak institutions make flexibility all the more imperative.

Much of the ability of judicial punishment to address wide-ranging wounds and to accommodate other restorative practices depends on the institutions through which it is carried out. Traditional courtroom trials, including international tribunals, national courts and hybrid courts, are typically strong in their rule of law standards, carry authority and prestige that enhance the censure of injustices and are best suited to try the perpetrators of the most serious crimes and the architects of atrocity, that is, those who sit atop hierarchies and issue enabling orders. Their weaknesses are a truncated exposure of truth, lack of empathetic acknowledgement of victims and often a remoteness from the populations who wish to see justice and on whose assent the legitimacy of nascent institutions depends.

Community justice forums, for their part, encourage popular participation, a textured revelation of truth, the acknowledgement of victims and their suffering, contrition and apology on the part of perpetrators, forgiveness, a tailoring of punishment to the needs of restoration and the rebuilding of communities whose inhabitants, in many places, have little choice but to live together again. They are weak on procedural standards, often local in their influence and best suited for comparatively less serious crimes.

Perhaps the best recommendation to emerge from this analysis is the development of models of local forums that manifest higher standards of the rule of law and are enabled to take on more serious crimes in a responsible fashion. Trials of the leading masterminds of atrocity, though, ought to be reserved for the highest-level courts, which communicate censure, deliver punishment and depose the standing victory of injustice most authoritatively. Here, Christian restorative punishment converges most with the international community's Nuremberg Dream.

Further reading

Llewellyn, Jennifer and Daniel Philpott, eds. *Restorative Justice, Reconciliation, and Peacebuilding* (Oxford: Oxford University Press, 2014).

Lu, Catherine. *Justice and Reconciliation in World Politics* (Cambridge: Cambridge University Press, 2017).

Marshall, Christopher D. *Beyond Retribution: A New Testament Vision for Justice, Crime and Punishment* (Grand Rapids: Eerdmans, 2001).
Murphy, Colleen. *A Moral Theory of Political Reconciliation* (Cambridge: Cambridge University Press, 2010).
Murphy, Colleen. *The Conceptual Foundations of Transitional Justice* (Cambridge: Cambridge University Press, 2017).
Murphy, Jeffrie and Jean Hampton. *Forgiveness and Mercy* (Cambridge: Cambridge University Press, 1988).
Philpott, Daniel. *Just and Unjust Peace: An Ethic of Political Reconciliation* (Oxford: Oxford University Press, 2012).
Tutu, Desmond. *No Future Without Forgiveness* (New York: Random House, 1999).
Volf, Miroslav. *Exclusion and Embrace: A Theological Exploration of Identity, Otherness, and Reconciliation* (Nashville: Abingdon Press, 1996).
Zehr, Howard. *Changing Lenses: Restorative Justice for Our Times* (Harrisonburg, VA: Herald Press, 2015).

21 The weight of judgment

Nathan S. Chapman

Christianity entails a call to discipleship, an ethic of following and becoming like Jesus Christ. This poses a quandary for Christians who participate in the government's exercise of criminal judgment: how can a follower of Jesus, who taught his disciples to "turn the other cheek" and who himself was unjustly convicted by a Roman kangaroo court, participate in the State's punishment of wrongdoers? Most of this volume has proceeded from the assumption that Christianity is at least compatible with criminal law, if not supportive of it. But is following Christ compatible with the violence, and inevitable mistakes, of criminal judgment?

Christians have given different answers through the centuries. Early Christians, German Anabaptists and contemporary Christian pacifists have concluded that discipleship precludes participation in the government's machinery of criminal judgment. The classical view, restated by the Protestant Reformers and many contemporary theologians, is the "two-swords" or "two-kingdoms" view of human authority. God has given authority to the temporal government to punish wrongdoing, and has given separate authority to the Church to make disciples. Although Christians should not avenge personal grievances, they may, indeed should, participate in God's use of the civil authority to avenge wrongdoing. Although both of these views have deep roots in Scripture, tradition and theology, they appear to be mutually exclusive. Christians may either participate in the government's exercise of criminal judgment, or they may not.

The government's exercise of criminal judgment, in particular, is an apt focal point for ethical inquiry. The New Testament plainly states that God authorises temporal rulers to judge wrongdoers (Rom. 13:1–8). Christians in a liberal democracy find it difficult, if not impossible, to avoid participating in criminal judgment at some level. The duty to vote or to serve on a criminal jury turns even a decision to *not* participate in criminal judgment into an affirmative act with meaningful repercussions on the criminal justice system. Yet, the government's exercise of criminal judgment is not as morally unproblematic as many two-kingdom theorists suggest. Criminal judgment is not only inherently imperfect in all the ways familiar to scholars, practitioners and victims; human government itself, though used by God, strains against the yoke of Christ. Those called into a kingdom of self-giving love must yet bear the weight of temporal judgment.

This chapter begins by explaining and critiquing the separatist and two-kingdoms theories. Based on this critique, the chapter argues that Christians may participate in criminal judgment consistent with discipleship. The theological premises that reorient a Christian's participation in criminal judgment are that temporal government is the locus of ongoing rebellion from God and that, as an act of grace, God nevertheless uses that government to mitigate the effects of that rebellion. It is a gracious stop-gap for a season of human rejection of God's rule, not an inherent aspect of human society with God. The chapter then explores three ways that this understanding of government should shape a Christian's participation in criminal judgment. Because Christians have modest hopes for the criminal justice system, they are free to acknowledge its shortcomings, including their own shortcomings within it, and to insist on *truthfulness* – about law, facts and motives. Because Christians are called to witness to the free gift of God's mercy in Christ, they are likewise called to explore avenues of *mercy* within the criminal justice system that declare God's kingdom and make space for it to flourish. And because Christians long for the conclusion of judgment in God's eternal society, they endure the imperfections of criminal judgment as a form of *suffering* that facilitates faith, hope and love.

21.1 "Separatist" and "two-kingdoms" ethics

The central principle of Christian discipleship is the call of Jesus: "If any want to become my followers, let them deny themselves and take up their cross and follow me" (Mark 8:34; see also Matt. 10:38, 16:24; Luke 9:23, 14:27; Rom. 8:30; Gal. 5:24, 6:14).[1] Christ declared that his kingdom was "not of this world", forgave rather than punished wrongdoers and declined the use of force to defend himself from unjust punishment. Likewise, his followers are "called" to "follow in his footsteps" of enduring suffering for doing right (1 Pet. 2:21). Christians should expect that the government, under the influence of spiritual forces opposed to God, will sometimes persecute them (Rev. 13; see also 2 Tim. 3:12).

Yet, the New Testament makes it clear that God uses earthly government to punish wrongdoers. Christ instructed his followers to "Give to the emperor the things that are the emperor's, and to God the things that are God's" (Mark 12:17). While the Apostle Paul exhorts the Christians at Rome to "never avenge yourselves, but leave room for the wrath of God" (Rom. 12:19; see also 1 Cor. 6:1–6), he likewise explains that the government "[has] been instituted by God" (Rom. 13:1) and "is the servant of God to execute wrath on the wrongdoer" (Rom. 13:4; see also 1 Pet. 2:13–17).

The tension between forsaking vengeance and trusting that God uses the government to execute wrath raises a question: may a follower of Jesus participate in the government's exercise of criminal judgment? Christians have generally answered the question in two ways. Many Christians have believed that, although

1 All scriptural citations are to the New Revised Standard Version.

God uses the government for wrath, disciples of Jesus must not participate in it. The early Church, a small but growing minority within the Roman Empire, was ambivalent about whether Christians could serve as magistrates or soldiers (those responsible for executing criminal law). Some Christian bishops refused baptism to magistrates and soldiers.[2] After Constantine made Christianity the empire's official religion, Christian leaders such as Ambrose and Augustine maintained that Christians could serve as magistrates, but urged them to exercise mercy.[3] Through the mediaeval era, the "religious" orders – monks and nuns – largely eschewed violence out of personal piety.

The Protestant Reformation rekindled an interest in discipleship among lay people. *The Schleitheim Articles*, adopted by German Anabaptists in 1527, proclaimed that "The sword is an ordering of God outside the perfection of Christ". Although the sword "punishes and kills the wicked and guards and protects the good", "within the perfection of Christ only the ban [excommunication] is used for the admonition and exclusion of the one who has sinned".[4] The principal reason a Christian may not "hold a position of governmental authority" is that "Christ should have been made a king, but he rejected this", so "we should do likewise and follow him".[5] Anabaptists across Europe and the United States maintain this tradition.

In the past half-century, several influential American theologians have made the case for one or another form of Christian pacifism. They seek to remind Christians that the Church is called to bear witness to a kingdom that eschews violence in favour of patience, forgiveness and unjust suffering.[6] While Christian pacifists rarely directly address the extent to which a Christian may participate in criminal judgment, a commitment to non-violence implies that Christians may not participate in a process that is inherently physically coercive. We shall return in a moment to the difficulties this raises for Christians in liberal democracies.

The mainstream view of Western Christians since the fourth century has been that Christians may – and in many cases should – serve as a minister of the government in criminal judgment. Christian thinkers have articulated the conceptual relationship between temporal society and the Church in various ways, but most have maintained that God authorises the temporal government and the Church

2 See Oliver O'Donovan and Joan Lockwood O'Donovan, "The Patristic Age", in Oliver O'Donovan and Joan Lockwood O'Donovan, eds., *From Irenaeus to Grotius: A Sourcebook in Christian Political Thought 100–1625* (Grand Rapids: Wm. B. Eerdmans, 1999), 2–3.

3 Ambrose of Milan, "Letter 50", in ibid., 83–4; Augustine of Hippo, "Letter 153", in ibid., 119–31.

4 "The Brotherly Agreement of Some Children of God Concerning Seven Articles", in ibid., 635.

5 Ibid.

6 See John Howard Yoder, *The Politics of Jesus* (Grand Rapids: Wm. B. Eerdmans, 1994); Stanley Hauerwas, *The Peaceable Kingdom: A Primer in Christian Ethics* (Notre Dame: University of Notre Dame Press, 2016); Richard B. Hays, *The Moral Vision of the New Testament: Community, Cross, New Creation: A Contemporary Introduction to New Testament Ethics* (San Francisco: HarperOne, 1996).

as "two swords" or "two kingdoms" with different yet compatible ends. After Constantine made Christianity the official religion of the empire, an increasing number of officials and magistrates were Christians. Many took it for granted that a Christian could serve as a magistrate. Indeed, in a society in which the vast majority are baptised, who else would do so? Some focused instead on *how* a Christian should exercise judgment, emphasising, as did Ambrose and Augustine, the call to exercise mercy.

As Richard Hooker argued in the late sixteenth century, the commonwealth and the Church are by nature distinct societies. They have different origins, purposes and ends. But this does not mean they must be composed of different persons. In a commonwealth composed of Christians, these societies will overlap. As the commonwealth and Church have different functions and purposes, so their members have different functions and purposes when they serve variously as magistrates and church members.[7] As a member of the commonwealth, a Christian may carry out criminal punishment against one who has violated the commonwealth's law. As a follower of Christ, however, the same Christian must decline revenge against one who harmed her. Drawing on Augustine, Luther and Calvin, most Catholic and Protestant theorists continue to articulate some version of this "two-kingdoms" view.[8]

Christians in liberal democracies are in a historically unique situation. Like the early Christians, many are a minority in a society that gives little to honour God. It is unsurprising that some find pacifism or other forms of social "retreat" attractive.[9] The separatist view emphasises the demands of Christian discipleship as an alternative to capitulating to an increasingly non-Christian culture. In a society of functional specialisation, it may seem relatively easy to avoid participating in the State's exercise of violence: simply decline to serve as a government official.

Unfortunately, the separatist view goes beyond what Scripture demands. The New Testament forbids Christians from taking vengeance themselves, but enjoins them to pray for and to financially support those whom God uses to exact his vengeance. Separatists do not give a convincing case for why Christians could not participate in the government's exercise of criminal judgment, since doing so is implementing God's vengeance, not their own.[10] Indeed, there is a case to be

7 Richard Hooker, *Of the Laws of Ecclesiastical Polity*, ed. Arthur Stephen McGrade (Cambridge: Cambridge University Press, 1994), 132–4.

8 See, e.g. Oliver O'Donovan, *The Ways of Judgment* (Grand Rapids: Wm. B. Eerdmans, 2005), 85; David VanDrunen, "Justice Tempered by Forbearance: Why Christian Love Is an Improper Category to Apply to Civil Law", in Robert F. Cochran, Jr. and Zachary R. Calo, eds, *Agape, Justice, and Law: How Might Christian Love Shape Law?* (Cambridge: Cambridge University Press, 2018), 144–5.

9 See Rod Dreher, *The Benedict Option: A Strategy for Christians in a Post-Christian Nation* (New York: Sentinel, 2017).

10 See John Calvin, *Institutes of the Christian Religion*, ed. John T. McNeill, trans. Ford Lewis Battles, 2 vols. (Philadelphia: Westminster Press, 1960), 4.20.10, 12, 18–20.

made that participating in the government's exercise of judgment on behalf of society is a form of love.[11]

The separatist view likewise fails to account for the political responsibility of members of liberal democracies. All members have a political duty to participate in criminal judgment by voting for representatives who will make criminal law and for prosecutors and judges who will enforce it. Many may vote directly on legislative referenda that would have an effect on criminal judgment, or to serve on a grand jury or criminal trial jury. Some are members of the criminal justice system by profession – lawyers, police officers, judges, prison officials and the like. These tasks are what Christians in liberal democracies owe to their political communities, along with taxes, honour and prayer. Why should Christians ask God to use their neighbours to protect society without lifting a finger to do so themselves?

While the two-kingdoms view rightly holds that a Christian may participate in the government's exercise of criminal judgment, its advocates sometimes ignore the difference that following Jesus ought to make. Consider Oliver O'Donovan's account in *The Ways of Judgment*. O'Donovan's thesis is that God authorises the secular government to do one thing: judgment. For O'Donovan, judgment includes the specification, identification, regulation and punishment of wrong-doing.[12] Central to his theory is the view that persons may engage in judgment only in their official capacity – not as private persons. His clearest direction to Christians who participate in secular judgment is a quote from Martin Luther: "Do you want to know what your duty is as a prince or a judge or a lord or a lady, with people under you? You do not have to ask Christ about your duty".[13]

O'Donovan's engagement with Scripture downplays government's ambiguous relationship to human morality. He says nothing about Genesis 3, which depicts "the knowledge of good and evil", i.e. human morality, as the fruit of deception, distrust and rebellion. He considers the city founded by Cain, the first murderer, as a provision of God's protective grace, rather than an act of continued faithlessness and rebellion (Gen. 4).[14] O'Donovan ignores 1 Corinthians 6, where Paul chastises the church at Corinth for taking a property dispute before secular judges. He does not wrestle with Christ's forswearing of violence, even in the face of an unjust arrest and conviction. Romans 13 apparently provides all he needs to know about a Christian's role in government: when the Christian acts as a governmental officer, he acts with God's authority to enter judgment; when he acts as a private party, he must "judge not".[15]

11 Paul Ramsey, *Basic Christian Ethics* (Louisville: Westminster/John Knox Press, 1993), 182: "One should do for others what one may not do for one's self". See also Rom. 12:9–21, 13:8–14; Lev. 19:11–17.

12 O'Donovan, *Ways of Judgment*, 5–8.

13 Ibid., 85 (quoting Luther's commentary on the Sermon on the Mount).

14 O'Donovan, *Ways of Judgment*, 66.

15 Ibid., 85.

O'Donovan admits that governmental judgment may be "shaped by the presence of a society [the Church] in which redemption is taking effect and assuming a social form" and thus "point indirectly to the living hope of which [secular judgment] cannot speak directly".[16] How might the Church "shape" secular judgment? One way, surely, would be through the participation of Christians. Yet, O'Donovan suggests that Christ's call has little – perhaps nothing – to say about how Christians ought to do so. In the wheels of secular judgment, Christians and non-Christians are interchangeable cogs. The view that there is nothing distinctive about Christian participation in government is altogether unsatisfying in light of the polyphonic witness of Scripture and the Church through the ages to the unique call of Christians "to do justice, to love kindness, and to walk humbly with your God" (Micah 6:8; see also Zech. 8:16).

The remainder of this chapter sketches an outline of a Christian ethics of participating in government with an eye for concrete implications for criminal judgment. Christians who participate in government should work to approximate truthfulness; seek opportunities to exercise mercy; and suffer the imperfection of human judgment. While all of these practices entail the development and exercise of the spiritual virtues of faith, hope and love, this chapter unfortunately cannot provide a more thorough exploration of the relationship between these virtues and those of truthfulness, mercy and suffering.[17]

21.2 A "two-kingdoms" genealogy, with ethical implications

All is not as it should be, or will be. Outside of Christ, whose government is one of self-giving love, human government has a sordid past, a challenging present and no future. According to the Genesis account, God made humans to live under God's gracious rule. God gave humans "dominion", or lordship, over creation, but not over one another. God gave them one rule: do not eat the fruit of the tree of the knowledge of good and evil. That fruit – the knowledge of good and evil – was not meant to be part of the human experience. Instead, God made people for faithful obedience, life with one another and with God, and care for creation.[18] Human judgment – the act of distinguishing right from wrong – is only fully human when it flows from loving obedience to God.

Craving equality with God, Genesis continues, humans disobeyed. They gained "the knowledge of good and evil" and lost intimacy with God, with one another and with all of creation (Gen. 3; Rom. 1–2). According to the New Testament

16 Ibid., 88.

17 See, e.g. Charles Mathewes, *A Theology of Public Life* (Cambridge: Cambridge University Press, 2007); L. Gregory Jones, *Transformed Judgment: Toward a Trinitarian Account of the Moral Life* (Notre Dame: University of Notre Dame Press, 1990).

18 Human "dominion" over creation (Gen. 1) should be understood in light of Christ's explanation and example that true "lordship" is service of others (Mark 10:41–44).

and the Christian tradition, this story depicts why, and how, all humans are sinful, their wills bent away from God and towards themselves. The very act of pursuing morality, because it comes at the cost of abandoning their Creator in distrust, destroys their capacity to judge rightly.[19]

Genesis recounts the origin of human government only in light of the perversion of human judgment. The man and woman's first son, Cain, murders his younger brother, Abel, out of jealousy for God's favour. Cain admits he deserves death, but God mercifully preserves Cain even as he punishes him. God curses Cain from the ground, so that he will be destined to roam the earth, but places a mark upon him so no-one will avenge Abel's murder. In light of the foregoing story of the fall, and of God's continuing attempt to reclaim a relationship with creation, the mark is best understood as an invitation for Cain to trust God. Yet, Cain rejects this invitation. Rather than wander the earth, trusting God's protection, Cain founds the first city. From Cain springs all of the cultural arts. His grandson, Lamech, boasts that in his might he will disproportionately avenge any harm done to him, completing the rejection of God's protection-in-judgment. Thus, Augustine identifies Cain as the founder of the earthly "city", the society of those who remain alienated from God, seeking the joy of God's city in all the wrong places.[20]

Scripture thus presents the origin and ends of human government as a rejection of God's rule – not only because government protects the innocent against the wrongdoing that springs from human sinfulness, but also because government itself arises from a rejection of God's offer of protection and vengeance. Human government is not only a result of, but is also a part of, the "futility" to which God has subjected creation because of human sinfulness.

Yet, this is not the last word. Scripture throughout insists that God uses human government, despite its inherent rebelliousness, for God's purposes. God declared to Noah the principle that God would demand punishment of those who take human life, and apparently authorised humans to effect that punishment (Gen. 9). God called the children of Abraham, Isaac and Jacob, giving them the law as a moral guide and as a means of re-entering a relationship of faithfulness. God raised up judges and kings to enforce the law and protect them from enemies. When Israel and Judah were unfaithful, God used heathen empires to execute judgment upon them, to correct them and to rebuild Jerusalem. God's prophets promised a future leader, whose "delight shall be in the fear of the Lord", and who "shall not judge by what his eyes see, or decide by what his ears hear; but with righteousness he shall judge the poor, and decide with equity for the meek of the earth" (Isaiah 11:3–4). The New Testament declares that Jesus was this promised judge (Luke 4:21).

19 See Nathan S. Chapman, "Law Asks for Trust", (2011) 85.2 *St. John's Law Review* 521–43.

20 Augustine, *The City of God Against the Pagans*, ed. and trans. R.W. Dyson (Cambridge: Cambridge University Press, 2002), 15.17.

The New Testament does not speak unambiguously, however, to Christians who may bear responsibility for human government.[21] Christ clearly distinguished between duties owed to the emperor and to God, admonishing his followers to give to each his due. And he told his disciples to give up everything to follow him. He inaugurated a kingdom of peace and righteousness through the power of the Holy Spirit rather than through physical coercion. He and his apostles suffered violent and unjust punishment for their commitment to the kingdom of God. Revelation presents human empire as an ongoing threat to the people of God, a "beast" and a "harlot" raging, like Cain and Lamech, opposed to God's good rule. Yet, the Apostle Paul insisted that, though Christians were not to avenge themselves, God would exercise vengeance against wrongdoers through the existing governmental authorities. Therefore, Christians were to pay taxes, and to honour and pray for officials. Yet, it seems equally clear that "earthly polities", in God's ordering of human affairs, are "stop-gaps".[22] The government executes God's wrath against wrongdoers, but will not survive the resurrection of the dead, the final judgment or the recreation of all things. Although used by God for penultimate judgment, government is premised upon, and composed of, human judgment that rejects the fear of the Lord and that will eventually be subsumed into a wave of perpetual worship in the new creation.

This genealogy of human government is decidedly less sanguine than that of many two-kingdoms theorists. Human judgment, and the government it has birthed, is soaked in self-love, wretchedly disordered. There is a radical difference between God's judgment in Christ, who judges with righteousness and equity, and the attempt of humans to save themselves through a political community apart from faithful obedience. Yet, God uses human judgment not only in the woof and warp of salvation history, as a dramatic backdrop for Israel's faithlessness, the Incarnation and the apocalypse, but also to execute God's own vengeance against wrongdoers. Christians are called to see this farrago for what it is, and to participate, in whatever way God calls them to do so, accordingly.

In some ways, liberal democracies today require very little of most Christians. Those who are categorically opposed to fighting may be excused from military service. Those who cannot conscientiously sit in judgment may likewise be exempt from jury duty. (Indeed, in the United States, those who object to the death penalty are ineligible to serve on a capital jury.) No-one must vote. Taxes, of course, are certain.

Yet, these governments *ask* for citizens to participate in government – including the criminal justice system – far more extensively than the vast majority of governments through history. Christians must choose whether to vote. At the moment, the U.S. House of Representatives has passed, and the Senate is considering, a bill that would dramatically reduce sentences for many federal crimes.

21 See Chapter 10 this volume, Nathan S. Chapman, "Christianity and Crimes Against the State", pp. 153–169.

22 Robert W. Jenson, *Systematic Theology*, vol. 2 (Oxford: Oxford University Press, 1999), 76.

Some Senators oppose the bill, fearful of backlash from their constituents. Christian voters, therefore, have a very real effect on the contours of the criminal justice system – whether they abstain, or whether they express support or opposition for sentencing reform. In some cases, voters have an even more direct say over legislation that would affect criminal justice. Voters in Florida, for instance, recently passed a ballot initiative that lifted restrictions on the voting rights of felons. And, of course, jurors play an integral role in the disposition of criminal cases. Lawyers, judges and other government officials play an even more intimate and extensive role in criminal judgment.

Given the ubiquity of a liberal democracy's call for citizens to participate in criminal judgment, the question for Christians is not whether, but how to participate. The remainder of this chapter considers three ways that Christians may participate in governmental judgment with faith that human government is not only bent away from God in self-love, but also used by God as an instrument of judgment. For each – truthfulness, mercy and suffering – the chapter considers concrete applications to criminal justice.

21.3 Truthfulness in judgment

As God has established government for vengeance, it should strive "within the limits of human understanding, [to] judge of a thing as God has judged of it".[23] This entails speaking truthfully about what acts the community should consider to be wrong, and entering judgment that squares with the law and the facts of a case. A commitment to truthfulness in judgment is commonplace in Western jurisprudence, yet the imperfectability of human judgment has important implications for the Christian's participation in criminal judgment.

Christians can witness to the reasons, and all of the ways, that human judgment is untruthful. Every government is composed of those whose "knowledge of good and evil" is twisted. In many cases, humans struggle to know right from wrong. Divine law, natural law and virtues of practical judgment go only so far. As Paul understood and Augustine elaborated, human perception is broken, turned inward by disordered desire. Every political community's will is bent towards idols, whether of freedom, wealth, security, equality or glory. With all others, Christians bear these weaknesses, groaning towards repentance and the healing of their desires. Christians have no monopoly on the non-spiritual virtues of truthfulness, equity and judgment that make for a relatively just society. Yet, because they know the origins, and the ends, of government, the citizens of the eternal city may serve the secular community's good without trusting it for their salvation, and thus without pushing it beyond its ken.

Christians should take care to develop and exercise the virtues of truthfulness.[24] As those freed from the tyranny of self-justification, Christians may see and speak

23 O'Donovan, *Ways of Judgment*, 16.
24 Bernard Williams, *Truth and Truthfulness* (Princeton: Princeton University Press, 2004).

truthfully about their own sinfulness and the sinfulness of their communities. This is a starting point for helping their communities exercise judgment in particular cases as truthfully as possible. Take, for instance, sentencing reform in the United States. Many white Christians have failed to speak honestly about their political community's responsibility for slavery, Jim Crow, housing segregation, the secularisation of social welfare and the effects of these historical and ongoing injustices on persons of colour. Besides a scandal to the Church, this is a failure of truthfulness in judgment. Christians must participate in the local and national conversations about sentencing and prison reform with a candour made possible by Christ's offer of forgiveness, and with an insistence on the spiritual and moral equality of all people on the basis not only of God's love, but also of God's coming judgment in Christ.

Christians must also insist on truthful judgment in particular cases. Criminal judgment should accord with the community's moral norms, should identify what happened as accurately as possible and should sincerely apply the community's norms to what happened. Consider each in turn.

Christians who participate in the law-making process should strive to ensure that the criminal law, and the sanctions the government imposes for violations, accord as much as possible with the community's moral norms. This should take into account, as discussed above, the community's particular moral shortcomings. What about a court in particular – what is its responsibility for determining a community's moral norms and implementing them in criminal judgment? This is a question about the court's role within the political community, about the extent to which the community has authorised it to make, rather than merely to apply, the law. At a minimum, the criminal procedural apparatus in most jurisdictions allows for prosecutors, judges, sentencing officers and juries all to play a role in implementing the community's moral norms, often at different stages of judgment. Prosecutors investigate cases based on the community's policing priorities and pursue charges (and plea agreements) based on the community's punitive priorities. Judges (and sometimes juries) implement the community's moral norms, according to law, by assigning a sentence.

Christian judges and jurors must also strive to enter judgment based on an accurate account of what happened, i.e. the facts of a case. Many procedural and evidentiary rules of the Anglo-American criminal jury trial are meant, in part, to facilitate accurate judgment. Some are meant to reduce the effects of bias, even as they reduce the availability of evidence that may be relevant to determining the facts. The result is an elaborate social process for approximating accurate judgments in the run of cases, though the process itself may obscure the historical facts in any given case. With others, Christians should pursue the calibration of rules of procedure and evidence most likely to generate accurate knowledge about past events, even as they take account of the inevitable shortcomings of human intellect and judgment. As they participate in individual cases, Christians should model a commitment to rigorous presentation and examination of the evidence of a case, sensitive of the sinful tendency of advocates to exaggerate, judges to grow impatient and jurors to grow weary. As often as not, the enemy of truthfulness in criminal judgment is not *insincerity* on the part of those participating in the system of justice, but the myriad temptations to cut corners on a careful evaluation of evidence from time pressures and lack of intellectual focus.

A particular practice of the American criminal justice system warrants careful consideration on this score. The vast majority of criminal charges now end in a plea bargain. The defendant confesses guilt to one or more charges rather than take the case to trial. In exchange, the prosecutor drops some charges, recommends a reduced sentence or both. In most cases, the prosecutor has had virtually unfettered discretion in selecting the charges (though the defendant may have been indicted by a grand jury). The prosecutor has little time for trial and, depending on the facts of the case, trial may present the defendant with little but the risk of a more onerous sentence. The court enters judgment by accepting the prosecutor and defendant's bargain, by giving it the weight of law and sometimes by assigning a sentence. Unsurprisingly, studies suggest that in many cases a plea bargain does not reflect a truthful application of law to the defendant's conduct.[25] At best, it reflects a cost–benefit analysis by both parties. At worst, an abuse of power.

Christians should accordingly be sceptical of the breadth of the practice of plea bargains. No system of judgment should countenance procedures that so manifestly exacerbate the weaknesses of human intellect and will by incentivising exaggerated charges and false confessions. The foundational rule of the common law was that no-one could be a judge in his or her own case. Plea bargains put the parties in the judge's place, with predictable results for judgment's reliability. When criminal convictions eschew accurate judgment, not only do they fail to reflect the community's moral norms, but they also make it impossible for the community to accurately assess the effect of those norms on society. Plea bargains mask the costs of enforcing those norms, in dollars and cents, and in human suffering.

Relatedly, truthful judgment requires prosecutors, judges and juries to sincerely apply the community's norms. The judgment must accord with the participant's own view of the case. Prosecutors have a unique responsibility within the unfolding of judgment. When a prosecutor enters a charge without believing that the defendant committed the crime, the prosecutor exercises that responsibility insincerely, a failure of truthfulness.

Recently, prosecutors and defendants have colluded to present a new temptation to judges: "fictional plea bargains".[26] The prosecutor and defendant agree that the charges to which the defendant is confessing are inaccurate – the

25 See Lucian E. Dervan, "The Innocent Defendant's Dilemma: An Innovative Empirical Study of Plea Bargaining's Innocence Problem", (2013) 103.1 *Journal of Criminal Law and Criminology* 1–48.

26 See Mark Sullivan, "Opinion Letter re: *Commonwealth of Virginia v. Ayala, Case No. FE-2018-541*", 20 July 2018; Thea Johnson, "Fictional Pleas", (forthcoming) *Indiana Law Journal*.

defendant is not in fact guilty of them. They then present it for the judge's approval. Aside from the inaccuracy of these deals, they also seek to implicate the court in a fraud on the public – a judgment that not even the judge believes to be true. Among other problems, such untruthfulness is inconsistent with the role of a judge, who takes an oath to uphold the law. Such insincerity likely springs from a systemic problem that may be frustrating judgment in the run of cases. The judge's business is to identify and ameliorate problems within the judicial system, not to exacerbate them with phony shortcuts.

21.4 Three facets of mercy

In addition to striving for truthful judgment, Christians are also called to "love kindness", traditionally translated as "mercy" (Micah 6:8). The Old and New Testaments emphasise God's care for the vulnerable, and call God's followers to do the same. Yet, the call to "do justice" and to "love mercy" raises an important question about how the two are related. One conception of mercy is that it is a departure from just deserts. God's justification of sinners in Christ, for instance, is in spite of their merit, not because of it. Some two-kingdoms theorists thus argue that the government, authorised to do justice, should have nothing to do with mercy, which is a departure from its demands.[27] Alternatively, some conceive of mercy as the reduction of punishment based on mitigating facts. As Jeffrie Murphy has rightly noted, however, this is best understood as an aspect of equity, a demand of *justice*, understood as the requirement to give each his due. "In short: mercy is either a vice (unjust) or redundant (a part of justice)".[28] For now, rather than attempting to sort out the true or best meaning of mercy based on Scripture or logic, I would like to briefly explore three facets of the call to "love mercy": mercy as equity; mercy as forgiveness; and mercy as compassion for the needy.

Christian theorists agree that those responsible for criminal judgment should temper that judgment with equity. Judgment should take account of mitigating facts. As William Perkins explained in the late sixteenth century, Christian judgment does not insist on the most rigorous punishment the law permits; it rather looks sympathetically for the mildest possible application of the law, consistent with the demands of justice.[29] As discussed above, this form of "mercy" is, strictly speaking, a requirement of justice, of *accuracy* in judgment. It has nothing to do with whether the offender is repentant, apologises or the like.

Perhaps the most well-known example of the exercise of mercy-as-equity is in sentencing. Courts have historically taken mitigating (and aggravating) factors into account when deciding a sentence that must ordinarily fall within a

27 O'Donovan, *Ways of Judgment*, 98–100; VanDrunen, "Justice Tempered by Forbearance".
28 Jeffrie G. Murphy, "Mercy and Legal Justice", (1986) 4.1 *Social Philosophy and Policy* 5–6.
29 William Perkins, "A Treatise of Christian Equitie", in O'Donovan and O'Donovan, *From Irenaeus to Grotius*, 772–7.

statutorily prescribed range. Some jurisdictions publish detailed guidelines to ensure that like cases are treated alike, that a court will not take a mitigating factor into account in one case and not in another, either deliberately or subconsciously. Inevitably, one's view of the goal of punishment, whether it is to be principally retributive, deterrent or restorative, influences one's view of which factors ought to mitigate judgment. Most jurisdictions today base punishment on a variety of these purposes and so allow courts to take a variety of factors into account. Christians involved in criminal sentencing, including prosecutors, judges and, in some jurisdictions, jurors, should reckon mitigating factors with what Jeffrie Murphy, elsewhere in this collection of essays, calls the virtue of humility. This entails paying "attention" to those who inhabit different circumstances, "the recognition of one's own luck" and "empathy". It involves remaining "open to the possibility that the offender has failed us because to some degree we have failed him".[30]

Where the law no longer reflects the community's moral norms, Christians should be attuned to the possibility of institutional responses that structurally affect mercy-as-equity. Consider the English criminal jury during the early modern era. Death was the only punishment for many serious crimes, so the jury often acquitted or convicted of lesser offences, probably because the jurors believed the punishment for the charged crime too harsh.[31] An executive officer may grant clemency or pardon for much the same reason. This is not mercy per se. It is rather a reflection that the lawful punishments are out of step with the community's moral sense. Such judgments, though inaccurate about the legal description of what happened, may nevertheless accurately reflect the community's judgment, by telling the truth about the gravity of the offence. These may be understood as structural, rather than individual, exercises of equity. When they are systematic, they call for a revision of the law to better approximate the community's moral norms. The current sentencing reform movement in the United States likely reflects a laudable attention to the demands of mercy-as-equity.

Christian theorists tend to disagree more about whether mercy-as-forgiveness has any place in secular judgment. For these theorists, the Christian call to forgive one's enemies and forego vengeance belongs to the realm of personal relationships. Christians who serve as governmental officers have a responsibility as such to exercise judgment and forego forgiveness. This presumes, however, that a political society could not, or perhaps should not, authorise officials to exercise forgiveness on its behalf in at least some cases. Put differently, supposing God authorises the government for vengeance, does it necessarily follow that the government may not exercise mercy-as-forgiveness? The answer turns on a

30 In Chapter 17 this volume, Jeffrie G. Murphy, "Punishment, Forgiveness and Mercy", pp. 269–282.

31 John H. Langbein, Renée Lettow Lerner and Bruce P. Smith, eds., *History of the Common Law: The Development of Anglo-American Legal Institutions* (New York: Aspen, 2009), 622–9.

more comprehensive analysis of the meaning and purpose of the "vengeance" for which God uses the government (is it strictly retributive, etc.) and on the meaning of mercy-as-forgiveness.

The Anglo-American criminal justice system has historically incorporated a semblance, at least, of mercy-as-forgiveness into the executive pardon power. Separate from the judgment and sentencing phases, the executive, usually at the suggestion of the judge or an executive committee, has the authority to issue a pardon which absolves the offender of legal guilt. Depending on the jurisdiction, the officer may issue the pardon before or after conviction. Would it be possible for Christian norms to guide executive pardons? God's forgiveness is offered freely to all who look to Christ for their salvation. Should pardons be equally available to all who show true repentance and remorse (assuming the officers can reliably assess sincerity)? What of the demands of justice? What if the offender, though truly repentant and remorseful, remains a threat? If not repentance and forgiveness, then what? As Al Alschuler has noted in an essay in this volume, U.S. presidents have recently reserved pardons mostly for political allies.[32] Christian forgiveness proceeds upon the presumption of enmity, not friendship. Christians should give more thought to whether, and how, society should exercise the virtues of mercy-as-forgiveness. As I will discuss below, the tension between the competing demands for government to do justice and for Christians to forgive poses a challenge for those called to both.

In the biblical tradition, in addition to the forgiveness of debt, mercy may also refer to empathy and acts of compassion towards the needy and vulnerable.[33] A criminal justice system that seeks to implement this notion of mercy would carefully craft and enforce laws designed to protect vulnerable populations, and would execute punishment in a way that respects the dignity of offenders and makes space for their reformation.

The Fourteenth Amendment of the United States Constitution requires states to provide the "equal protection of the laws". The motivation for this provision was the protection of recently freed blacks in the South after the Civil War. The former Confederate states had enacted black codes to institute legal apartheid. Private groups like the Ku Klux Klan, often counting government officials among their members, committed atrocities against blacks to terrorise the black community into submission. Officials winked at the wrongdoing. One of the principal purposes of the Equal Protection Clause was to require state governments to extend the protection of the law – not only of legal rights but also the enforcement of the law – to the black community. While the provision has never been used to this full effect (indeed, evidence suggests that black Americans are disproportionately subject to prosecution and punishment), the provision should

32 In Chapter 18 of this volume, Albert W. Alschuler, "Justice, Mercy and Equality in Discretionary Criminal Justice Decision-making", pp. 283–300.

33 See Michael Welker, "The Power of Mercy in Biblical Law", (2014) 19.2 *Journal of Law and Religion* 225–58.

remind American governments that, for communities uniquely vulnerable to private violence, equal protection of the laws may require more protection than others. Courts and prosecutors should likewise be attuned to inequities in the imposition of punishment based on the victim's association with an unpopular or vulnerable community.

One of the most vulnerable populations in many countries are those subject to criminal punishment. At a minimum, as Jeffrie Murphy has suggested in this volume, Christians should demand forms of punishment that do not expose offenders to degrading or violent treatment at the hands of officers or other offenders.[34] The offender justly subject to criminal judgment remains the object of God's extravagant love, the one for whom Christ died. A form and theory of punishment that seeks to avenge wrongdoing and express the love of God to the offender would be one that, at a minimum, seeks the offender's good consistent with the demands of justice. While criminal judgment may not lead an offender to reformation, it may make space for it. This was Augustine's argument to a Roman magistrate tasked with executing an offender adjudged worthy of death. Augustine appealed to the example of Christ and the woman caught in adultery. Christ, who had no need of mercy, extended it alongside the command to "go, and sin no more" (John 8:11, KJV).

> Since ... God shows such great patience and mercy toward sinners that are not damned forever if they amend their conduct in this life ... it follows that we men ought to be such toward other men, for, whatever praise we heap up on this life of ours, we never say that it is without sin.[35]

Even in the task of criminal judgment, Christians may witness to the undeserved mercy at the heart of the gospel.

21.5 Conclusion: suffering the imperfectibility of judgment

This chapter closes with a brief reflection on the weight of judgment, the burden of participating in an imperfectible, penultimate task. The government's criminal judgment is not God's first-best. It is a response to wrongdoing born of humanity's rejection of God. As we have seen, Scripture suggests that human government itself reflects this rebellion, though God uses it to execute vengeance. Government teems with seduction – to self-righteousness and to the receipt of honour that belongs to God alone. Christ's coming kingdom, by contrast, is one of perfect judgment in submission, forgiveness and self-giving; it needs, and makes, no place for the sword.

Christians participate, and *should* participate, in God's use of government to serve their neighbours, but they do so knowing that governmental judgment is

34 Murphy, "Punishment, Forgiveness and Mercy".
35 Augustine, "Letter 153", 122.

not only imperfect, but also imperfectible. A community's moral norms are always turned towards self-love and vainglory. The earthly city, with its proliferation of moral and political judgments, is a monument to attempted self-sufficiency, to distrust of God's promised protection. Language, reason, evidence – these often raise as many hurdles as they lower for true judgment.

Christians participating in criminal judgment bear not only the tension between perfect and imperfect judgment, but also the tension between the responsibility to execute justice and the call of Christ to forgive. The classic two-kingdoms account of the ethics of governmental judgment, that Christians wear two ethical hats, one as a Christian and one as an official, requires ethical bifurcation that produces an under-appreciated psychological, emotional and spiritual tension. One potential remedy for this tension is abnegation of governmental responsibility. Yet, this seems contrary to Christian love. There is simply no avoiding the suffering of participating in governmental judgment. As all creation endures the futility of sinfulness, Christians participating in criminal judgment must do so with faith that God is using their work, often despite appearances, for his purposes. Christians thus bear the weight of judgment as they do all other forms of suffering – by groaning for resurrection (Rom. 8:18–25).

Augustine astutely observed this tension. "We do not know why an innocent man can leave the court not only unvindicated, but actually condemned, either oppressed by the injustice of his judge or overwhelmed by false evidence".[36] For Augustine, the judge who knows his methods of interrogation will, in some cases, produce false verdicts, should weep for that injustice.[37] Yet, he maintained that "divine doctrine conduces to our salvation even in circumstances where divine justice is not apparent".[38] To see the criminal justice system as an expression of God's love takes eyes of faith; to participate in that system calls for the hope of glory.

Further reading

Augustine. *The City of God Against the Pagans*, ed. and trans. R.W. Dyson (Cambridge: Cambridge University Press, 1998), Books 19 and 20.

Calvin, John. *Institutes of the Christian Religion*, ed. John T. McNeill, trans. Ford Lewis Battles, 2 vols (Philadelphia: Westminster Press, 1960), Book 4, ch. 20.

Gregory, Eric. *Politics and the Order of Love: An Augustinian Ethic of Democratic Citizenship* (Chicago: University of Chicago Press, 2008).

Hauerwas, Stanley. *The Peaceable Kingdom: A Primer in Christian Ethics* (Notre Dame: University of Notre Dame Press, 2016).

Mathewes, Charles. *A Theology of Public Life* (Cambridge: Cambridge University Press, 2007).

36 Augustine, *City of God*, 20.2.

37 Ibid., 19.6.

38 Ibid., 20.2.

Murphy, Jeffrie G. "Mercy and Legal Justice", (1986) 4.1 *Social Philosophy and Policy* 1–14.
O'Donovan, Oliver. *The Ways of Judgment* (Grand Rapids: Wm. B. Eerdmans, 2005).
O'Donovan, Oliver and Joan Lockwood O'Donovan, eds. *From Irenaeus to Grotius: A Sourcebook in Christian Political Thought 100–1625* (Grand Rapids: Wm. B. Eerdmans, 1999).
VanDrunen, David. *Divine Commandments and Moral Order: A Biblical Theology of Natural Law* (Grand Rapids: Wm. B. Eerdmans, 2014).
Wolterstorff, Nicholas. *Justice in Love* (Grand Rapids: Wm. B. Eerdmans, 2011).

Index

For Product Safety Concerns and Information please contact our EU representative GPSR@taylorandfrancis.com
Taylor & Francis Verlag GmbH, Kaufingerstraße 24, 80331 München, Germany

www.ingramcontent.com/pod-product-compliance
Ingram Content Group UK Ltd.
Pitfield, Milton Keynes, MK11 3LW, UK
UKHW022008180926
475701UK00003B/249
* 9 7 8 0 3 6 7 4 9 5 7 8 7 *